Philosophical and Radical Thought in Marketing

Philosophical and Radical Thought in Marketing

A. Fuat Fırat
Appalachian State University

Nikhilesh Dholakia
University of Rhode Island

Richard P. Bagozzi
University of Michigan

Lexington Books
D.C. Heath Company/Lexington, Massachusetts/Toronto

Library of Congress Cataloging-in-Publication Data

Philosophical and radical thought in marketing.

  1. Marketing 2. Consumers. I. Fırat, A. Fuat.
II. Dholakia, Nikhilesh, 1947–   . III. Bagozzi, Richard P.
HF5415.P485   1987   658.8   86-45791
ISBN 0-669-14301-4 (alk. paper)

Published simultaneously in Canada
Printed in the United States of America
International Standard Book Number: 0-669-14301-4
Library of Congress Catalog Card Number: 86-45791

The paper used in this publication meets the minimum requirements of American National
Standard for Information Sciences—Permanence of Paper for Printed Library Materials, ANSI
Z39.48-1984.∞ ™

87 88 89 90 91 8 7 6 5 4 3 2 1

Dedicated to
  Ömer Fehim Fırat
  Johan Arndt
  Edward L. Bagozzi

Contents

Acknowledgments

The idea for this book originated as we were discussing the possibilities of founding a journal (which could be called the *Journal of Radical Marketing Thought*) that would serve as a forum in which marketing and consumer behavior scholars, as well as other interested scholars, consumers, and practitioners, could introduce novel and exciting perspectives, theories, and ideas. Such a journal would also allow discussion of these ideas through commentaries and polemical exchanges. Its purpose would be to open the field to creative thinking that could run counter to and rebel against mainstream paradigms and set ways of academic practice. We still feel that this is an achievable goal, but recognize that it needs more time. This book is a step towards creating such an exciting forum in marketing.

A book of this type could only be realized through the contributions of the most active and creative minds in the discipline—those who seek truly exciting growth in and meaningful contributions to human knowledge. We thank our contributors—all of whom fit this description—for responding to our call and providing original, path-breaking ideas. Their work gives us the greatest hope for a meaningful future in marketing and consumer behavior.

We also wish to thank the publishing crew at Lexington Books, especially Caroline McCarley and Marsha M. Finley, for making this publication process interesting and fun. They have been most helpful, competent, and professional.

Introduction: Breaking the Mold

A. Fuat Fırat
Nikhilesh Dholakia
Richard P. Bagozzi

Seeds of Change

The need for new perspectives and worldviews in marketing has been expressed by many scholars in marketing and consumer behavior fields; it is not a novel thought. Free minds begin to feel constrained after a while when they are asked to produce for a specific audience, for a specified purpose, or even for a specified understanding. This is not only true for minds in marketing; it has happened to people of all kinds—philosophers, poets, physicists, revolutionaries—throughout history. We are not presenting this idea as a universal fact, but as a historical recurrence whose causes could be systematically investigated. This approach, looking for systematic understanding of historical events rather than trying to establish invariate universal truths, is one of the underlying considerations that led us to think of this book. The discipline of marketing has endeavored to establish theories, facts, and truths about the behaviors of marketers and buyers under specific but implicit assumptions which regard a certain worldview, historic juncture, and social system as perpetual. We in marketing have not been critical of our conditions even in the simplest sense of scientific skepticism and inquisitiveness, let alone for the purpose of changing these conditions.

The Logic of the Market

Many may argue the necessity for such critical questioning in terms of having to establish a discipline. The establishment of an applied discipline, such as marketing, requires practical utility for at least one segment in society. For marketing, this has been the managerial segment. Of course, this reasoning is especially true in a market system where success is measured and established in terms of utility that sells. Practicality in a market system is judged in terms of who can pay for this utility the most. And marketing as a discipline is a cornerstone supporting the logic of practicality of the market system. In a way, therefore, the reasoning has some circularity to it. Systemic hurdles make it difficult to break out of both the reasoning and the traditional practices of the marketing discipline.

Inquiring minds have the right, however, to question such a logic, even if it is so smugly circular and widely accepted. But can such questioning voices be heard? What practical utility do these voices have for those with effective demand and organization in the market as well as the ability to pay? Do new and critical approaches to marketing have any practical utility for any segment of society? Such questions bring to mind the principles of scientific knowledge generation generally accepted in the natural sciences:

1. Scientific value and development cannot be assessed on the basis of immediate practical utility. In general, the history of scientific development bears out this principle. Many major discoveries in science were the results of seemingly impractical research and thought.

2. Since immediate practicality cannot be the touchstone of scientific knowledge, the second principle is that society must support many esoteric scientific knowledge enterprises. This is the principle that initially gave rise to state funding agencies, although many state funding agencies no longer serve such a lofty purpose.

The principles of scientific knowledge generation and the logic of the market system are seemingly at odds with one another. If no practical purpose is to be served,and if utility of the endeavor is questionable even in the long run (that is, if there is no demand and, therefore, the free market is not willing to support such activity), should society allocate its resources to these activities? Immediately, the need arises to critically examine our conceptualizations of demand, free market, and social purpose. Such examination brings into perspective that the state, in allocating its funds (tax revenues,for example) to such scientific endeavor, is also part of the "free market" and, therefore, the market is in a way willing to pay. However, the decisions made by society through its state are political, and political-influence processes have largely been excluded as subjects for study in the marketing discipline—clearly a step away from reality. (For an exception, see Kotler 1986.) Just this one example of how the marketing discipline has dealt with only part of reality is sufficient, in our minds, for a critical examination of its history and its nature. Yet, maybe, even a greater need for critical marketing thought derives from the fact that many segments and individuals in society cannot effectively participate in the market because they lack the buying power and the required organization. They are especially powerless to influence knowledge generation and research processes and projects in applied disciplines such as marketing.

Currents of Change in Consumer Behavior

Consumer behavior scholars, especially an emerging vanguard of socially conscious ones, are seeking ways, conceptual and methodological, to generate knowledge that pertains to the consumption experience of individuals, households, and communities, regardless of the direct consequences of such experiences for market exchange or buying-selling processes (Belk 1984; Hirschman 1986; Holbrook and Hirschman 1982; Levy 1981; Olson 1983). They are questioning the validity of research done solely for consulting purposes for the marketing organizations. They are further arguing that marketing management implications of their research should not be a criterion of evaluation of their work. Finally, these scholars are seeking ways to become an independent consumer science discipline, separate from marketing. Similar movements among the academics of the marketing discipline are also found. These movements seek a scientific marketing discipline rather than a technological one, wish to become independent of a purely business approach, and try to find alternative paradigms (Dholakia and Arndt 1985). If there is no strong effective demand in the market for critical marketing thought, there surely is much feeling for such thought within the academic ranks. This critical, philosophical, and radical literature, however, barely finds place in the pages of the major journals in the discipline. This book is an attempt to articulate such philosophical and radical scholarship and to launch critical investigations into the history, present, and possible future of the discipline.

Tendency toward Compartmentalization

It is no coincidence that the discipline of consumer behavior is a spin-off from marketing. It was the need for marketing organizations (businesses in particular) to know about the attitudes, behaviors, personalities, and psychologies of consumers as buyers of products that launched the investigations into what came to be termed "consumer behavior." Only recently is there a recognition that not "consumer" but "buyer" behavior has been the focus in the field. The question is being raised: Can we study consumer needs, experiences, and behavior independent of their implications for marketing management? (Firat 1984; Hirschman 1983; Holbrook 1984). Underlying this question might very well be the concern that science and academic research ought to be usable by all segments in society. The purpose of *scientific* endeavor is not to inform some interest groups in society about other groups; such purpose is more in line with the goals of intelligence and police apparatuses.[1] When the consumer behavior discipline opens itself to all kinds of knowledge regarding consumption behavior and experiences, we willingly or inadvertently enter the whole realm of human behavior. This is not, per se, an unacceptable intrusion into other disciplines. All social sciences interest themselves in human behavior. The lines between the disciplines are drawn primarily based on their *perspectives* in studying human behavior. Sociology, for example, studies the structure and development of interpersonal and intergroup (social) behavior, while political science looks at power relationships between institutions and people. In many respects, unfortunately, the social science disciplines have concentrated their efforts not around the perspectives which initiated them but on only certain variables, groups, or institutions as their subject matters. The subject matter of any social science is the human being and the totality of the environment in which humans live. Limiting the human being to only one of the existential dimensions (economic, social, political, and so forth) or partitioning the human environment into interest fields only leads to partial understanding, removal from reality, and irrelevance to the human condition (Marcuse 1964). Under the pressures of technological and methodological precision (a consequence of the industrialized technological society and its accompanying approach to science characterized by positivism/rationalism/logical empiricism), the social science disciplines have compartmentalized themselves and lost touch with the total reality in favor of token precision.

A Holistic Approach

A holistic approach to understanding human needs (what the marketing concept advocates) and how they are (or are not) satisfied would require breaking the boundaries of traditional social science disciplines. By breaking disciplinary walls, we can understand the human being in its totality. Such total understanding is necessary because needs are the products of total historical human experience. Attempts at creating new holistic perspectives will push the boundaries of knowledge further if the required transformations in the knowledge system are arrived at through critical analyses of the times. Such perspectives, no matter how refreshingly relevant when first conceived, may become stale as times change. We must seek meaningful transformations in knowledge but not become so attached to them that we cannot let go when it becomes appropriate.

At a Crossroad

We in the disciplines of marketing and consumer behavior are presently standing at a crossroad. There is all the potential to develop into a social science discipline of some relevance to the human condition on this planet. There is also the impetus to lose contact with the human condition, to become overly one-dimensional in the interests that are served, and, thus, to fall into oblivion as an instrument of control, becoming socially irrelevant in the long run. This strong impetus is fostered by the tendency in contemporary popular ideology to moralize rather than analyze. There is a dialectic relationship between the scientific/academic enterprise and popular ideology in society. It is, therefore, not possible to expect that the scientific enterprise will continue on its route of criticism, self-criticism, rationality, analysis, and reconstruction of knowledge without any influence from the moralistic tone of contemporary popular ideology. But a knowledge-generation enterprise cannot break out of its lull and its self-determined (and, therefore, self-justified) limitations through moralizing. Rather, a critical and radically analytical orientation is needed. The history of scientific thought provides strong evidence in this respect. If marketing and consumer behavior disciplines, as they stand, are not challenging the imagination, and if so many scholars in the disciplines are feeling the urge to break free of stifling disciplinary boundaries, then the path to take is one of radical analysis and criticism of where we stand, our history, and the forces that have shaped our discipline.

Call for a Radical Deconstruction

Today, marketing needs a thorough deconstruction. Through a process of criticism and self-criticism, it is possible to move to a novel reconstruction based on philosophical and analytical investigations into the assumptions, premises, and proclaimed truths that we have taken for granted for so long. For a healthy process of criticism and deconstruction, we must not be afraid to pose as questions what we assumed were answers, and we must not pull back from being radical in every sense.

By "radical," we mean having a particular concern with substance and history. Specifically, a substantive theory (or discipline) is taken to connote one addressing the fundamental and essential aspects of a phenomenon; further, it is taken as axiomatic that such a theory or discipline can only be understood as it has evolved and continues to evolve. We thus feel that "radical" implies a synthesis between essence and change. The goal of radical theorizing is to bridge the lacuna between naive or biased presuppositions and reality. This requires that existing theories be continually reexamined, challenged, and ultimately replaced with one or more new theories revealing deeper substantive roots and more valid historical descriptions.

To be radical, then, means to go to the roots and seek the essential realities (relationships, processes, or dimensions) which are not necessarily apparent or reflected at the surface. Furthermore, to be radical means to be ready, not afraid of, and willing, if necessary, to break with the predominant cultural, political, and social beliefs and values in order to investigate the essential realities that they conceal.

We must go to the very roots of existence of the knowledge enterprise we call marketing and question those roots, asking questions that will enable a thorough and robust understanding of those roots. We must be radical in seeking novel and revolutionary alternatives to our set ways, ways that tend to frustrate some of the brightest minds in the discipline. Marketing is not unique in necessitating such revolutionary perspectives. The world feels the staleness of the tried ways, whether they be in political, economic, or social affairs, be they in the less developed or developed regions. Novel perspectives and alternatives are sought throughout the international bodies in financial institutions, international relations, and developmental processes. But novelty, experimentation, and untried ways are detested by some. There is insistence, on the part of some interest groups, to revert to the old solutions to new problems. The moral force of what was once successful is invoked to tarnish and blur the bright potential of alternative solutions, perspectives, and realities. To advance a radical perspective, therefore, is always an act of struggle.

Barriers to Holistic and Critical Research

As marketing stands at a crossroad, the rest of the social sciences are in crisis. This crisis is observed in two ways. First, the social science disciplines can neither explain nor enhance the understanding of major events in the world. Many unsatisfactory and inadequate theories remain in the literature and sometimes in popular media. Second, much of the work in these disciplines does not even address the major events and problems of contemporary human condition. There is much piecemeal work that is not somehow united and for which syntheses are not available. Such work fails to contribute to solutions of problems that are holistic, not only within disciplines but in interdisciplinary terms. That is, no major problem is just social, economic, political, cultural, or psychological, but rather total. Solutions, therefore, require multidisciplinary and multidimensional perspectives that concentrate on ways of looking at issues and cut across disciplines. The reality of the studies in the social science disciplines is, on the other hand, one of concentrating on tractable variables and testing of narrow hypotheses. Such work, strewn in the pages of "academic" journals and books, is fostered by the dominant positivist-empiricist method which seeks precision within narrow bounds, as well as by funding institutions which can handle such limited studies but are petrified by studies that may rock the boat by having major political or social repercussions. Consequently, the scholars in their disciplines withdraw into their academic cocoons, develop their own research programs, and talk to each other about their little studies, using their exquisitely coded jargons. This whole enterprise of self-satisfaction is greatly reinforced by the academic environments in the disciplines. A publish-or-perish atmosphere in major universities leaves little chance for time-consuming, substantive research. The pressures of academic evaluations for promotion and tenure lead to an emphasis on quantity of publication in certain journals rather than on substantive contribution. While these are ills well-recognized among many scholars in the disciplines, the rules of the game are difficult to change given the established system of rewards and the evasiveness of criteria for judging substance.

Indications are there that maybe this entire system requires a new assessment and transformation. For those who have gained respect and positions of authority and power within the system, however, it is embarrassing and difficult to reject what has enabled them to get where they are. An almost vicious circle is present. Where and how it can be broken is in need of investigation. But, broken it must be if relevance to the realities and predicaments of human society is of any importance. The chapters in this book are, to various degrees, attempts to break out of this circle.

Reinventing Relevance

Sooner or later, any attempt to put forth a radical conceptualization will run up against the powerful criterion of "relevance." Radicalism degenerates into nihilism unless it is relevant. For traditional marketing thought, "managerial relevance" provides an unambiguous if manifestly narrow touchstone. For the new thinkers in marketing and consumer behavior represented in this book, we feel a broader, more global kind of relevance is needed. But for this, we must first be clear about the prevailing, global human condition.

The Global Predicament

The contemporary human predicament is indeed global owing to developed communications systems as well as internationalization of markets, interests, and problems. One does not need to detail the extent and nature of the global problems that surround human existence since they are well known and frequently heard. Poverty, which dominates the lives of a large majority of Earth's inhabitants, is one of the most critical. But its importance is realized in marketing studies only when the focus of the investigations is the human condition. This is because it is this poverty, its nature, and its creation that most affect the ability to satisfy human needs. Much studying of poverty, however, has been one-dimensional and ideological, both in terms of how poverty is defined and how it is operationalized. Marketing has the great potential, as an integrating social science discipline, to bring enlightening perspectives to this overwhelming problem. Many other global predicaments are directly or indirectly related to this problem.

The Search for Solutions

The pollution of the environment, ecological imbalances, advent of nuclear power and the bomb, undernutrition and malnutrition, ongoing wars, and ethnic, sexual, and cultural discrimination are only some of such global problems which, maybe surprisingly to some, seem to intensify with the "advancement" of technology. Technology, perceived by many to be the answer to all human problems, does not per se provide the solutions. This is only one indication as to why, in marketing, the solutions cannot be sought only in marketing management technology. Rather, it becomes increasingly clear that the solutions require well-rounded and integrated philosophical, political, social, economic, cultural, psychological, and ecological—that is, multidimensional—answers.

One thing that marketing can still boast about is the fact that while its students and scholars have taken off along its different dimensions (narrowing their perspectives in the process), as a field of study it still remains multidisciplinary. This is a strength rather than a weakness, and ought to be built on through critical-analytical philosophies. For such growth and development, we very much need a critical forum that allows for the infusion, critical discussion, and assessment of radically different ideas. This book is a step in that direction; however, it is only a beginning. To reach its global audience, the discipline needs more powerful and permanent forums, such as a journal for such purpose. In the meantime, one can only hope that editors, reviewers, and other gatekeepers will see fit to encourage dissent, radicalism, and novel orientations. We are confident that such developments will occur. The currents of change in marketing thought point in this direction.

The purpose of this book is not to present one philosophy or one radical approach. On the contrary, it is to break the limitations and allow many different yet critical and vigorous perspectives and orientations to be heard. We hope that in the pages of this book you will find a refreshing variety of approaches, critiques, and frameworks.

Notes

1. We note in passing that marketing scholars have no qualms in labeling the study, surveillance, and monitoring of competitors as *intelligence* operation (Montgomery and Weinberg 1979). But when the objects of study, surveillance, and monitoring are consumers, we prefer to parade the euphemism of *consumer research* or *market research*.

References

Belk, Russell W. (1984)."Manifesto for a Consumer Behavior of Consumer Behavior," in *Scientific Method in Marketing*, P.F. Anderson and M.J. Ryan, eds. Chicago: American Marketing Association, 57–60.

Dholakia, Nikhilesh, and Johan Arndt, eds. (1985), *Changing the Course of Marketing: Alternative Paradigms for Widening Marketing Theory*, Greenwich, Conn.: JAI Press.

Fırat, A. Fuat (1984), "A Critique of the Orientations in Theory Development in Consumer Behavior: Suggestions for the Future," in *Advances in Consumer Research*, vol. 12, E.C. Hirschman and M.B. Holbrook, eds. Provo, Utah: Association for Consumer Research

Hirschman, Elizabeth C. (1983), "Aesthetics, Ideologies and the Limits of the Marketing Concept," *Journal of Marketing* 47 (Summer): 45–55.

———, (1986), "Humanistic Inquiry in Marketing Research: Philosophy, Method and Criteria," *Journal of Marketing Research* 23 (August): 237–249.

Holbrook, Morris B. (1984), "The Consumer Researcher Visits Radio City: Dancing in the Dark," in *Advances in Consumer Research*, vol. 12, E.C. Hirschman and M.B. Holbrook, eds. Provo, Utah: Association for Consumer Research.

Holbrook, Morris B., and Elizabeth C. Hirschman, (1982), "The Experiential Aspects of Consumption: Consumer Fantasies, Feelings and Fun," *Journal of Consumer Research* 9 (September): 132–140.

Kotler, Philip (1986), "Megamarketing," *Harvard Business Review* 64 (March-April): 117–124.

Levy, Sidney J. (1981), "Interpreting Consumer Mythology: A Structural Approach to Consumer Behavior," *Journal of Marketing* 45 (Summer): 49–61.

Marcuse, Herbert (1964), *One-Dimensional Man*. Boston: Beacon.

Montgomery, David B., and Charles B. Weinberg (1979), "Toward Strategic Intelligence Systems," *Journal of Marketing* 43 (Fall): 41–52.

Olson, Jerry C. (1983), "Presidential Address—1981: Toward a Science of Consumer Behavior," reprinted in *Marketing Theory*, S.D. Hunt, ed. Homewood, Ill.: Richard D. Irwin, 395–405.

Part I
Problems of Contemporary Marketing Thought

1

Consumers, Markets, and Supply Systems: A Perspective on Marketization and Its Effects

Kjell Grønhaug
Nikhilesh Dholakia

Several parties are interested in consumers. For marketers, consumers represent their *raison d'être*. For marketing researchers, consumers represent the basic research arena. For educators, consumers constitute the prime target groups. For government authorities, consumers imply votes, pressure groups, and human interests which have to be taken into account and served as best as possible.

Researchers from several disciplines such as economics, policy sciences, consumer studies, psychology, sociology, and marketing have devoted considerable time, energy, money, and talent to study *how* and *why* consumers behave as they do and, to some extent, how they *should* behave. Scope, concepts, and constructs vary across disciplines. The disciplinary orientations influence how consumers are perceived and the aspects of consumer behavior that are emphasized in research studies.

This chapter begins with a brief review of the notion of "market" (i.e., collectivities of consumers) which reveals the diversity of perspectives. Markets are then viewed from a consumer perspective and classified by the types of transactions consumers engage in. Some evolutionary trends are observed in the emergence of various transaction systems. Finally, markets are compared with alternative supply systems and some consumer policy implications are presented.

Markets

The notion of a *market* represents an important arena in the study of consumers. The effectiveness of the market exerts influences on consumer satisfaction and well-being. Marketers and economists believe satisfaction of the ultimate consumer to be the final goal of all productive and distributive activities, which is in concordance with the focus on consumer well-being in consumer policy (Thorelli and Thorelli 1977). However, as noted in the literature on consumer satisfaction/dissatisfaction (Hunt 1977) and on the disadvantaged consumer (Andreasen 1975), consumers are not always satisfied, nor do the products and services offered in the marketplace always reflect real consumer wants (Rothenberg 1968). In other words, markets seem to function at less than ideal levels of effectiveness.

Review of literature reveals several definitions of the concept of "market," focusing on different aspects of this concept. A marketer's definition is that "a market is the set of all actual and potential buyers of a product" (Kotler 1980, p. 21). This definition obviously reflects the interests of the marketer. The marketer is interested in the consumer as a *buyer*. Goods and services are exchanged for money, enabling the marketer to make a profit and stay in business.

An industrial-organizational definition of this concept is "a collection of firms each of which is supplying products that have some degree of substitutability to the same potential buyers" (Koch 1974, p. 13). Here the focus is mainly on the *supply side*, viewed from an industry perspective (i.e., all firms offering products to the same market). Porter's (1980) work on competitive strategy has broadened this perspective to include indirect competitors, potential new entrants, and others influencing the supply of a product.

An economist's definition is "all the people who buy or sell a commodity in the ordinary course of their affairs" (Dorfman 1967, p. 21). This definition focuses on both the *seller* and the *buyer*. Moreover, the market is, according to this definition, "a constantly shifting group of people rather than a place or an identifiable social institution" (p. 21).

The implicit or explicit definitions underlying the concept of market will influence which aspects are considered. A great deal of the research on consumer behavior has been conducted in a marketing context, from a marketer's perspective, viewing the consumer as an "object" (Arndt 1976).[1] We would like to view markets from a *consumer* perspective.

A Consumer Perspective on Markets

Very few attempts have been made to consider the market from the consumers' point of view. When considering the notion of "market" from this perspective, it emerges that consumers participate in multiple markets and that consumers may face a variety of barriers when attempting to enter or leave a market.

Many markets.   Consumers enter not one but *many* markets. In a modern society, consumers have to form a variety of buyer-seller relationships in order to acquire the products and services needed. As we argue later, the evolution of contemporary societies is characterized by a steady increase in the *market* relationships that consumers enter into (and a corresponding decline in pre-market and nonmarket relationships). Some of these relationships may be long-lasting and others may entail short-term, one-shot transactions. Various resources such as knowledge, time, and economic means are needed to perform transactions. Due to differences across markets, consumers require new insight and learning to enter new markets.

Barriers. Barriers may exist in both entering and leaving markets for producers as well as consumers. From a consumer's point of view, the following types of barriers may be of crucial importance:

The *economic resources* needed to become a buyer or to stop being a buyer.

The *problem-solving capacity* of the consumer.

The *time* required to plan, transact, and consume purchases.

The *access* of the consumer to distribution outlets.

The *social contacts* through which help and advice are available.

The importance of *economic resources* is self-evident. A certain amount of money or buying power is needed to enter a given market. Even exit from certain markets requires resources. People with cars can escape the market for public transit; people with money to travel can temporarily exit from the markets of their local town.

Variations in *problem-solving capacity* of consumers influence their ability to obtain and analyze purchase-related information and to form buyer–seller relationships. Such variations also exert an impact on the outcome of transactions. In the purchase of consumer durables, for example, not all people have the capacity to obtain information from consumer-testing services, figure out price–quality trade-offs, and enter the market armed with a superior bargaining strategy.

Time is a limited resource. Buying and consuming are part-time activities. The fraction of the time-budget allocated to such activities varies among consumers. The time devoted to such activities is partly restricted by the total load of activities attached to the individual and by the perceived importance of buying (Jacoby 1978). To some degree, time spent on buying can be minimized by simplifying the buying process (e.g., buying in a full-service department store), but there is usually a cost attached (e.g., premium prices).

Access to distribution points and, thus, the ability to take various product and price alternatives into account depend on factors such as health (in terms of mobility), access to transportation, and distance to the buying alternatives.

Thus, being handicapped or lacking access to a car may force a consumer into localized monopolist seller–buyer relationships.

Access to *relevant social networks* enables consumers to obtain purchase-related information and to function effectively as consumers. Advice seeking and help in performing buying activities have been found to be of great importance to the consumer. The access to relevant social networks differs across consumers. More affluent and capable consumers usually have better access to social networks.

Classification of Markets

Both marketers and consumer representatives assume—in most cases, implicitly—that markets are *open*—if consumers have the necessary economic means, the market is open to them. In other words, markets seem to be thought of as *visible* and *commercialized* (Houg 1980). By extending the perspective to include not-visible and not-commercialized markets, we can form the matrix of transactional systems depicted in figure 1–1.

The visibility dimension is viewed from the consumers' perspective. Marketing as presented in textbooks and taught in the classrooms is focused on making the exchange partners (sellers) visible to the consumers and easing the conditions under which transactions may take place.

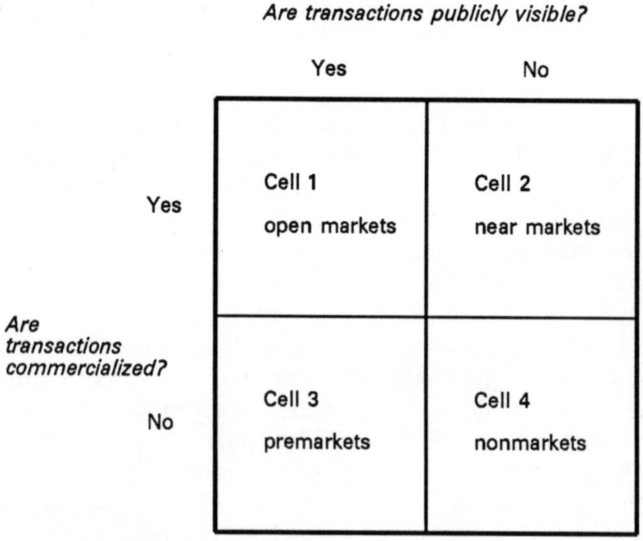

Are transactions publicly visible?

		Yes	No
Are transactions commercialized?	Yes	Cell 1 open markets	Cell 2 near markets
	No	Cell 3 premarkets	Cell 4 nonmarkets

Figure 1–1. Transactional Systems Described by Visibility and Commercialization

Cell 1 of the figure represents transactions that are both visible and commercialized. It describes the typical, commercialized markets open to most consumers. This is the arena of competitive marketing activities.

Cell 2 includes transactions that are commercialized but not visible in the legitimate, public domain. It represents illegal, tax-free transactions of goods and services. This is the arena of "the underground economy," the black market which constitutes an important part of the total economy in many countries (Henry 1978). The consumer may benefit considerably in terms of immediate economic advantage or immediate gratification by entering such markets. Access to such markets, however, is not equally distributed among consumers, so such markets may contribute to increased economic inequities among consumers. Direct risks (getting caught and facing criminal charges) and indirect penalties (through increased taxes and corruption) are also associated with transactions in cell 2.

Cell 3 represents transactions that are visible but not commercialized. It includes various public goods, such as free education and free medical care. In the U.S. and most European countries, there is currently a strong trend toward privatization of many public services (converting cell 3 markets into cell 1 markets).

Cell 4 represents transactions that are neither commercialized nor visible. It includes exchange of private services in established social networks (such as mutual baby-sitting and helping a neighbor with garden work one day in exchange for assistance another day). The relative importance and usefulness of such transactions depends on access to relevant social networks as well as individual resources and capabilities. Those with good access to social networks and many exchangeable resources benefit from such relationships. In traditional societies, such private exchanges need not rely on strict *quid pro quo*; obligatory reciprocity is the norm. As societies modernize, *quid pro quo* requirements grow stronger.

Evolution of Markets: Marketization

To facilitate discussion, the contents of the cells in figure 1–1 can be labeled. Cell 1 represents open markets; cell 2, near markets (sometimes functioning as black markets or shadow markets); cell 3, premarkets; and cell 4, nonmarkets. Collectively, these cells represent the transactional systems occurring in a society.

An evolutionary process, observable especially in capitalist societies, is the movement of transactional systems from cells 3 and 4 to cells 1 and 2—transformation of nonmarkets and premarkets into open markets and near markets (Polanyi 1957). While the actual processes of market transformations are complex and vary across societies, the direction of change is unmistakable: it is from the lower cells (3 and 4) to the upper cells (1 and 2).

This process of commoditization or "marketization" is pervasive in its global reach (Taussig 1980). Yet, it is one of the least understood of market-related phenomena. Based on our limited understanding of this phenomenon, the following tentative hypotheses can be offered regarding the evolution and transformation of markets:

1. Nonmarkets move into the category of open markets by passing through the intermediate category of premarkets. This happens through a progressive *depersonalization* leading to increased visibility of the exchange relations. There is movement from cell 4—via cell 3—to cell 1.

2. In societies characterized by traditional ties, premarkets are more likely to be transformed into near markets than into open markets. In many third world countries, for example, public services turn into a shadow market through corruption—there is a price (bribe) for every category of service. A part of the explanation is that estabished social ties are used as a point of departure in establishing powerful networks for moderating exchanges (Johanson and Mattsson 1985).

3. In advanced capitalist societies, there is pressure to transform premarkets. This is partly due to the fact that public goods are made private by allowing the price mechanism to work. The deregulation and privatization movements in the United States and several European countries can be interpreted in this manner. Also, theories of monopoly capitalism suggest that continued capital accumulation requires that newer spheres of human activity be marketized. (See Baran and Sweezy 1966.)

4. In advanced capitalist societies, there is pressure to create more legitimate forms of near markets (lobbying, public relations, and "megamarketing") rather than illegitimate forms of near markets (bribery, corruption). This is because of 1) the rising concentration of economic interests and 2) the strong legal system which enhances the public scrutiny of transactions in general.

It is hoped that these tentative generalizations will lead to further research on and exploration of the phenomenon of marketization. The process of marketization is not only important from a historic standpoint, it is also an ongoing phenomenon in advanced industrial societies. Without an understanding of marketization, we cannot assess how markets and other supply systems of contemporary societies have evolved and how these systems interact.

Supply Systems

Our discussion of the market so far has been from a micro perspective. At the macro level, the market may be viewed as one form of control and steering system for economic activities. In classical economics, markets were assumed to be atomistic. They involved large numbers of buyers and sellers ("free" or "pure" competition). Basic assumptions underlying this model are that the producers are rewarded on the basis of their contribution to the value added, and that how consumers spend their incomes signals producers their priority of wants. Thus conceived, markets may be viewed as incentive and information systems, as well as coordination mechanisms. The key structural attributes of markets are impersonal, decentralized exchanges.[2]

The market is, however, only one of several systems of steering and coordinating exchanges. The bureaucracy represents another steering system in the economic arena (Ouchi 1980). Table 1–1 contrasts the two economic steering systems and compares them to representative democracy and party-based socialism, steering systems existing in the political arena.

Table 1–1 is to be read in the following way. Each of the four steering systems is described by four characteristics: system type, initiative, steering criteria, and information system. The characteristics are used to portray the ideal types. In the ideal or perfect market, the consumer initiates production by expressing wants. In the ideal representative democracy, voters initiate choices by expressing preferences and interests. The interests of the central authorities lead to the actions in the ideal bureaucracy. The interests of the masses (articulated by the party) lead to actions in the ideal form of party-based socialism. In a similar view, the steering criteria in the ideal types of market, representative democracy, bureaucracy, and party-based socialism are profit maximization, maximization of votes, maximization of careers through implementation and adjustment to rules, and maximization of party or class interest,

Table 1–1
Four Steering Systems Described by Initiative, Steering Criteria, and Information System

	Steering System			
	Perfect Market	*Representative Democracy*	*Traditional Bureaucracy*	*Party-based Socialism*
Type of System:	Economic	Political	Economic	Political
Initiator:	The Consumer	The Voter	The Central Authority	The Party Leader
Steering Criteria:	Profit maximization	Maximization of votes	Maximization of career through implementation and adjustment to rules	Maximization of party or class inerest
Information System:	Price system	Voting	Expertise	Party membership

respectively. The information systems in these ideal systems are based on the price system, voting, expertise, and party membership, respectively.

Most consumers operate in a *variety* of supply and steering systems. In most countries, the public sector covers an important and often increasing fraction of all goods and services consumed. Public goods cater to basic needs such as health, education, safety, and transportation. Public goods are often supplied through bureaucratic systems. Thus, in the conduct of their life activities, consumers are often confronted with both markets and bureaucracies.

Neither a perfect bureaucratic nor a perfect market supply system will always be able to respond to the consumers' wants. In a study, Grønhaug and Arndt (1979) found that perceived dissatisfaction and voiced complaints were less frequent for goods distributed through the public, bureaucratic systems as compared to goods distributed through the private, market system. These findings do not allow, however, the conclusion that the bureaucratic system is superior to the market supply system. In that study, the nature of services offered had only modest variability in service quality and level. This probably caused only small variations in expectations—and, thus, less reasons for complaints. In a bureaucratic, centralized supply system, there are no alternative suppliers; thus, the exit option is less relevant (Hirschman 1970). It should also be noted that the no-buy option may sometimes be violated due to authoritative decision making, such as mandated purchase of seat belts in car buying. Such authoritative decisions may be distributed through both markets and bureaucracies.

The Articulation of Consumer Interest

Viewed in the ideal ("pure") forms, markets as supply systems fit into cell 1 (open market) of figure 1–1 and bureaucracies fit into cell 3 (premarket). The articulation of consumers' interests (priorities, preferences, wants, etc.) in the ideal market system is achieved through the price mechanism. In the bureaucratic system, the articulation of consumer interest is through the central authority—the bureaucrats. In the ideal representative democracy, the articulation of political interest occurs through the voting process. In the ideal party-based socialism, it occurs through popular participation in party affairs.

The articulation of consumer interest occurs directly through the economic supply systems, namely, markets and public-sector bureaucracies. But indirect articulation of consumer interest through the political system is also important. Governments (either elected or party-based) influence the economic supply systems (markets or bureaucracies) and are supposed to check the behavior of these supply systems. Presumably, if the economic supply systems do not serve consumer interest well, then the consumers can exercise political power and impel the markets and bureaucracies to become more proconsumer.

These modes of articulation are the ideal types. Real-life articulation may follow quite different patterns. Political processes are used a lot more for articulation of (or to prevent articulation of) consumers' economic interest than economic theory would suggest. Lobbying and advocacy campaigns are used extensively in the United States. Loyalty to the party line is often a way of advancing one's economic interest in socialist societies. Corruption and nepotism as ways of furthering one's economic and political interest seem to flourish in underdeveloped societies. The absence or paucity of other legitimate channels (markets, bureaucracies, parties, elections, etc.) also seem to encourage the growth of various forms of influence peddling and corruption. Just as consumer's participation in markets is affected by the various barriers we discussed earlier, articulation of consumer interests through other systems (bureaucracies, parties, elections) is affected by comparable barriers that impact these systems. These barriers are usually the products of social conditions and, in most cases, reinforce each other. Those who can effectively articulate their economic interests are usually also able to forcefully articulate their political interest. Any overall judgment on how consumer interests in a society are served must be based on a comprehensive understanding of the prevailing economic and political supply systems. Insights into these modes of articulation are needed to understand how markets work (or do not work). Such understanding will lead to the improvement of marketers' performance, leading to an overall increase in consumer satisfaction.

There is an important distinction between market-based and bureaucratic (as well as party-based) articulation of consumer interest. In market systems, consumers with the most monetary resources are able to articulate their interest most effectively and openly. Markets confer a high degree of openness and legitimacy on the articulation of demand-backed consumer self-interests. That rich live the good life and the poor do not is an accepted fact of life. In bureaucratic systems, the articulation of consumer interest is through influencing the bureaucrats. In terms of transactional systems, this may entail nonmarket, premarket, and shadow-market transactions. Connections and corruption matter, in addition to the legitimate championing of the interests of a class of consumers by socially concerned bureaucrats. This last form of articulation (by idealistic bureaucrats or party functionaries) is perhaps the least understood by consumer researchers. It will be interesting to study conditions under which bureaucratic articulation remains in genuine consumer interest or gets corrupted in favor of the powerful and the resourceful.

The conclusions to be drawn are that consumer interest is articulated through many complex transactional systems and that there are often politically and economically strong forces preventing the articulation of consumer interests. Solutions to the problems of consumers cannot merely be sought in the chimerical realm of efficient and open markets because open markets (efficient and inefficient) are only a subset of the transactional systems in which consumers participate. Political processes of various types seem particularly important for the articulation of consumer interests.

Conclusion

Individual consumer resources have been described in the chapter in terms of economic means, problem-solving capacity, allocation of time, reach, and size and quality of accessible social network. Due to inequalities across consumers, skewed distributions of resources are often the case. Furthermore, interactions among various resources may occur—consumers high in problem-solving capacity may also be high in economic resources and have access to a high-quality social network. Such skewed and intercorrelated distributions of resources lead to inequality among consumers. Redistribution of income and improvements in consumer education may be regarded as means to improve the situation of the individual consumer by fostering greater equality among the members of society. This is what consumer policy tries to accomplish in Scandinavia, for example. It should also be noted that the not-visible and not-commercialized markets and the distributions of access to such markets have been neglected in consumer policy and marketing research; thus, important arenas contributing to individual economic and social welfare have been overlooked.

From a consumer policy point of view, the distribution of access to various supply systems as well as the sensitivity of the various supply systems in serving consumer interests should be considered. Relevant criteria for judging the performance of various supply systems are needed. Furthermore, it should be noted that the process of marketization is constantly transforming the character of supply systems in a society. A consumer policy formulated under one assumption of the supply system (e.g., that educational services are public and free) may become irrelevant if that assumption no longer holds.

The supply-system perspective advanced in this chapter has cross-cultural research implications. In comparing consumer behavior across cultures (nations), the unit of analysis should be shifted from the individual to the social system, including the degree of marketization and the type of supply systems prevailing. So far, cross-cultural research has largely focused on the individual consumer and, thus, missed the boat by omitting important social and structural factors.

Notes

1. Rogers (1976) applied a similar parties-involved perspective to explain the proinnovation bias in the research on diffusion of innovations.

2. In the past few years, this basic paradigm has been challenged. See Arndt's (1979) description of domesticated markets, Chandler's (1977) treatment of visible actors, Lindblom's (1977) discussion of various market and authority systems, and Williamson's (1979) exposition of transactional costs.

References

Andreasen, A. (1975), *The Disadvantaged Consumer*. New York: Free Press.

Arndt, J. (1976), "Reflections on Research in Consumer Behavior," in *Advances in Consumer Research*, vol, 3, B.B. Anderson, ed. Ann Arbor, Mich.: Association for Consumer Research, 213–221.

———, 1979), "Toward a Concept of Domesticated Markets," *Journal of Marketing* 43 (Fall): 69–75.

Atkinson, A.B. (1975), *The Economics of Inequality*. Oxford, England: Clarendon.

Baran, P.A. and P.M. Sweezy (1966), *Monopoly Capital*. New York: Monthly Review.

Bauer, R.A., and S.A. Greyser (1967), "The Dialogue That Never Happens," *Harvard Business Review* 45 (November-December): 2–12.

Chandler, A.D. (1977), *The Visible Hand*. Cambridge, Mass.: Harvard University Press.

Dorfman, R. (1967), *Prices and Markets*. Englewood Cliffs, N.J.: Prentice-Hall.

Ferguson, C.E. (1969), *Microeconomic Theory*. Homewood, Ill.: Richard D. Irwin.

Grønhaug, K. (1977), "Exploring Consumer Complaint Behavior: A Model and Some Empirical Results," in *Advances in Consumer Research*, vol. 4, W.D. Perrault, ed. Ann Arbor, Mich.: Association for Consumer Research, 159–65.

Grønhaug, K. and J. Arndt (1979), "Consumer Dissatisfaction and Complaining Behavior as Feedback: A Comparative Analysis of Public and Private Delivery Systems," in *Advances in Consumer Research*, vol. 7, J.C. Olson, ed. Ann Arbor Mich.: Association for Consumer Research, 324–28.

Henry, S. (1978), *The Hidden Economy: The Context and Control of Borderline Crime*. London: Martin Robertson.

Hirschman, A.O. (1970), *Exit, Voice, and Loyalty*. Cambridge, Mass.: Harvard University Press.

Houg, T. (1980), "Households and Markets: Theories and New Research on Consumption Activities," *Acta Sociologica* 23(1): 21–31.

Hunt, H.K. (1977), "CS/D — Overview and Future Directions," in *Conceptionalization and Measurement of Consumer Satisfaction and Dissatisfaction*, H.K. Hunt, ed. Cambridge, Mass.: Marketing Science Institute, 455–88.

Jacoby, J. (1978), "Consumer Research: State of the Art Review," *Journal of Marketing* 42 (April): 87–96.

Johanson, J., and L.G. Mattsson (1985), "Marketing Investments in Industrial Networks," *International Journal of Research in Marketing* 2: 185–95.

Koch, J.V. (1974), *Industrial Organization and Prices*. Englewood Cliffs, N.J.: Prentice-Hall.

Kotler, P. (1980), *Marketing Management, Analysis, Planning, and Control*, 4th ed. Englewood Cliffs, N.J.: Prentice-Hall.

Leiss, W. (1976), *The Limits of Satisfaction.* Toronto: University of Toronto Press.

Lindblom, C.E. (1977), *Politics and Markets.* New York: Basic Books.

Olander, F. (1977), "Can Consumer Dissatisfaction and Complaints Guide Public Policy Research," *Journal of Consumer Policy* 1: 124–37.

Olshavsky, R.W. (1977), "Nonbehavioral Reactions to Dissatisfaction," in *Consumer Satisfaction, Dissatisfaction and Complaining Behavior*, R.L. Day, ed. Bloomington, Ind.: Indiana University, 159–62.

Ouchi, W.G. (1980), "Market, Bureaucracies, and Clans," *Administrative Science Quarterly* 25 (March): 129–41.

Polanyi, K. (1957), *The Great Transformation.* Boston: Beacon.

Porter, M.E. (1980), *Competitive Strategy.* New York: Free Press.

Rogers, E.M. (1976), "A Personal History of Research on the Diffusion of Innovations," in *Public Policy and Marketing Thought*, A.A. Andreasen and S. Sudman, eds. Chicago: American Marketing Association, 65–76.

Rothenberg, R. (1968), "Consumer Sovereignty," in *International Encyclopedia of the Social Sciences*, D.L. Selss, ed. New York: Macmillan and Free Press, 326–35.

Sheth, J.N. (1972), "The Future of Buyer Behavior Theory," in *Proceedings of the Third Annual Conference*, M. Venkatesan, ed. Ann Arbor, Mich.: Asssociation for Consumer Research, 562–75.

———, (1979), "The Surpluses and Shortages in Consumer Behavior Theory and Research," *Journal of the Academy of Marketing Science* 7 (Fall): 414–27.

Sheth, J.N., and N.J. Mammana, (1974), "Recent Failures in Consumer Protection," *California Management Review* 16 (Spring): 64–72.

Taussig, M. (1980), *The Devil and Commodity Fetishism in South America.* Chapel Hill, N.C.: University of North Carolina Press.

Thorelli, H.B., and S.K. Thorelli (1977), *Consumer Information Systems and Consumer Policy.* Cambridge, Mass.: Ballinger.

Uusitalo, L., and J. Uusitalo (1980), "Scientific Progress and Research Traditions in Consumer Research," in *Advances in Consumer Research*, vol. 8, K.B. Monroe, ed. Ann Arbor, Mich.: Association for Consumer Research, 559–63.

Williamson, O.E. (1979), "Transaction Cost Economics: The Governance of Contractual Relations," *Journal of Law and Economics* 22 (October): 233–61.

Zaltman, G., and M. Wallendorf (1979), *Consumer Behavior: Basic Findings and Managerial Implications.* New York: John Wiley & Sons.

2

The Social Consumer: Institutional Aspects of Consumer Decision Processes

Aharon Hibshoosh
Franco Nicosia

he early contributions to the emergence of the discipline of consumer
behavior were from microeconomics and social psychology. By the late
sixties, a growing emphasis on psychological constructs and processes
became evident—for example, the dominance of the attitude research era,
followed by the information processing era, the short-lived era of the left versus
the right hemispheres of the brain, and the countercognitive revolution including the rediscovery of motivation (e.g., Nicosia 1979) and, more recently, of
emotions (e.g., Aaker and Stayman 1986). This focus has led to the relative
overlooking of the roles of the social environment in consumer behavior. Yet,
consumers act not only in a commercial environment (with stimuli such as
product and package designs and prices) but also in a social environment (with
stimuli such as norms from formal and informal institutions)—see the stream
of writings by S.J. Levy from 1959 through 1981.

The practical necessity to address our thoughts to the consumer's social
environment is frequently stressed. (See, e.g., Bartos 1982; Bogart 1982.) How
do social stimuli and contexts bear upon the consumer's thought, feelings, and
activities? Which are the sources of social stimuli; to what extent do these
sources of social stimuli act independently; and how are these stimuli coordinated so as to ensure that a consumer can "function"? The study of these and
other questions has led to useful knowledge—for instance, in the areas of child
development (e.g., the socialization of a child in a patriarchal versus a nuclear

Richard Lutz, Alladi Venkatesh, Raymond Horton, Roland Artle, Kenneth Mackenzie, Jinyong
Lee, and others gave us incisive, attentive, and meaningful reactions. Harold Kassarjian proved to
be the very warm "chaperon" that he has been for so many of us. We also acknowledge John
Myers's and Richard Holton's points.

family versus a commune) and school design and management (including the realization that the stimuli and contexts provided by the family must be coordinated with the stimuli and contexts provided by the school).

For some types of problems, the psychological focus of current consumer research is useful. To visualize a consumer behaving in a space of perceptions of, and preferences for, product attributes (characteristics) does provide actionable information to brand managers, creators of product and package designs, and advertising strategists. For such problems, it is legitimate to assume that the social environment and its norms of conduct are given. In fact, it has been argued for a long time that, for such problems, cultural values and institutional norms of conduct are meaningful once they have been internalized in the psychological processes underlying consumer behavior (e.g., Nicosia 1966, pp. 84-85, 137-140).

Yet, there are types of longterm strategic problems usually facing corporate managers and public policy makers where knowledge about the role of the social environment in affecting what consumers do, think, and feel is necessary. Two examples of the relevance of such knowledge suffice. A few years ago, projected sales of personal computers (and the related investments by the private sector) were based on several hunches; one of these was that sales of PCs for home use and at the workplace would interact synergetically (Venkatesh and Vitallari 1986a). This synergetic effect can occur if some *hidden* assumptions about the working of the social environment are correct—for example, that the norms prevailing at the workplace can change fast enough to allow people to work at home (Venkatesh and Vitallari 1986b). Another example is public policy makers' attempts to affect conservation of natural resources and decrease pollution (Henion and Kinnear 1979; Antil 1984). From local to federal levels, efforts have been made to persuade consumers to drive less, but the institutional contexts of driving activities creates a problem: a human is locked into at least two institutions—the family and the office—usually located in different parts of town and having norms of behavior that may conflict with relocation. After decades of traffic jams, families' norm still tend to prescribe that a dwelling in the suburbs is preferable to a downtown highrise. Without changes in the *norms prescribing this preference ordering*, the psychological effects of information campaigns about driving less, no matter how well conceived and executed, are bound to be limited. (See, e.g., Nicosia 1978.)

Purpose. We propose a social psychological inquiry into the nature of and the ways in which the social environment of a complex, postaffluence society may directly and indirectly be associated with what consumers do, think, and feel. There is a vast literature on society, its institutional organization, and its possible relationships with human activities. We plan to distill from this literature a few key constructs *and* some relationships among them. We will then examine the role of these relationships in guiding consumer behavior.

Given known psychological processes (e.g., cognition, motivation, and learning), these proposed relationships *describe the functioning* of a social *and* psychological consumer.

Building a Model. The proposed description of a functioning consumer is encoded in a formal language (a linear control system). The model is a *prototype* with a focus on the consumer's *institutional* aspects. The specific definitions of the chosen constructs, of the chosen relationships among the constructs, of the chosen dynamic aspects (time lags and leads), and of the stipulations on these relationships are given in the next two sections. The prototype and its boundaries are thus precise and internally consistent representations of some ideas in the literature.

The implications of these ideas as encoded in the model are systematically identified and discussed in the subsequent section. Here, we derive a number of consequences and insights, for instance: the reasons why the content (and change) of consumer preferences may be related to institutional norms rather than only product/brand attributes; the reasons why consumer behavior may occur in a space of norms and activities rather than only in a product/brand attributes space; the reasons why, in a complex society, finetuning of norms and activities bearing on consumer behavior may fail, whereas controlling the principal components of norms may succeed; the precise conditions for stability in consumer norms and activities; and a conclusion that the same stable level of consumer norms and activities will be obtained with different time lags (delays) of consumer feedbacks of norms/activities into consumer values. In addition, for purposes of empirical research, we have deliberately chosen a discrete rather than a continuous form for known advantages; for instance, use of socioeconomic time series data and availability of methods of identification and of control (specifically, ability to infer about norms from estimation of activities). Such methods (e.g., those based on Kalman filter) can also be used if the prototype model were to be extended to some nontime invariant cases (e.g., changes in social institutions and norms, social costs and optimal design, technological change, and uncertainty).

The construction of the model in the next two sections and the subsequent discussion and derivations follow conventional style. (In the social sciences, see examples ranging from Lazarsfeld 1954 and Simon 1957 to Boudon 1979, Coleman 1979, Oberschall 1979, and Glazer 1986.) For the nonmathematically inclined reader, this style of presentation may require some "faith and patience" in reading these sections and some careful examination of the subsequent section, *Discussion of the System*, to identify and assess the very precise derivations presented there.

All in all, for many decades, a number of basic disciplines have argued about the role of the social environment and its organization in shaping human behavior. Efforts to consider explicitly both social and psychological aspects of consumer decision processes have been reported for a long time, as by White 1959, Fisk 1963, Bauer (ed.) 1966, Rokeach 1968, Zaltman and Sternthal (eds.) 1975, Arndt 1976, Douglas and Isherwood 1979, Fırat and Dholakia 1982, Sherry 1983, Manson 1984, Sheth 1985, and Belk in this book. These and other efforts indicate that consumer researchers are ready to take a constructively radical step—that of modeling some of the knowledge pointed out by these efforts. The proposed model draws from the ideas in Nicosia and Glock (1968), Nicosia and Mayer (1976), Mayer and Nicosia (1981), and Nicosia (1986). However, to share commonalities with others' definitions, the model makes only minimal stipulations and it provides specific boundaries. Thus, it offers clear bases for disagreements with (1) the definitions of the chosen constructs, (2) the relationships postulated among these constructs, and (3) the substantive *derivations from* and *interpretations* of the choices in (1) and (2). By engaging in clearer and involved dialectics, we can move together toward more precise and accurate conceptual and empirical research.

Choice of Constructs and Their Relationships

We select from the literature a few constructs and their possible relationships. From the many available, we chose very specific definitions; the postulates are minimal to build a robust prototype model. The presentation is organized along verbal propositions stating constructs and their relationships. The substantive interpretations are in *Discussion of the System*.

Proposition 1

The first proposition considers three constructs: cultural values (*v*) institutions (*I*), and norms (*n*) formulated by institutions. The specific definitions of these constructs are from Nicosia and Mayer (1976).

Cultural Values. This construct appears in most social science literature. (See, e.g., Pitts and Woodside 1984; McCracken 1986.) On the one hand, it invariably implies stable and enduring elements of any culture; for instance, one reads of values of Western culture or of the Judeo-Christian tradition. On the other hand, the construct's specific domain varies a great deal within and across disciplines. For our purpose:

> Cultural values (1) are widely held beliefs, (2) affirm what is desirable, and (3) have some direct or indirect impact on consumer activities (Nicosia and Mayer 1976, p. 67).

Examples of cultural values that may characterize a contemporary Western society are: success through individual achievement, freedom of choice, active use of time, orientation toward the future, active mastery of the physical environment, and "terminal and instrumental" values. (See, e.g., the literature ranging from Riesman *et al.* 1950, and McClelland 1961, through Henry 1976, and Inglehart 1977, to Belk 1985, and others.)

Institutions. The content of this construct varies in degree and, often, kind across various disciplines, ranging from institutional economics to law and sociology, to name a few. For our purpose, it is useful to define an institution as follows:

> An institution is a set of specific activities performed by specific people in specific places through time (Nicosia and Mayer, 1976, p. 67).

This definition is related to, and it includes, the notion of "situation" as used in marketing literature. Examples of an institution as defined here are the family, the workplace, the place of worship, and the place of learning (school). Note that the worker is not the factory, the consumer is not the family, and so on. What characterizes each of these institutions is its unique *pattern* of interaction among certain specific *activities*, by specific *people*, at specific *places* through time.

Institutional Norms. Institutions create and implement *specific* norms to guide *specific* activities toward consistency with achievement of certain cultural values (e.g., Salkins 1976; Quimby 1978; and Fox and Lears 1983). Norms interpret cultural values in the context of specific activities. For example, the value "achieving" in the context of the family is spelled out into specific norms to guide specific activities such as to go to bed early, to do school work before going to play with friends, and to clean the room (Nicosia and Mayer, 1976, p. 67).

Note that we model only three functions of institutions: translation of cultural values into norms, maintaining norms, and governing performance of activities. These three functions are represented below by the operators G, H, and A, respectively.

> *Proposition 1*: Cultural values (v) are translated by a set of different institutions (I) into specific norms (n), by operator G.
>
> Graphically: $v \xrightarrow{\quad G \quad} n$

At this moment, we propose only that the number of independent cultural values v is smaller than the number of independent norms n. Further discussion of this operator G will follow; for example, we shall see in proposition 6 that the operator G also reflects the effect of the feedback of consumer activities into cultural values.

Proposition 2

The construct of institution is usually explicated on many dimensions such as "structure," "technology," and "function." In proposition 1, we modeled the specific function of translating cultural values by producing norms. In proposition 2, we stipulate that institutions tend to retain or maintain the produced norms.

> *Proposition 2*: Institutions tend to retain the produced norms through time, by operator H.

$$\text{Graphically:} \quad n^k \xrightarrow{\quad H \quad} n^{k+1}$$

where n^k, n^{k+1} represent the norms produced over the period k, $k + 1$.

At this moment, we propose that for the window of time to be considered, the number of norms remains the same through time, that is, H is a square matrix. Also, we require that H is a matrix with its largest eigenvalue less than one in absolute value; that is, we want to model the case where the efforts of retaining the previous norms are less than perfect (a case of "decay"). In addition, we require H to be full rank and diagonalizable.

Proposition 3

The construct of activity was already alluded to in the definition of institutional norms in proposition 1. Our definition of activity is any observable overt behavior (e.g., writing a check, choosing to wear a pair of shoes, calling a repair person, asking a coworker where a tie was bought, storing leftovers in a refrigerator, bringing aluminum cans to a dump site). Accordingly, we model not only the traditional activity of purchasing, but also prepurchase and, more importantly, postpurchase activities. Crucial in our modeling is that an activity is the object of a norm.

> *Proposition 3*: Institutional norms (n) govern the performance of activities (a) as they occur within each institution, by operator A.

$$\text{Graphically:} \quad n \xrightarrow{\quad A \quad} a$$

At the moment, we allow for any one norm to apply to more than one activity. The operator A is a block diagonal matrix; that is, we postulate that each block is associated with one institution and that, in each institution I, the number of activities a is greater than the number of norms n.

Proposition 4

The mechanism described so far guides the consumer to purchase and "consume" a basket of activities that presumably should satisfy the given or prevailing cultural values. Accordingly, we need a translation of the "units" of activities performed into "units" of values obtained.

> *Proposition 4*: The consumption of a basket of activities (a) leads to obtaining some units of cultural values (v'), by operator F.

$$\text{Graphically:} \quad a \xrightarrow{\quad F \quad} v'$$

At the moment, we assume that the dimension of v' is equal to that of v, and that every cultural value is realized to some extent. Note that, from the previous propositions, the dimension of a is greater than the dimension of v'. We do not postulate the possible roles of institutions in this translation.

Once a certain amount of cultural values (v') has been obtained, at least two more operations must be considered to model consumer feedback—namely, to describe a *functioning* of the social psychological consumer.

Proposition 5

In the normal course of events, the obtained value v' will differ from the "commandments" prescribed in v. We propose that some type of comparisons will occur between the obtained values (v') and the initial values considered in proposition 1. We stipulate that the initial values are and will remain given through a window of time, that is, they are ($\bar{v}$). This comparison can be conceptualized as a monitoring operation.

> *Proposition 5*: The monitoring consists of a comparison of the obtained values (v') with the initially given values ($\bar{v}$), by operator D.

$$\text{Graphically:} \quad (\bar{v}, v') \xrightarrow{\quad D \quad} u$$

where u is the result of the comparisons performed by the operator D, and is the measure of the "discrepancy" between obtained and desirable values. The comparisons may be performed by a variety of entities, ranging from biopsychological processes to a dictator or an elected body such as Congress, or even the invisible hand. In this chapter, we do not want to model explicitly the entities presiding the comparison. For simplicity, we stipulate that the operator D produces a variable $u = (\bar{v} - v')$, and that D is fixed over the time period under consideration.

Proposition 6

Recall that we began modeling the feedback of the system with proposition 4 (the obtaining of certain values v') and proceeded with proposition 5 (the comparisons of $\bar{v}$ with v'). The result of the comparisons, u, is here modeled as the system's control variable; that is, in order to create norms leading to activities that may obtain $\bar{v}$, the institutions use the control variable u to create changes in the norms n.

> *Proposition 6:* The gap between desired $(\bar{v})$ and obtained (v') values serves as the control variable u that is translated by the operator G into a change in norms, by operator G.

$$\text{Graphically:} \quad u = (\bar{v} - v') = (\bar{v} - Fa) \xrightarrow{\;\;G\;\;} n$$

where, in addition to the dimensional stipulations in proposition 1, the operator G is fixed in the time window here modeled.

Representation of the System

The choices of the constructs and of their relationships presented in the above six propositions can be represented as a linear control system. Graphically:

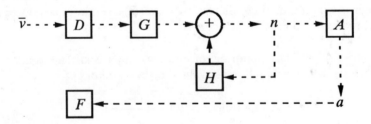

We now expand the system by considering the *dimension of time*. Given our focus on the institutional aspects of consumer behavior, we select as a unit of the time dimension the length of time for H to complete its operation. (See proposition 2.) For the operator F, we assume that its operation may take any length of time $d \geqslant 0$. For D and A, we assume that the effect of their operations is instantaneous, and the operation in G take one unit of time. We rewrite the six propositions with these stipulations on time:

1. $Gv \rightarrow n^k$, for v evaluated at time k

2. $Hn^k \rightarrow n^{k+1}$

3. $An^k \rightarrow a^k$

4. $Fa^k \rightarrow v'$, for v' evaluated at time $k + d$

5. $D(\bar{v}, v') = D(\bar{v}, Fa^{k-d}) = \bar{v} - Fa^{k-d}$, at time k

6. $G(\bar{v} - Fa^{k-d}) \rightarrow n^{k+1}$

Combining the preceding propositions, we write:

A. $n^{k+1} = Hn^k + G(\bar{v} - Fa^{k-d})$

B. $a^k = An^k$

for $v = \bar{v}; k > d;$ and $d \geqslant 0$.

As in all other applied disciplines, we shall not consider how the system (equations A and B) came into existence. The focus is on a functioning system in a time window beginning at a period k_0 greater than or equal to $d + 1$. Accordingly, the *initial* conditions for the functioning of the system during the time window here considered are known; they are

$$n^{k_0-1}, \ldots, n^{k_0-d}.$$

By substituting equation B into equation A, we obtain the system,

C. $n^{k+1} = Hn^k - GFAn^{k-d} + G\bar{v}$

D. $a^k = An^k$

We have purposefully chosen n as the state variable and a as the output, for our inquiry is focused on the *institutional* aspect of consumer decision processes. As mentioned, the proposed model captures only some ideas in past and current literature. Given the state of the art and extant knowledge, our purpose is certainly not to build a general case. On the contrary, we are only constructing a representative prototype of the institutional aspects of consumer behavior. At the moment, all we need is to agree that the substantive aspects of consumer behavior embedded into the six propositions can be translated into the two equations above.

Discussion of the System

In the following discussion of this prototype system (equations A and B), we shall probe carefully into the substantive meanings and implications of the ways in which norms may affect themselves through time (see operator H), the ways in which consumer activities may affect the functioning of the consumer (see operator A), and the ways in which activities' feedbacks affect cultural values and norms (see operators F, D, and G). Finally, we state and discuss the meaning of the conditions for a prototype system of the type here proposed to have stable equilibrium. For each operator, we first characterize formally the operator and then provide substantive interpretations.

The Management of Norms by Institutions

Institutions produce and maintain norms so as to obtain certain cultural values (propositions 1 and 2). We consider the case where the institutional efforts to enforce (retain) norms are less than perfect; that is, we want to model the case of decay in norms. (See the stipulations regarding the operator H.) We shall discuss, first, two basic ways in which norms may decay and, then, three types of social organization in which such decays may occur.

Types of Decay. In the absence of any other inputs (see the feedback and control mechanism in F, D, and G), a decay process implies the disappearance not only of norms but also of institutions, namely of the basic mechanisms through which a society can inform and coordinate human activities. It is plausible and, we believe, reasonable, to assume that institutional efforts to retain norms are less than perfect, and that decay occurs for norms both prescribing and forbidding certain activities. We discuss two basic ways in which decay occurs in real life and cast them in algebraic terms.

Norms may decay in a *gradual* way. Among recent examples, we may recall "wear a jacket and a tie at work" and "gambling is not allowed." If the decay of any norm n_i is independent of the decay of all other norms, and vice versa, then a gradual, unidirection, nonoscillatory decay can be captured by the condition that for n_i, its eigenvalue λ_i of H be $0 < \lambda_i < 1$. The path by which norms may decay could also be *oscillatory*. A case in point concerns the length of men's hair: a clean look was a crew cut; then, the norm was long hair; and eventually the length of hair tended to become an unregulated choice. This oscillatory type of decay is captured by the condition that for an independent norm n_j to decay in oscillatory fashion, it must be $-1 < \lambda_j < 0$, for λ_j of H.

In a social environment comprising a variety of institutions and norms bearing on consumer activities, it is likely that combinations of these two types of decay exist. This more reasonable possibility—different ways in which different institutions may manage their efforts to retain norms—is captured by the requirement that the eigenvalues of the operator H satisfy the condition $|\lambda_s| < 1$, for $s = 1, \ldots, n$.

In this subsection, we have derived from a vast verbal and empirical literature one particular way in which institutional norms may impinge on the psychological functioning of a consumer, namely, by a gradual and/or oscillatory decay process. This process is now characterized very specifically and quantitatively. In fact, if one were to believe that processes other than decay do exist, and were to characterize them specifically, then we know from the above discussion that the eigenvalue(s) of such processes would have to be greater than one.

The quantitative characterization of the decay process here modeled has strong implications for measurement. If reasonable realizations of this decay process were available, then estimates of the operator's eigenvalues would provide the percentage of the norms' impacts on consumer behavior from prepurchase to postpurchase activities. For example, if one were to measure a very rapid decay in norms' intensity, one could predict (in the absence of feedbacks; see below) that a consumer would eventually "function" in a normless social environment. Can one imagine a psychological consumer functioning in a normless society? In this subsection we have provided some information that will become relevant to this question in a later discussion. (See the discussion of stability conditions below.)

Coordination of Norms within and across Institutions. There may be variations in the coordination of norms within and across institutions. We can identify in the literature three types of societies (primitive, simple, and complex) depending on variations in institutional organization and functioning. The proposed model can characterize these three different social environments as they govern consumer activities.

A Primitive Institutional Organization. In this case, the result of the institutional effort to retain a norm guiding a consumer activity is independent of the result of the efforts to retain any other consumption norm. If this independence of the results of the efforts applies within and across institutions, the operator H capturing this independence is a diagonal matrix. To illustrate, consider two norms about health ("Brush your teeth before going to bed" and "Wear your shoes") and two about proper appearance ("Wear a tie at work" and "Do not have a beard at work"). It is conceivable that the results of the efforts to retain these norms by institutions such as the family and the place of work would each be independent of the other. Yet, in recent decades, it appears that the decrease in the efforts' intensity to retain all four norms have been highly dependent, at least *empirically*.

A Simple Institutional Organization. The intensity of retaining a norm may be related to the intensity of retaining other norms in a functioning society. One may conceive of a society where the institutional effort to retain any norm n_i is equal to the effort of retaining any other norm n_j. This case of dependency can be represented by a nondiagonal symmetric operator H.

It is plausible to think of a social group where norms guiding both consumption and nonconsumption activities could be retained by efforts represented with a nondiagonal symmetric operator H. To illustrate, consider a small village isolated from other social groups. There is the institution of family (say, about twenty families), one general store, and one place of worship. As life unfolds, the three institutions review the degree of success by which their norms lead activities toward the satisfaction of the group's cultural values. If changes in the intensity to retain the group's norms are necessary, it would be relatively easy to implement such changes in a symmetrical fashion.

We now raise a question. Would it also be relatively easy to implement changes in the efforts to retain desirable norms in a society where there are many institutions (families, schools, workplaces, places of worship, political parties, courts, etc.) and many units of organizations in each institution (many families, many schools, etc.)? An answer may be found by examining another type of society.

A Complex Institutional Organization. Consider a highly complex society —one with a very specialized and differentiated social organization in terms of many types of institutions, and with many units operating within each institution. As the institutions review the performance of past activities so as to satisfy a set of cultural values, the necessary changes in the efforts to retain norms would have to be implemented simultaneously within and across institutions because of the norms' dependencies.

This simultaneous implementation would not be feasible for a number of well-known lag structures, even in a highly centralized society. These lag structures are associated with the monitoring of cultural values obtained by consumer activities, the evaluations leading to possible changes in the efforts to retain desirable norms, and, last but not least, the applications of such changes by many types of institutions onto the many units in each institution.

We want to suggest that the functioning of institutions guiding consumer activities in complex societies is captured by a nondiagonal asymmetric operator H. This implies that at any point in time we would observe a wide variety in the efforts' intensity of retaining norms within and across institutions and data would thus appear to be "messy."

If this situation were to occur, conclusions could be drawn to the effect that institutions are failing in their efforts to lead activities to achieve the satisfaction of a society's values. Very likely (as seems to have occurred historically), new and more precise regulations (norms) would be issued to guide more strongly and in more detailed manner an increasing number of activities.

Yet, if the messy data were the manifestation of the working of a nondiagonal asymmetric operator H, these "interventions" would most likely disturb the natural and slow process of adjustment due to the above lags performed by the institutions. In due time, we would most likely observe either an "implosion" or an "explosion" of both the society's institutional organization and of consumer and nonconsumer activities.

In fact, such data would be a blessing, for they would help in estimation and realization. They would give the observer the opportunity to study the parameters of the operator H and, specifically, the opportunity to search for the independent principal components underlying the societal norms (as done in other control systems applications). If the studies result in successful realizations, then, rather than increasing fine-tuning of individual extant norms, control efforts could be focused on such independent components to reach more efficiently the system's goals (a society's set of values). It is important to note that in the case of H being a nondiagonal asymmetric operator, the sign of λ_c (where c denotes a principal component) indicates whether the decay is gradual or oscillatory, and the size of $1 - |\lambda_c|$ indicates the rate of the component's decay.

In this subsection, we have characterized a type of institutional environment that may impinge upon the functioning of a consumer in a complex society. We have seen that a proliferation of institutions and norms creates problems of coordination and, thus, problems of relevance to public policy strategies. In particular, the conclusion has been derived that public policy should not be focused on fine tuning, for this would not provide an institutional environment facilitating the functioning of the psychological consumer. At this moment, we should appreciate that the increase in institutions and their norms, the difficulty in coordinating such norms, and the intrinsic lags in coordination would lead a consumer to perceive contradictions among norms and across institutions and, ultimately, to sense a configuration about which norms and activities are or are not appropriate in supporting the self, especially self-identification with social groups and society. In the next section, we shall examine how a consumer psychologically handles confusion among norms and across institutions.

From Norms to Activities

We have just concluded the description of how institutions retain norms (operator *H*) in the case of a complex society. It wil be useful to specify further our meaning of a complex society on the dimensions of norms and activities as we turn to the discussion of proposition 3, namely, that institutional norms guide consumer activities through the operator *A*.

Perhaps in a historical evolutionary sense, we see a complex society emerging from a primitive one (e.g., a pastoral society) through the following events. As the population of a social group grows, an increasing number of new institutions are formed to assume governance of sets of activities previously performed by groups such as the family. Schools are created to guide educational activities; places of worship emerge to preside over religious activities; and factories, offices, and retail stores come to govern work activities. The implication of these events is that consumer activities may now occur in different institutions. More importantly, growing complexity is paralleled by growing affluence, which, in turn, allows an explosive increase in types of consumer activities not previously possible—for instance, in a primitive society, the norm "do not be wasteful" may apply to eating and dressing activities, but in a complex and affluent society, the same norm is to guide new activities such as use of electricity and gas at home as well as use of gasoline in driving to school, resorts, and movies. Accordingly, we have postulated (see proposition 3) that in a complex society, the number of activities is greater than the number of norms.

In a complex society, to understand the functioning of the consumer, we must ideally understand (1) how norms affect activities, (2) how activities may affect the institutions' generation of norms, and (3) how institutions "manage" norms.

How can such understanding be gained? In our review of the literature, we have not identified strong insights or empirical studies about these three processes. Especially in the consumer behavior literature, the emphasis has been on understanding consumers' perceptions of, and preferences for, characteristics (attributes) of goods, taking the domain of activities and norms as given. Our modeling of the institutional consumer suggests that consumer decision processes operate in a more fundamental domain (that of activities and norms) rather than only in the domain of perceptions of, and preferences for, product attributes. Vis-à-vis prevailing orientations in consumer research, the proposed model suggests that the latter domain is imbedded in the former. The implications of this derivation from the literature are fundamental.

From the model's perspective, research on norms and activities becomes a key to the understanding of the psychological consumer behaving in complex and affluent societies. As for norms, published literature has not focused on norms governing consumer activities, for consumer research appears to have assumed that norms are given. In our opinion, from a strict measurement point of view, it should be useful to consider norms as the unobserved state variables and to concentrate on the measurement of activities *in the context of* institutions. This would allow estimation and inference—if not of norms directly—at least of the functioning of combinations of norms and their effects on consumer activities.

As for consumer activities, we need conceptual and empirical knowledge of these activities as they occur in specific institutional contexts. The current available knowledge is not sufficient for at least three reasons: inappropriate classifications and recording of consumer activities; overlooking that the same activities are performed in different institutions; and very inadequate observations of postpurchase activities.

Some empirical knowledge of consumer activities is misguiding, for it is based on inappropriate classification schemes. One inappropriate classification is the lumping of consumer activities along similarities that hide the dissimilarity related to where (which institutions) activities are performed. The well-known recent difficulty in regulating transportation activities in the United States may be explained by the fact that transportation activities are lumped together, although they relate to vastly different institutions and specific norms—driving to school is different from driving to work, place of worship, and the movies. Different institutional norms may guide seemingly similar driving activities.

In addition, research has overlooked the fact that in complex societies, similar sets of activities occur in different institutions. Recall that in a pastoral family, consumption, work, and other activities were guided by the family's norms. The family management of norms so as to obtain activities reaching certain cultural values could be relatively consistent over time. In a complex society, consumer activities occur in the family and several other institutions. The so-called dichotomy of work and leisure hides the fact that such activities can occur not only in their related institutions, but in numerous others as well.

One of the consequences of this state of affairs is that any one consumer activity tends to be performed in different institutions and, thus, be the object of different institutional norms. Accordingly, the utility and the ordering of preferences for a set of activities performed in one institution may differ from those emerging in other institutions. Any consumer is thus likely to experience conflict. Concurrently, the coordination among the norms of different institutions necessary to obtain a set of cultural values is bound to be slow and complex. Both of these processes—conflict and coordination—may cause instability within each consumer and within the societal fabric.

Finally, very little is known about consumer activities. For decades, published literature has concentrated on the study of the activity of buying. Undoubtedly, this activity, a fugitive instant in time, is relevant for legal and accounting purposes. Yet, for understanding consumer decision processes, especially their institutional aspect, knowledge about buying activities is not sufficient. There is some knowledge about prepurchase activities (consumer information obtained through mass media, shopping, and word of mouth). Yet, to the extent that *the verb to buy differs in kind from the verb to consume*, our modeling indicates that we should learn also about postpurchase consumption activities—storing, using, maintaining, repairing, and disposing (Nicosia and Mayer 1976; Belk 1987)—for they are the very core of consumer behavior in postaffluence (of an alive consumer functioning over time). (See, e.g., the recasting of consumer satisfaction as a postpurchase process in Tse 1984 and Wilton and Nicosia 1986.)

Consumer research has been given an opportunity to focus on consumer activities as early as the sixties. (See, e.g., Becker 1965; Foote 1966; Linder 1970; and Lancaster 1971, pp. 47–49.) Yet, the tendency has remained to study a consumer behaving in the domain of product attributes rather than in the larger domain of the activities that a person chooses and, thus, the set of attributes that may appear more likely to satisfy the chosen activities. More importantly, all activities should be observed in the context of the specific institutions and their specific norms, for different institutional norms may lead to unique and conflicting considerations, choices, and performances of different sets of activities.

Another implication of the modeling proposed must be made explicit. The consumer's choice of a set of activities does lead to the related *use of time*— namely, the allocation of the scarce resource called time to one rather than another *basket of activities*. Following the discussion of a complex society, different institutions may press for different and usually conflicting ordering of activity preferences and, thus, call for different *time-allocation* schemes. (See, e.g., Deighton, Nicosia, and Wind 1983; Hawes 1986.) Here, we find again the potential of psychological conflict in the institutional consumer. We shall not pursue further the question of time allocation to different baskets of activities (and eventually different baskets of product attributes) in this inquiry.

In concluding the discussion of the operators *A* and *H*, the proposed modeling of the institutional consumer calls for recasting consumer research into the domain of institutional norms and consumer activities and viewing norms and activities as primary sources of psychological conflict. This radical recasting may lead to theoretical results different from those we currently accept, that, although possibly not relevant to a brand manager, are in our professional experience relevant to corporate managers and public policy makers.

Feedback and Control Processes

To model a "living" (functioning) consumer requires at least a feedback process and a control process. As illustrated earlier by the flow chart of the model, the feedback and control mechanism are modeled by the operators F, D, and G. Specifically, the operator F transforms the performed activities into units of values v'. In turn, the operator D compares the obtained units v' with the initially given values $\bar{v}$, and the gap between the two values is signified by the system's control variable u. This control variable is then translated into changes of norms' intensity by the operator D.

In this chapter, space allows us to focus only on modeling the institutional aspects of a consumer. Thus, the stipulations on the operators F and D were purposefully kept simple. However, they do allow characterization of different socioeconomic systems and their differential impacts on the institutional consumer.

Richer stipulations would require modeling at least three aspects of these two operators. First, one should explicitly consider the entities that may enact the controlling mechanism—be it an elective body such as the U.S. Congress, a benevolent dictator, supreme court, consumer union, or the invisible hand. Second, one would have to consider how different controlling entities go about their tasks. Finally, the modeling of the "who" and the "how" would have to proceed with considerations of the related "costs" and, eventually, of designing optimal F and D.

In concluding a discussion of the feedback and control mechanisms F, D, and G, one must notice some related implications of our analysis of the previous operators H and A. Recall that, if any one activity meets the requirement of any institutional norm, then it is legitimate to consider such norm as given. However, if some performed activities do not meet the norms of one or more institutions, then the modeling of this case would have to be addressed to the unraveling of basic complexities.

One central consequence of the modeling of H and A would be to consider the additional feedback of consumer activities directly into institutions. That is, the conflicts between activities and norms within and across institutions would become one of the factors pushing toward changes in norms and/or even in the very nature of some institutions. Eventually, such conflicts would have to lead to changes in extant entities and/or creation of new entities presiding over institutional conflict resolution (ranging, e.g., from small claims courts to black markets), for failure to do so would not provide the social environment in which a psychological consumer can function.

Modeling the feedback of consumer activities directly into institutions would naturally raise the perennial question in many social sciences: To what extent do individuals and their activities lead to the creation of institutions, and, concurrently, to what extent do institutions and their norms inform and shape human activities? (See, e.g., Blau 1960; Tannenbaum and Bachman 1964; and Coleman 1986.) The flow chart of the model clearly indicates that we do not intend in this chapter to model and examine feedback of activities into institutions and entities presiding over control mechanisms.

Dynamics of the Institutional Consumer

The preceding discussion and the early stipulations indicate the commitment to model an institutional consumer within a time window where the structure of the decision process is fixed (the operators H, A, F, D, and G are fixed). Within these limits, an analysis of the dynamics of the model reveals further insights.

The Functioning of the Institutional Consumer. Recall that we chose as a unit of time the length of time for H to perform its operations, and that the time delay associated with the operation of F may assume various values of $d \geqslant 0$. For the case of $d = 0$, the feedback of activities through F is instantaneous. The combined operations of D and G take one unit of time. Thus, the intensities of the norms in the next period $k + 1$ (see equation C) depend ultimately only on the intensities of the norms at time k, given the cultural values. For the case of time delay $d > 0$, the intensities of the norms at time $k + 1$, n^{k+1}, ultimately depend on n^k and n^{k-1} through n^{k-d}.

Empirically, it is worth stressing that depending on the actual time span for the feedback of activities into the social control mechanism, a very large variety of fluctuations—dynamic paths—may occur. The estimation of the actual time span for H and F has very clear actionable implications for both private and public management, for one would gain insights into the lag structures mentioned previously.

System Equilibrium. We can now conclude the discussion of the proposed modeling of the institutional aspects of the consumer with a note about the system equilibrium. From equations C and D it follows that a sufficient condition for stable equilibrium of both norms and activities is that every eigenvalue λ_i of the matrix $(H - GFA)$ satisfies $|\lambda_i| < 1$. The equilibrium levels for norms and activities are provided in equations E and F respectively:

$$\text{E.} \quad n_{eq} = [I - (H - GFA)]^{-1}G\bar{v}$$

$$\text{F.} \quad a_{eq} = An_{eq} = A[I - (H - GFA)]^{-1}G\bar{v}$$

Furthermore, the dynamic path of norms and activities would vary from model to model based on different values of time lags of feedbacks. Nevertheless, the different models consistent with our system still require the same equilibrium conditions and still predict that the same equilibrium levels of norms and consumption activities will be reached.

Some substantive interpretations of the equilibrium conditions and values are warranted. Recall that social consumption is likely to be characterized by processes whereby norms of different institutions generate conflicting preferences for activities and, ultimately, for consumption commodities. Yet, at least when dealing with major aggregates of products, their consumption tends to be quite stable over time. To the extent that a trend is exhibited, it is a rather smooth one. Our framework can help explain such observation. The equilibrium conditions of norms and activities place certain requirements on the relationship among institutional mechanisms, namely that the joint net retaining effort of any norm must be imperfect. This effort is comprised of direct retaining effort through H combined with indirect efforts through activity feedback into cultural values by GFA. Hence, it can be thought that no given norm's intensity can exercise lasting effect on the intensity of norms that are dated far into the future. However, through the retaining efforts, future intensity of norms is gradually formed by society's continuous reference to its cultural values.

Some Concluding Remarks

Over decades, mainstream consumer research has been successful in its study of psychological processes governing the behavior of consumers, and it has been useful in solving problems concerning brand management, product management, advertising management, and so on. We have proposed to look at the social environment of a consumer, especially the ways institutional arrangements of a society may bear on the psychological consumer.

We have distilled from a vast body of literature about society and its institutional organization a few constructs and their relationships that in our professional experience appear to be central in governing the behavior of the institutional consumer. We have constructed and discussed a prototype system representing an institutional consumer, and we have developed a number of insights about its functioning in a complex, postaffluence society.

Among these insights, we stress four. As the number of institutions and the number of consumer activities increases, and as consumer activities are performed in many different institutions, fine tuning—efforts to create more and more norms—may lead to impossible problems of social coordination within and across institutions. Identifying and focusing efforts on the main components of institutional norms may be a more efficient way if not the only possible way for society to guide consumer activities toward obtaining a desired set of cultural values.

Related to this is a second insight. As consumer activities may be performed in various institutions, differences in norms across institutions may lead to different preference rankings for consumer activities. Coping with such differences leads consumers to experience psychological conflicts in their choices of a satisfying basket of activities (and, eventually, bundles of product attributes). We did not attempt to model or discuss in general the resolution of such conflicts at either the individual or the institutional and societal levels. It is clear, however, that if these two insights and their implications were to occur empirically in modern affluent and postaffluent societies, then conceptual modeling and empirical research in the direction of these two insights may contribute to the framing and solution of a number of strategic problems facing private and public managers.

A third insight concerns the basic debate in the literature about whether cultural values have an effect, and the magnitude of the effect, on buying and other consumer activities. (See, e.g., Pitts and Woodside 1984; Munson 1984; Mayer and Nicosia 1981; and Horton 1986.) The conceptual view underlying this debate is that "buying is a function of cultural values." This view may be too parsimonious. It ignores the literature that suggests the importance of institutional processes that either intervene (see, e.g., the operators H and A) and/or follow (see, e.g., the operators F, G, and D) the postulated relationship of cultural values with consumer activities. These overlooked processes may amplify and/or dampen the measured impacts of the parsimonious relationship (see, e.g., equations C and D) and, thus, would usually lead to bias in the estimates of the impact of cultural values on consumer behavior. In addition, *omission* of such processes will lead to low goodness of fit statistics; that is, one would observe that a great variability in consumer activities would not be explained by cultural values.

A fourth contribution of our modeling efforts is the provision of strong *measurement* bases to work in consumer research. Thus, for example, we chose to encode our ideas in a discrete linear control system in order to relate closely to current empirical measures such as those in the national income accounts and cost of living surveys. More generally, our efforts were dedicated to the identification of "restrictions" implicitly posed by the literature on properly specified models of the ways in which institutional environments impinge upon the psychological consumer. As for the measurement of activities and time allocation to activities, we stress again that there are available methodologies that have been used successfully. Finally, the choice of a discrete rather than a continuous system was made to facilitate future research incorporating consideration of social costs, optimization of design, environmental shocks, uncertainties, and technological changes.

The expository system we have proposed has one explicit exogeneous vector variable—the cultural value v. The operators of the system were assumed to be time-invariant so as to gain insights into the working of norms and activities. This time-invariance should be gradually relaxed in future research since a vast amount of literature suggests events that may make for changes in such operators. One of these events is the rapid succession of technological changes that have affected the functioning of work institutions and their norms. More recently, some research has been addressed on how, over the long term, technological changes have affected the operation and the norms of a family (e.g., Venkatesh and Vitallari 1986b; Nicosia 1983) and related institutions (Venkatesh and Vitallari 1986a; Nicosia 1986).

All in all, the very basic thrust of our efforts has been to explore relatively uncharted areas and to suggest new and exciting directions of future research to complement and strengthen the discipline of consumer behavior.

References

Aaker, D., D.M. Stayman, and M.R. Hagerty (1986), "Warmth in Advertising: Measurement, Impact and Sequence Effects," *Journal of Consumer Research* (March).

Antil, J.H. (1984), "Socially Responsible Consumer: Profile and Implications for Public Policy," *Journal of Macromarketing* (Fall): 18–39.

Arndt, J. (1976), "Reflections on Research in Consumer Behavior," in *Advances in Consumer Research, Vol. 3*, B.B. Anderson, ed., 213–221.

Bartos, R. (1982), "Social Research Redefines Marketer's Target Audience," *Marketing News* (May 14).

Bauer, R.A., ed. (1966), *Social Indicators*, Cambridge, Ma: MIT Press.

Becker, G.S. (1965), "A Theory of Allocation of Time," *Economic Journal* (September).

Belk, R.W. (1985), "Materialism: Trait Aspects of Living in the Material World," *Journal of Consumer Research* 12 (December): 265–280.

Blau, P.M. (1960), "Structural Effects," *American Sociological Review* 25: 178–193.

Bogart, L. (1982), "Research Total Ad Environment as Media Choices Expand," *Marketing News* (May 14).

Boudon, R. (1979), "Generating Models as a Research Strategy," in R.K. Coleman, and P.H. Rossi, eds. *Qualitative and Quantitative Social Research: Papers in Honor of Paul F. Lazarsfeld*, New York: Free Press.

Coleman, J.S. (1979), "Purposive Actors and Mutual Effects," in Merton, Coleman, and Rossi, *op. cit.*

———, (1986), "Social Theory, Social Research and a Theory of Action," *American Journal of Sociology* 19 (6): 1309–35.

Deighton, J., F.M. Nicosia, and Y. Wind (1983), "Exploration into the Time-Money Tradeoff: Concepts and an Application," in *Strategic Planning: A Theory of the Past or a Necessity for the Future?* Proceedings, European Society of Marketing Research, Japan Marketing Research Association, Japan Marketing Association, American Marketing Association (April).

Douglas, M., and B. Isherwood (1979), *The World of Goods: Toward an Anthropology of Consumption*. New York: Norton.

Fırat, A.F., and N. Dholakia (1982), "Consumption Choices at the Macro Level," *Journal of Macromarketing* 2 (Fall): 6–15.

Fisk, R. (1963), *Leisure Spending Behavior*. Philadelphia: University of Pennsylvania.

Foote, N.N. (1966), "The Time Dimensions and Consumer Behavior," in *On Knowing the Consumer*, J.W. Newman, ed. New York: Wiley.

Fox, R.W., and T.J. Lears, eds. (1983), *The Culture of Consumption: Critical Essays in American History*: 1880–1980. New York: Pantheon.

Glazer, R. (1986), "A Holographic Theory of Decision-Making," working paper. New York: Graduate School of Business, Columbia University.

Hawes, D.K. (1986), "Time Budgets and Consumer Leisure-Time Behavior: An Eleven-Year-Later Replication and Extension," in *Advances in Consumer Research*.

Henion, K.E., and T.C. Kinnear, eds. (1979), *The Conserver Society*. Chicago: American Marketing Association.

Henry, W. (1976), "Cultural Values Do Correlate with Consumer Behavior," *Journal of Marketing Research 13* (May): 121–127.

Horton, R., and P.J. Horton (1986), "Organ Donation and Values: Identifying Potential Organ Donors." Bethlehem, Pa.: Department of Marketing, Lehigh University.

Inglehart, R. (1977), *The Silent Revolution: Changing Values and Political Styles among Western Publics*. Princeton, N.J.: Princeton University Press.

Lancaster, K. (1971), *Consumer Demand, A New Approach*. New York: Columbia University Press.

Lazarsfeld, P.F., ed. (1954), *Mathematical Thinking in the Social Sciences*. New York: Free Press.

Levy, S. (1959), "Symbols for Sale," *Harvard Business Review 37* (July-August): 117–124.

———,(1981), "Interpreting Consumer Mythology: A Structural Approach to Consumer Behavior," *Journal of Marketing 45* (Summer): 49–61.

Linder, S.B. (1970), *The Hurried Leisure Class*. New York: Columbia University Press.

Mayer, R.N., and F.M. Nicosia (1981), "Social Organization and Changing Consumer Values," in *Management under Differing Value Systems*, G. Duglos and K. Weirmair, eds. Berlin: Walter de Gruyter.

McClelland, D.C. (1961), *The Achieving Society*. New York: Free Press.

McCracken, G. (1986), "Culture and Consumption: A Theoretical Account of the Structure and Movement of Cultural Meaning of Consumer Goods," *Journal of Consumer Research* (June).

Merton, R.K., J.S. Coleman, and P.H. Rossi, eds. (1979), *Qualitative and Quantitative Social Research: Papers in Honor of Paul F. Lazarsfeld*. New York: Free Press.

Munson, J.M. (1984), "Personal Values: Considerations on Their Measurement and Applications to Five Areas of Research Inquiry," in *Personal Values and Consumer Psychology*, R.E. Pitts, Jr., and A.G. Woodside. Lexington, Mass.: Lexington Books.

Nicosia, F.M. (1966), *Consumer Decision Processes*. Englewood Cliffs, N.J.: Prentice-Hall.

——— , (1978), expert witness testimony, California Senate.

——— , (1979), "What Happened to Motivation in Consumer Psychology?" National convention, American Psychological Association, New York.

——— , (1983), "Technology, the Family, and Consumer Behavior: Implications for Strategic Marketing," in *Strategic Planning: A Theory of the Past or a Necessity of the Future?* Proceedings, European Society of Marketing Research, Japan Marketing Research Association, Japan Marketing Association, American Marketing Association, April.

——— , (1986), "The Post-Affluence Consumer: Consumer Decision Processes Revisited," in K.E.K. Möller, ed., *Proceedings*, Annual Conference, European Marketing Academy, Helsinki (June).

Nicosia, F.M., and C.Y. Glock (1968), "Marketing and Affluence: A Research Prospectus," in F.W. Webster, ed., Fall Conference Proceedings, American Marketing Association, Chicago.

Nicosia, F.M., and R.N. Mayer (1976), "Toward a Sociology of Consumption," *Journal of Consumer Research* (September).

Oberschall, A. (1979), "Social Exchange and Choice," in Merton, Coleman and Rossi, *op. cit.*

Pitts, R.E., Jr., and A.G. Woodside, eds. (1984), *Personal Values and Consumer Psychology.* Lexington, Mass.: Lexington Books.

Quimby, I., ed. (1978), *Material Culture and the Study of Material Life.* New York: Norton.

Riesman, D., N. Glazer, and R. Demney (1950), *The Lonely Crowd.* New Haven, Conn.: Yale University Press.

Rokeach, M. (1968), *Beliefs, Attitudes, and Values.* San Francisco, Calif.: Jossey-Bass.

Saklins, M. (1976), *Culture and Practical Reason.* Chicago: University of Chicago Press.

Sherry, J.F., Jr. (1983), "Gift Giving in Anthropological Perspective," *Journal of Consumer Research* (September).

Sheth, J.N. (1985), "Broadening the Horizons of ACR and Consumer Behavior," *Advances in Consumer Research*, Proceedings, Association of Consumer Research, Annual Conference.

Simon, H.A. (1957), *Models of Man.* New York: Wiley.

Tannenbaum, A., and G. Bachman (1964), "Structural versus Individual Effects," *American Journal of Sociology* 69: 585–95.

Tse, D.K. (1984), *A Model of Consumer Post-purchase Processes, Ph.D. Dissertation.* Graduate School of Business Administration, University of California at Berkeley.

Venkatesh, A., and N. Vitallari (1986a), "Computing Technology for the Home: Product Strategies for the Next Generation," *Journal of Product Innovation and Management 3* (December).

Venkatesh, A., and N. Vitallari (1986b), "A Longitudinal Analysis of Home Computer Use," working paper. University of California at Irvine.

White, I.S. (1959), "The Functions of Advertising in Our Culture," *Journal of Marketing* (July).

Wilton, P.C., and F.M. Nicosia (1986), "Emerging Paradigms for the Study of Consumer Satisfaction," *European Research* (January).

Zaltman, G., and B. Sternthall, eds. (1975), *Broadening the Concept of Consumer Behavior.* Association of Consumer Research.

3

Changing Asymmetry in Marketing

Meir Karlinsky

> Customers do have limited information and limited capacity to process it. This is the way of the world.
>
> —R.A. Bauer and S.A. Greyser

> The reasonable man adapts himself to the world; the unreasonable one persists in trying to adapt the world to himself. Therefore all progress depends on the unreasonable man.
>
> —George Bernard Shaw

The first epigraph (Bauer and Greyser 1969) exemplifies marketing theory, current philosophical view about consumers—a view that, as is shown below, has had a considerable impact on the development of marketing theory and research. The second, taken from Shaw's *Man and Superman*, embodies the author's belief in the need for, and usefulness of, radical thought—especially those thoughts whose time has come.

The purpose of this chapter is to point out the asymmetric development of marketing theory and research with respect to marketers and consumers, trace this development's roots and reasons, and suggest that the time is ripe for a change toward a more symmetric approach.

Asymmetry in Marketing

Before delineating what asymmetry in marketing is all about, it is useful to discuss why and how the symmetry concept is used. It should be claimed at the outset that there is nothing sacred about symmetry *qua* symmetry. It is used here only as a diagnostic and instrumental device of criticism and constructive change.

The author wishes to thank David Aaker, Paul Anderson, Shelby Hunt and the editors of this volume for helpful comments on an earlier version of this paper. John Myers is especially acknowledged for his patient and constructive help.

Symmetry

In the classical Helenic era, the term *symmetry* belonged to a group of terms and phrases that designated harmony, rhythm, balance, equipoise, stability, good proportions, and evenness of structure. It was a dominant trait in Sophist statements on moral, social, and political issues (Guthrie 1969).

Symmetry, as wide or as narrow as one may define its meaning, is one idea by which human beings through the ages have tried to comprehend the created order, beauty, and perfection (Weyl 1952). Symmetries, if broadly conceived, seem to occur everywhere and anywhere in nature, in cognition (even in perception), in moral and religious tenets, in aesthetic expressions and aspiration, and generally in mimetic experiences of any kind (Wiener 1973). In particular, when one observes asymmetry or lack of symmetry, the possibility of symmetry is usually invoked. If such symmetry is indeed desirable or warranted, the symmetry perspective seems to be quite productive in suggesting what to symmetrize and how.

For example, symmetry relates to invariance and conservation laws which are the core concepts of present-day physics. New and deeper understanding of the properties of matter are achieved by advance notions of dynamic symmetry and supersymmetry.

In economics, treating both consumers and producers in a symmetric fashion (namely, modeling both as maximizing agents) yields a powerful paradigm for analyzing economic behavior (Debreu 1959). Considerations of asymmetry of information in the marketplace led to the modeling of market failures (Akerlof 1970) and started a productive stream of research on informational asymmetries, agency theory, and the like.

In psychology, taking a symmetric perspective by comparing the layperson's causal-inference abilities to those of the scientist resulted in the so-called intuitive scientist hypothesis (Kelley 1967, 1973). Research on this hypothesis has revealed profound, systematic, and fundamental errors in people's judgments and inferences (Nisbett and Ross 1980; Tversky and Kahneman 1974, 1981). These findings, which are very important for the general theory of decision making, might have been slower to come by, had the hypothesis not started with the symmetry perspective.

The moral that seems to emerge from this discussion is that taking a symmetric perspective in marketing might be useful for analysis, research, and change.

Normative and Positive Research

In recent years, there has been a debate about the proper philosophy of science for marketing (Bush and Hunt 1982; Anderson and Ryan 1984; Dholakia and Arndt 1985). While scholars differ significantly in whether they support positivist or relativist approaches to marketing theory development, they seem to agree on two issues. The first is that exchange is the core concept of marketing (Hunt 1983; Peter and Olson 1983). The second is that the development of marketing theory and research, as exemplified in textbooks and journal articles, is dominated by the managerial approach (Arndt 1985; Hunt and Speck 1985).

From a symmetry perspective, these two issues are not conformable to one another. The concept of exchange (Bagozzi 1975) or transaction (Kotler 1972) is inherently symmetric. For marketing to be the science of the exchange in its broad meaning, the exchange concept has to be defined in symmetric terms. Bagozzi, for example, when defining exchange, uses symmetric terms such as *actors* and *social parties*, rather than the asymmetric expressions of *buyer* versus *seller* or *supplier* versus *customer*.

The managerial approach or, in Tucker's (1974) words, "through the eyes of the channel captain," is inherently asymmetric (Anderson 1983). This asymmetry becomes more apparent if we characterize it in terms of the normative–positive dichotomy in marketing (Hunt 1976), a dichotomy that is well known and much debated (Etgar 1977; Robin 1977, 1978; Hunt 1978). According to Hunt (1983), positive marketing adopts the perspective of attempting to describe, explain, predict, and understand marketing activities and phenomena. This perspective examines what *is*. In contrast, normative marketing adopts the perspective of attempting to prescribe what marketing organizations and individuals ought to do. That is, this perspective examines what *ought to be* and what organizations and individuals *ought to do*.

There are two kinds of normative "ought": the ethical and the rational. The former prescribes what is morally correct. The latter prescribes the best possible way of achieving given goals under given conditions.

An examination of the list of issues and problems under the normative–positive classification (Hunt 1983, pp. 10–11) reveals that while firms are treated both positively and normatively (mainly rationally), consumers are almost exclusively treated positively. If there are normative issues regarding consumers, they are of the ethical type, for example, "Is consumer sovereignty desirable?" rather than "How to find the best buy?" which is of the rational type.

In recent years, most of the research in marketing has been of the rationally normative type when it comes to firms and managers, but strictly positive when it comes to consumers. There is some positive research on managers, but, as Lutz (1979, p. 5) noted: "we have virtually ignored (in a scientific sense) the behavior of the party selling to the consumer. . . . This is simply not good science." The situation is even worse when it comes to rationally normative research for consumers—there is none. Of course, there is positive research that can be used to enhance consumer welfare (for example, Malhotra 1984), much as there is other positive research that can be used to improve managerial decision making. But there is no rationally normative research making direct use of the positive research for consumers' benefit.

Asymmetry

The asymmetry in the development of marketing theory and research is that of rationally normative research for managers but only positive research on consumers. This is exactly the managerial approach to marketing: The marketing manager needs to have a good understanding of the market (positive consumer research) before employing the recommended means (rationally normative research) to achieve desired goals.

This is an approach that some marketing scholars believe to be appropriate for marketing science: "My perspective is that of a marketing scientist. My goal is to study marketing phenomena and to develop theory and methodology which help managers better understand the environment in which they operate in order to use marketing strategies proactively to maximize profit" (Hauser 1985).

Evidence for such an asymmetric state of affairs is abundant, though scattered, in marketing textbooks and journal articles. An example of such general evidence is the popularity of the "managerial relevance" institution found at the end of many articles. There are, however, two relevant specific testimonies. First, in surveying the first four decades of the *Journal of Marketing*, Grether (1976) has found the topical areas of marketing management, marketing mix variables, and marketing research to command the highest continuing interest. Second, comparing the two editions of Bartels' (1962, 1976) book on the historical development of marketing thought, one finds a new chapter titled "Marketing Management." Bartels also observed that many general marketing courses had been superseded by courses in marketing management. A parallel phenomenon occurred with marketing textbooks. Lichtenthal and Beik (1984), for example, argue that Howard's text *Marketing Management: Analysis and Decision* (1957) hallmarks the arrival of the marketing management era. Also in 1957, Wroe Alderson introduced *Marketing Behavior and Executive Action*, where he identifies the need for theory in marketing as stemming from the "ever increasing demands from business executives" (p. 4).

Reasons for Asymmetry

I would argue, however, that the roots of the managerial approach to the development of marketing thought lie much deeper. There seem to be four related reasons for that: Interests of early scholars, the received economic view of consumers, business education, and the technology of decision making.

Early Scholars

Although the formal history of marketing starts at about 1900 (Bartels 1976), there were some important writers in the field of marketing prior to 1900. Frank Coolson (1960) has identified Edward Atkinson, David A. Wells, and Henry and Arthur B. Farquhars, as the *Laissez faire* economists of the late nineteenth century whose contributions to marketing theory have been significant and influential.

Of the four, Atkinson and Arthur B. Farquhar were businessmen. The latter collaborated with his brother Henry, a government statistician. Wells was chairman of the U.S. Revenue Commission and later chairman of the New York State Tax Commission. These four liberal-minded economists became interested in marketing phenomena as part of their search for an answer to the question: How can the American people obtain the greatest total abundance from the land of boundless resources? However, their viewpoint was business-oriented, to a large extent because of the era and their occupations. In a time characterized by overproduction and steadily declining prices, the consumer was not a problem; conducting an efficient business of distribution was the main issue.

Similarly, of the twenty pioneer marketing scholars listed in Converse's (1959) survey of the 1900–1923 period, at least thirteen were, in one stage or another, businessmen. As Converse noted, making the distinction between the teachers and the businessmen was not easy since many of the pioneers rotated between these vocations. Taking the channel captain viewpoint on marketing phenomena was, for these early scholars, almost inevitable. And indeed, the then emerging approaches to studying marketing (commodity, institutional and functional) were all intimately related to the commercial channel and only remotely to consumers. In so far as the direction of marketing thought has been determined by these early scholars, it could not but develop asymmetrically.

Received Economic View of Consumers

At its inception, marketing was considered to be a branch of applied economics which, although new, had roots that went back as early as the economic thought of Plato (Cassels 1936). Converse (1945) polled teachers and researchers of marketing who entered the field prior to 1920 or in the early 1920s as to the importance of older fields of knowledge for marketing. Grading the first choice 1, a second choice 2, and so on to 6, the first three average ratings were 1.5 for economics, 2.7 for management, and 3.2 for psychology, attesting to the impact that economics has had on marketing thought.

Towards midcentury, it was still strongly argued that "A marketing course devoid of economic theory is sterile; the student is presented with a superfluity of facts and descriptive material without the economic framework needed to analyze and evaluate the marketing structure" (Seelye 1947). Recently, Steiner (1984) argued that "there is an urgent need to return to the tradition of the earlier marketing/economics thinkers and to build a descriptive and theoretical analysis of the consumer goods economy on the solid base they had begun to erect."

Thus, it is clear that the view economics has of consumers should have had a determinant impact on the development of marketing thought. But what exactly is this view?

Seemingly, it is an honorable and a complimentary one. It starts with the founder of modern economics, Adam Smith (1776/1937, p. 625) who stated: "Consumption is the sole end and purpose of all production; and the interest of the producer ought to be attended to, only so far as it may be necessary for promoting that of the consumer. The maxim is so perfectly self-evident, that it would be absurd to attempt to prove it." This early description of what is known today as "consumer sovereignty" is sometimes expressed as "producers dancing to the tune of consumers" (Mansfield 1980, p. 53).

The problem with such an approach is that it views consumption as something basic, natural, and driven by more or less fixed tastes, while production and distribution seem to be complementary, artificial, and dynamic. In other words, the view is that consumption and choice thereof come naturally and need no further improvement, while production and distribution are recent inventions that need attention and help to improve and perfect. After all, if it was not for the snake, Adam and Eve and their descendants would have been choosing and consuming without ever producing.

It is not only that the economic view does not see the need for a (rationally) normative help for consumers, but that it is ideologically against it. For example, the concept of consumer sovereignty rests on two fundamental postulates concerning human behavior:

1. Consumers make choices among alternatives in a manner consistent with their own evaluations of their self-interest.

2. Given that adequate information is available, consumers are the best judges of their own self-interest.

Economists (e.g., Quirk 1976, p. 60) believe the first statement to be a scientific one and testable, but regard the second postulate as an ethical belief or a value judgment. This point of view is expressed even more strongly by Henry David Thoreau in his epic *Walden* (in the first chapter, "Economy"), "If I knew for certainty that a man was coming to my house with the conscious design of doing me good, I should run for my life." While clearly this view is against ethical "ought to" policy and not against rational "ought to" advice, it had its influence on the latter as well.

Note, however, that in economics, there is not a parallel normative reservation with regard to producers. The theory of the firm is unbashfully normative, as the following story attests: In one of the leading business schools, a student pointed out to a distinguished economics professor that he was observing the behavior of his fellow students and that they did not seem to be profit maximizers. "By the time they leave this school, they will be," answered the professor dryly.

Closely related to these postulates of consumer behavior is the Arrow-Debreu (1954) general equilibrium model of perfect competition. This model, because of its Pareto optimality feature, serves as a standard of comparison for other, more realistic, models. One of its unrealistic assumptions is that of "perfect information." This is a somewhat misleading term. It is better called "perfect effective knowledge" since it actually assumes not only the availability of full information, free of charge to all economic agents, but much more. It assumes that all agents have acquired the relevant information, have internalized it, and have actually utilized it effectively when making decisions.

While this view of a consumer is refuted again and again in marketing and consumer behavior research (e.g., Olshavsky and Granbois 1979), the economic legacy of the omniscient consumer who is naturally endowed with efficient and effective tools for choice and consumption prevails in the guiding philosophy of research in marketing. An extreme example of such view is found in an advertising campaign run by Scott Paper Company hailing the American housewife as "The Original Computer. . . . [A] strange change comes over a woman in a store. The soft glow in the eye is replaced by a steely financial glint; the graceful walk becomes a panther's strike among bargains. A woman in a store is a mechanism, a prowling computer" (Feldman 1976, p. 35). Portraying the consumer as king or queen, while flattering, has resulted in a view of a passive element of the economic system that need not change or improve its natural inheritance of choice and consumption competence.

Business Education

Scholars and students of marketing are found in business and management schools. Whether vocational or, to use a more dignified term, professional, these schools prepare most of their students for business careers. It is only natural that the business viewpoint will dominate their thought. In fact, the emergence of business schools was the result of demand for trained businesspeople when the conduct of business became too complex and dynamic to allow for training on the job.

Early courses in marketing were almost entirely descriptive. The material was obtained from businesspeople through personal interviews (Hagerty 1936; Litman 1950) or by studying first-hand and physically following shipments of commodities (Weld 1941). Choice and consumption, though, were not considered a relevant part of the observation.

The descriptive approach has changed to a normative one as a result of two factors. The first was the application of Taylor's scientific management to marketing, mainly by businesspeople (La Londe and Morrison 1967). The second was the explicit recommendations of Ford Foundation and Carnegie Foundation studies on business education. Beside recommending going beyond the then current business practices, they suggested, backing the suggestion with appropriate funds, the extensive usage of behavioral and quantitative methods, thus creating a common knowledge and methodological base which (while shared by marketing scholars and the newly trained businesspeople) is beyond consumers' comprehension. Although such knowledge has become much less common since then (Myers, Massy, and Greyser, 1980), it is far more common than the knowledge shared with the average consumer.

Technology of Decision Making

Though the formation of business policy was always influential in marketing thought, only in recent years has emphasis been placed upon marketing management as a decision-making process (Bartels 1976). Of the new technological inventions, the computer is the one most used for advancing decision making. It is also the technological device that until recently was shared by academia and business, but not by consumers.

This common access to a decision-making and research tool increased the mutual interest and common language of marketing scholars and management. Decision support systems (Little 1979), multivariate methods, and scanner data are part of this common interest made possible by the computer. So strong is this relationship, that some marketing scientists predict as a result a coming revolution in marketing theory, a revolution that would be most beneficial to managers (Hauser 1985).

If science is indeed marketing of ideas in the form of substantive and methodological theories—as Peter and Olson (1983) argue—then it is easy to understand why marketing thought has developed asymmetrically. Not only is there a "product fit" between academic production and business demand, due to business education, but there is also a very efficient distribution channel for such a product in the form of computer technology—a channel which, until recently, has not reached the consumers.

Consequences of Asymmetry

The environment becomes more and more complex, both for managers and for consumers. To borrow from a recent set of provocative papers in economics

(Heiner 1983, 1985), it is characterized by a genuine gap between an agent's decision-making competence and the difficulty of the decision problems.

Not surprisingly, this fact has been considered by marketing scholars for some time now. On the normative side, research has concentrated on enhancing the managers' competence by decision aids and on reducing the difficulty of the problems by conceptual modeling and development of data-gathering and data-reduction methods. On the descriptive side, research examined and tried to predict the behavior of consumers when faced with the difficult problems of making purchase and consumption decisions.

Heiner's (1983) main point is that the wider the gap between competence and difficulty, the more predictable the behavior would be. This conjecture might seem paradoxical, but can be demonstrated with a simple marketing example. Consider two consumers, one who does not suffer from the above competence-difficulty gap, and the second with a wide gap. Both need to choose in a product class with a large number of available brands. While the first consumer has a large consideration set which, because of superior competence, can be thoroughly scanned and evaluated, the second consumer, unable to process it all, would have a much smaller set. Assuming the two sets are known, it is easy to see that without any further information, we have better chances in predicting the choice of the second consumer than that of the first one. In particular, we can know for sure that some brands, those excluded from the second consumer's evoked set, will not be chosen. No such deterministic inference can be made with regard to the first consumer.

Thus, we see that the asymmetry in marketing theory and research (namely, normative research for marketers and positive research on consumers) leads to asymmetric distribution of benefits. Consumers become more predictable and firms become better in exploiting this predictability. The argument that what is good for marketers is also good for the consumers because of improved efficiency which is ultimately transferred to consumers in the form of reduced prices is, at best, only partially true. Recalling the perfect-information assumption, or as it was renamed, "perfect effective knowledge" in the Arrow-Debreu model, it is clear that lack or nonuse of full knowledge will normally prevent consumers from acquiring that combination of goods with the greatest benefit to them. If transactions are entered into on the basis of inaccurate or inadequate information, then the contention that buyers prefer to get what they actually got is open to doubt.

Furthermore, as Holton (1981, p. 145) argues, the worsening of the consumer information problem arises because of the success of our economic system: increasing income per capita enables consumers to buy more goods and services, more alternatives are available, and technological changes are accelerating. In short, this asymmetry in the marketplace has a tendency to increase as a result of the asymmetry in marketing research—better models for managers, further revelation of consumer shortcomings.

This leads to distortion of resource allocation both at the level of the individual consumer and at the society level. Consumers cannot get their "first best" choices because of the difficulty of the choice process itself and because the fruits of research in which society invests are distributed asymmetrically between consumers and marketers.

Increasing the efficiency of market activities of both consumers and marketers calls for expertise and specialization. However, recent trends of women ceasing to specialize in homemaking by seeking work outside the household, the fragmentation on the consumer side (into single parents, swingles, and single elderly) versus recent megamergers occurring on the marketer side (e.g., G.E. with RCA, Phillip Morris with General Foods, R.J. Reynolds with Nabisco) are evidence for further asymmetry in the marketplace.

The situation is probably best described by a statement attributed to Holton: "The consumer is a part-time amateur buyer facing full time professional sellers." It would be hard and, in all likelihood, unjustified to attribute it all to research philosophy and priorities of marketing scholars. However, it is clear that the asymmetry in marketing theory and research is not harmonious with the current demands and opportunities available to marketing as a discipline (Bartels 1983).

The Symmetrization Proposal

It is apparent that consumers need help to improve their market decision making. The usual means of education and legislation have their flaws and limitations (Karlinsky 1986). In particular, they do not help consumers to overcome their cognitive limitations. The observation that managers have similar cognitive problems suggests that we could learn from whatever has been done for managers so as to facilitate the improvement of consumers' decision making. This is the basis for the symmetrization idea: *Do for consumers as you do for managers.* Note that this idea, due to the symmetry perspective, is not only about *what* to do but also about *how* to do it. But first we have to examine if such a proposal is viable and possible under the ensuing conditions.

Changing Conditions

In examining again the reasons for the asymmetry in marketing, we find that, to some extent, they are no longer valid and, thus, call for a change or at least point to the possibility of one.

While many of the early scholars were businessmen with business orientation, many of the current marketing scholars (for example, those who are engaged in basic research in consumer behavior or macromarketing) have much less direct contact with, or commitment to, the business world. This suggests that the channel captain perspective might not be as essential or as inevitable as before.

The received economic view of consumers is being modified (Belk 1984). Consumers, more recently, have been regarded as engaged in problem solving and decision making, much the same as managers (Bettman 1979). This opens up the opportunity to treat consumers as we have treated managers.

Most marketing departments are in business schools, and it could be argued that their first obligation is to business. Nevertheless, many marketing researchers are concerned with firm regulation which helps consumers. This concern has little to do with the training of managers except possibly from a moral perspective. Hence, if the marketing community already accepts research in regulation as part of their curriculum, the idea of direct research for consumers should be accepted as well.

Last but not least, the main tool of the technology of decision making—the computer—is no longer the exclusive property of academia and the business sectors. Home computers and telecommunication are easily accessible to consumers.

What seems to emerge from this discussion is that the time is ripe for change with regard to research activities in marketing. However, changing paradigms in a scientific discipline is not a simple matter.

Changing Paradigms

The idea that in changing a historically and currently well-entrenched paradigm, one needs to resort to radical means, has gained considerable popularity since Kuhn (1962) presented the notion of revolutionary changes in science. However, descriptively speaking, it seems that this revolutionary metaphor is at best colorful exaggeration (Toulmin 1970). Normatively, Kuhn's analysis does not contain the prescription that all disciplines resolve their differences in a revolutionary manner. Furthermore, new paradigms do not necessarily replace the old; they seem to coexist (Venkatesh 1985). It is the latter kind of change that is advocated here.

Symmetrization

Building on the symmetry perspective, we can now suggest a change in marketing theory and research that, on the one hand, may seem radical (the opposite of what is currently done), but, on the other hand, is capitalizing on what has already been done in marketing.

Using our own terminology, the proposed change is more of a concentric diversification than a conglomerate diversification. Such a change makes better sense from the point of view of resource utilization and adoption of innovations by the marketing community.

In its most simplistic form, the symmetrization proposal is that of adding to the current practice of normative research for managers and positive research *on* consumers, a stream of direct normative research *for* consumers. Philosophically, it means to do research from the perspective of the consumer, rather than from that of the channel captain. Operationally, it means that researchers can use the symmetry perspective and start by examining (1) what can be transferred from normative managerial research to normative consumer research and (2) how can it be best achieved.

For example, can the idea of decision support systems be adapted and adopted for direct consumers' usage in their purchase and consumption decisions? Can we build an interactive computer program that will offer consumers a menu of retail outlet attributes, and, after they choose those attributes of interest to them, represent a map or some other helpful classification representation of the relevant stores? Or maybe we can use conjoint analysis or other choice or preference models, not to predict consumers' choice but rather to help them find their best buy in an efficient and effective way.

Note that these ideas go beyond the simple supply and format of information which are the usual subjects in research for public policy on informational issues (Capon and Lutz 1979, 1983). Rather, they are about interactive aid in processing and utilizing market information, much the same as is done for managers. Furthermore, these consumer-decision–aid systems (CDAS), like those for managers, rely on computers and remote information services as a medium for dissemination and serve as devices that improve the effectiveness and efficiency of consumer decision making.

Such normative research will have to draw on existing positive consumer research as well. For example, in eliciting consumers' preferences in order to search for them in a large and difficult product class (e.g., life insurance), attention should be given to possible induced biases (Kahneman, Slovic, and Tversky 1982). This means that such consumer decision aids should also be debiasing devices, unlike their managerial counterpart (consumer models) which are used for measurement and prediction only. Of course, we will need also new and specific positive research to facilitate the proposed normative research. For example, how will consumers perceive, interact with, and adopt such aids? For whom and for what product classes are CDASs most beneficial? On a more macro level, we might want to know how marketers might adapt to the usage of CDAS by consumers.

There is also a whole host of questions on the supply side. Who will build and supply the CDAS service? Who will update it? Who will guarantee its quality and integrity? How will all of this be done? Answering these questions, even partially, is beyond the scope (and the page limit) of this chapter. However, as a hint, it is suggested that the symmetrization idea be invoked at yet another level: Why not view CDAS as a new product design problem and proceed analogically? An example of CDAS design that adopts a modified form of Urban and Hauser's (1980) methodology for new product development can be found in Karlinsky (1986).

Viewing consumer normative research in general (and CDAS research in particular) as a new product design problem suggests that this is simply a new business opportunity made possible by the new technology of home computers. Even moderate estimates of market potential are staggering. Thus, there might be a market incentive for the development and launching of such systems. As F. Scott Fitzgerald said: "The cleverly expressed opposite of any generally accepted idea is worth a fortune to somebody."

Thus, we may be able to use the business sector to support such development and capitalize on the effectiveness of the market mechanism to promote consumer welfare. It is clear that producing, promoting, and selling such decision-making services will involve issues of reputation, perceived effectiveness, credibility, and similar nontangible features—a marketing challenge indeed.

Conclusion

Using symmetry, an important notion in the development of many sciences, we were able to identify asymmetry in marketing theory development—assymetry that refers to the development of normative research for marketers, but a lack of normative research for consumers. Similar asymmetry exists in the marketplace. Marketers make better decisions due to effective decision resources, while consumers resort to simplified decision rules and suboptimal heuristics.

The development of new information technology, including the home computer and electronic communication, provides the opportunity for advancing the state of normative research for consumers and improving consumer decision making. In a sense, this is what Russo (1978) called "research directed to the jointly optimal cell of the [environment-strategy] matrix: the simultaneous education of consumers and improvement in the environment that will lead to a global maximum for consumer performance" (p. 72).

It is sometimes argued that a recurrent phenomenon in social sciences is that of failing to anticipate the problems to be faced. Possibly one such problem is consumers' utilization of the home computer as an extension of the mind. We might ask ourselves if ignoring such research area is not some kind of marketing myopia. It seems that it would be better to help things happen than wonder what happened.

Unlike the controversy on broadening the concept of marketing, the proposed research is well within Luck's (1969) bounds of marketing and within Carman's (1980) definition of marketing. It is concerned with and related to market transactions as well as being related to resource allocation. Indeed, it proposes to enhance their efficiency.

The proposed symmetrization is also in the spirit of "Is Science Marketing" (Peter and Olson 1983), concerning the creation of useful knowledge. It is, in fact, the ultimate application of the marketing concept to our own research by truly and directly catering to consumer needs.

References

Akerlof, G. (1970), "The Market for Lemons: Qualitative Uncertainty and The Market Mechanism," *Quarterly Journal of Economics* 84 (August): 488–500.

Alderson, Wroe (1957), *Marketing Behavior and Executive Action.* Homewood, Ill.: Richard D. Irwin.

Anderson, Paul F. (1983), "Marketing, Scientific Progress and Scientific Method," *Journal of Marketing* 47 (Fall): 18–31.

Anderson, Paul F., and Michael J. Ryan, eds. (1984), *1984 AMA Winter Educators' Conference: Scientific Method in Marketing.* Chicago: American Marketing Association.

Arndt, Johan (1985), "The Tyranny of Paradigms: The Case for Pluralism in Marketing," in *Changing the Course of Marketing: Alternative Paradigms for Widening Marketing Theory,* N. Dholakia and J. Arndt, eds. Greenwich, Conn.: JAI Press.

Arrow, K.J., and G. Debreu (1954), "Existence of an Equilibrium for a Competitive Economy," *Econometrica* 22: 265–90.

Bagozzi, Richard P. (1975), "Marketing as Exchange," *Journal of Marketing* 39 (October): 32–39.

Bartels, Robert (1962), *The Development of Marketing Thought.* Homewood, Ill.: Richard D. Irwin.

———, (1976), *The History of Marketing Thought,* 2nd ed. Columbus, Ohio: Grid.

———, (1983), "Is Marketing Defaulting Its Responsibilities?" *Journal of Marketing* 47 (Fall): 32–41.

Bauer, R.A., and S.A. Greyser (1969), "The Dialogue That Never Happens," *Harvard Business Review* (January-February): 122–28.

Belk, R.W. (1984), "Manifesto for a Consumer Behavior of Consumer Behavior" in *1984 AMA Winter Educators' Conference: Scientific Method in Marketing,* Paul E. Anderson and Michael J. Ryan, eds. Chicago: American Marketing Association.

Bettman, James R. (1979), *An Information Processing Theory of Consumer Choice.* Reading, Mass.: Addison-Wesley.

Bush, Ronald F., and Shelby D. Hunt, eds. (1982), *Marketing Theory: Philosophy of Science Perspectives.* Chicago: American Marketing Association.

Capon, N., and R.J. Lutz (1979), "A Model and Methodology for the Development of Consumer Information Programs," *Journal of Marketing* 43 (January): 158–67.

Capon, N., and R.J. Lutz (1983), "The Marketing of Consumer Information," *Journal of Marketing* 47 (Summer): 108–12.

Carman, James M. (1980), "Paradigms for Marketing Theory," in *Research in Marketing.* vol. 3, J.N. Sheth, ed. Greenwich, Conn.: JAI Press, 1–36.

Cassels, J.M. (1936), "The Significance of Early Economic Thought on Marketing," *Journal of Marketing* 1 (October): 129–33.

Converse, Paul D. (1945), "The Development of the Science of Marketing—An Exploratory Survey," *Journal of Marketing* 1 (July): 14–23.

———, (1959), *The Beginning of Marketing Thought in the United States With Reminiscence of Some of the Pioneer Marketing Scholars.* Austin Bureau of Business Research, University of Texas.

Coolson, Frank G. (1960), *Marketing Thought in the United States in the Late Nineteenth Century.* Lubbock: Texas Tech Press.

Debreu, G. (1959), *Theory of Value: An Axiomatic Analysis of Economic Equilibrium.* New Haven, Conn.: Yale University Press.

Dholakia, N., and J. Arndt, eds. (1985), *Changing the Course of Marketing: Alternative Paradigms for Widening Marketing Theory.* Greenwich, Conn.: JAI Press.

Etgar, Michael (1977), "Comment on the Nature and Scope of Marketing," *Journal of Marketing* 41 (October): 14, 16, 146.

Feldman, L.P. (1976), *Consumer Protection: Problems and Prospects.* New York: West.

Grether, E.T. (1976), "The First Forty Years," *Journal of Marketing* 40 (July): 63–69.

Guthrie, W.C. (1969), *A History of Greek Philosophy.* Cambridge, England: Cambridge University Press.

Hagerty, J.E. (1936), "Experiences of an Early Marketing Teacher," *Journal of Marketing* 1 (July): 20–27.

Hauser, John R. (1985), "The Coming Revolution in Marketing Theory," in *Marketing in an Electronic Age.* R.D. Buzzell, ed. Boston: Harvard Business School Press.

———, (1986), "Theory and Application of Defensive Strategy," in *The Economics of Strategic Planning.* L.G. Thomas, III, ed. Lexington, Mass.: Lexington Books.

Heiner, R.A. (1983), "The Origin of Predictable Behavior," *American Economic Review* 73: 560–95.

———, (1985), "The Origin of Predictable Behavior: Further Modeling and Applications," *American Economic Review* 75: 391–98.

Holton, R.H. (1981), "Public Regulation of Consumer Information: The Life Insurance Industry Case," in *Regulation of Marketing and The Public Interest.* F.E. Balderston, J.M. Carman, and F.M. Nicosia, eds. New York: Pergamon Press.

Howard, John A. (1957), *Marketing Management: Analysis and Decision.* Homewood, Ill.: Richard D. Irwin.

Hunt, Shelby D. (1976), "The Nature and Scope of Marketing," *Journal of Marketing* 40 (July): 17–28.

———, (1978), "A General Paradigm of Marketing: In Support of the Three Dichotomies Model," *Journal of Marketing* 42 (April): 107–10.

———, (1983), *Marketing Theory: The Philosophy of Marketing Science.* Homewood, Ill.: Richard D. Irwin.

Hunt, Shelby D., and Paul S. Speck (1985), "Does Logical Empiricism Imprison Marketing?" in *Changing the Source of Marketing: Alternative Paradigms for Widening Marketing Theory.* N. Dholakia and J. Arndt, eds. Greenwich, Conn.: JAI Press.

Kahneman, D., P. Slovic, and A. Tversky, eds. (1982), *Judgment Under Uncertainty: Heuristics and Biases.* Cambridge, England: Cambridge University Press.

Karlinsky, Meir (1986), "Towards Consumer Decision Aid Systems: The Case of Decisions Under Risk," unpublished Ph.D. dissertation. Graduate School of Business, University of California at Berkeley.

Kelley, H.H. (1967), "Attribution Theory in Social Psychology," in *Nebraska Symposium on Motivation*. vol. 15, D. Levine, ed. Lincoln: University of Nebraska Press.

———, (1973), "The Process of Causal Attribution," *American Psychologist* 28: 17–28.

Kotler, Philip (1972), "A Generic Concept of Marketing," *Journal of Marketing* 36 (April): 46–54.

Kuhn, Thomas S. (1962), *The Structure of Scientific Revolutions*. Chicago: University of Chicago Press.

La Londe, J.B., and E.J. Morrison (1967), "Marketing Management Concepts Yesterday and Today," *Journal of Marketing* 31 (January): 9–13.

Lichtenthal, David J., and Leland L. Beik (1984), "A History of the Definition of Marketing," in *Research in Marketing*, vol. 7, J.N. Sheth, ed. Greenwich, Conn.: JAI Press.

Litman, Simon (1950), "The Beginnings of Teaching Marketing in American Universities," *Journal of Marketing* 15 (October): 220–23.

Little, J.P.C. (1979), "Decision Support Systems for Marketing Managers", *Journal of Marketing* 43 (Summer): 9–26.

Luck, David (1969), "Broadening the Concept of Marketing—Too Far," *Journal of Marketing* 33 (July): 53–55.

Lutz, J. (1979), "Opening Statement" in *Conceptual and Theoretical Developments in Marketing*, O.C. Ferrell, S.W. Brown, and C.W. Lamb, Jr., eds. Chicago: American Marketing Association.

Malhotra, N.K. (1984), "Reflections on the Information Overload Paradigm in Consumer Decision Making," *Journal of Consumer Research* 10: 436–40.

Mansfield, E. (1980), *Economics: Principles, Problems, Decisions*, 3rd ed. New York: W.W. Norton.

Myers, John G., William F. Massy, and Stephen A. Greyser (1980), *Marketing Research and Development*. Englewood Cliffs, N.J.: Prentice-Hall.

Nisbett, R., and L. Ross (1980), *Human Inference: Strategies and Shortcomings of Social Judgment*. Englewood Cliffs, N.J.: Prentice-Hall.

Olshavsky, R.W., and D.H. Granbois (1979), "Consumer Decision Making—Fact or Fiction," *Journal of Consumer Research* 6 (September): 93–99.

Peter, J. Paul, and Jerry C. Olson (1983), "Is Science Marketing?" *Journal of Marketing* 47 (Fall): 111–25.

Quirk, J.P. (1976), *Intermediate Microeconomics*. Chicago: Science Research Associates.

Robin, D.P. (1977), "Comment on the Nature and Scope of Marketing," *Journal of Marketing* 41 (January): 136–38.

———, (1978), "Comment on the Nature and Scope of Marketing," *Journal of Marketing* 41 (July): 6, 42.

Russo, E.J. (1978), "Comments on Behavioral and Economic Approaches to Studying Market Behavior," in *The Effect of Information on Consumer and Market Behavior*. Andrew A. Mitchell, ed. Chicago: American Marketing Association, 65–74.

Seelye, A.L. (1947), "The Importance of Economic Theory in Marketing Courses," *Journal of Marketing* 11 (January): 223–27.

Smith, Adam (1776/1937), *An Inquiry into the Nature and Causes of the Wealth of Nations*. New York: Random House.

Steiner, Robert L. (1984), "Basic Relationships in Consumer Goods Industries," in *Research in Marketing*. vol. 7, J.N. Sheth, ed. Greenwich, Conn.: JAI Press.

Toulmin, S.W. (1970), "Does the Distinction between Normal and Revolutionary Science Hold Water?" in *Criticism and Growth of Knowledge*, I. Lakatos and A. Musgrove, eds. Cambridge, England: Cambridge University Press.

Tucker, W.T. (1974), "Future Directions in Marketing Theory," *Journal of Marketing* 38 (April): 30–35.

Tversky, A., and D. Kahneman (1974), "Judgment under Uncertainty: Heuristics and Biases," *Science* 185: 1124–31.

Tversky, A., and D. Kahneman (1981), "The Framing of Decisions and the Rationality of Choice," *Science* 211: 453–58.

Urban, G.L., and J.P. Hauser (1980), *Design and Marketing of New Products*. Englewood Cliffs, N.J.: Prentice-Hall.

Venkatesh, Alladi (1985), "Is Marketing Ready for Kuhn?" in *Changing the Course of Marketing: Alternative Paradigms for Widening Marketing Theory*, N. Dholakia and J. Arndt, eds. Greenwich, Conn.: JAI Press.

Weld, L.D.H. (1941), "Early Experience in Teaching Courses in Marketing," *Journal of Marketing* 4 (April): 380–81.

Weyl, Herman (1952), *Symmetry*. Princeton, N.J.: Princeton University Press.

Wiener, Phillip P. (1973), *Dictionary of the History of Ideas*. New York: Scribner.

4

Ethical Consciousness and the Competence of Product Management: Beyond Righteousness, Rituals, and Rules

Michael P. Mokwa

A Nissan 300ZX sportscar is very exciting;
An MTV music video episode can be very entertaining;
But, ethics are truly awesome!

When we are asked to think about products, our tendency is to consider images of basic consumer goods—soap, cereal, soft drinks, cosmetics, automobiles, and so forth. When we are asked to think about product management, our images tend to focus on large consumer goods organizations and their formal product or brand management structures. If we are asked to think about ethics, our images tend to converge on rules or ideals that demarcate "right and wrong" or "good and bad." If we challenge surface images, our perspectives often change.

The purpose of this chapter is to challenge our surface images of products, product management, and the ethics of product management, and to encourage us to enrich our ethical consciousness and commitment. First, we explore the nature of contemporary products and their management. Next, we present a consciousness of ethics that is relevant and meaningful for contemporary

A sincere thanks to the editors for their invitation and their conscientious review work, and to Professors Gene Laczniak of Marquette University, Pat Murphy of University of Notre Dame, Richard Mason of Southern Methodist University, and Mark Pastin of Arizona State University's Center for Ethics. I appreciate their personal encouragement and respect their genuine concern for ethics in marketing and management practice.

product management. Finally, we consider some areas of leverage to create and enrich ethical product management consciousness and competence.

Contemporary Products and Their Management

We find tremendous breadth, diversity, and complexity in the nature and meaning of contemporary products (Levy 1978). To illustrate, let us consider both the product meaning and the product management responsibilities related to: fine art or pornography; aspirin tablets or organ transplant surgery; wooden blocks or home computers with video games; generic prescription drugs or "synthetic" cheese on a restaurant's pizza; industrial pesticides for the farm or industrial-strength pesticides under the kitchen sink; a child's reading primer without any value orientation or an executive M.B.A. degree without any debate over different value orientations; nuclear power, waste, or warheads; and bioengineering, psychotherapy, or transcendental meditation.

Our products absorb and project the diversity, complexity, and uncertainties of our technologies, markets, cultures, and life-concepts. They also mirror the conflicts and paradoxes within and across our life-concepts, life-styles, and life-quality (Levy and Zaltman 1975). As such, complexity and controversy have become common product features (Mitroff and Kilmann 1984).

Further, we find that product management is a very complicated and fluid process (Wind 1982). Few organizations have a single product or product line. An organization might produce and market everything from soft lights for bedroom lamps to industrial power systems to the world's most efficient machine guns. Moreover, most organizations become involved with other organizations in the design, production, and marketing of their products. They explicitly purchase chemical components or detailed blueprints, and implicitly buy the laboratory tests or engineering knowledge underlying these resource components. They subcontract production runs of their designer-label jeans when their own plants are at capacity producing private-label jeans for a large department store chain. Another department store chain markets a vast assortment of merchandise that it has purchased for resale after other department stores could not sell the same merchandise during its first-run season. An appliance store hires independent local union tradespeople to deliver, install, and service their products. A national department store chain hires local dentists to work in its in-house dental clinics.

Business groups, product line portfolios, multimarket domains, and interconnected distribution (or market) systems characterize the contemporary marketplace and the contemporary diversified organizations cooperating and competing within it.

At a more personal level, we find that product management involves many people in diverse roles *within* an organization and *across* its markets and environments. There are design engineers, production personnel, and quality control inspectors. There are financial planning staffs allocating resources and mandating rigorous bottom-line demands, government regulators establishing industry packaging and labeling standards, and a sales agent interpreting the package and label persuasively to sell a prospective consumer. Then, there are consumers buying, storing, giving, receiving, using, evaluating, and discussing products. Sometimes consumers do it all quite well, and sometimes they do it poorly or even abusively.

Product management involves all these product stakeholders and others (Emshoff 1980; Mitroff 1983). It involves all their intentions, actions, and influences as these meld in the creation, enactment, use, and evaluation of a product. Inherently, the tasks and responsibilities of product management are diffused widely.

Some organizations adopt formal management processes and complementary organizational structures, attempting to anchor responsibilities and rewards in complex product management roles (Buell 1975; Clewett and Stasch 1975; Hise and Kelley 1978). Typically, these roles charge relatively young, aspiring managers to prove themselves by creating, coordinating, and executing successful market campaigns for their assigned products. Corporate objectives and constraints, as well as market pressures, bear intensely on these roles. To illustrate, a newly appointed product manager may be asked to defend the market share of a "bread-winning" product in a stagnating mature market. Each share point is worth hundreds of thousands of dollars in profit or contribution. There are several well-entrenched aggressive competitors who are seeking to increase their share points through promotional warfare. Competitors' marketing budgets are larger, and consumers are starting to switch their loyalties. The reward for a few successful years as the product manager in this struggle is a product group vice presidency. The struggle will be fierce, and the stakes are high for both the product manager and the corporation. Potential conflicts will abound. Clearly, product management roles are filled with pressures, stress, and make-or-break consequences generating conflict. These must be confronted carefully by both the incumbent product manager and the executives who are charged to lead, guide, and protect an organization's culture and its market presence.

Formal product management processes and structures, however, are not the norm except within a few industries. Many organizations manage products ad hoc, informally, or reactively. Managerial product attention is focused only on select dimensions of the total process or during periods of crisis. As such, product management responsibilities become fragmented formally—a serious design flaw is discovered but never reported; a warranty claim is exaggerated in promotional materials; product quality erodes over time, yet consumer complaints are disregarded by a customer service representative; the genuine dissatisfaction of a market is not heard until a consumer advocate attacks the company on national news. Managerial product responsibilities can be difficult to find and define in many organizations. More importantly, product concern, commitment, and care can be difficult to generate, nurture, and sustain in such organizational cultures, regardless of the inherent value or quality of the organization's products.

In review, let us reconsider some critical points. All organizations have products and compete in markets. Thus, all organizations confront product management challenges. Contemporary products have become increasingly complex. Controversy is a common product feature. Most organizations have multiple product lines, operate across multiple markets, and interact with other organizations to produce and market their products. Many people in many different roles have stakes in the product management process. Broadly speaking, all stakeholders are involved in product management. Prospects for confusion or conflict are high given the diversity of product portfolios and the interdependencies of multiple stakeholders. Some organizations enact formal product management systems, but most organizations manage products relatively informally. Regardless of an organization's style, product management involves an increasing number of perplexing questions, tough challenges, turbulent contexts, and tight corners. When we consider that our products embody and symbolize our life-styles, life-concepts, and life-quality, we realize that ethics is an immanent dimension of product management.

Ethical Consciousness, Competence, and Collaboration

We believe that there is no simple meaning of ethics, nor any simple formula to enact or realize its significance.[1] We find that complexity, paradox, and depth pervade the meaning and significance of ethics.

Ethics is our consciousness of human ecology, and it is our competence exploring, appreciating, enacting, and enriching this consciousness and unfolding it into a harmony of human conditions. As such, ethics is a continuous collaborative dialectic process involving all humanity's search for, conversations about, and realizations of quality human consciousness and quality human conditions (Churchman 1979, 1982). It is a complex dialectic of inquiry and action, of thoughts and feelings, of purposes and passions, of cooperation and conflicts, of conduct and consequences, of competence and incompetence. Moreover, the dialectics of ethics are grounded deeply in the paradoxes of human nature—the perceived dualities of human nature—our consciousness and aconsciousness; our aspiring minds and our expecting bodies; our basic goodness and its dark shadows; our innate suffering and simple joys; our objective constructions and subjective valuations; our personal freedom and collective interdependencies; our manifest conditions and latent potentials; our material realizations and spiritual liberations (Bateson 1972, 1980; Hampden-Turner 1982; Wilber 1980). Ethics is an awesome subject, yet it is pervading and practical.

The Spirit and Stuff of Ethics—Consciousness and Competence

c reotional potential

To engage ethics seriously and competently, "heroic spirit" awakening and encouraging human commitment, purpose, systemic consideration, and collaboration are necessary. Heroic spirit is deeply within each of us (Huxley 1944; Jung 1966; Trungpa 1984; Wilber 1980). As such, ethics emerges from penetrating human awareness and deep human respect that emanate genuine human responsibility and motivate human enlightenment and enrichment (Hayward 1984; Trungpa). This consciousness is the stuff of ethics, and it is the essence of each heroic self which actively confronts the human struggle to develop sensitively, empathetically, and sympathetically into competent selflessness (Walsh and Vaughn 1980; Wilber 1983).

Ethics is an energy, a deep tension within human consciousness and within human conditions as consciousness and conditions interpenetrate and interplay in rhythms of human order and conflict (Jung 1956; Mitroff 1983; Prigogine and Stengers 1984). The tensions surface across the variety and diversity of our evolving human capacities and potentials, and the tensions emerge within and between active *personal* human nature and interactive *social* human ecology. Thus, ethics is a heroic epic in which our fundamental spirit and stuff struggle to become enlightened and actualized selves, and in which heroic selves struggle to enact and enrich our human ecology. Ethics is natural, but it is not easy.

Sadly, we find that many contemporary discussions of ethics, particularly of "professional" ethics, have severe limits and, thus, must be considered cautiously (Laczniak 1983; McCoy 1983). In professional literature and policy statements, ethics is often conceptualized only in terms of its shadows—rules and rituals that constrain, avoid, or protect against isolated "evils," or codes and committees that project images of righteous conduct and correct concern without much vision, depth, or genuine sensitivity. In actual policy formulation and discussion of policy methods, ethics is frequently considered as a situational contingency or constraint surfacing in an anticipated or manifest belief confrontation, and our attention is directed to avoiding, getting around, or getting out of the situation and saving face or looking good after the confrontation. Also, there is infatuation with separating ethics from other life-concepts such as morality, law, or even philosophy and with generating differentiated and customized ethics across life-domains such as distinct professions—a medical ethics, a business ethics, a product managers' ethics, a lawyers' ethics, a judges' ethics. Ethical confusion might be more common than ethical confrontation.

We do recognize, however, that life-challenges are differentiated, and they often are perceived and treated as distinctive or even unique. But we believe that ethics is an immanent force pervading all life-concepts and all life-challenges in which our human nature, our human interconnections, and our human conditions are the subject. Thus, our life-concepts, life-styles, life-conditions, and life-prospects are the substance confronting an immanent and pervading ethics. These life-expressions and life-experiences are our relative contingencies, and ethics is our pervading drive for human competence—competence to draw upon quality consciousness, constructive consideration, compassionate collaboration, and correct conduct to permeate our contingencies and challenges and to promote quality human conditions which radiate our evolving human community. As such, ethics is not ego, not righteousness, not rituals, not rules. Ethics decries righteous egos, ritualistic demarcations, shallow rules, and expedient remedies. These are the dark shadows, the surface facades, the contingencies, and the situational separations by which a pervading ethics can be hidden, ignored, distorted, or perverted. Ethics is energy and ultimately substance within personal consciousness and across collective consciousness. Although ethics often endures entrapment in our consciousness, it always awaits enlightenment and release into our enduring human ecology. Ethics is heroic human spirit thrusting itself over and over into consciousness, competence, and community.

Ethics functions through personal human awareness and effort, shared human consciousness and consideration, and substantive human collaboration and construction, across all human being and human becoming. Ethics functions to envision, consider, and construct quality human conditions that protect and promote integrative personal and collective human development and, as such, radiate human harmony. Ethics is the valuation and expression of human consciousness and human conditions in a fluid interplay seeking and manifesting continuous evolutionary equilibria—an ecology within consciousness and across conditions. Thus, ethics is our belief, trust, commitment, and investment in human ecology and human competence. It is deeply personal and totally collective, reaching into each of us and across all of us.

In figure 4–1, we symbolize our general ecological perspective of ethics, sketching it as an evolving dialectic process in which human capacities, potentials, and consciousnesses unfold projectively and reflectively with human conditions (Jantsch 1980). As such, ethics is a tension and, ultimately, energy or drive within human personal capacities for self-awareness, self-respect, and self-development and within human collective competencies for collective consciousness, collective compassion, and collective enrichment. Human ethical consciousness expresses itself *throughout* our considerations, construc-

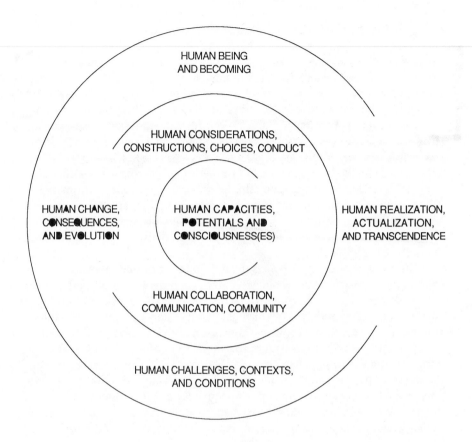

Figure 4–1

tions, choices, and collaborations *into* our communications, conduct, and communities *across* our human challenges, contexts, and conditions.

Ethics involves a poetic—a purposive, committed search for human quality, appropriateness, and responsiveness. It requires and releases heroic human spirit in a dialectic of our human being and our human becoming. Yet, ethics also involves a practical perspective—a search for as well as enactment, experience, and evaluation of our inquiry, intentions, influences, actions, and impacts. Ethics involves practical problems of motivation and valuation to inquire and to act appropriately, responsively, effectively, and aesthetically within ourselves and in collaboration with all others (Churchman 1971, 1982). Let us explore more carefully the enactment or practice of ethics.

The Practice of Ethics—Commitment and Collaboration

To engage ethics seriously, competently, and practically, heroic spirit must become heroic stuff. Heroic stuff is immanent within us all. It is the human respect, empathy, compassion, and joy that can be felt and expressed when a genuine self emerges and engages the essential quality and harmony of our human ecology. This is the heroic self—our fundamental spirit and complex, paradoxical natures in balance emitting quality consciousness, meaningful considerations, significant conduct, and compassionate collaboration (Hayward 1984). While the emergence and sustention of a heroic self is natural, it is not easy. It is a heroic struggle, and this heroic struggle parallels the practice of ethics—an ethics guiding, nurturing, and expressing human competence and human collaboration, yet an ethics understanding and even tolerating human incompetence and egotistic human boundaries (Walsh and Vaughn 1980; Wilber 1981, 1983).

The practice of ethics pervades the development of both personal human character and social human ecology. Our ethical practice is predicated on our belief in active human purpose, our trust in human experience developed constructively and reflectively through inquiry, and our involving human commitment to guide and serve one another. Simply, we share belief and trust in active, purposive human competence and collaboration to know, experience, value, and form or shape human character and human conditions. Our orientations, perspectives, and intentions, our inquiring and action complexes, and our social arrangements and consequences are the conduits of ethical practice. We use these conduits to envision and direct our ethical practice; to design, communicate, and enact it; and to evaluate, develop, and transform it. Or, we can use these conduits to inhibit our ethical practice and evolution.

Quality ethical practice is achieved through heroic struggle (Jung 1956; Stevens 1982). This involves the development of competent selves and their collaboration to sustain and enrich evolving human ecology. Quality ethical practice, thus, requires active and penetrating orientations that envision the pervading and immanent ethical core of human development and its reach throughout human ecology. It also involves purposive and seriously committed intentions: to eradicate ignorance, manipulation, and repression of heroic human stuff; to seek personal human enlightenment and development; and to transform and integrate personal development responsibly and responsively within human social ecology. As such, we express, enrich, and actualize our individual selves and our human ecology interactively. Quality ethical practice, thus, emerges from penetrating orientations and serious intentions that ground and motivate multiperspective inquiry and action across the interacting domains of personal human development and social human ecology (Habermas 1984; Mason and Mitroff 1981; Mitroff and Mason 1981).

Inquiry and action, therefore, emerge as pivotal methods of ethical practice. The dialectic rhythms across and within human inquiry and action manifest the heroic struggle of ethical practice to actively encounter, seriously understand, and competently transcend the immanent paradoxes of human nature and its potential (Churchman 1971, 1979). Inquiry can generate, valuate, and discipline action. It operates projectively, responsively, and reflectively through streams of personal and collective consciousness, of critical and constructive consideration, and of individual and collaborative effort. Action can engage, translate, and transform inquiry carefully, wisely, and effectively. Or, inquiry and action can repress, ignore, or even pervert human spirit, value, effort, and quality. This raises an essential ethical paradox—the "practice" paradox.

Simply, our practice *in* ethics is also our realization *of* ethics. And practice is always a human struggle for competence—a dialectic of trial and error, of problem and perceived resolution, of learning and teaching, of listening and debating, of convention and change, and essentially of being and becoming. Thus, ethical practice is our serious and shared commitment to inquiry and action that can envision, value, negotiate, choose, and enact quality human character and ecology from paradoxical human nature and potential. And, because our practice is our reality, we have *no guarantee* (Churchman 1971, 1979). There is no guarantee to be or to become ethically competent, except our serious and purposive commitment to our heroic spirit, stuff, and struggle, and to collaboration.

Collaboration is an essential ethical practice and a very difficult competence (Hayward 1984). It is a fundamental, but profound human capacity, potential, and need. Collaboration is grounded deeply in our shared yet personal human consciousness; it is unfolded complexly throughout our conditions. Collaboration emerges from the frightening awareness, consoling acceptance, and then motivating respect of our isolated, intimate, and limited personal human natures in contrast with our potential involving, evolving, sustaining, nurturing, and emerging collective human ecology and potential. As such, we each recognize intimately our apparent human isolation and natural limits as well as our motivation and potential for individuation and self-actualization within a human ecology rich with variety, diversity, and community.

We know our paradoxical struggle is to find and enact our distinctive personal self-identity and to find and express our dynamic social ecological niches simultaneously and interactively. We know our fundamental sameness and differences, and we recognize that our ethical wealth is to be found in our sameness across our variety, diversity, and its ecology. We know and feel our needs for collective security, nurturing, mentoring, and development as well as our needs for personal identification, recognition, expression, and contribution. We know and feel the fluid interplay and intermingling of personal and collective needs. We confront the capacity and need for collaboration, but we feel the conflict and confusion of negotiating and expressing our uniqueness and our sameness, our selves and our communities, our communities and our collective ecology. Thus, we know and feel the "responsibility paradox," and we encounter and observe all others struggling through it: Are there genuine limits to our human personal and human collective consciousness and competence to envision, accept, appreciate, respect, enact, and enrich our human personal and collective nature? This enduring question frames the responsibility paradox (McCoy 1983; Wilber 1981). Confronting the question moves heroic spirit, stretches collaborative wisdom, and encourages a continuous human experiment manifest in our commitment to practice quality inquiry and action.

The Styles of Ethics—Formative or Restrictive

Our practice of ethics is a process of realizing and resolving the responsibility paradox by developing and expressing quality human consciousness personally and collectively. Thus, ethical practice is primarily a *formative process* in which each human self emerges, matures, and seeks its natural individuation and actualization as well as its natural contribution and integration within human ecology. As such, the human ego and its dark shadows are apprehended, understood, and transformed into a human self on its path to selflessness.

Ethical arrest, ignorance, distortion, or perversion, however, are not uncommon throughout our human ecology. And, the tensions within human ecology can generate confusion, frustration, and other fearful reactions which entrap and impound heroic spirit and stuff while producing ethical disillusionment, defensiveness, and avoidance. Moreover, the human self is fragile and fluid, while the human ego is forceful and primitive. The ego makes boundaries, exploits limits, enjoys control, and seeks to dominate. The ego protects itself vigorously and asserts itself aggressively. Thus, our ethical practice often drifts into infatuation with restricting or ignoring our ego and our shadows, or pretending to restrict or arrest these, by masking them in patterns of rules, rituals, or righteousness. As such, we recognize that the practice of ethics manifests differentiation in orientation, form, and quality as well as in commitment and content.

We find that archetypal styles of ethical practice can be observed throughout the human ecology. In table 4–1, we present ethical styles as distinctive patterns of human orientation, intention, inquiring, and action perspectives, and ordering values. There are two general types of ethical patterns: restrictive and formative. Both types manifest at least three identifiable styles. Let us explore each.

Table 4–1
Archetypical Styles of Ethics

			Parameters for Studying Ethics			
Ethical Styles	Orientations	Intentions	Inquiring Perspectives	Action Perspectives	Ordering Values
Restrictive					
Ethical gamesmanship	Egocentric and narcissistic	Distorted, ignorant, or perverted	Ego-limited, ego-driven, shallow, blind-emotive, and conniving	Greedy, demanding, ambitious, manipulative, and destructive	Righteousness
Ethical repression and suppression	Ego-compliant and fearful	Defensive, avoiding, and disillusioned	Limited, reflexive, depressed, entrapped, and frustrated	Alienated, apathetic, inconsistent, threatened and withdrawn	Ritual
Ethics of protection	Self-compliant and detached	Deferrent to convention	Bounded-rational, experiential, defensive, structured, authoritative	Obligating, maintaining, controlling, enforcing, and constraining	Rules
Formative					
Ethics of responsibility	Self-emergent and purposive	Internalized respect and empathy	Trusting, feeling, vigilant, guided, communal	Investing, appreciating, nurturing, teaching/learning, and adjusting	Care
Ethics of service	Self-actualizing and expressive	Expressed empathy and compassion	Believing, engaging, expressing, cooperating, and helping	Interchanging, sharing, exchanging, developing, and warranting	Enrichment
Ethics of wisdom	Selfless and involved	Serious commitment and sympathy	Penetrating, unfolding, aesthetic, collaborative, and ecological	Intensive, liberating, reflective, transcending, and enduring	Integrity

Restrictive Ethics. *Restrictive* ethical styles emerge from ego-orientations and produce limited, or even distorted ethical intentions, inquiries, and actions. These styles deal in ethical shadows and shadow values.

Ethical gamesmanship is an ignorant, distorted, or perverted ethical style. It consciously abuses ethics as a facade to propagate ego-behaviors and to profess ego-righteousness. This style is "anti-ethics" masked, often skillfully and very seductively, as ethics. Human ecology is treated as a competitive game in which human manipulation and exploitation are perceived as natural and, thus, as "righteous" human freedoms which can be justified pragmatically and seductively. It is a greedy and conniving expression of surface human consciousness distorted by narcissistic emotion chasing primitive ambition. Ethical gamesmanship is not only restrictive; it is threatening and potentially destructive. Sadly, it is accepted and practiced too commonly and too widely throughout our human ecology. It generates substantial human tension and ethical confusion or frustration.

Ethical repression or suppression is a response to ethical gamesmanship and other extreme tensions within our human ecology. It is ethical illness generated by confusion, frustration, or fear. It is usually manifest in alienation and apathy as well as avoidance of genuine self-development and responsibility. The ethically ill appear to be easily seduced, manipulated, and exploited within ethical "games" and easily constricted and directed by the authorities who practice ethical protection.

The hallmark of an *ethics of protection* is the illusion of "personal" detachment and its corollaries of *demarcation*—boundary building and boundary control. Detachment and demarcation might be ethical perversions; at least, these are significant distortions. Ethical protection usually transfers rituals and righteousness into rule structures, enforcement complexes, and systems of sanction and punishment. Ethical protection has a peculiar anchor in unquestioned human convention and control, as well as a frightening deference for human hierarchy built upon unchallenged convention and human control. Protection distorts and limits human respect, responsibility, and inquiry. It is a clear restriction of human potential and capacity which overaccentuates our primitive roots and remedies, while overusing a tightly bounded perspective of the human mind as human reason. The ethics of protection is an ethics of reason with natural roots that easily degenerates into reason over "evil" roots, one reason *over* another reason, one bounded remedy *after* another bounded remedy.

Ethical protection, however, can be and frequently is practiced with sincere intentions and well-reasoned inquiry and action. But, protection is primitive and restrictive, and reason is incomplete. As such, ethical protection should be a transitory state or supportive ethical style. However, it appears to be our most common connotation of ethics and, thus, our most widespread framework of ethical practice—an ethics restricting "evils" and "evil shadows" through rules and remedies.

Formative Ethics.   Formative ethics transcends the human capacity to detach or to demarcate. It promotes our human potential to emerge purposively, to enact wisely and cooperatively, and to endure harmoniously. It is ethical wellness and fitness challenging ethical illness, distortion, or perversion. Formative ethics operates through quality human orientations and intentions, serious human inquiry and action, and a commitment to genuine human collaboration. It is a melding of human integrity and human responsibility that generates human enrichment through human care and service guided by an inquiring complex that is wise and compassionate. The styles of formative ethics work together to enact and express personal human development and positive human social ecology.

The *ethics of responsibility* challenges directly the artificiality of personal detachment and the illusion of human boundaries (McCoy 1983). It is an ethics of community and *care* emerging from deep respect for our interdependence and its call for quality involvement and genuine commitment. An emerging self knows and feels deep human respect and its related tensions and energies that release empathetic competence and the purposive motivation to care and to enact care. Ethical responsibility is natural human trust generating, nurturing, enabling, and guiding personal development within and across human selves and human communities. It is a dynamic human responsiveness bonding all individuals and enabling each individual. It provides a secure foundation for directed human experience, expression, and exchange.

The *ethics of service* emerges from a foundation of responsibility and care. It surges beyond interdependence into *interchange*—collaborative development. Service ethics confronts our expressive and consumptive needs simultaneously and interactively. It acknowledges the variety and diversity of human needs and human competencies (our ethical wealth), and it encourages empathetically and compassionately matching needs and competencies through simple exchanges and complex interchanges—through sharing oneself with others for mutual and synergistic satisfaction and development.

Service ethics confronts directly the practice paradox. We each believe that we *can* make a difference and that we each *should* make a significant difference. We seek to find and enact our contribution. This requires serious commitment to self-valuation and self-expression as well as to their transformation into sharing processes in which we collaborate in valuation, expression, and consumption. Genuine service, thus, is a developmental dialectic interchange of ideas, efforts, time, values, and things; of expressing and involving; of having and giving; of getting and using of constructing, instructing, preserving, and destructing; of organization, production, distribution, and consumption.

Service is our serious commitment to cooperate and to choose to make a purposive difference. As such, we actively challenge the practice paradox enacting service as a transformative capacity and potential in which we must choose (and must learn to choose competently) how to express and exchange self and collective complexes of needs and capabilities. Our choice of service practice confronts us and consistently challenges us: which capabilities to deploy, enact, and develop; which potentials to envision, seek, and explore; what quality to consider, construct, and consume; what consequences to appreciate and approach, and which to know and understand but avoid or refrain from until a transformation is possible; how to collaborate and develop through collaboration; and, throughout it all, why?

Competent ethical choice involves enduring questions, and enduring questions are without guaranteed answers. Thus, without any guarantee, we each confront our responsibility to do our best to genuinely care and purposively serve. This process is critical to our personal human development and to our social human ecology. It is innately enriching! But, to know our best might be our most critical and enduring ethical challenge. This challenge transforms our questions of practice and responsibility into questions of human purpose and meaning.

The *ethics of wisdom* directly confronts our paradox of human purpose and meaning. It pervades all the paradoxical questions of human practice and responsibility as well as all those questions of our human nature and ecology that do not appear to be paradoxical until they are confronted wisely. Wisdom, itself, is a human paradox.

Ethical wisdom is our deep, penetrating consciousness of our radiant human capacities and our unfolding human ecology and potential (Churchman 1979, 1982; Hayward 1984). As such, ethical wisdom involves the human known and the unknown in dialectic rhythms which ground and define our knowledge and which generate our drive, maybe our purpose, to know and to express our knowledge. Ethical wisdom, thus, is our commitment and competence to know deeply and radiantly our personal and collective humanness, and it is our serious commitment to express, thus share and interchange our human knowledge—our human competence. Moreover, ethical wisdom generates and guides our human courage to apprehend and confront the unknown, to appreciate and respect it, and to seek and share its radiance unfolding. Ethical wisdom is the human known and the unknown being envisioned, felt, thought, and realized through each moment of personal mind and across the ecology of collective minds. This is an aesthetic moment, over and over, offering us our potential but engaging us in our practice.

Wisdom is our heroic ethical guide knowing human spirit, releasing human stuff, engaging human struggle, enabling human selves, and unfolding our human ecology. Ethical wisdom emerges from serious and sympathetic inquiry in which there is a purposive search for and an expression of our personal and collective ecological integrity. Wisdom is our integrity, and our integrity is human quality—deep and radiant, personal and collective, aesthetic and tional, liberating and enriching, selfless and enduring.

Ethical wisdom, thus, is manifest human quality found throughout human integrity. The release and grasp of ethical wisdom involves our best inquiring processes actively confronting, centering, penetrating, enriching, and unfolding our knowledge over and over through: intense purposive contemplation and envisioning; sensitive and constructive open communication and debate; considerate and compassionate intentional conduct (and its consequences); and critical collaborative reflection, valuation, and reconstruction. Our knowledge is closely related to human purpose and to human potential. Ethical wisdom is our best human knowledge, our best human practice, and our most challenging and critical human responsibility. It is our human potential pulling our human purpose through our human practice.

Formative Ethics and Product Management

Conventionally, the primary focus of product management has been the technologies of product design and market development. Typically, ethics is considered implicitly or contingently in terms of following norms, conventions, or codes. Ethics is treated explicitly in terms of avoiding confrontations with norms, conventions, and codes or when an overt belief confrontation erupts. We suggest that restrictive ethical perspectives dominate much of product management practice and theory. But also, we believe that formative ethics do exist throughout the product management space. More attention to formative ethics can deepen and enrich our consciousness to ground and guide product management thought and practice.[2]

Products are our shared human creations through which we interconnect our ideas, efforts, resources, and technologies as well as express our life-concepts, life-styles, and life-qualities. Every product is a complex of aspirations, expectations, experiences, expressions, and ethics. As such, ethics cannot be turned off and on throughout the product management process. Ethics is present always, and it always pervades.

Every product is a paradoxical mix of our ethical stuff and our ethical shadows—a distinctive construction of and, thus, commitment to an intermingling of our ethical stuff and its shadows. Ethical product management is grounded in confronting this challenge with quality consciousness, deep commitment, and constant vigilance. Ethical product management is grounded in confronting this challenge with quality consciousness, deep commitment, and constant vigilance. Ethical product management emerges through each caring, serving, and wise product market realization. It involves a heroic struggle masked in practical tensions.

Products are our shared human experiences. Every product is an expression of an organization's ethical consciousness and ethical character. Every product is an experience within a consumer's life and life-quality. Within our organizations, real people generate our product ideas and shape these into specific market offerings. Across our markets, real people buy and consume the costs and benefits of each product experience. Products interconnect organizations and markets as well as personal organizational contributions and personal consumption. Ethical product management involves considering each product in explicit terms of human experience and human character. Thus, ethical product management involves building, nurturing, and developing people, organizations, and markets simultaneously. It is a process of human interchange and relationship management through which care, service, and wisdom are exchanged to shape our best ideas into offerings and shape our product offerings into quality life-experiences.

Ethical product management can be enhanced practically by reflectively and creatively studying and learning about our markets and marketing practice, and sharing our marketing experience, knowledge, and methods. Knowledge is a powerful ethical potential. Careful inquiry and constructive education are vital to ethical product management. The better we know our markets, products, and marketing practice, the better we are able to construct and consider genuine product market options, and the better we are able to make and enact ethical product market choices.

Moreover, ethical product management can be enhanced practically by considering all products as being in a continuous process of development or "becoming"—a state of continuous potential for genuine renewal and enrichment. The process of *new* product development is managed carefully in many organizations (Takeuchi and Nonaka 1986; Wind 1982). Complex systems melding serendipity and creativity with pragmatic checks and balances are formally established to stimulate product innovations and to cautiously study, shape, and evaluate their viability and potential contribution. These systems typically include integrated organizational efforts, active participation of prospective consumers and other relevant stakeholders, and intensely focused attention on the evolving product market and market environment. A strong spirit of "making the product happen, if it should happen" epitomizes the process. As such, a genuinely new product is a collaborative result of constructively challenging conventions (or assumed conventions) and creatively breaking through personal, technical, economic, organization, and market barriers. The spirit and careful management practice exercised when developing new products provides a prototypic perspective for managing all products ethically.

Further, ethical product management considers the total product as being in a constant developmental state of potential enrichment, augmentation, and even transformation (Levitt 1980). Products are more than static bundles of basic features and characteristics. Products are complex and dynamic. Our productive and consumptive needs and desires are enfolded within each product, and they are unfolding through each product into functional and symbolic value constellations. The complex product constellation unfolds further through the functional and symbolic design and configuration of total product and total marketing programs. A "basic" product works as an anchoring, orienting, and organizing element in the total processes of organization-market interchange. A comprehensive marketing program complements, extends, and transforms the basic product into a total product expression and experience. Ethical product management involves careful integration and responsible interchange of the total marketing configuration—all products, price promotion, and delivery/access decisions and constructions—as expressions of ethical character and experiences of life-quality.

Ethical product management extends beyond the responsibility of comprehensive product market programs into the responsibilities of comprehensive and often diverse product market portfolios of programs, and beyond into the dynamics of market and program portfolio change. The ethical product manager often must orchestrate a complex harmony of product market exchanges across diverse, changing products and markets. Contemporary portfolio management theory can lead to mechanical analysis and decision making that promotes shallow examination and evaluation of product market investment and divestment decisions (Wensley 1981).

The ethical product manager must carefully consider each product and market in terms of an organization's competitive competence and the market's attractiveness, but also in terms of an organization's fundamental expertise and scope of capabilities, its ethical character and competence, and the ethical responsibilities and volatilities inherent in the market. Ethical product managers must look deeply into their products and markets and view wisely the scope, balance, and synergies of their portfolio. Broad awareness and deep sensitivity complemented with active and wise inquiry are vital competencies and necessary practice to manage product market portfolios ethically and effectively.

To conclude, product management is a social ecological process through which we collaboratively encounter and enact the complex and diverse realizations of our personal and collective human needs and their shadows—human drives and desires. As such, product management involves a dialogue between our fundamental spirit and our evolving human character as well as across our emerging purpose, responsibilities, and conduct. This dialogue is guided by the active quality of our "voice" and, particularly, our competence to listen to each others' voices empathetically and constructively. This dialogue involves all stakeholders and their needs and voices—hoping, trusting, helping, encouraging, and waiting—across time. Moreover, the dialogue involves the deep and expansive voice of nature and its time—whispering, singing, or even shouting to us. Finally, ethical dialogue involves action as well as conversation. Action is our augmented conversation. Action is our product. Therefore, our responsibility to care, our need to share and serve, and our potential to collaboratively know together actively ground ethical product management now and for the future.

Conclusion

When we think about products, we are thinking about ethics. When we manage products, we confront ethics expressively and experientially. Ethical product management practice involves no simple prescription nor any guarantee. It involves the process of recognizing and actualizing our potential by realizing our consciousness and competence collaboratively and carefully through our products and markets. Our best ethical stuff is responsibility, service, and wisdom. Our best products are grounded in ethical stuff.

Notes

1. The perspective of ethics presented throughout this section has emerged over an extended period. I have chosen to present it in a general manner, rather than to analytically detail its grounding and development. Moreover, citing and notes have been minimized. However, my perspectives of human ecology and formative ethics have many important influences, above all C. West Churchman (1979, 1982).

Churchman recatalyzed and has grounded my pursuit for ethical knowledge, illustrating and assuring our need for introspection as a vital and necessary form of scholarship and practice. Moreover, his work radiates the meaning and significance of ethical human ecology. Other fundamental influences include Carl Jung's (1956, 1966) search for the spirit in man and his confidence in the power of spirit and heroicism, Ken Wilber's (1980, 1983) powerful insight into consciousness and human becoming, Gregory Bateson's (1972, 1980) grasp of the ecological features of human mind, Erich Jantsch's (1980) peek into the evolutionary process and its implications for human practice, Richard Mason and Ian Mitroff's (1981) practical development of dialectic processes, Mitroff's (1983) passion for understanding the real nature of problems, and Chogyam Trungpa (1984) and Jeremy Hayward's (1984) teaching of Eastern mysticism in practical, lucid presentations.

2. This section can be approached best in a contemplative frame of mind. Carefully consider the nature and dynamics of your personal and organizational products and product management processes. Introspective analysis into one's personal performance of product management responsibilities is the catalyst for mature ethical product management.

References

Bateson, Gregory (1972), *Steps to an Ecology of Mind*. New York: Ballantine.
———, (1980), *Mind and Nature—A Necessary Unity*. New York: Bantam.

Buell, Victor (1975), "The Changing Role of the Product Manager in Consumer Goods Companies," *Journal of Marketing* 39 (July): 3–11.

Churchman, C. West (1971), *The Design of Inquiring Systems*. New York: Basic Books.

———, (1979), *The Systems Approach and Its Enemies*. New York: Basic Books.

———, (1982), *Thought and Wisdom*. Seaside Calif.: Intersystems.

Clewett, Richard M., and Stanley Stasch (1975), "Shifting Role of the Product Manager," *Harvard Business Review* (September-October): 65–73.

Emshoff, James (1980), *Managerial Breakthroughs*. New York: AMACOM.

Habermas, Jürgen (1984), *The Theory of Communicative Action*. Boston: Beacon.

Hampden-Turner, Charles (1982), *Maps of the Mind*. New York: Collier.

Hayward, Jeremy W. (1984), *Perceiving Ordinary Magic—Science and Intuitive Wisdom*. Boulder Colo.: Shambhala.

Hise, Richard T., and J. Patrick Kelley (1978), "Product Management on Trial," *Journal of Marketing* 42 (October): 28–33.

Huxley, Aldous (1944), *The Perennial Philosophy*. New York: Harper.

Jantsch, Erich (1980), *The Self-Organizing Universe*. New York: Pergamon.

Jung, Carl G. (1956), *Symbols of Transformation*. Princeton, N.J.: Princeton/Bollingen Paperbacks.

———, (1966), *The Spirit in Man, Art and Literature*. Princeton, N.J.: Princeton/Bollingen Paperbacks.

Laczniak, Gene R. (1983), "A Framework for Analyzing Marketing Ethics," *Journal of Macromarketing* 3 (Spring): 7–18.

Levitt, Theodore (1980), "Marketing Success through the Differentiation of Anything," *Harvard Business Review* (January-February): 83–91.

Levy, Sidney J. (1978), *Marketplace Behavior—Its Meaning for Management*. New York: AMACOM.

Levy, Sidney J. and Gerald Zaltman (1975), *Marketing, Society and Conflict*. Englewood Cliffs, N.J.: Prentice-Hall.

Mason, Richard O., and Ian I. Mitroff (1981), *Challenging Strategic Planning Assumptions*. New York: Wiley Interscience.

McCoy, Bowen H. (1983), "The Parable of the Sadhu," *Harvard Business Review* (September-October): 103–8.

Mitroff, Ian I. (1983), *Stakeholders of the Organizational Mind*. San Francisco: Jossey-Bass.

Mitroff, Ian I., and Richard O. Mason (1981), *Creating a Dialectic Social Science*. London, England: Reidel.

Mitroff, Ian I., and Ralph Kilmann (1984), *Corporate Tragedies*. New York: Praeger.

Prigogine, Ilya and Isabelle Stengers (1984), *Order Out of Chaos*. Boulder Colo.: Shambhala.

Stevens, Anthony (1982), *Archetypes—A Natural History of the Self*. New York: Morrow Quill.

Takeuchi, Hirotaka, and Ikujiro Nonaka (1986) "The New New Product Development Game," *Harvard Business Review* (January-February): 1986.

Trungpa, Chogyam (1984), *Shambhala—The Sacred Path of the Warrior*. Boulder, Colo.: Shambhala.

Walsh, Roger N., and Frances Vaughn (1980), *Beyond Ego—Transpersonal Dimensions in Psychology*. Los Angeles: Tarcher.

Wensley, Robin (1981), "Strategic Marketing: Betas, Boxes or Basics," *Journal of Marketing* 45 (Summer): 173–82.

Wilber, Ken (1980),*The Atman Project*. Wheaton Ill.: Theosophical.

———, (1981), *No Boundary* Boulder, Colo.: Shambhala.

———, (1983), *Up From Eden: A Transpersonal View of Human Evolution*. Boulder, Colo.: Shambhala.

Wind, Yoram J. (1982), *Product Policy: Concepts, Methods and Strategies*. Reading, Mass.: Addison-Wesley.

5

Marketing as Exchange in an Institutional Framework

Anil Pandya

In marketing literature on exchange, two contending schools of thought can be discerned. Based on their conception of exchange, one group can be called the "marginalists" and the other the "institutionalists." The marginalist paradigm is the dominant one and the institutionalist paradigm is the critical one in marketing.

The marginalists (Bagozzi 1977, 1979, 1985; Kotler 1972, 1983; Kotler and Levy 1969; Hunt 1983; Levy and Zaltman 1975) view exchange in the neoclassical microeconomic paradigm. They believe that material as well as symbolic exchanges are in the legitimate domain of marketing. The market is viewed as yielding benefits to all participants proportionate to their productive contributions because both buyers and sellers are assumed to be maximizers. The market is seen as a perfectly competitive, equilibrating, and efficient resource-allocating mechanism which resolves competing claims on scarce resources.

The institutionalists (Alderson 1965; Arndt 1981, 1983; Bartels 1968; Pandya 1985) believe that markets are rarely perfect. Market actors belong to institutions whose nature and functions have an effect on the form and outcome of transactions. Market actors do not always optimize and have multiple goals and imperfect information. Consumers have unstable preferences and often engage in transactions harmful to themselves.

The marginalist view fails to broaden the domain of marketing—the very reason for which the marginalist view was advanced. It fails to explain the behavior of the finished-goods market in market economies because these markets are imperfect, oligopolist, vertically integrated, and, thus, domesticated (Anderson 1982; Arndt 1981; Day and Wensley 1983). This view is of limited use in developing and socialist countries where finished-goods markets are weak, peripheral, or nonexistent. The broadening literature (Kotler and Levy 1969; Kotler 1972) and the social marketing literature (Bagozzi 1975; Kotler 1972) also fails because it reduces all forms of economic and noneconomic transactions to market exchange and equates all institutions to market institutions, instead of highlighting their differences and interconnections (Pandya 1985). On the other hand, the institutionalist perspective on understanding and explaining market behavior highlights differences among markets, hierarchies, and households and makes distinctions between market and nonmarket transactions.

This chapter presents an institutionalist framework for viewing exchange in marketing as an alternative to the dominant marginalist paradigm. Exchange is viewed as an interactive process occurring within and across institutions involving power, negotiations, and bargaining. This is in contrast to exchange being viewed as an end state of individual decision making. The chapter thus extends Arndt's (1981, 1983, 1985) political economy approach to marketing.

An essential feature of the political economy approach is the simultaneous and interdependent analysis of political and economic systems of production and consumption of resources. Economy refers to systems that transform inputs into outputs. Polity concerns the power and control systems of an organization or society. The major focus of this approach is to study how marketing institutions engage in exchange and how political processes influence and control exchanges.

The advantage of this perspective is that it provides better theoretical and practical support to the newer marketing areas of macromarketing, social marketing, and marketing in developing countries. It is a nonreductionist view of transactions which does not construe all forms of exchange as market exchange.

An Institutional Framework to View Exchange

The economic structure of a society consists of four types of institutions: households, private firms, public firms, and government institutions. Production and consumption occur within these institutions, while exchanges occur within and across them. Transactions take three forms: reciprocity, redistribution, and market exchange. Institutions in this model are thus linked with one another through transactional relations, some of which are considered desirable by society while others are socially undesirable.

Participants enter a transaction with expectations of achieving outcomes. When expectations and outcomes do not coincide, participants use negotiating power—a political process—to influence outcomes and achieve satisfaction. Those with greater negotiating power get more satisfaction than those with low negotiating power.

All transactions are not equally desirable for institutions and society. Therefore, institutions and society use formal and informal controls to encourage transactions they consider desirable and inhibit transactions they consider undesirable. Internal controls help institutions monitor and control their own behavior. External controls are imposed on institutions and these regulate transactions among institutions.

The institutional framework thus has an economic structure—a typology of institutions and transactions whose function and performance are governed by a political process consisting of negotiating power and control systems.

Types of Institutions

Table 5–1 describes and contrasts the four types of institutions. The household category includes single-parent, nuclear, joint, and extended families in rural and urban areas. Private firms include large and small privately, publicly, and cooperatively held companies engaged in production of goods and services as well as small entrepreneurs, craftspeople, and artists who sell their skilled products and services in the market. Public firms are state-owned organizations engaged in producing private goods and services. Examples include companies such as British Steel, Amtrak, Renault, and the State Bank of India. Government institutions include local, state, and federal agencies providing a variety of services at the local, state, and national levels.

These institutions all perform functions such as planning, searching, risk taking, producing, and purchasing and do not differ from each other on account of these functions. What separates them is the content of these functions. For instance, both households and restaurants are engaged in the production of food. What differentiates the household from the restaurant are the

Table 5–1
Types of Institutions and Their Functions

Types of Institutions	Members	Types of Transactions
Household	One or more members related by kinship ties. Hierarchically organized.	Exchange in markets, gifts to households, and allocation within households.
Private Firm	Individual members unrelated by kinship ties. Hierarchically organized economic bureaucracy.	Exchange in markets and allocation within firms.
Public Firm	Individual members unrelated by kinship ties. Hierarchically organized state-owned economic bureaucracy.	Exchange in markets, allocation within firms, and allocation to other public firms.
Government Institution	Individual members unrelated by kinship ties. Hierarchically organized state bureaucracy.	Exchange in markets, allocations within institutions, and allocation to and from households and firms.

motive for production, the technology of production and the organization for production.

Consumption processes also differ across different institutions. Households produce goods and services in response to their internal consumption needs. Private and public firms respond to market signals and do not normally consume their own final products. Government institutions produce goods and services in response to the internal needs of the rest of society and these products are jointly consumed by members of a society.

Goods and services produced within all these institutions are distributed in three ways: they are shared, they are given as gifts, or they are exchanged for other goods and services. These three forms of transactions are called reciprocity, redistribution, and exchange.[1]

Households, for example, are connected to other households through reciprocity, to private and public firms through market exchange and to the government through redistribution. Similarly, private and public firms use market exchange to transact business with each other and use redistribution in their transactions with government. Because they are state-owned, public firms often engage in redistributive exchange with other firms, somewhat like the member firms of a large private conglomerate. Government institutions purchase services and goods from the market (from households and firms) but then redistribute the outputs back to households, firms, and other institutions. To understand the complexity of this system of transactions, it is important to highlight the differences between reciprocal exchange, redistribution, and market exchange.

Reciprocal Exchange

Reciprocity is a form of gift exchange whereby members belonging to a reciprocal network are obliged to give and receive gifts of goods and services (Mauss 1974). The obligation to give or receive is usually implicit. The closer the members of one group feel toward one another, the greater is the tendency to develop reciprocal relations (Polanyi 1957). The greater the reciprocal gift giving, the closer are the feelings toward one another. Gifts of goods and services are exchanged, usually among friends, relatives, and neighbors and rarely among strangers. Gifts are given to strangers out of a sense of obligation toward the whole community. The closer the reciprocal relations, the less explicit are the rules governing transactions (Sahlins 1972). For example, how much and what a family should give to a distant relative for a wedding is governed by customary rules of etiquette. But when parents give to their children, the expectation of a return gift is not as clear.

Figures 5–1 through 5–3 show three forms of transactions. In figure 5–1, members of group *A* establish reciprocal relations with members of group *B* and perhaps with group *C* as well, such that members of *A* give to *B*, *B* to *C*, and

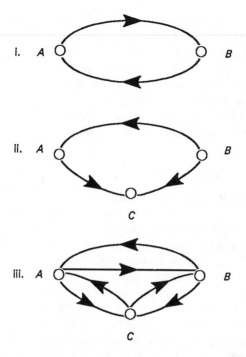

Figure 5–1. Reciprocal Transactions

C in turn to *A*. Whatever the sequence, reciprocal gift exchanges occur in a network of households. The network is maintained by a regular flow of gifts and becomes a source of comfort and strength for the household. In modern urban societies, the networks consist of both relatives and friends with whom contact is frequent. Gifts of goods and services are exchanged constantly to strengthen the bonds of the network. The network thus becomes a system of support in an uncertain world and a source of comfort in times of certainty.

As Banks (1979) and Belk (1979) have shown, gift giving has great economic significance. Conservative estimates show that gifts account for nearly 10 percent of retail sales in North America; many retailers estimate that 30 to 40 percent of their net sales occur in the holiday season of November and December. In Britain, gifts accounted for 5 percent of GNP in 1972. In developing countries, gifts have traditionally played a significant part in weddings, birth observances, and religious ceremonies. No wedding in India is complete without the bride's dowry, which can include gifts of gold, clothes, utensils, furniture, and occasionally a car or house, depending upon the economic status of the family. Reciprocal exchanges dominate market exchanges in developing countries where markets do not produce all the necessities of goods and services required by households. In developed countries, (though market exchanges dominate) reciprocal transactions still persist and are highly valued by individuals and households because they perform symbolic and psychological functions which market exchanges cannot.

One cannot understand demand, supply, or marketing in any economy without reference to reciprocal exchange. Whenever gifts are bought for money, or when ingredients to make gifts are bought for money, market exchanges occur, but in these cases, the logic of reciprocal exchange rather than the logic of market exchange drives the market.

Redistributive Exchange

For redistribution to occur, there must be a *group* of members (households, firms, associations, or government bureaucracies) defined by a rule of inclusion and a *center* where allocation decisions are made.

The main mechanism for redistribution is sharing. As shown in figure 5–2, members of a group (*A*, *B*, or *C*) first pool all or part of their production at a center (*N*). The pooled product is then shared according to some distributive rule. Rules of pooling and redistribution vary according to the principles of hierarchy where each member assumes some rank. If all ranks are equal, then everyone pools an equal share; if ranks are unequal, then unequal shares are pooled. If all ranks are equal, the members receive the redistributed products equally, but if some ranks are unequal, then some members receive more than the others. Take, for example, the right to use public goods and services. In modern democratic or socialist countries, all citizens theoretically have the same rank and enjoy the same access to public goods. In South Africa, however, the black majority does not have the same rights and access to public goods. The political system of apartheid maintains the system of unequal access and consumption. If blacks are to have equal access to public goods and services, then this political system needs change. Clearly, the question of rank is a political one, whereas the principle of sharing is an economic one.

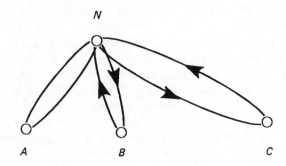

Figure 5–2. Redistributive Transaction

Redistribution is an important form of exchange in marketing. Social marketing can be better understood within the structure of redistribution by identifying the group, the center, and the allocation and membership rules. Redistribution describes social marketing better than market exchange because it deals with transfer, cooperative sharing, and public goods—concepts that are outside the vocabulary of market exchange. For example, India has a democratic government; legally and constitutionally, all Indians have the same rights to public goods. But a vast majority of traditionally poor and backward castes and tribes are discriminated against and are often denied access to such goods. Similarly, in the United States, after the civil rights movement of the sixties, blacks have had the same rights to public goods and services, yet blacks are often discriminated against. In both these cases, social marketing can contribute to improvement in consumption of the socially handicapped groups by providing information and changing attitudes.

Redistribution is important for the study of regional development, public sector marketing, strategic planning, comparative marketing, and marketing in socialist countries because planning and internal resource allocation are suited to redistributive exchange. Resource allocation by a central authority, according to hierarchical rules, to achieve regional, corporate, or national goals is redistributive behavior. For example, Indian development plans now have *tribal subplans* and *special component plans* which preempt expenditures and programs to benefit the really poor and socially discriminated-against tribes and castes. Affirmative action programs are used in the United States and India to help disadvantaged groups get access to jobs. Thus, political and economic processes are used to correct historical inequalities faced by certain groups in getting access to opportunities and public goods. The state uses its political authority to remove inequalities in redistributive ranks so that all citizens have equal rights and entitlement to public and private goods.

Market Exchange

As shown in figure 5–3, market exchange is the simultaneous transaction of goods and services between any two parties in a market. A market is a specialized and institutionalized set of such regularly occurring transactions.

Market transactions are specialized by the types of goods and services exchanges, such as the packaged goods market, labor market, and capital market. Such transactions are institutionalized by custom and law. Product markets are categorized as factor, commodity, and final goods markets. Market transactions are segmented by types of buyers; examples of these market segments include institutional, government, and international markets. Marketers have traditionally studied transactions of final goods and services in these different market segments, but have not studied factor or commodity markets.

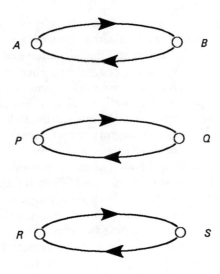

Figure 5–3. Market Exchange Transaction

A Critique of Marginalist Exchange

The marginalist conception of exchange is appropriate for the study of factor and commodity markets because these markets more closely resemble perfect market conditions. Marketers, however, have traditionally stayed away from the factor and commodity markets where economists clearly enjoy a differential advantage.

In western market economies, finished-goods markets are generally imperfect, oligopolist, vertically integrated, and domesticated (Arndt 1981). Here, the marginalist view of exchange is of little use. Power, negotiation, and bargaining play a greater role in these markets.

Conceiving marketing as the marginalists do also leaves out the study of transactions in countries that do not have institutionalized markets, but instead have planned economies; countries where markets are peripheral or nonexistent; and countries where only labor and commodity markets predominate. Socialist countries such as China and Soviet Union are experimenting with peripheral markets, while some developing countries have both planned and market sectors; these require an understanding of market exchange in conjunction with other forms of exchange.

As these arguments suggest, the marginalist view of exchange plays an incomplete role in the development of marketing theory and practice. The institutional framework better captures the reality of transactions of goods and services, accommodates market and nonmarket transactions, and can handle a diversity of political and economic institutions which meet human consumption needs.

Transactions and Institutional Relations

Transactions occur within and across institutions. For example, households buy goods from the market and redistribute these within the household. A mother may buy a new dress for her child or pass on the dress of an older child to the younger one. At the same time, she may buy sweets and share them with the family. Thus, the household is connected to the dress store and the candy store through a market exchange relation and within the household through a redistributive relation. Similarly, when a brother buys a gift for his sister, the household is externally linked to the gift store through market exchange and internally through a reciprocal relation. A private manufacturing firm buys factors of production from the market through an external market exchange relation, allocates these through redistribution to manufacture products, and markets the finished product to outside markets. These are the normal, everyday, legitimate transactions sanctioned by society. But often households and friendships break up, firms (instead of competing) begin to collaborate, and government officials and others give or take bribes. Such transactions are considered illegitimate and prohibited by institutions and government. The marginalist perspective does not explain these failures. The institutionalist framework presented here is capable of describing and explaining both legitimate and illegitimate transactions.

Legitimate Transactions

Consider figure 5–4. Households are in reciprocal relations with other households (cell 1). Households sell labor to the other three institutions through the market (cells 2, 3, and 4) and pay taxes to the government through a redistributive relation (cell 4). Private firms exchange their products with all other institutions (cells 5, 6, 7, and 8) and pay taxes to government institutions (cell 8).

Public firms are in an exchange relation with both households and private firms (cells 9 and 10), but are in an exchange or redistributive relation with other public firms. For instance, if a government-owned refinery provides oil to a government-owned petrochemical firm, the transaction could either be a market exchange or merely a book transfer. Public firms by definition are state-owned and, therefore, are in a redistributive relation to government institutions.

The transaction matrix in figure 5–4 suggests that societies with different mixes of institutions will have different patterns of transactions. In the United

	Households	Private firms	Public firms	Government institutions
Households	Reciprocity 1	Exchange 2	Exchange 3	Exchange Redistribution 4
Private firms	Exchange 5	Exchange 6	Exchange 7	Exchange Redistribution 8
Public firms	Exchange 9	Exchange 10	Exchange Redistribution 11	Redistribution 12
Government institutions	Redistribution 13	Redistribution 14	Redistribution 15	Redistribution 16

Figure 5–4. Legitimate Pairwise Transactions across Institutions

States, the transaction pattern is dominated by market exchange followed by redistribution and reciprocity. In socialist China, it is dominated by redistribution followed by reciprocity and market exchange. In India, reciprocity dominates, followed by redistribution and market exchange. These patterns shift with changes in the institutional structure and functions of these economies.

As a developing country industrializes, the production mix of the households will change and market exchange or redistribution will begin to replace reciprocal transactions. As the role of the state increases in a developed country, redistribution will replace market exchange. As the state begins to decontrol in socialist or mixed economies, market exchange replaces redistribution. Macroplanners and regulators can influence the pattern of exchanges or its rate of change with the help of this institutional model.

Illegitimate Transactions

Consider figure 5–5. Households are linked by market exchange, firms are linked by reciprocity and redistribution, and government institutions are linked to others by market exchange and reciprocity.

The normal state of exchange between two households is a reciprocal one, but sometimes households do engage in market exchange with each other directly. Yard sales are examples of such transactions, though such relations are often inconsequential and governed by custom rather than law.[2] Consumer protection laws in the United States protect consumers from companies or dealers who sell shoddy products or deceive consumers. Such laws are an instrument for empowering the household in relation to a private or public

	Households	Private firms	Public firms	Government institutions
Households	Exchange	Reciprocity	Reciprocity	Reciprocity
Private firms	Reciprocity, redistribution	Reciprocity, redistribution	Reciprocity, redistribution	Reciprocity
Public firms	Reciprocity	Reciprocity, redistribution	Reciprocity, redistribution	Exchange
Government institutions	Exchange	Exchange	Exchange	Exchange

Figure 5–5. Illegitimate Pairwise Transactions across Institutions

firm. These laws are usually not applicable when consumers buy from or sell to other consumers.

Similarly, the usual legitimate transaction relation between any two firms is market exchange. Reciprocal and redistributive relations are discouraged by society because these help some firms gain unfair advantage over rivals or consumers and undermine competition. The antitrust laws in the United States and the Monopolies and Restrictive Trade Practices Acts in India and Britain are designed to prevent firms from monopolizing the market (leading to market failure) by forming cartels, developing discriminatory reciprocal relations (sweetheart deals), by price fixing, and vertical integration. These laws thus protect competition and prevent reciprocal or redistributive relations among firms. Individual members of firms are said to commit a breach of trust (conflict of interest) when they receive gifts or payments from other firms to strike favorable deals and preempt the market.

Finally, attempts by government institutions to sell public goods (such as the sale of public lands, forests, or waterways) are often seen as illegitimate even though such sales are limited and regulated. These sales reveal the replacement of normal redistributive transactions by market exchange. Such transactions often convert irreplaceable public goods into private goods and, thus, restrict and reduce private consumption. Such transactions also tend to bring social inequalities and conflicts to the forefront because not all members of the society have the same capability of purchasing or utilizing these goods. Therefore, such transactions are considered illegitimate.

The Political Side of Exchange

Exchanges of all types—reciprocal, redistributive, and market—represent *economic* behaviors in different institutional contexts. But the *conditions* precipitating such exchanges and the *consequences* of exchange behavior are usually political. With the exception of channel literature, the political side of exchange is usually ignored. This is a serious flaw because economic analysis of exchange, even when blended with sociopsychological insights, is a partial representation of the phenomenon being studied. Two political aspects of exchange—negotiating power and control systems—are discussed here to show the depth of understanding achieved by focusing on the political side of exchange.

Power in Negotiations

Exchanges among institutions are usually negotiated settlements or contracts (Alderson 1965). The party with greater negotiating power tends to benefit more than the party with lesser negotiating power. An uncontrolled monopolist supplier enjoys great power over a buyer without an alternative source of supply. Such an exchange is unbalanced because one party gains at the expense of the other.

Pandya (1985) traces the source of negotiating power to institutional factors such as technological strength and organizational complexity. These factors enable firms to achieve market dominance in the long run. If an institution is simple and uses low technology (for example, a peasant household), it has the lowest comparative negotiating power because of lack of control over raw materials or markets. A complex organization using high technology has the highest relative negotiating power for exactly the opposite reasons. AT&T and IBM are examples of organizations with high negotiating power because of control over technology and markets.

Accordingly, the higher the technological strength and the higher the organizational complexity of an institution, the greater will be its negotiating power, as shown in figure 5–6. Participants who find themselves in vulnerable negotiating situations are likely to try and enhance their technological strength and organizational complexity to increase their negotiating power.

Consider, for example, the case of technology transfer from developed to developing countries. Technology markets are imperfect and highly skewed in favor of suppliers. This has led many third world governments to create institutional mechanisms to purchase technology from abroad. In India, government officials, jointly with buyers from private and public firms, negotiate purchases of technology, often increasing organizational complexity to improve their bargaining power vis-à-vis the sellers (Pandya 1982). OPEC and the EEC are also examples of organizations attempting to increase negotiating

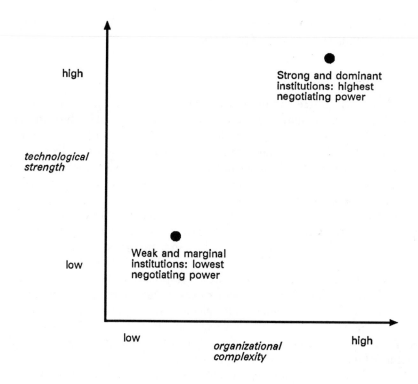

Figure 5–6. Technology, Organization, and Negotiating Power

power by organizing joint purchase and sale of their products in the international market.

Developing countries often erect barriers against foreign competition in order to protect local industries and maintain better control over markets and resources. Public relations and political maneuvering are often of little use in fighting import barriers, as Pepsi Cola discovered in its attempts to enter the Indian market recently. In such situations, a cooperative strategy that enhances rather than subverts local interests may work better.

These examples of the consequences of imbalances in market power are drawn from international trade between developed and developing countries because this trade, unlike domestic trade, is not regulated by a central authority. In domestic markets, however, national governments recognize the problems of power imbalances in transactions and regulate imperfect markets through consumer protection and antitrust laws. International markets, on the other hand, are governed by bilateral and multilateral treaties expressing the relative economic power of different countries. International courts and domestic courts can only interpret the treaties under which trade is carried on. The only recourse that injured parties have in international trade is to either abstain from trading or erect selective barriers. Burma is a recent example of the former strategy and India an example of the latter.

Control Systems

Control systems enforce and protect legitimate institutions and transactions, while inhibiting illegitimate ones. Laws and incentives offered by the state and federal governments encourage entrepreneurs; the law and order agencies try to prosecute the Mafia; consumer protection and other regulatory legislation intervenes in markets; and firms and households use rules, values, and beliefs to regulate and pattern internal transactions. Control systems function within a redistributive framework of transactions.

Redistribution performs the major control function in a society. It maintains the corporate structure of society and subordinates its members to a central authority. This subordination is done in many ways: through coercive enforcement of a body of law; by ritual, which is the collective performance of well-recognized acts by members to reinforce notions of inclusion and sharing; and by ideological communication which evokes and communicates images of sameness and otherness to maintain the group boundary and legitimacy of the center. By these means, redistribution acts as an integration process, generates a spirit of unity and centricity, and codifies the ranked and hierarchical structure of the corporate body (Sahlins 1972).

A legal system is an example of a control system orchestrating transactions in society. It is an external and formal method of enforcing decisions internal to institutions. Some examples of these are truth-in-advertising, product safety, and antitrust laws. But each institution has its own rules and policies, both formal and informal, which are internal to the institution and govern the actions and decisions of its members. Examples are formal codes of ethics and informal norms of behavior which exist in most institutions as well as the newspaper ombudsperson who monitors deviations from these set norms. Other informal mechanisms influencing transactions include the values of participants, peer pressure, and gossip.

Figure 5–7 presents a two-dimensional classification matrix of control systems, along with some examples. The two classifying dimensions are methods of control (formal and informal) and locus of control (internal and external). The first dimension addresses the question of explicitness of a control system; the second fixes the location of the controlling authority. The informal/internal control mechanisms (such as personal values, beliefs, socialization, and acculturation) ensure the orderly running of institutions through honest and moral behavior. Breakdown of these control systems leads to corruption and illegitimate transactions. Informal/external controls (such as peer pressure and gossip) bear upon institutional transactions, enforce uniform behavior, and define acceptable and unacceptable group norms. Formal/internal rules

Locus of Control

		Internal	External
Methods of Control	*Informal*	Values, beliefs, socialization, and culture	Group pressure, gossip, and appearances
	Formal	Codified rules and policies	Legal systems and regulations

Figure 5–7. Control Systems

guide internal transactions by codified policies such as personnel and wage policies or a ban on trade with South Africa. Finally, the formal/external control system consists of the national legal framework which guides all institutional business and defines legitimate and illegitimate transactions.

Households usually use internal/informal systems, while government institutions tend to use formal/internal and formal/external control systems. Private and public firms use both formal and informal controls to deal with their members and clients. Formal controls tend to increase with an increase in the number of private and public firms; consequently, the use of informal systems tends to decrease. Control systems encourage legitimate transactions and discourage illegitimate ones; different institutions respond to different controls. The framework enables policy makers to identify areas where controls are needed and suggests alternative methods of controlling transactions.

Summary and Conclusion

The concept of exchange in marketing, dominated by the marginalist paradigm, is a limiting perspective for the marketing discipline. Marketers have traditionally studied final goods markets (which are especially amenable to the marginalist view) and not factor or commodity markets. This perspective does not deal with market failures in market economies, nor is it useful in nonmarket economies or economies where markets are weak. Nor is the marginalist view of much use in the newer areas of strategic market planning, macromarketing, social marketing, and developmental planning.

The institutional framework, based on the political economy approach, presents an alternative view of exchange where four institutions (households, private firms, public firms, and government institutions) are linked by three forms of exchange (reciprocity, redistribution, and market exchange).

Transactions are influenced by negotiating power, conceptualized as control over markets and raw materials. Monopoly power, technological strength, and organizational complexity increase the negotiating power of institutions. Those institutions that find themselves in a weak negotiating position attempt to increase their strength through upgraded technology, organization, or government protection.

Society approves and legitimizes some transactions and disapproves of others. Institutions use formal or informal and internal or external mechanisms to promote or inhibit transactions.

The framework is comprehensive and interdisciplinary. It deals with transactions in both market and nonmarket economies and allows for the comparative study of different marketing systems. It deals with economic and noneconomic transactions. By adjusting institutional factors, development planners and macromarketers can use the framework to influence transactions and institutions. The framework is better suited to the reality of international markets, the current practice of marketing, and the development of marketing theory. It uses an inductive and open approach as opposed to the closed, deductive, idealistic, and ethnocentric approach used by the marginalists.

Notes

1. These terms are used here as defined in economic anthropology literature, as in Polanyi (1957) and Sahlins (1972).

2. In some towns where yard sales have become widespread, ordinances are enacted by town governments banning, limiting, or otherwise controlling such transactions.

References

Alderson, W. (1965), *Dynamic Marketing Behavior*. Homewood, Ill.: Richard D. Irwin.

Anderson, Paul F. (1982), "Marketing Strategic Planning and the Theory of the Firm," *Journal of Marketing* 46 (Spring): 15–26.

Arndt, Johan (1981), "The Political Economy of Marketing Systems: Reviving the Institutional Approach," *Journal of Marketing* 41 (Fall): 36–42.

——— (1983), "The Political Economy of Paradigm: Foundations for Theory Building in Marketing," *Journal of Marketing* 43 (Fall): 44–54.

——— (1985), "Changing the Course of Marketing: Alternative Paradigms for Widening Marketing Theory," in *Changing the Course of Marketing*, N. Dholakia and J. Arndt, eds., Greenwich, Conn.: JAI Press: 1–25.

Bagozzi, Richard P. (1975), "Marketing as Exchange," *Journal of Marketing* 39: 32–39.

———— (1977), "Is All Social Exchange Marketing? A Reply," *Journal of the Academy of Marketing Sciences* 5 (Fall): 315–26.

Banks, Sharon (1979), "Gift Giving: A Review and an Interactive Paradigm," in William Wilke, ed., Advances in Consumer Research, Vol. 65 Ann Arbor, Mich.: Associatin for Common Research, 319–324.

———— (1985), "Marketing as Exchange: Is It Distinguishable from Social Psychology?" in *Changing the Course of Marketing*, N. Dholakia and J. Arndt, eds., Greenwich, Conn.: JAI Press, 257–62.

———— (1979), "Towards a Formal Theory of Marketing Exchanges," in O.C. Ferrel, S.W. Brown, and C.W. Lamb, Jr., eds. *Conceptual and Theoretical Developments in Marketing*, Chicago: American Marketing Association, 431–37.

Bartels, Robert (1968), "The General Theory of Marketing," *Journal of Marketing* 32 (January): 28–33.

Belk, Russell (1979), "Gift Giving Behavior," *Research in Marketing* Vol. 2: 95–126.

Day, George S., and Robin Wensley (1983), "Marketing Theory with a Strategic Orientation," *Journal of Marketing* 47 (Fall) 79–89

Hunt, Shelby D. (1983), *Marketing Theory: The Philosophy of Marketing Science.* Homewood, Ill.: Richard D. Irwin.

Kotler, Philip (1972), "The Generic Concept of Marketing," *Journal of Marketing* 36 (April): 46–54.

———— (1983), *Principles of Marketing*, Englewood Cliffs, N.J.: Prentice-Hall.

Kotler, Philip, and Sidney J. Levy (1969), "Broadening the Concept of Marketing," *Journal of Marketing* 33 (January): 10–15.

Lemann, Nicholas (1986), "The Origins of the Underclass," *The Atlantic* (June): 31–61.

Levy, Sidney J., and Gerald Zaltman (1975), *Marketing and Conflict in Society.* Englewood Cliffs, N.J.: Prentice-Hall.

Mauss, Marcel (1974), *The Gift: Forms and Functions of Exchange in Archaic Societies.* London: Routledge & Kegan Paul.

Pandya, Anil (1982), *Managing the Technology Purchase Decision Process in the Indian Public Sector*, unpublished Ph.D. dissertation. Ahmedabad: Indian Institute of Management.

———— (1985), "Reflections on the Concept of Exchange: Marketing and Economic Structures," in *Changing the Course of Marketing*, N. Dholakia and J. Arndt, eds. Greenwich, Conn.: JAI Press, 235–55.

Polanyi, Karl (1957), "Economy as an Instituted Process," in *Trade and Markets in the Early Empires: Economics in History and Theory*, Karl Polanyi, C.M. Arensenberg, and H.W. Pearson, eds. New York: Free Press, 243–69.

Sahlins, Marshall (1972), *Stone Age Economics.* Chicago: Aldin, Atherton.

Williamson, Oliver E. (1975), *Markets and Hierarchies: Analysis and Antitrust Implications.* New York: Free Press.

Part II
Marketing and Knowledge Systems

6

The Poverty of Ahistorical Analysis: Present Weakness and Future Cure in U.S. Marketing Thought

Ronald A. Fullerton

> You cannot step twice into the same river.
> —attributed to Heraclitus

Disquietude in Marketing Thought

> There comes a moment when the atmosphere changes, [when] the significance of the unreflectively utilized [orthodox] viewpoints becomes uncertain and the road is lost in the twilight. . . . Then scholarship too prepares to change its standpoint and its analytical apparatus and to view the streams of events from the heights of thought. It follows those stars which alone are able to give meaning and direction to its labors.
>
> —Max Weber

Discontent with the narrowness and rigidity of U.S. marketing thought has been rising for several years now, as expressed by established scholars as well as by newer entrants (e.g., Arndt 1985; Bartels 1983; Deshpande 1983; Wind and Robertson 1983; Webster 1981). There is a growing agreement that the logical positivist approach which has dominated marketing thought for the past quarter-century inhibits both scholars' and practitioners' understanding of the full dimensions of marketing. A major example of such inhibition that has scarcely been mentioned in the literature of discontent is orthodox marketing thought's lack of a well-developed awareness of time, change, and context. Because it lacks this awareness, current marketing thought is "ahistorical"— which has disquieting consequences for its ability to understand and explain marketing phenomena.

This paper has benefitted from comments by Leonard Carlson, Edward Cundiff, Luis Dominguez, and the editors of this book. Research was aided by a grant from Rhode Island College, where the author previously taught.

Markets, marketing activities, and marketing thought itself are all historical phenomena; ahistorical approaches cannot elucidate them either fully or accurately. Because it is ahistorical, a considerable part of contemporary marketing thought risks having no more power to explain marketing than the notoriously ethereal analytical arabesques of classical economic thought can explain economic life. But where classical economists are indifferent to the irrelevancy of their work, marketers are not.

Marketing thought should not be, and does not have to be, ahistorical. It can develop the missing sense of time, change, and context by studying the philosophy and methods for dealing with these issues that have been devised by historians, historical sociologists, and philosophers of history.

The remainder of this chapter will amplify the arguments made here. It will also show how and why U.S. marketing thought became ahistorical.

Historical versus Ahistorical Thought

A sense of history does not necessarily mean an interest in the long ago; more important here is how one views the present and the future—as static or as in flux. The essence of the historical perspective is a thorough, systematic, and sophisticated awareness of change—or lack of it—over time, and of the context(s) of place, situation, and time in which change—or continuity—occurs. It is important to mention continuity here because the passage of time is not synonymous with change; the relationship between time and change is extremely complex.

"Historically" oriented thought emphasizes complex flux and the uniqueness of any single phenomenon in time. "Ahistorical" thought, on the other hand, generalizes across time and place, seeks simplicity ("parsimony"), and either ignores historical flux or assumes that it follows known and regular patterns.

The Ahistorical Nature of Current U.S. Marketing Thought

Current marketing thought in the United States is clearly and overwhelmingly ahistorical. Its dominant tendencies are to ignore change, to deny that there is enough change to be of much concern, or to assume that it follows simple, structured, and categorical patterns.

Marketing models, for example, are presented as if valid everywhere and at all times. They presuppose, to borrow a phrase from the French historian Braudel (1958, p. 37), "the perpetually fixed moment, which is, as it were, suspended above time." For another example, time and context should be intrinsic to empirical research in marketing, yet they are largely ignored; the work aspires instead to establish universals above time—about "the industrial saleswoman," "product quality," or "market share," for instance. Anyone who has ever tried to apply such results to a specific marketing program will recognize how little pertinence they commonly have. A third example derives from the short-term orientation characterizing much of U.S. marketing thought as well as practice. Since it is widely (though incorrectly) assumed and asserted that little change can take place during short-term periods (those of up to a year or so) and since the short-term preoccupation in effect eliminates most consideration of longer time periods, the effect of short-term analysis as presently practiced is to minimize the possibility of change *over any term*. Wind and Robertson (1983, p. 14) find that the bulk of contemporary marketing thought takes for granted "an essentially stable, continuous environment . . . [and] an existing set of brands and perceptions." Stewart and Punj (1982) observe that consumer researchers typically treat consumers' evoked sets as static. Their own treatment of these sets as fluid reflects a sophisticated awareness of time and change that is rare in today's marketing thought.

More representative, unfortunately, is the widespread custom of using research results from varied dates without seriously considering how the time and context in which they were done might effect their current applicability. For example:

Cron (1985) and Cron and Slocum (1984) papers on the career stages of industrial sales people rely heavily upon a model of career stages done in 1957 and taken as fixed by later researchers. Considering the widely reported changes in attitude toward careers and in career patterns since 1957, the current applicability of the early work should be addressed. It is not. Further, the possibility that differences in results on salespeople obtained by researchers from 1960 to 1983 are due in part to temporal differences is not even considered.

Writing about the size of trading areas in his 1982 work on marketing and economic development (pp. 17–19), Kaynak draws upon sources published between 1959 and 1967. No attempt is made to adjust these older results to the much-changed reality of the early 1980s.

Kotler (1984, pp. 136–139) presents several psychological theories, from Freud's through Herzberg's, without mentioning the social and cultural contexts out of which they were developed. The contexts may effect the theories' current applicability. Freud's ideas, for example, reflect concerns of upper-middle class Central Europeans in the socially and sexually restrained environment of the late nineteenth century. This is not to say that these ideas have no use today—many older ideas certainly do—but, rather, to caution that the use must take the origin of ideas into account. It should consciously explain why and how much of the ideas still apply.

Such examples abound in the marketing literature. Researchers in marketing evidently assume that marketing knowledge is a cumulative (just as knowledge in the hard sciences is said to be) and, therefore, that earlier results may be built upon without question as to their present relevance. They thus assume that all research results, empirical or conceptual, have somehow arisen in the same basic milieu (Arndt 1983b); the only differences noted concern such matters as sample size rather than time or context. If work done before 1960 is seldom cited today, it is only because of the questionable (see Fullerton 1985) but widespread belief that no one knew anything about marketing that far back.

There are a few streams of marketing thought that do attempt to deal with change over time: Case research, dynamic modeling, longitudinal studies, and descriptive analyses of new marketing and marketing-related phenomena such as generic products and major legal or demographic changes.

All of this work together, however, is but a fraction of the marketing literature. Moreover, it usually lacks a genuinely strong, thorough, and sophisticated historical awareness. Case studies do convey the intricacy of change well and provide a welcome infusion of concrete presentation rather than generalizing presentation. On the other hand, case research is held in low esteem by many researchers, and case studies as usually written are not intended to provide fully developed analyses—there are intentional gaps and digressions to challenge students, who are expected to do most of the analyzing. The flexible and sophisticated research underlying some cases could be utilized in serious analysis but at present is not: case-based works such as Bonoma's (1985) seem intended for pampered, mentally indolent executives. Logitudinal studies have been rarities so far in the marketing literature. They have not even had much "longitude," twelve to fourteen months being a typical span covered (e.g., Moschis and Moore 1982). Descriptive studies of new marketing phenomena tend to present them as permanent additions to the marketing universe rather than as the transient, ever-evolving phenomena they more likely are; recent examples include generic products (whose sales were reported down even before the 1985 article by Harris and Strang appeared) and the supermarket shopper segments discussed by Zeithaml (1985).

Contemporary marketing thought's most ambitious attempts to deal explicitly with change over time are found in dynamic modeling, in mathematical forecasting techniques, and in process-oriented concepts such as the family and product life cycles and the diffusion of innovations. Drawn heavily from other disciplines, these approaches emphasize the importance of change. Yet, they are largely ahistorical because of their implicit assumptions that change over time follows known, regular patterns and that the underlying relationships among variables are constant. Statistical forecasting assumes that past patterns will continue. The family and product life cycles and the diffusion of innovations assume that change will—indeed, must—follow a known sequence. Dynamic modeling assumes that social phenomena follow some "orderly and predictable" logic (Huckfeldt, Kohfeld, and Likens 1982, p. 7). None of these methods can cope with the historical realities of discontinuities and seemingly irrational alteration. Hence they distort change into excessively categorical patterns.

Contemporary marketing thought, it is clear, is overwhelmingly ahistorical. The phenomena that it attempts to explain, on the other hand, are characterized by complex flux. They are historical.

Marketing Is a Historical Phenomenon

The statement that marketing is a historical phenomenon applies to marketing, to marketing thought, and to the very nature of marketing itself. Bringing about change in buyer behavior is a fundamental goal of much marketing practice, especially now as competition intensifies still further in numerous markets. (See Stewart and Punj 1982.) To alter buyer behavior, new institutions and tactics are devised. Partly in response to these, and partly in response to other stimuli, buyers do alter some of their behavior. Many product markets have shown marked volatility during the past dozen years—anyone who believes in a glacial pace of market change ought to study automobile sales figures (aggregate, by type, and by brand) for the United States or any Western European country since 1973. Yet, during the same period, in other product markets, change has come slowly. Some of today's most popular designs of sterling flatware, furniture, and china have been on the market continuously for a century or more.

Thus, markets in the aggregate are in flux—*complex flux*. They do not all change at the same rate, in the same ways, or in accordance with economic rationality. Behind some of the bewildering flux seen in markets and marketing behavior lie complicated and unexpected environmental changes. The dismal prediction record of large econometric models in recent years has been due largely to an onrush of unforeseen shifts in underlying economic relationships which the models had assumed to be stable. Although they are commonly trivialized and made to seem somehow unworthy of scholarly attention by breathless journalistic accounts, environmental shifts can be profound. The German historical sociologist Elias (1978/1939) showed how fundamental behavior patterns changed over time in Europe; today, the pace of such change is almost certainly faster than it was in the period Elias described.

The very nature of marketing itself changes over time. While marketing in its most basic sense of exchange activity is universal across time and context, its degree of development, specific methods and institutions, vigor, and efficacy can and do differ over time (Fullerton 1984). Some of the differences are epochal.

Marketing, then, is a historical phenomenon. This has major implications for marketing thought.

The Poverty of Ahistorical Thought in Marketing

To attempt to understand and interpret a historical phenomenon—marketing—with an ahistorical analytical approach is to doom marketing scholarship to results that are incomplete at best and distorted at worst. Yet, this is the current state of U.S. marketing thought. Marketing systems are social systems; social systems, according to the German philosopher Habermas (1976/1969, p. 141), being in continual and complex flux, simply cannot be grasped by means of analytical approaches developed to study "repetitive systems" (systems in which change follows repetitive patterns). Much of today's marketing arsenal, as we have seen, assumes repetitive systems. Again, the criticism which Elias (1978/1939, p. xv) directed at historical sociological analysis in the 1930s applies very well to marketing thought in 1987:

> But since every historical phenomenon, human attitudes as much as social institutions, did actually once "develop," how can modes of thought prove either simple or adequate in explaining these phenomena if, by a kind of artificial abstraction, they isolate the phenomena from their natural, historical flow, deprive them of their character as movement and process, and try to understand them as static formations without regard to the way in which they have come into being and change?

Another argument made against ahistorical sociology (Bendix 1984, p. 9) also extends to marketing: the assumption that knowledge is cumulative is weakened, if not destroyed, by the fact that social and historical phonemena may change too much over time for earlier results to apply today.

The best that ahistorical approaches can do when applied to historical phenomena is to illuminate their state at a single point in time. Some of our current approaches do this very well. The approaches that presuppose categorical patterns and rates of change can do well when environmental conditions are stable, as, for example, they were during much of the 1950s and 1960s in the United States and Western Europe. The historical data used to justify such approaches are nearly always taken from these decades. Complacent and now-obsolete assumptions of slow and predictable change developed during the 1950s and 1960s underlie much of what is being taught as the *sine qua non* of marketing today. If, on the other hand, we develop models based upon today's turbulence, they will not necessarily apply in the future; it would be surprising if they did, in fact. The point is that, in social phenomena such as marketing, neither the patterns nor the pace of change is known categorically in advance. Models, theories, and survey results alike apply best to when and where they have been done, not to all times and all places.

But this is heresy! It contradicts one of the most sacred assumptions to the dominant logical positivist paradigm in marketing—the principle of uniformitarianism, according to which laws—or at least generalizations—valid for all times and places can be discovered. The hold of this principle over current marketing thought is typified by Hauser's (1985, especially p. 352) serenely confident assertion that marketing "scientists" are on the verge of developing, from scanner data and quantitative virtuosity, eternal mathematical theorems about marketing phenomena. These theorems will apply to all times, and they will not be challengeable by any new empirical data. Justifying his bold assertions with references to the history of science, Hauser never demonstrates a convincing connection between the stability of subject matter in science and that in marketing. The fact that an atom of a given type will always behave in a given way at a given altitude and temperature neither proves nor disproves that two consumers will behave in the same way given the same denomination coupon for the same brand of mayonnaise. Describing both behaviors with mathematical formulae makes no difference. Consumer behavior is likely to change over time whatever the formula; that of an atom will not.

If it were possible to relate the behavior of atoms making up consumers to their buying behavior, then the principle of uniformitarianism might apply equally to marketing. Under the present level of knowledge, it is not possible. Moreover, we cannot stabilize or regularize market behavior merely by attaching "timeless" mathematical formulae to it. The presumption of timelessness that often accompanies mathematical analysis in marketing is fatuous. In sum, the fact that the principle of uniformitarianism applies to mathematics and physics does not mean that it applies to a social science such as marketing. The evidence seems overwhelming that it does not apply, except sometimes at a very high level of abstraction, and then usually only for similar cultures.

Uncritically applied as it has been to marketing thought, the principle of uniformitarianism encourages researchers to minimize the significance of historical change and context. Its uncritical acceptance contributes heavily to the ahistorical tenor of contemporary marketing thought. It encourages researchers toward the ahistorical—and chimerical—goal of discovering timeless laws and generalities, and away from the goal of elucidating the present nature of marketing reality. Ahistorical aspirations are a major contributing factor not only to the shortcomings of marketing thought discussed above, but also to several other shortcomings which have been pointed out during the past few years: (1) vacuous abstraction and generalization in place of concrete analysis (Arndt 1983a, 1985; Fırat 1985), (2) oversimplification of marketing realities, such as imputing rationality to all actions (Pascale 1984), (3) underrating the temporal, spatial, and other contexts of marketing behavior (Black, Ostlund, and Westbrook 1985; Savitt 1982), (4) a weak sense of time and change which lends to static assumptions by academics and consultants and, in turn, to strategic mistakes by practitioners (Wack 1985), and (5) a false sense of progress in marketing because of ignorance of past marketing thought and practice (Hollander 1986).

Discussed in isolation from one another in the literature to date, these problems all stem wholly or partly from marketing's dominant ahistorical assumptions to seek general truths transcending time, change, and context, a propensity that should now at last be judged in light of the argument that Max Weber first published over eighty years ago:

> The more comprehensive the . . . scope . . . of a term, the more it leads us away from the richness of reality, since in order to include the common elements of the largest possible number of phenomena, it must necessarily be as abstract as possible and hence *devoid* of content. In the cultural [social] sciences, the knowledge of the universal or general is never valuable in itself. (1949/1904–5, p. 80)

Let me illustrate Weber's point. Envision a model of a trade show, an empirical experiment on the relationship between money spent and inquiries received in the trade show, and a homiletic piece along the lines of "Ten Ways to Make Trade Shows Pay" (replete with a hodgepodge of examples). Would any of these typically generalizing and ahistorical treatments tell us as much about a trade show as this historical passage from Kidder about a 1979 show?

> Sperry had a big new machine and a slide show all about it. Burroughs had erected a small theater, with chairs set up to face a rank of computers in big white cases that looked like nothing so much as dishwashers and refrigerators; a recording of trumpets playing fanfares ushered you into this homely spectacle. The main thing memorable at National Cash Register was the pair of golden-haired women, identical twins, posing at its booth. "The bipolar blondes," said Jon Blau . . . [in] a fairly witty remark drawn from the language of semiconductor technology. (1981, p. 239)

The passage applies to one show in one industry at one time—1979. It supplies the kind of rich detail and context that is so basic to the marketing process— and so absent in our literature. To write it requires genuine and sustained cerebral activity in the form of expert powers of observation and literary skill.

How It Got to Be This Way: The Development of Ahistorical Thinking in U.S. Marketing

> If research was once founded on a Heraclitean kind of assumption that all is in flux, . . . it is now based on an Eleatic idea. The Eleatics, it is said, imagined the flight of an arrow as a series of states of rest; actually, it seemed to them, the arrow does not move at all.
>
> Norbert Elias (1978/1939, pp. 233–234)

Given its historical development, it is hardly surprising that U.S. marketing thought has become ahistorical. It has drawn much of its personnel as well as its methodological assumptions and apparatus from the mainstream variants of Anglo-American social sciences, especially economics, psychology, and sociology, where the dominant mentality has long been ahistorical (Bernal 1965, pp. 1087–88, 1139; Elias 1978/1939, pp. 230ff, appendix; Fırat 1984; Savitt 1982; Stone 1981, pp. 8ff; Weber 1949/1904–5, pp. 85ff).

Still, into the 1950s, U.S. marketing thought showed some awareness of time, change, and context. Its emphasis upon accurately and thoroughly describing marketing activities and deducting general concepts from these descriptions paralleled some methods of historical research. A quality introductory text such as that of Beckman, Maynard, and Davidson (6th ed., 1957) explained more about the actual marketing phenomena of *that* time than does one of today's quality texts for *this*. Behind the description was considerable careful observation and analysis of why things happened as they did.

But in the late 1950s existing thought in marketing (and other business disciplines) was deemed mindlessly inadequate by three economists who authored reports of enormous influence upon business education (Gordon and Howell 1959; Pierson 1959). It did not seem to matter that these men had neither researched nor taught business, but rather were trained in a discipline that at times actually glories in its remoteness from and irrelevance to the realities of actual business phenomena. Though based upon biased questioning and dogmatic assumptions, these economists' reports set a new direction for marketing thought. The emphasis, according to Gordon and Howell (p. 186), for instance, had to be on analysis based upon the work of the social science; description was to be kept to "some irreducible minimum" (p. 287). Why discuss real products in real markets when "widgets" in imaginary ones reflected a higher order of scholarship? Pierson (p. 93) intoned that techniques for dealing with specific contexts were of little use to business. The generalizing approach of U.S. social science with its universal and eternal—and, therefore, ahistorical—paradigms was infinitely preferable.

Had academic marketing developed a critical orientation, especially one that would look beyond work published in English and in the United States, the existence of the strong historically oriented social science tradition of Germany and Italy might have been recognized. But this did not happen even when the contemporary critical work of Adorno and Habermas and the classical work of Elias and Weber became available in English translation (e.g., Adorno 1976; Elias 1978; Hebermas 1976; Weber 1949). Similarly, strong criticism of the dominant ahistorical approach by social science dissidents in the English-speaking world (e.g., Dopfer 1979; Hudson 1972) has not attracted the interest of many marketers. Only within the past few years have marketing scholars began to systematically probe the limitations of the "received" view of hard science upon which the dogmas of social science methodology are uncritically grounded (e.g., Fırat 1984, 1985b; Zaltman, LeMasters, and Heffring 1982). At present, mainstream U.S. social science is still predominantly ahistorical, and it still continues to shape marketing thought (Arndt 1983b).

The Remedy: A Historical Approach

An ahistorical approach has narrowed the range and limited the explanatory power of contemporary marketing thought; a historical one can correct these shortcomings—without jeopardizing the very real advances in standards of scholarship that marketing has made in the past twenty-five years. By a "historical approach" is meant both the process of studying change over time and the approaches developed to do this.

The historical approach presented here is drawn from three disciplines which have devoted themselves to exploring the ramifications of time, change, and context—history (especially social and economic history), historical sociology (e.g., Bendix 1984; Elias 1978), and the philosophy of history (e.g., Collingwood 1956; Mink 1979). The work of social historians and historical sociologists is especially relevant to marketing. Even this work, however, has different aims than does the marketing discipline, which is why the approach presented here, representing a composite/consensus of historical approaches, will doubtless require further modification to achieve its full potential within marketing thought. Our goal here is to demonstrate how marketing can *begin* developing the sophisticated sense of "history" which it so clearly needs.

Although history has been studied and written about for over two thousand years in the Western world, the historical approach used today dates largely from the nineteenth century. It is older than marketing as a discipline, but only by several decades. Like marketing, the historical disciplines, especially history, have experienced important methodological advances in recent decades (Burke 1980; Gilbert and Graubard 1972; Hexter 1979; Iggers and Parker 1979; McClelland 1975; McCullagh 1984; Stone 1981).

The Philosophy of the Historical Approach

The philosophy of the contemporary historical approach is made up of five core sets of ideas. These hang together closely. The ideas focus on: historicism, complexity, empirical reality, assessment of causation, and differences between social and natural sciences.

Historicism. Historically oriented minds are intensely conscious of the passage of time, which is believed to be intimately associated with change; the only disagreements are on what—if any—pattern(s) change follows. Strong awareness of time and change, which can only be heightened by consciously studying historical examples, has produced the philosophical perspective of historicism, whose tenets are explicitly or implicitly accepted by most twentieth century historians and historical sociologists. In the German sociologist Mannheim's (1924, p. 2, translated by this author) classic definition, historicism means perceiving concepts and theories as well as institutions and customs "as always in flux, as phenomena (*Potenzen*) which are coming from somewhere in time and pressing on toward somewhere [in time]." From the perspective of historicism, an analytical construct such as "equilibrium" is bizarre and erroneous nonsense. Social systems do not tend to equilibrium, but rather to flux. Nothing human is beyond time and change, and nothing human can entirely transcend its temporal context. General laws of the type that mainstream social science and marketing aim to discover are distrusted: "The essence of historicism is the substitution of a process of individualizing observation for a generalizing [and timeless] view of human forces in history" (Meinecke 1972/ 1936, p. lv). Historicism emphasizes the *uniqueness* that to some extent characterizes every phenomenon in time, and also the *context* in which a phenomenon occurs. Clark (1967, p. 25) argues that "to neglect the context of historical evidence is to misunderstand its meaning;" an event at one time and situation is not identical to any outwardly similar event at another time and in another situation.

Taken to their extremes, the emphases on uniqueness and context would deny the possibility of any generalizations, much less of any theory or quasi-theoretical construct or model being able to elucidate more than one event at one point in time (Troeltsch 1922). Some historians have gone to such an extreme. More common among historians for the past two decades, however, is the view that there are enduring and also recurring patterns of causation which yield *probabilities* of analogous (not completely identical) response. These patterns exhibit too much subtle variation over time to be fitted into the categorical formulations of universal laws (Chandler 1984; Clark 1967, pp. 24–25; Gerschenkron 1968, pp. 40–56; McClelland 1975, pp. 72–79; McCullagh 1984, Chapter 6; Stone 1981, p. 85). Historical sociologists have tended to derive more generalities and to impose more structure upon history than historians, but they too stress the ultimate transience of both (e.g., Elias 1978).

Whether or not change over time follows recurrent patterns has long been debated among the historically oriented. The classical historicist position was articulated by the philosopher-theologian Troeltsch:

"[History] is . . . an immeasurable, incomparable profusion of always new, unique, and hence individual tendencies, welling up from undiscovered depths, and coming to light in each case in unsuspected places and under different circumstances." (1923, p. 14).

In other words, there is no strong underlying pattern to historical change. Contemporary English novelist Graham Swift expresses this very well: History "goes in two directions at once. It goes backwards as it goes forwards. It loops. It takes detours. Do not fall into the illusion that history is a well disciplined and unflagging column marching unswervingly into the future" (1985/1983, p. 102).

Applied to marketing phenomena, such ideas are a valuable corrective to the unreflective assumptions of underlying rationality and stability in which most marketing scholars have been trained. The statements of Swift and Troeltsch can be backed up with considerable historical evidence. They challenge the too-simple assumptions that change comes either slowly and predictably or not at all. They encourage us to consider marketing thought and practice as historical phenomena which are always subject to unforseen change —in bewildering directions. Above all, they challenge us to think seriously about change over time and in differing contexts.

Two other sets of ideas on patterns in history are also valuable correctives to the ahistorical thrust of marketing thought. They have been developed by serious historical thinkers. First is the idea of *dialectics* originated by the nineteenth century German philosophers Hegel and Marx. In the dialectical view of history, there is near-perpetual turbulence. The inevitable clash of opposed cultural, economic, and political tendencies (*thesis* versus *antithesis*) resolves itself in a new *synthesis* of institutions and beliefs. This, in time, generates antagonistic tendencies within itself, continuing the dialectic. Dialectical analysis has been significant in continental European social science, which offers a vigorous counterpoint to logical positivist (e.g., Adorno 1976/ 1969) and has been used by both American and European historians (e.g., MAHRO 1984). The fact that dialectics is associated with Marxism in no way lessens its value to marketing analysis, since the core idea is about change, not politics. Sophisticated dialectics offers great promise in understanding marketing change, especially that brought about through competition. It is a far superior analytic device to the simplistic "insights" from military strategy (Clausewitz, samurai, kung-fu, etc.) currently being purveyed to practitioners by nonacademic word processors.

Another substantive change paradigm was developed by the recently deceased French historian Braudel (Braudel 1984; Iggers and Parker 1979, p. 177; Hexter 1979, pp. 93–94). Braudel believed that changes of long, medium, and short duration go on *simultaneously*, each at a different velocity. Long-run changes are slow and take centuries, even millenia, to come to completion; examples include geological and climatic changes. Major cultural, economic, and social changes are of medium duration and velocity, while political changes show rapid velocity and short duration. All three types of change are going on and effecting one another at any given time. Applied originally to sixteenth century Mediterranean Europe, the Braudel scheme certainly should not be taken literally for today, when velocities of change are faster even for long-run phenomena. Rather, it should be modified into a framework for conceptualizing the simultaneous coexistence of many changes going on at different rates. Hardly simple, it nevertheless does make sense of the extremely complex and otherwise chaotic reality of marketing and its environment.

A third change paradigm worth considering here is very old. It is the concept of *teleology*, according to which historical development moves inevitably toward some predestined goal. The goal may be miserable or beatific, secular or religious, in nature; there are many teleologic schemes. Almost all American marketers have been exposed to the teleologic scheme in which business struggled through several ages of crude ignorance (the production era, the sales era) on its way to the marketing era in which the marketing concept governs business life. Growing scepticism within the marketing community that it really happened that way (Fullerton 1985; Hollander 1986) underscores the major problem with teleologic schemes—they are better as expressions of faith than as guides to the empirical actuality of historical development.

Complexity. Historical researchers, particularly historians, tend to see and seek complexity, and then to compound it further by emphasizing that "the factors which make up the complexity of an historical situation are always changing" (Clark 1967, p. 23). Parsimony is equated with the simplistic (e.g., MAHRO 1984, p. 80; Stone 1981, p. 40). Complex psychological theories like those of Freud are preferred to simpler, newer ones because they seem to explain rather than conceal the observed complexity of behavior change. Stone (p. 41) describes historical explanation as "a nonlinear, multiple loop feedback system, with many semi-independent variables, each responsively reacting to the influence of some, or all, of the others."

Obviously, such explanation lacks the mechanical precision possible with controlled experimentation, but controlled experimentation is not always a possibility. Should phenomena be ignored because they do not lend themselves to experimentation? The historical approach can offer rich results. Wasserman (1985) finds that the development of long-distance telephone transmissions was complicated and convoluted far beyond anything that current models of the innovation process portray. At times, theory generation overlapped chronologically rather than proceeded experimentation, for example.

An example of complexity in the development of a market is given by my work (1977, 1979) on the growth demand for commercial "pulp" fiction among urbanized workers and their families in Germany from about 1870. In moving from rural areas to industrial cities, the German working class not only earned higher wages, but also broke away psychologically from old customs such as the oral tradition of telling and retelling unwritten fairy tales (*Maerchen*) as a major form of amusement. These developments combined with the growing ability to read engendered by state elementary education to create potential demand for inexpensive, thrilling pamphlets. Meanwhile, advances in technology brought inexpensive wood pulp paper and high-speed presses; it became possible to publish large number of inexpensive pamphlets at a profit. Most book publishers, however, disdained the lower-class market, just as their ancestors would have. The men who finally began to publish and market pulp literature were aggressive entrepreneurs who were able to enter publishing after the old restrictions on entry into trades were abolished as a result of political agitation in the 1860s. Behind the new entrepreneurs were decades of growth of an aggressive marketing mentality in once placid Germany. The publisher-entrepreneurs who produced pulp for the masses' latent demand also worked vigorously to stimulate that demand, employing, for example, the now inexpensive technique of color lithography to reproduce paper covers with gripping scenes of mayhem and romance. Finally, the story content of the pulp literature was heavily influenced by the American dime novels of the Wild West. German receptivity to such stories in part reflected centuries-old popular beliefs about freedom and adventure in the land where the Indians roamed.

Thus, the demand for a specific product, the pulp pamphlet, was due to the actions and interactions over time of economic, technological, demographic, psychological, and cultural causes. Contrast this explanation to a (hypothetical) demand schedule following the traditions of microeconomics. The schedule would focus upon the relationship between price and demand; income levels, literacy levels, and the prices of other goods could be included. But the psychological impact of urbanization, changes in the ethos of marketing, and myths about the United States—all well-documented historically—would be left out. Precision would be obtained at the heavy cost of oversimplification. Most of the techniques of marketing demand analysis described by Hughes (1973) pay this heavy cost; they deal only with a small number of causal variables.

Empirical Reality. Historical researchers' propensity toward complexity is grounded in their emphasis upon clear and full study of all empirical (observed and reported) factors pertaining to a phenomenon at hand. Among historians, the goal of describing history "as it actually happened" (*wie es eigentlich gewesen war*) laid down in mid-nineteenth century by the German historian von Ranke still guides much practice today. Where mainstream social scientists would assume rationality, purpose, and even parsimony, for example, historians would want concrete evidence of them. Applied to marketing, the historical approach would be to determine how different markets actually develop—however strange and complex that development might be by the light of received assumptions.

Assessment of Causation. Historical researchers today stress determining why things happened as well as what happened. Unable perforce to use controlled experimentation, they have developed sophisticated methods based on comparison of analogous situations, applying theories of behavior, and other devices. Such explanations of causation are probabilistic, to be sure, but, if carefully done, are highly probable. They are certainly preferable to assuming away or ignoring the many areas of behavior—present as well as past—that cannot be interpreted by controlled experimentation. Restricting research to survey, experimentation, and quantification, argues the German philosopher Habermas (in Adorno 1976/1969, p. 199), means that "whole problem areas would have to be excluded from discussion and relinquished to irrational attitudes, *although . . . they are perfectly open to critical discussion*" [emphasis added].

In contrast to the range of critical methods for assessing causation used by historical researchers, marketers swerve between the extremes of experimentation and unsubstantiated guru-babble ("People want holes, not drill bits.") with little in between. Critical and systematic assessment of nonexperimental, nonquantifiable causation variables needs to be introduced to marketing thought.

Subject Matter and Goals Different from Those of Natural Science. There is a long tradition to this belief, which sees historical knowledge as unique and time-bound in contrast to science's universal and timeless norms, and which judges historical knowledge to be noncumulative and scientific knowledge to be cumulative (e.g., Adorno 1976/1969; Clark 1967, chapter 4; Iggers 1983, pp. 147–167; Weber 1949/1904–5). Some of the differences have been exaggerated (McCullagh 1984, pp. 129–130). But the distinction has freed historical researchers from the compulsion to imitate hard science uncritically and thereby has allowed them to develop approaches suitable to their own difficult subject. If it is to comprehend its social and historical character, marketing must grant itself similar freedom.

Historical Method

Current historical method follows logically from the philosophy of the historical approach. Compared to marketing methodolgy, it is richer, more flexible, and less formal. Capable and extended discussions are available in Burke

(1980), Clark (1967), Iggers and Parker (1979), McClelland (1975), McCullagh (1984), and Stone (1981). The basic elements of the method are:

1. *Systematic doubt*. Every aspect of research (sources of evidence, theories that may help explain what happened, other accounts, and the researcher's own assumptions) should be methodically and thoroughly questioned. The intent is to develop the most accurate and objective account possible from available sources. If skillfully done, systematic doubt enables lucid and plausible results even from fragmentary, biased, and intellectually low-grade sources.

2. *Flexible use of analytical tools*. A wide array of tools is used now, ranging from statistics, modeling, and social science theories, through semiotics, to techniques unfamiliar to most marketers (e.g., hermeneutics and impressionist analysis). Researchers take a flexible attitude toward techniques, using them flexibly as they appear suitable.

3. *Multiple data sources*. Social historians in particular feel that critical evaluation of a wide range of data sources is needed to reveal the richness and uniqueness of historic phenomena. For example, to study the growth of ostentatious consumption among upper-middle class Americans in recent years, social historians would scrutinize popular literature and periodicals (including advertisements), study products as artifacts of culture, conduct interviews, review demographic and economic statistics, and look for past analogies in the scholarly literature.

4. *Synthesis*. This involves the coherent recreation of what happened, enriched by interpretation of why it happened and its significance. Collingwood (1956, p. 242) described synthesis as "a web of imaginative construction stretched between certain fixed points provided by [critical interpretation of source material]." The process is creative, but also critical. The coherence imposed must be consistent with the full range of evidence employed.

5. *Mode of presentation*. How should change be presented when so many of the critical and interpretive concepts employed are better suited to present analyses of fixed points in time. There is growing agreement that the traditional literary form of the narrative has not been equalled in presenting change over time and across context. But narrative is extremely difficult to do well.

Conclusion

"Narrative," "literacy," "creative"—lush variety of data and multiplicity of analytical tools—can there be any value to such a different methodology? Can any reliance be placed on the findings it purports to uncover? Should level-headed marketers take all—or any—of the historical approach seriously?

The answer to each of these questions is yes, and for good reasons. The historical approach described here has more substance—and the conventional, ahistorical, logical positivist approach less—than may seem to be the case at first, unreflective glance. Historians value impartiality, objectivity, and, especially, faithfulness to evidence; according to Kuhn's still-valid 1972 essay (pp. 159–92), they share these values with the natural scientists who are so often presented as the quintessence of scholarship. They share the experience of making breakthroughs by means of creative synthesis of fragmentary, even conflicting, evidence. Of course, many of their methods and philosophical tenets are different from those of natural scientists—they *should be*, given the great differences in subject matter. The historical approach offers careful analysis of social phenomena in complex flux, a subject with which the hard sciences do not even pretend to deal. Scholarship is best judged by the degree to which it develops an approach appropriate to its subject matter, not by the degree to which it uncritically apes a more prestigious discipline.

Uncritical aping of Anglo-American social science, which in turn has unreflectively imitated the hard sciences, has brought marketing thought rigor and pretention, but at the expense too often of substance and flexibility. There are too many timeless and vacuous generalities, produced by elaborate methodological devices which seem incapable of dealing with many observable aspects of marketing—especially with time, change, and context.

Marketing is a historical phenomenon. If we deny this, we risk drifting off into the analytical Cloud Cuckoo-Land which the classical economists posit in place of actual markets. The historical approach offers hope in elucidating time, change, and context in marketing. Conventional marketing thought does not and cannot.

Adopting a historical orientation will increase the complexity of marketing analysis and will shatter the certitude of some dearly held beliefs. These difficulties are outweighed by the advantages, however. Since the "historical" dimension of marketing is a vital aspect of the subject, and since a means of beginning to deal with this aspect is available, it would be both irresponsible and unnecessary to perpetuate the present impoverishment of ahistorical thought.

References

Adorno, Theodor W., et al., eds. (1976/1969), *The Positivist Dispute in German Sociology*, translated by G. Adey and D. Frisby; London: Heineman.
Arndt, Johan (1983a), "The Political Economy Paradigm: Foundation for Theory Building in Marketing," *Journal of Marketing* 47 (Fall): 44–54.

———, (1983b), "Review of Hunt's *Marketing Theory,*" *Journal of Marketing* 47 (Fall): 145–146.

———, (1985), "On Making Marketing Science More Scientific: Role of Orientations, Paradigms, Metaphors, and Puzzle-Solving," *Journal of Marketing* 49 (Summer): 11–23.

Bartels, Robert (1983), "Is Marketing Defaulting Its Responsibilities?" *Journal of Marketing* 47 (Fall): 32–35.

Beckman, Theodore N., H.H. Maynard, and W.R. Davidson (1957), *Principles of Marketing,* 6th ed. New York: Ronald.

Bendix, Reinhard (1984), *Force, Fate, and Freedom: On Historical Sociology.* Berkeley: University of California Press.

Bernal, J.D. (1965), *Science in History, Vol. 4: The Social Sciences.* Cambridge, Mass.: MIT Press.

Black, W.C., L.E. Ostlund, and R.A. Westbrook (1985), "Spatial Demand Models in an Intrabrand Context," *Journal of Marketing* 49 (Summer): 106–113.

Bonoma, Thomas (1985), *The Marketing Edge: Making Strategies Work.* New York: Free Press.

Braudel, Fernand (1972/1958), "History and the Social Sciences," in *Economy and Society in Early Modern Europe,* P. Burke, ed. New York: Harper & Row, 11–42.

———, (1984), *Capitalism and Civilization, 15th–18th Century, Vol. 3: The Perspective of the World,* translated by S. Reynolds. New York: Harper & Row.

Burke, Peter (1980), *Sociology and History.* London: Allen & Unwin.

Chandler, Alfred D., Jr. (1984), "Comparative Business History," in *Enterprise and History,* D.C. Coleman and P. Mathias, eds. Cambridge, England: Cambridge University Press, 3–26.

Clark, G. Kitson (1967), *The Critical Historian.* New York: Basic Books.

Collingwood, R.G. (1956/1946), *The Idea of History.* New York: Oxford University Press.

Cron, William L. (1985), "Industrial Salesperson Development: A Career Stages Perspective," *Journal of Marketing* 48 (Fall): 41–52.

Cron, William L., and J.W. Slocum (1984), "Career Stage Effects in the Industrial Salesforce," in *1984 AMA Educators' Proceedings,* R.W. Belk et al., eds. Chicago: American Marketing Association, 148–52.

Deshpande, Rohit (1983), "Paradigms Lost': On Theory and Method in Research in Marketing," *Journal of Marketing* 47 (Fall): 101–10.

Dopfer, K. (1979), *The New Political Economy of Development.* New York: St. Martin's.

Elias, Norbert (1978/1939), *The Civilizing Process: The History of Manners,* translated by E. Jephcott. New York: Urizen.

Firat, A. Fuat (1984), "Marketing Science: Issues Concerning the Scientific Method and the Philosophy of Science," in *1984 AMA Winter Educators Conference: Scientific Method in Marketing,* P.F. Anderson and M.J. Ryan, eds. Chicago: American Marketing Association, 22–25.

———, (1985a), "Ideology vs. Science in Marketing," in *Changing the Course of Marketing: Alternative Paradigms for Widening Marketing Theory,* N. Dholakia and J. Arndt, eds. Greenwich, Conn.: JAI Press, 135–46.

——, (1985b), "A New Approach to Science and Research in Marketing: An Historical Necessity," in *Marketing in the Long Run*, S.C. Hollander and T.R. Nevett, eds. East Lansing: Dept. of Marketing and Transportation, Michigan State University, 317–28.

Fullerton, Ronald A. (1977), "Creating a Mass Book Market in Germany: The Story of the 'Colporteur Novel' 1870–1890," *Journal of Social History* 10: 265–83.

——, (1979), "Towards a Commercial Popular Culture in Germany: The Development of Pamphlet Fiction 1871–1914," *Journal of Social History* 12: 489–511.

——, (1984), "Capitalism and the Shaping of Modern Western Marketing," presented to the 9th International Macromarketing Seminar.

——, (1985), "Was There a 'Production Era' in Marketing History? A Multinational Study," in *Marketing in the Long Run*, S.C. Hollander and T.R. Nevett, eds. East Lansing: Dept. of Marketing and Transportation, Michigan State University.

Gerschenkron, Alexander (1968), *Continuity in History and Other Essays*. Cambridge, Mass.: Harvard University Press.

Gilbert, Felix, and S.R. Graubard, eds. (1972), *Historical Studies Today*. New York: Norton.

Gordon, Robert A., and J.E. Howell (1959), *Higher Education for Business*. New York: Columbia University Press.

Habermas, Jürgen (1976/1969), "The Analytical Theory of Science and Dialectics," in *The Positivist Dispute in German Sociology*, T.W. Adorno, ed., translated by G. Adey and D. Frisby. London: Heineman, 131–62.

Harris, B.F., and R.A. Strang (1985), "Marketing Strategies in the Age of Generics," *Journal of Marketing* 49 (Fall): 70–81.

Hauser, John R. (1985), "The Coming Revolution in MarketingTheory," in *Marketing in an Electronic Age*, R. Buzzell, ed. Boston: Harvard Business School, 344–65.

Hexter, J.H. (1979), *On Historians: Reappraisals of Some of the Makers of Modern History*. Cambridge, Mass.: Harvard University Press.

Hollander, Stanley C. (1986), "The Marketing Concept—A Deja View," in *Marketing Management Technology as Social Process*, G. Fisk, ed. New York: Praeger, 3–29.

Huckfeldt, R.R., C.W. Kohfeld, and T.W. Likens (1982), *Dynamic Modeling*. Beverly Hills: Sage.

Hudson, Liam (1972), *The Cult of the Fact*. London: Jonathan Cape.

Hughes, G. David (1973), *Demand Analysis for Marketing Decisions*. Homewood, Ill.: Richard D. Irwin.

Iggers, George G. (1983), *The German Conception of History*, rev. ed. Middletown-,Conn.: Wesleyan University Press.

Iggers, George G. and H.T. Parker, eds. (1979), *International Handbook of Historical Studies: Contemporary Research and Theory*. Westport, Conn.: Greenwood.

Kaynak, Erdener (1982), *Marketing in the Third World*. New York: Praeger.

Kidder, Tracy (1981), *The Soul of a New Machine*. Boston: Little, Brown.

Kotler, Philip (1984), *Marketing Management*, 5th ed. Englewood Cliffs, N.J.: Prentice-Hall.

Kuhn, Thomas (1972), "The Relation between History and History of Science," in *Historical Studies Today*, F. Gilbert and S.R. Graubard, eds. New York: Norton, 159–92.

Mannheim, Karl (1924), "Historismus," *Archiv fuer Sozialwissenschaft und Sozial-politik* 52: 1–60.

McClelland, Peter D. (1975), *Causal Explanation and Model Building in History, Economics and The New Economic History*. Ithaca and London: Cornell University Press.

McCullagh, C. Behan (1984), *Justifying Historical Descriptions*. Cambridge, England: Cambridge University Press.

Meinecke, Friedrich (1972/1936), *Historism*, translated by J.E. Anderson. London: Routledge & Kegan Paul.

Mid-Atlantic Radical Historians' Association (MAHRO) (1984), *Visions of History*. New York: Pantheon.

Mink, Louis O. (1979), "Philosophy and Theory of History," in *International Handbook of Historical Studies: Contemporary Research and Theory*, G.G. Iggers and H.T. Parker, eds. Westport, Conn.: Greenwood, 17–27.

Moschis, G.P., and R.L. Moore (1982), "A Longitudinal Study of Television Advertising Effects," *Journal of Consumer Research* 9 (December): 279–86.

Pascale, Richard T. (1984), "Perspectives on Strategy: The Real Story Behind Honda's Success," in *Strategy and Organization: A West Coast Perspective*, Glenn Carroll and D. Vogel, eds. Boston: Pitman, 38–63.

Pierson, Frank C. (1959), *The Education of American Businessmen*. New York: McGraw-Hill.

Savitt, Ronald (1982), "A Historical Approach to Comparative Retailing," *Management Decision* 20 (4): 16–23.

Stewart, David W., and G. Punj (1982), "Factors Associated with Changes in Evoked Sets among Purchasers of New Automobiles," in *An Assessment of Marketing Thought and Practice: 1982 Educators' Conference Proceedings*, B.J. Walker et al., eds. Chicago: American Marketing Association, 61–65.

Stone, Lawrence (1981), *The Past and the Present*. Boston, London: Routledge & Kegan Paul.

Swift, Graham (1985/1983), *Waterland*, New York: Washington Square Press.

Troeltsch, Ernst (1922), *Der Historismus und seine Probleme*. Tüebingen: J.C.B. Mohr.

———, (1923), *Christian Thought*, translated by F.V. Huegel et al. London: University of London Press.

Wack, Pierre (1985), "Scenarios: Shooting the Rapids," *Harvard Business Review* 63 (November-December), 139–50.

Wasserman, Neil H. (1985), *From Invention to Innovation: Long-Distance Telephone Transmission at the Turn of the Century*. Baltimore and London: Johns Hopkins University Press.

Weber, Max (1949/1904–5), *Max Weber on the Methodology of the Social Sciences*, trans. and ed. by E.A. Shills and H.A. Finch. Glencoe, Ill.: Free Press.

Webster, F.E., Jr. (1981), "Top Management's Concerns about Marketing Issues for the 1980's," *Journal of Marketing* 45 (Summer): 9–16.

Wind, Yoram, and T.S. Robertson (1983), "Marketing Strategy: New Directions for Theory and Research," *Journal of Marketing* 47 (Spring): 12–25.

Zaltman, Gerald, K. LeMasters, and M. Heffring (1982), *Theory Construction in Marketing: Some Thoughts on Thinking*. New York: Wiley.

Zeithaml, Valerie (1985), "The New Demographics and Market Fragmentation," *Journal of Marketing* 49 (Summer): 64–75.

7
Historical Method: Toward a Relevant Analysis of Marketing Systems

Erdoğan Kumcu

Paradigm Choice in Marketing

It is important to recognize that the dominant logical empiricist worldview in social sciences has clearly and strongly influenced researchers both in economics and in marketing (Bagozzi 1980; Hausman 1984; Hunt 1983, 1976; Zaltman, Pinson, and Angelmar 1973). Additionally, the dominant economics paradigm, neoclassical microeconomic theory, has set the research tone in marketing and some of its subfields from the beginning (Arndt 1981, 1983). Incidentally, both of these paradigms are modeled after the natural sciences (*Naturwissenschaften*) and aspire to the predictive powers of the sciences of the physical universe—"naturalistic determinism" (Scholtz 1974, p. 1142).

However, these models and methods faced serious criticism from philosophers (Feyerabend 1975; Lakatos 1970) as well as recently from economists (see overviews in Eichner 1983; Hausman 1984) and researchers in marketing (Anderson 1983; Arndt 1981, 1983; Fırat 1985b; Sauer, Nighswonger, and Zaltman 1982). These criticisms are primarily based on the verification-falsification problems and the applicability of paradigms of natural sciences to the social/human sciences. Indeed, social sciences generally (and marketing particularly) involve complex socioeconomic relationships in a socially and culturally specific environment that go beyond the determinist Newtonian-type cause-effect or stimuli-response models (Scholtz 1974; Weingartner 1967; Sauer, Nighswonger, and Zaltman).

As a result, a more serious and general criticism is that the methodological approach in marketing is ideological (unscientific), meaning that researchers in marketing reach generalizations from temporal and contextual truths, abstracting the phenomena from their history (Fırat 1985b). Another critical problem stems from the ethnocentricity of most of the North American researchers in marketing. They believe in the superiority of the North American social, political, and economic systems and attempt to export these to other societies, ignoring the need to establish the universal validity of the generalizations of their findings.

In view of these criticisms, new paradigms and/or methodologies are being sought in social sciences. For example, institutionalism is proposed in economics (Dugger 1984; Stanfield 1983) and in marketing (Arndt 1981, 1983) as an alternative/complementary paradigm. In this chapter, I shall propose the historical method as a viable solution for research in marketing.

Historical Research in Marketing

Researchers in marketing have given little and rather discrete attention to historical research. In more than two decades, one can only find a relatively small amount of historical literature in marketing. This rather scarce literature presents three major streams of study dealing with company/industry histories, history of marketing thought, and historical analysis as a method and its application.

The first type of historical research in marketing has both company and industry histories as its content. Examples of this approach can be found in Williamson (1963) and, more recently, in the volumes edited by Hollander and Savitt (1983) and by Hollander and Nevett (1985). These studies are, to a great extent, confined to the operations of the subject companies without relating the events to their environment and context. Also, most of these works are descriptive rather than explanatory.

The second group of studies deals with the history of marketing thought. Among these works, Bartels' research (1976) is the most prominent. This type of study concentrates on documenting the major academic contributions since the turn of the twentieth century. They are historical to the extent that they are chronological, but do not employ either analytical or comparative methods (Savitt 1980, pp. 53–54).

The third group of studies marks a more recent attempt to discuss historical analysis as a method and to apply it to marketing. Savitt (1980, 1983) develops a formal five-step methodological diagram for historical research in marketing, while discussing problems relating to historical data. In his 1984 work, he applies his proposed method to comparative retailing. Fullerton (1983), discussing the positive contributions of the method to scientific inquiry, applies it to demand analysis. Kumcu (1985) underlines the various definitions and uses of the historical research, attempting to apply it to the comparative analysis of marketing channels. Essentially, these works are relevant for the purposes of this chapter. They are more methodological in nature and represent the first incomplete attempts to accentuate the usefulness and contributions of historical method in complementing available research methods in marketing. However, what is lacking is a comprehensive application of the historical method.

The inappropriateness and/or shortcomings of historical research in marketing dictate that at least the following tasks be undertaken:

1. Historical analysis should be defined clearly and its variations pointed out.
2. In order to identify their characteristics, historical perspectives should be compared and contrasted with dominant research methods in marketing.
3. A strong historicist perspective should be presented and its need accentuated.
4. A historical perspective framework should be developed for, and applied to, marketing systems.

The purpose of this chapter is to elaborate on these issues.

Historical Study as a Method

Background and Definition

The historical school sees all social and cultural reality as being dominated by change. Therefore, historicism is defined as "the belief that an adequate understanding of the nature of anything and an adequate assessment of its value are to be gained by considering it in terms of the place it occupied and the role it played within a process of development" (Mandelbaum 1967, p. 24). It should be noted that this definition does not characterize historicism as a worldview, but rather as a methodology concerning explanations of phenomena.

Originally, historical method was introduced in Germany around the midnineteenth to the turn of the twentieth century. It rose from the extensive criticisms of the applicability to Germany of classical economic theories first developed in England and France. Indeed, the historical school voiced its criticism against empiricist and classical theories based on four important issues (Ingram 1878): (1) Isolation of issues from their broader social, economic, and political contexts, (2) extensive abstraction of concepts and phenomena, (3) abuse of deductive method, and (4) claims of arrival at absolute/ universal theoretic and practical conclusions.

The older historical school represented by Roscher and Knies, the newer school of Schmoller and his followers in Germany, and even Leslie and Toynbee in England adopted the historical study of political economy and attempted a detailed description and explanation of the social and economic institutions of nations (Gide and Rist 1915; Oser 1970; Toynbee 1884). For the historical school, institutionalism was concerned with how society is organized to integrate wants and to translate them into actions. Therefore, historicism is considered to be the forerunner of modern institutionalism (Wonnacott and Wonnacott 1986).

Terminology

Authors of historical literature in marketing have used a variety of terms interchangeably to designate sometimes identical and sometimes unlike concepts. The most commonly used terms are *historical research, historical perspective, historical study, historical approach*, and *historical analysis*. Parallel to the main streams of research discussed earlier, I propose to distinguish two concepts from one another: Historical research and historical perspective.

The term *historical research* could be used to denote the study of a subject during an earlier time period, thus emphasizing the understanding of the past (Kumcu 1985). Using written documents and other material to study the emergence of, for example, new grocery outlets during the thirties in the United States would be historical research. In contrast, historical perspective is the study of a subject in light of its earlier phases and subsequent evolution (Lawrence 1984, p. 307). In this sense, historical perspective "provides a description of the change as well as the means for understanding the process of change" (Savitt 1984, p. 149). Using the historical information about the thirties and the emergence of different grocery stores to explain the problems of developing new retailing systems elsewhere today is historical perspective. According to Lawrence, historical research provides the raw materials for historical perspective. In this chapter, the term *historical perspective* is used to describe this dynamic approach, and *historical method* is proposed to include both historical research and historical perspective. The substantial differences between logical empiricism/neoclassical economic theory and historical method warrant elaboration.

Logical Empiricism versus Historical Method

Logical empiricism and historical method, as depicted in table 7–1, represent two completely different worldviews (*Weltanschauung*). Logical empiricism and the neoclassical theory of economics employ Newtonian deterministic thinking on equilibrium mechanisms.

Even though historicists reject the resemblance of their paradigm with the natural sciences, the closest to their understanding is the Darwinian evolutionary thinking. Therefore, historical explanation is radically different from naturalistic explanation in physical sciences, because "human sciences"

Table 7–1
A Taxonomy of the Empiricism/Neoclassical Theory and the Historical
Method

Basic Characteristics	Logical Empiricism/ Neoclassical Theory	Historical Method
Natural science analogy	Newtonian thinking on equilibrium mechanisms	Darwinian evolutionary thinking
Variable relations	Deterministic cause	Probable cause
Dominant mode of logical reasoning		
Theory development	Primarily deduction based upon abstraction	Primarily induction based upon observation
Testing	Empirically comparing deductions with observation	Empirically comparing hypothesized institutional structures with observation
Validity of laws	Universal/absolute	Relative
Perspective of theory	Cosmopolitan and ethnocentric	Context-bound or culturally relevant
Design of study	Primarily normative	Primarily descriptive/ explanatory
Scope of study	Isolated treatment of issues	Treatment of issues as part of an integrated whole
Model type	Mainly a static model: emphasis on status quo	Dynamic process model: emphasis on change

Source: Arndt 1981; Dugger 1984; Gide and Rist 1915; Ingram 1878; Oser 1970; Savitt 1980; Stanfield 1983.

(*Geisteswissenschaften*) cannot be modeled after the natural sciences and cannot achieve their deterministic and predictive power (Weingartner 1967; Scholtz 1974, p. 1142). Human and institutional behavior is greatly formed by environment, and changes according to persistent conditions. Therefore, it is mainly probabilistic.

A variety of marketing examples illustrate these points depicted in table 7–1. Stages of marketing evolution, family life cycle, product life cycle, industrial and consumer buyer behavior models, retail-change models (such as the wheel of retailing and retail life cycle), and others follow deterministic logic and attempt to predict future events by taking the cultural/historical setting as given or as static. They would fail when the present settings, cultural context, and/or other conditions change or when all variables—including the ones that are assumed as given—are taken as independent variables. Consider for instance, the retail-change theories. (For overviews, see Savitt 1984; Markin and Duncan 1981.) The primary purpose of these theories is to describe the present status and predict the future patterns of retail development. To accomplish this task, these theories define stages through which the retail establishments should pass during their lifetime—emerge, grow, and finally decline and "die."

These theories are presented as if this process is uncompromisingly determined by some uncontrollable factors and as if it is valid in all industries and at all times. Further, they give no indication regarding why the retail systems evolve as described. Indeed, as social institutions, retailing systems are formed and transformed through interaction with their environment. Therefore, they appear in various configurations in different societies and/or at different times in the same society. The simplistic and deterministically mechanical explanation by retail-change theories fails to see the retailing change phenomenon as part of the integrated social, cultural, and economic whole of societies (Markin and Duncan, p. 61).

Further, because of the theories' normative character and claims of universal validity, they are presented in such a way that the described patterns of change are independent variables which all retailing organizations must follow (Savitt 1984, p. 151). In fact, the changes are dependent variables which are determined by marketing and managerial action (Markin and Duncan 1981, p. 61; Dhalla and Yuspeh 1976). Consequently, changes and the conditions influencing them cannot and should not be studied as a given.

In addition, the perspective of the models having the logical empiricist approach are cosmopolitan and ethnocentric, aiming at absolute/universal laws which are valid across time and space as a consequence of their premise of naturalist determinism. This view is static and considers all cultures to be uniform. In contrast, the historical method consists of a dynamic process model and claims historical relativism. It studies phenomena in their culturally relevant contexts. Indeed, "cultural relevance is a prerequisite to policy relevance" (Stanfield 1983, p. 198). This method encourages more holistic and informative theorizing, although it is less universal as well as less hypothetical and less abstract, as shown in table 7–1.

In empiricism, the logical reasoning in theory development is primarily deductive on a highly abstract level. Various sets of factors explaining differences/similarities and the structure of marketing systems are discussed independently of each other. Then, these individual analyses are aggregated and/or abstracted, and used in a deductive manner to predict phenomena. Empirical testing is done by comparing deductions. This concept is depicted in figure 7–1.

The theory of relating economic development to the marketing systems of various societies is an excellent example to illustrate this last point. As Bartels (1981, p. 23) points out, this theory depicts "that *economic development is* [the] *determinant* of a number of actions and conditions in marketing. From this it is deduced that with industrialization, economic systems and personal behavior in developing countries tend to become like those in already developed countries" [emphasis in original].

As illustrated in figure 7–1, the available information from different countries which observe different development levels are aggregated. From this, it is deduced that the phenomena experienced in the United States will occur elsewhere. Methodological and logical problems of such works are reviewed in El-Ansary and Liebrenz (1982). Some authors contend that the marketing systems in those countries *will* and/or *ought to* look more like the North American structure. Consequently, they recommend that institutions and marketing practices of advanced countries should be introduced into other economies (Mallen 1975; Bennett 1966; Cundiff 1965; Slater 1965; Wadinambiaratchi 1965; Hall, Knapp, and Winsten 1961).

Influenced by the stages of the economic development model of Rostow (1960), this literature implies that all economies are likely to move through the same stages as they develop, and that a country or industry moves strictly from one stage to the next through time. Further, the paradigms used are a product of, and are culture-specific and context-bound to, the North American environment and economic conditions (Dholakia, Fırat, and Bagozzi 1980). Consequently, this literature implicitly assumes not only a cultural and economic similarity between various countries, but also a parallelism in their historic and future development, which is highly doubtful (Kumcu 1985). The marketing literature offers many examples showing that diverse social and cultural environments shape and limit institutions' structures and their relationships differently (Barksdale and Anderson 1982; Stern and El-Ansary 1982; Boddewyn 1981). Indeed, "the developing countries are growing in an environment quite different from that in which the United States and other industrialized countries developed" (Holton 1963).

One should recognize that the ahistorical use of the temporal models, such as the stages of economic development model, as assumed and applied in marketing, is a misrepresentation of reality and creates more confusion than understanding of the solution of economic development problems. In addition, such use represents an excellent example of the ideological approach to marketing.

In contrast, logical reasoning in the historical method is primarily inductive and based upon observation. (See figure 7–2.) Factors influencing change are related to individual marketing systems in different time periods—including the carryover effects represented by the solid and broken arrows in the figure. Sets of factors, various marketing systems, as well as the relationships among these are analyzed in their social and cultural contexts and used in an inductive manner. The hypothesized changes of structures and processes are compared with observation. (See table 7–1.) The analysis of "domestic marketing systems" (Cox 1965; Mulvihil 1967) of various countries and the use of findings in an inductive way would be an illustrative example of this explanation. Indeed, the historical method with its holistic approach, inductive reasoning, and context-bound perspective can better explain many of the problematic issues in marketing.

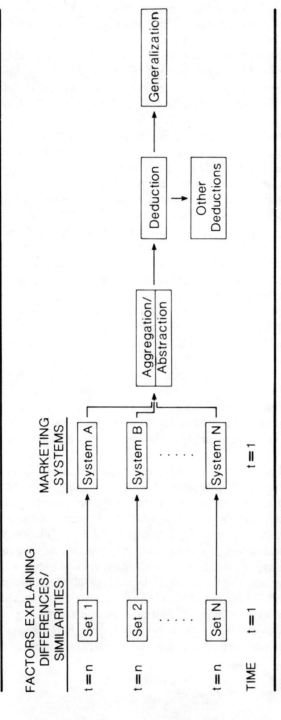

Figure 7–1. Naturalistic Deduction/Generalization of Phenomena

NOTE: One specific set of factors and marketing systems are taken from different industries , countries, or geographical areas of the same country.

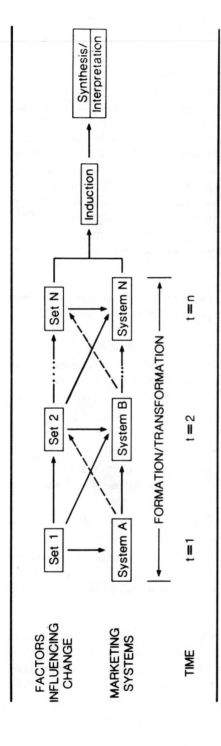

NOTE: The set of factors and marketing systems may relate to the same society or to different cnes in different time periods.

Figure 7–2. Darwinian Interpretation of Phenomena

Rationale for Historical Analysis in Marketing

Although it is argued by Oser (1970, p. 185) that the historical inductive method has become generally accepted in economics as complementary to the abstract deductive approach, many contributions in marketing remain to present the basic problems of such an approach. As I discussed elsewhere (Kumcu 1985) and other authors contended explicitly (Fırat 1985a, 1985b), research in marketing and in consumer behavior tends to (1) be ethnocentric, (2) make unjustified assumptions of dependent and independent variables, (3) generalize partial findings across time and space, and (4) emphasize a managerial-predictive orientation, thus reducing its scientific-theory–building mission. The reader should note that these criticisms closely resemble the discussions around the turn of the century. Historical analysis is one of the possible methods to overcome such criticisms in research in marketing.

The benefits of historical analysis in social sciences and in marketing can be summarized in six points:

1. By taking into account key variables that are otherwise assumed to be given (ceteris paribus) in a particular cultural setting, it will enable researchers to gain an understanding of the effects of large-scale social and historic factors on human behavior (Lawrence 1984; Williamson 1963).

2. By encouraging researchers to study the processes of institutional changes in societies, it can broaden research horizons and correct the ahistorical tendencies of current research in marketing (Fırat 1985b, Lawrence 1984).

3. By studying the marketing institutions in light of their earlier phases and subsequent evolution, it will anchor findings more clearly to their historic and social origins, thus bringing them into clearer focus (Lawrence 1984).

4. By introducing a different method of knowledge pursuit, it will help to identify and compensate for some significant weaknesses in the now-used analytical apparatus (Fullerton 1983).

5. By employing its basic premises, it will question generalizability of findings across time and cultural settings (Kumcu 1985).

6. By providing some idea of where and what the status of marketing theory building is, it will help to establish an identity for the discipline. It will relate the marketing discipline to its own past and to other disciplines (Savitt 1980).

The historical method, with its priority of studying the institutional change and economic development in various parts of a society and in different countries, easily lends itself to producing broader interpretative frameworks of socioeconomic development and comparative marketing. These frameworks will hopefully be conducive to generating more meaningful concepts.

A Historical Perspective Framework for Marketing Systems

It is broadly accepted that social institutions are neither static nor given, but rather change through time. Indeed, as a social institution, marketing is itself subject to historic change and evolution. Therefore, the historic method would provide guidance in understanding and explaining the structural change in marketing systems and in anchoring its relations with other institutions to their social and economic origins.

Although critics might argue that historic changes are essentially superficial and that underlying realities are permanent, I contend that the employment of the historical method would capture also the status of substantial underlying variables in social relationships. Indeed, as illustrated in the examples above, present research in marketing takes variables such as change, development, values, consumer choices, and various guiding principles as given. Yet, essentially it is these variables that determine the actual context of marketing processes and that need to be studied. In fact, it is the empiricist approach and not the historical method that "examines epiphenomena and ignores the underlying phenomenal structures" (Stanfield 1983, p. 191). One of the major issues we now must understand and explain, therefore, is the formation and transformation of particular marketing systems, institutions, and processes in various time periods, places, and countries.

For the purposes of this chapter, I will approach this problem through a conceptualization of three sets of variables. These are:

1. The underlying social, cultural, political, and economic structures and their historic development,
2. The production relations, and
3. The marketing systems that enable allocation of goods and services in the society, plus the constitution of the market—consumer profiles as well as behavior and consumption patterns.

The relations proposed from a historical perspective regarding these variables are depicted in figure 7–3. This framework is based upon various premises. First, marketing systems attempt to satisfy consumption needs and wants of consumers and/or societies through exchange transactions (Bagozzi 1975) as well as other modes of want satisfaction (Enis 1973). Second, marketing system formation and transformation rests primarily on social relations, not on natural events or on characteristics and isolated attempts of units in the system. That is, the changes in marketing systems can be best understood in terms of the tensions and contradictions among the units of the system, and between them and the production relations in society. Finally, to understand

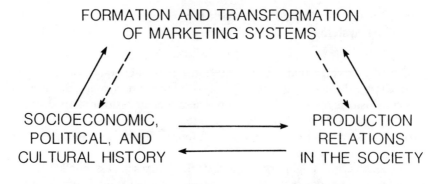

FORMATION AND TRANSFORMATION
OF MARKETING SYSTEMS

SOCIOECONOMIC,
POLITICAL, AND
CULTURAL HISTORY

PRODUCTION
RELATIONS
IN THE SOCIETY

NOTE: In developing this concept and figure, I benefited
from discussions with A. Fuat Firat and
Stanley J. Shapiro.

Figure 7–3. Historical Perspective Framework of Marketing Systems

these changes, the link of historically and contextually specific marketing phenomena must be established with general socioeconomic, cultural, political, and historic processes in the society.

Figure 7–3 illustrates how the *societal-macro context* formulates and limits the formation and transformation of marketing systems. Indeed, the needs, values, goals, and interests of the market participants such as consumers, manufacturers, and distributive organizations are defined by the value systems, institutionalizations, and use of resources in the society of which they are part. It is also necessary to look at the culture, power structure, (such as forms of government), and economic system (Firat and Kumcu 1984).

Although a superficial analysis might suggest that the process explained appears to work at the present only, the set of factors do operate over time historically—there are significant carryover effects. For instance, consider the consumption patterns of the middle-class American families in the 1980s. When these families wish to satisfy, for example, their transportation needs, the *first* choice of most of them is a car. This behavior appears to be the "natural" result of the *present* social environment (distant social contacts), cultural environment (self-actualization), and economic environment (cars are often the only transportation mode), as well as of the nature of production. However, the choice, as well as the present context determining it, have been shaped by changes in the society over the past sixty or more years.

Indeed, the same transportation need was satisfied in significantly different ways in the past, is now being satisfied differently in various parts of North America, and may be satisfied still differently in the future or in other societies.

For instance, the *primary* choice of a European family of comparable social class would probably be another solution, perhaps public transportation. Likewise, many urban commuters in the United States prefer public transportation to work. Still other societies satisfy their transportation needs through different means. For example, although the Netherlands and People's Republic of China have clearly different historic developments and present economic conditions, natives in both countries use the bicycle as the major transportation means. These and other phenomena need substantial analyses. As these examples suggest, there are close links between the variables of the framework that need to be interpreted with respect to the historic processes depicted in figure 7–2.

Production relations in society are important to the extent that they shape and limit the marketing systems as well as the historic context. (See figure 7–3.) In this framework, production relations demonstrate how the society organizes production and how it controls the means of production. Also, the nature and volume of production are critical in these relationships. The means of production are organized and owned differently in various sectors of the economy (industry and farming, small businesses and corporations). Organization and ownership have been changing in various societies in different ways over time. Obviously, small farming (at or just above subsistence levels in many developing societies) shapes the marketing systems differently than in kibbutz farming in Israel. Consequently, successful cooperatives and marketing boards are created in Israel in contrast to assemblers in many developing countries. Similarly, the type of industry and production volume influence marketing systems, most significantly the marketing channels. Small-scale manufacturing encourages strong wholesaling, while large-scale production may support vertical marketing channels. These relationships are dynamic and are influenced, in turn, by the transformation of marketing systems. The broken feedback arrows in figure 7–3 indicate the reciprocal nature of the relationships among these variables.

Finally, the third element of this framework is *the formation and transformation of the marketing systems*. As figure 7–3 illustrates, this variable is influenced by both of the main elements of the framework. Also, the dynamic changes and innovations—brought about by the units of the marketing system and their relationships with each other—work formatively on the marketing system itself as well as on the other elements of the framework.

An analysis using this historic perspective framework will demonstrate that, for example, the characteristics and the dominant role of vertical marketing channels in North America resulted from the historic period during which they emerged. Similarly, wholesaler-sponsored voluntary retail chains appeared as a response to the competition of large chain stores. Therefore, they are neither customary in North America nor may they be normatively the best for other countries. In other countries, different distribution channels have emerged, such as TNUVA (an Israeli marketing board of agricultural products) and cooperatives in Scandinavia and many other places. (See essays in Izraeli, Izraeli, and Meissner 1976.) With the constructive purpose of creating competitive forces in the marketplace, recommending, for instance, the introduction of voluntary retail chains in developing countries may prove futile if the necessary socioeconomic and cultural conditions and production relations are not present.

In fact, the question is not to recommend institutions or structures that elsewhere appear the best normatively, but rather to find out what the necessary conditions are to permit a pertinent marketing system to emerge.

Conclusion

Although rare, the questioning of the relevance of the neoclassical economic theory and logical empiricism in social sciences and especially in marketing is encouraging. Among other paradigms, the historical method offers a viable and applicable alternative methodology perspective for marketing theory building. The use of the historical method in the analysis of marketing structures and processes could successfully be applied to various marketing phenomena such as comparative marketing, consumer behavior, marketing channels, and retailing systems.

This framework aids, first, in anchoring the formation and transformation of marketing systems more clearly to their historic origins, thus advancing our understanding and explanation of such structures and relationships. Second, it brings the contemporary state of marketing systems into clearer focus, be it domestic or foreign. Although culture has a strong influence on the formation and transformation of marketing structures, these may have been affected more importantly and directly, for example, by production relations and consumption patterns or simply by historic factors.

Finally, in the historical method, marketing structures and processes that are different from the *present* North American system will not be labeled backward or inefficient, but an attempt will be made to understand the specific characteristics and potentials. What appears well suited or inappropriate according to North American standards may—or may not—be working at acceptable levels in a different context. Apparently, domestic and international development experts as well as marketing researchers, policy makers, and managers could benefit from the historical perspective framework of marketing systems in understanding its basic structures and processes. Further, this framework could enable them to produce and implement more relevant and useful practices and public policies.

References

Anderson, Paul F. (1983), "Marketing, Scientific Progress, and Scientific Method," *Journal of Marketing* 47 (Fall): 18–31.

Arndt, Johan (1981), "The Political Economy of Marketing Systems: Reviving the Institutional Approach," *Journal of Macromarketing* (Fall): 36–47.

——— , (1983), "The Political Economy Paradigm: Foundation for Theory Building in Marketing,"*Journal of Marketing* 47 (Fall): 44–54.

Bagozzi, Richard P. (1975),"Marketing as Exchange," *Journal of Marketing* 39 (October): 32–39.

——— , (1980), *Causal Models in Marketing*. New York: Wiley.

Barksdale, C.H. and L.M. Anderson (1982), "Comparative Marketing: A Review of the Literature," *Journal of Macromarketing* (Spring): 57–62.

Bartels, Robert (1976), *The History of Marketing Thought*, 2nd ed. Columbus, Ohio: Grid.

——— , (1981), *Global Development and Marketing*. Columbus, Ohio: Grid.

Bennett, Peter D. (1966), "Retailing Evolution or Revolution in Chile?" *Journal of Marketing* 30 (July): 38–41.

Boddewyn, J.J. (1981), "Comparative Marketing: The First Twenty-Five Years," *Journal of International Business Studies* 12 (Spring-Summer): 61–79.

Cox, R. (1965), "The Search for Universals in Comparative Studies of Domestic Marketing Systems," in *Proceedings of the 1965 Fall Conference: Marketing and Economic Development*, P.D. Bennett, ed. Chicago: American Marketing Association, 143–162.

Cundiff, Edward W. (1965), "Concepts in Comparative Retailing," *Journal of Marketing* 29 (January): 59–63.

Dhalla, N.K., and S. Yuspeh (1976), "Forget the Product Life Cycle," *Harvard Business Review* 54 (January-February): 102–122.

Dholakia, Nikhilesh, A. Fuat Fırat, and R. Bagozzi (1980), "The De-Americanization of Marketing Thought: In Search of a Universal Basis," in *Theoretical Developments in Marketing*, C.W. Lamb and P.M. Dunne, eds. Chicago: American Marketing Association, 25–29.

Dugger, William (1984), "Methodological Differences between Institutional and Neo-classical Economics," in *The Philosophy of Economics: An Anthology*, D.M. Hausman, ed. Cambridge, England: Cambridge University Press, 312–22.

Eichner, Alfred S. (1983), *Why Economics Is Not Yet a Science*. Armonk, N.Y.: M.E. Sharpe.

El-Ansary, A.I., and M.L. Liebrenz (1982), "A Multistage Approach to Comparative Marketing Analysis," *Journal of Macromarketing* 2 (Fall): 59–65.

Enis, Ben (1973), "Deepening the Concept of Marketing," *Journal of Marketing* 37 (October): 57–62.

Feyerabend, Paul (1975), *Against Method: Outline of an Anarchistic Theory of Knowledge*. London: New Left Books.

Fırat, A. Fuat (1985a), "A Critique of the Orientations in Theory Development in Consumer Behavior: Suggestions for the Future," in *Advances in Consumer Research*, vol. 12, E.C. Hirschman and M.B. Holbrook, eds. Provo, Utah: Association for Consumer Research.

———, (1985b), "Ideology vs. Science in Marketing," in *Changing the Course of Marketing: Alternative Paradigms for Widening Marketing Theory*, N. Dholakia and J. Arndt, eds. Greenwich, Conn.: JAI Press.

Fırat, A. Fuat, and E. Kumcu (1984), "Towards Developing An Integrative Framework in the Study of Distribution Channels," in *Developments in Marketing Science*, vol. 7, Jay D. Lindquist, ed. Kalamazoo, Mich.: Academy of Marketing Science.

Fullerton, Ronald A. (1983), "Historical Analysis as an Aid to Understanding Current and Future Demand," in *First North American Workshop on Historical Research in Marketing: Proceedings*, S.C. Hollander and R. Savitt, eds. East Lansing, Mich.: Michigan State University, 128–135.

Gide, C., and C. Rist (1915), *A History of Economic Doctrines* (translated from the 1913 ed.). Boston: D.C. Heath.

Hall, M., J. Knapp, and C. Winsten (1961), *Distribution in Great Britain and North America*. London: Oxford University Press.

Hausman, Daniel M. (1984), *The Philosophy of Economics: An Anthology*, Cambridge, England: Cambridge University Press.

Hollander, Stanley C., and Ronald Savitt, eds. (1983), *First North American Workshop on Historical Research in Marketing, Proceedings*, East Lansing, Mich.: Michigan State University.

Hollander, Stanley C., and Terence Nevett, eds. (1985), *Marketing in the Long Run: Proceedings of the Second Workshop on Historical Research in Marketing*. East Lansing, Mich.: Michigan State University.

Holton, Richard H. (1963), "Discussion of 'Effective Marketing Institutions for Economic Development,'" in *Toward Scientific Marketing: Proceedings of the Winter Conference*, S.A. Greyser, ed. Chicago, Ill.: American Marketing Association, 405–8.

Hunt, Shelby D. (1976), *Marketing Theory: Foundations of Research in Marketing*. Columbus, Ohio: Grid.

———, (1983), *Marketing Theory: The Philosophy of Marketing Science*. Homewood, Ill.: Richard D. Irwin.

Ingram, John K. (1878), "The Present Position and Prospects of Political Economy," reprinted in *Readings in the History of Economic Thought* (1932), S. Howard Patterson, ed. New York: McGraw, 481–506.

Izraeli, Dov, D.N. Izraeli, and F. Meissner (1976), *Marketing Systems for Developing Countries*, vols. 1, 2. New York: Wiley.

Kumcu, Erdoğan (1985), "Historical Analysis of Distribution Systems: An International Research Agenda," in *Marketing in the Long Run: Proceedings of the Second Workshop on Historical Research in Marketing*. East Lansing, Mich.: Michigan State University, 98–111.

Lakatos, Imre (1970), "Falsification and the Methodology of Scientific Research Programmes," in *Criticism and the Growth of Knowledge*, I. Lakatos and A. Musgrave, eds. Cambridge, England: Cambridge University Press.

Lawrence, Barbara (1984), "Historical Perspective: Using the Past to Study the Present," *Academy of Management Review* 9 (April): 307–312.

Mallen, B. (1975), "Marketing Channels and Economic Development: A Literature Overview," *International Journal of Physical Distribution* 5 (5).

Mandelbaum, Maurice (1967), "Historicism," in *The Encyclopedia of Philosophy*, vol. 4, Paul Edwards, ed. New York: Macmillan and Free Press, 22–25.

Markin, Rom J., and C.P. Duncan (1981), "The Transformation of Retailing Institutions: Beyond the Wheel of Retailing and Life Cycle Theories," *Journal of Macromarketing* 1 (Spring): 58–66.

Mulvihil, Donald F. (1967), *Domestic Marketing Systems Abroad*. Kent, Ohio: Kent State University Press.

Oser, Jacob (1970), *The Evolution of Economic Thought*, 2nd ed. New York: Harcourt, Brace & World.

Rostow, W.W. (1960), *The Stages of Economic Growth*. Cambridge, England: Cambridge University Press.

Sauer, William J., N. Nighswonger, and G. Zaltman (1982), "Current Issues in Philosophy of Science: Implications for the Study of Marketing," in *Marketing Theory: Philosophy of Science Perspectives*, R.F. Bush and S.D. Hunt, eds. Chicago, Ill.: American Marketing Association.

Savitt, Ronald (1980), "Historical Research in Marketing," *Journal of Marketing* 44 (Fall): 52–58.

———, (1983), "A Note on the Varieties and Vagaries of Historical Data," in *First North American Workshop on Historical Research in Marketing, Proceedings*, S.C. Hollander and R. Savitt, eds. East Lansing, Mich.: Michigan State University, 30–34.

———, (1984), "An Historical Approach to Comparative Retailing," in *Comparative Marketing Systems*, E. Kaynak and R. Savitt, eds. New York: Praeger, 147–55.

Scholtz, G. (1974), "Historismus, Historizismus," in *Historisches Woerterbuch der Philosophie*, J. Ritter, ed. Basel, Switzerland: Schwabe, 1141–47.

Slater, Charles C. (1965), "The Role of Food Marketing in Latin American Economic Development," in *Marketing and Economic Development, Proceedings*, Peter D. Bennett, ed. Chicago: American Marketing Association.

Stanfield, J. Ron (1983), "Institutional Analysis: Toward Progress in Economic Science," in *Why Economics Is Not Yet a Science*, A.S. Eichner, ed. Armonk, N.Y.: M.E. Sharpe, 187–204.

Stern, Louis, and A.I. El-Ansary (1982), *Marketing Channels*. Englewood Cliffs, N.J.: Prentice-Hall.

Toynbee, Arnold (1884), "Selections from 'The Industrial Revolution of the Eighteenth Century in England'," reprinted in *Readings in the History of Economic Thought* (1932), S. Howard Patterson, ed. New York: McGraw, 530–33.

Wadinambiaratchi, G. (1965), "Channels of Distribution in Developing Economies," *The Business Quarterly* (Winter): 74–82.

Weingartner, Rudolf H. (1967), "Historical Explanation," in *The Encyclopedia of Philosophy*, vol. 4, Paul Edwards, ed. New York: Macmillan and Free Press, 7–12.

Williamson, Harold F. (1963), "Application of Historical Analysis to Marketing," in *Toward Scientific Marketing: Proceedings of the Winter Conference*, S.A. Greyser, ed. Chicago, Ill.: American Marketing Association, 319–23.

Wonnacott, Paul, and R. Wonnacott (1986), *Economics*. New York: McGraw-Hill.

Zaltman, Gerald, Christian R.A. Pinson, and R. Angelmar (1973), *Metatheory and Consumer Research*. New York: Holt, Rinehart and Winston.

8

Extensions of Bagozzi's Holistic Construal

Terence A. Oliva
R. Eric Reidenbach

In a 1984 *Journal of Marketing* article, Bagozzi presents a prospectus for theory construction in marketing. Bagozzi's viewpoint is consonant with other philosophy of science writers such as Whitehead, who observes that "the development of abstract theory precedes the understanding of fact" (1929, p. 75). The foregoing, of course, imply that we need a theoretical matrix to understand what we observe, a proposition which we support and is held by others (e.g., Lewis 1929; Popper 1959; Hayek 1952) under the general term of "factual relativity" (Weimer 1979). This is not to suggest we disagree with Bagozi's statement that one should "regard data and theory in an inseparable and reflexive way" (1984, p. 18). Hence, we do not take the extreme position that there are "facts" independent of thought.

From the foregoing perspective, we present five extensions regarding important focal issues touched on by Bagozzi. These are intended as additions, modifications, and caveats relating to the prospectus for theory construction. More specifically, we focus on: (1) a formalization of the construal approach, (2) the centrality of language, (3) the match between causality and system precursors in theory development, (4) an examination of limits and their effects on the canonical form, and (5) the importance of concept linkages in theory construction and analysis.

The authors would like to thank Professor Richard Bagozzi of the University of Michigan and Professor John O'Shaughnessy of Columbia University for their many insightful comments.

Extensions

Extension 1: Construals

Bagozzi's use of a construal approach is a step in the right direction for the development of theory in marketing. Clearly, people with different epistemologies or different academic bases often define the same object in different ways. Hence, Crest toothpaste may be viewed as a cash generator, chemical compound, product, health aid, or brand name. Each of these construes Crest in a different way. None of these is incorrect, nor is any one of them completely descriptive. Each of these is, then, a construal of the referent object. What a construal does is to allow for differences while recognizing that there is in some sense a constant, the object in reality. From this perspective, any marketing theory may be viewed as a construal of some referent marketing phenomenon. However, no matter how cleverly devised, a single construal cannot completely describe the phenomenon perfectly. Thus, the use of a single construal for paradigm development can create the very problem that it is trying to alleviate (Arndt 1985).

What follows is a more generalized approach than that proposed by Bagozzi, which includes his format as a subset. Because it is more generalized, it supports more paradigmatic approaches than does the holistic construal. The formal approach presented here is adapted from Marchal's (1971) work.

C is a construal of a marketing phenomenon M if:
1. $C = <E, R>$;
2. $\{E\}$ is a set of marketing elements (characteristics, attributes, concepts, etc.)
3. $\{R\}$ is a set of relations that hold between members of E;
   - 3.1 Where relations r $(r\varepsilon R)$ hold between the members of an element set $\{E\} \leftrightarrow \{R\}$ is decomposable into and threads E;
   - 3.2 R is a relation $\rightarrow (r)$ $(r\varepsilon R) \rightarrow (\exists\, a)(\exists\, b)$, $(r = <a, b>)$ where $<a, b>$ is an ordered pair $\{(a), (a, b)\}$;
   - 3.3 It is assumed that Zermelo's axiom of choice holds. (Marketing phenomena can be viewed as related wholes that may be considered ordered sets.)

The above formalized approach includes its own form of bias, namely, that the world of marketing theory (and ultimately marketing phenomena) is truly a combination of elements and relations. It should be apparent that this construal approach contains Bagozzi's as a subset. Specifically, his elements (identified by boxes and squares) are related to one another by arrows (the relation set). To get a more complete description of a given phenomenon, one needs to look at the set of proper construals of the phenomenon (e.g., using all the descriptors of Crest given above). Toward this end, Oliva (1976) developed the concept of a maximal construal as the best, most complete characterization of a theory of phenomenon possible.

MC is maximal construal of a marketing phenomenon $M \leftrightarrow$
$MC = \ <E, R>$, and if e belongs to an element set of any existentially related construal of S, then $e \varepsilon r$, and if r belongs to the relations set of any existentially related construal MC, then $r \varepsilon R$.

The term *existentially related* means that the existence of one construal implies the existence of the other. This ensures that they are proper construals. Notice the toothpaste brand Crest as a construal implies the existence of the construals: health aid and chemical compound. It would appear that the construal approach recognizes the limitations implied by both the Heisenberg uncertainty principle and Gödel's theorems, because it suggests the need to use multiple models (definitions) or theories. Hence, it allows different approaches to be used, consistent with different research interests, while at the same time maintaining connectivity with some view of the thing-in-itself (the underlying marketing phenomenon being modeled). The importance of using multiple construals can be seen by looking at Bagozzi's own presentation of the models of correspondence rules in scientific inquiry. The element set $\{e\}$ in each of the point form of the models is the same $\{p(x), E(x), R(x)\}$. Similarly, the relation set $\{R\}$ is fixed $\{\rightarrow, =, (\ )\}$. For the structural form an additional relation set $S(x)$ is included. This represents the meta rules, which may be thought of as a context or syntax for the relations set $\{R\}$. By changing $S(x)$, the interpretation (both theoretical and empirical) can change. Examples of this abound in mathematics, where simple restructuring of operator syntax generates differ-ent forms of analysis (e.g., Boolean or abstract algebra vis-à-vis standard algebra). For simplicity of exposition, we will use the point form of the specification. Each of the terms and symbols is defined below:

1. $P(x)$: theoretical property of x.
2. $E(x)$: experimental test procedure.
3. $R(x)$: result yielded.
4. $\rightarrow$: if, then.
5. $=$: if and only if.
6. $(\ )$: Closure.

If the above items are permuted, the three models of correspondence rules Bagozzi presents can be generated, viz, the operational definition model, the partial interpretation mode, and the causal indicator model. Furthermore, each of these model (construals) has its proponents (e.g., Bridgman 1927; Carnap 1956; and Bagozzi 1984, respectively). Assuming each position has merit in different research contexts, arguing for any one of them in a universal sense seems inappropriate. This last statement incudes the definition of *construal* presented here. After all, it is a construal of a construal. Our view, of course, is that it is a more parsimonious statement and has extended domain relative to other conceptualization. In comparison to Bagozzi's approach, it is less limited, because he specifies a form. At the same time, where that form is appropriate, his approach is equally good. At the same time, exclusive use of his approach (call it "the structural model paradigm of theory development") could lead to the kind of systematic error (method error, M) he warns us against. Even if this structure allows for an error check, the top-down (theory driven) approach can incorporate errors invisible to the error-checking procedure. This occurs because the specification of a structure creates a structural error not perceivable to the error-checking method. While Bagozzi's construal is a much-improved approach, relative to what has existed, it is only one of several possible structures. By permuting the relations as indicated above, several related structurally oriented construals can be generated. Beyond this, other totally different construals are possible and correct for different contexts. More importantly, the pluralistic approach avoids what Nagel would indicate is "a potential intellectual trap" (1979, p. 115).

Finally, the relationship between models and theory (Nagel 1979) fits the construal approach very nicely, particularly if one views each construal as a model. Models vary in form (structure—identified by $\{R\}$) as seen in the Bagozzi example cited earlier. As with theories, this arises from the processes used to develop them, as well as the purposes for which they are developed.

Extension 2: Language

Research in marketing tends to utilize symbolic rather than iconic or analog models. (For a typology of models, see Miller 1978; Murdick and Ross 1975.) The reason for this is the nature of the phenomena examined and the hypotheses tested in marketing. Simply stated, the economy of effort along with the effectiveness and efficiency of processing symbols generally makes such models superior to the other forms of models. Additionally, since many of the phenomena modeled contain constructs made up of other models and constructs— construals of construals (nested construals) as it were—the only practical form of modeling becomes symbolic.

The medium of symbolic models is usually a written language. Hence, to some degree a modified version "the medium is a lot of the message" of McLuhan's (1964) dictum is a critical factor in model and theory development. This is also evident from the canonical form presented by Bagozzi (1984). Models and theories are heavily dependent on and restricted by the language in which they are expressed. One only has to reflect on the differences between quantitative and qualitative (verbal) models to see the differences (e.g., a

Markov model of brand switching as opposed to the wheel of retailing). Each language has its advantages and disadvantages in terms of a given modeling or theorizing process. These depend heavily on the particular alphabet of primitive symbols and the nature of the syntax. (See, e.g., Skvoretz 1984; Chomsky 1963.) Note, that languages fit the construal approach presented earlier (primitives = $\{E\}$, syntax = $\{R\}$). In fact, the difference between English and Spanish is primarily in $\{R\}$. For German and English, it is primarily in $\{R\}$ and somewhat in $\{E\}$.

This brings us to the issue of metalanguages. (See Warfield 1979; Popper 1981; Oliva and Leap 1981.) The explicit metalanguage in the United States is English. We explain (teach) other languages (e.g., French, FORTRAN, calculus, Chinese) in terms of English. Of course, the same is true with regard to symbolic model building in that the symbols are explained in terms of English (as they were in Bagozzi's example above). For the quantitative model builder, it should be evident that ultimately set theory is the metalanguage, as it is the metalanguage of mathematics. However, it may not be so evident to the verbal model builder that set theory can be also utilized as a metalanguage for verbal model building through, for example, the statement calculus. While the purpose of this chapter does not permit a description of the statement calculus, the reader can easily get a feel for it by examining Stoll (1963, pp. 162–63).

The central idea here is that the modeler, in addition to obeying the syntax and notation of a given object language, should also look at the model's abstraction hierarchy (Oliva and Leap 1981). It implies that model specifications are hierarchically related. Typically, movement is from an object language (e.g., English) to an intermediate language (e.g., graphic) and ultimately the metalanguage (e.g., mathematics). Looking at Bagozzi's *TCO* approach, each component (T, C, O) has a linguistic structure which relates it to the others. Figure 8–1 uses the source credibility presentation to demonstrate the relationships. Clearly, the symbolic structure is verbal, vis: that greater source credibility leads to more positive attitudes. This is then translated to a digraph (directed graph; see Harary, Norman and Cartwright 1965; Warfield 1979) as shown in Bagozzi's figures 2 and 3 (1984, pp. 13, 15). The final result is the translation of the digraph to a causal indicator model structure. Language equivalents are English (objective), graphic sentences (intermediate), and set theory (meta). This mirrors the following modeling process. Typically, we get an idea (T), draw a picture (C), then specify a testable model (O). A clear implication is that, in part, model building is a search for the proper language. What is gained from this direct comparison of language forms is a crucial understanding of the translation process used. Notice that as one moves from the verbal (value-rich description) to the set theoretic (value-free), there are fewer problems with semantics. Hence, it lends itself to experimental testing. There is a cost, however—namely, that as one reduces semantic difficulties, there is a loss in richness. Also, there can be a false sense of precision. For

Symbolic model type	Language
Verbal	Object (English)
Digraph	Intermediate (graphic sentences)
Causal Indicator	Meta (set theoretic)

Examples of the three using source credibility:

    Verbal: Greater source credibility leads to more positive attitudes.

Digraph:

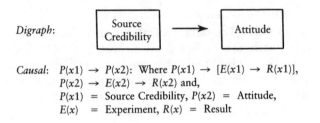

Causal: $P(x1) \rightarrow P(x2)$: Where $P(x1) \rightarrow [E(x1) \rightarrow R(x1)]$,
                    $P(x2) \rightarrow E(x2) \rightarrow R(x2)$ and,
                    $P(x1)$ = Source Credibility, $P(x2)$ = Attitude,
                    $E(x)$ = Experiment, $R(x)$ = Result

Figure 8–1. The Hierarchy of Language and Models

example, if the set theoretical formulation has an implicit flaw, that flaw will be processed perfectly by set theoretical operations. Use of set theoretical formulations is no guarantee of logical rigor. Furthermore, translation processes are entropic in the sense that as one translates from level to level, there is some loss (generally, richness for precision or vice versa).

Extension 3: Causality

The issue of causality is controversial and many times fraught with emotion. From a marketing perspective, the general view is that causality exists. In some sense, if this were not the case, marketers would have no reason to pursue the discipline at the applications level. At the same time, with the growing use of causal modeling by researchers who do not understand the key issues relating to the concept, we suggest that more formal study of the nature of causality in marketing be assessed. For our purposes here, we take Bunge's (1959) position that there is a hierarchy of determinism (a pluralist approach) in which causation (in the common sense usage of the term) is a member.

Bagozzi's prospectus for theory construction in marketing is highly suited for, though not limited to, causal linkages. In fact, his construal structure uses (as noted earlier) a causal modeling format. We would extend this somewhat by suggesting a compatible but different approach that looks at system precursors (Gray 1977). The central theme of this approach is that a system (or theory) is what forms when system precursors (preconditions and/or reasoning events) and reactive environment come together. In general, the theory has focused on self-referential systems (which marketing theory is). Figure 8–2 is

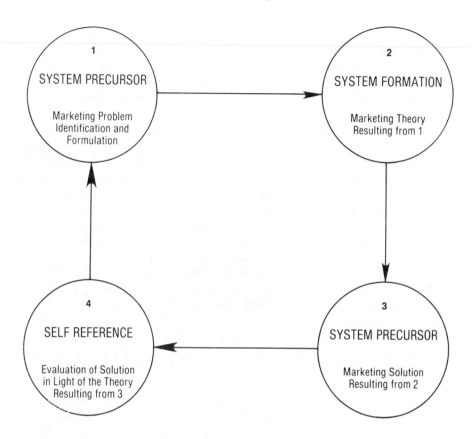

NOTE: The process in number 1 ultimately is the determining factor in theory development. Once the process starts, it continues to cycle alternating between precursor
and system formulation. Finally, this represents only part of the precursor
approach, clearly much more is involved.

**Figure 8–2. The Core Model of System Precursor Theory Applied to
Marketing**

the core (the minimum essential) system precursor model mapped onto a
generic marketing situation. From this perspective, what is important are the
preconditions (the marketing problem) that generate the system (a marketing
theory), rather than the system itself. In more concrete terms, the existence of a
criminal is not what is critical, but rather what conditions lead to the creation
of the criminal in the first place (Gray). Similarly, theory development is a
function of precursors that drive that development. The effect of Aristotle on
logic and those who followed dominated thought and development for centuries. St. Thomas Aquinas's integration of Aristotelian logic with Catholic

theology still has strong influence in that church's theological development. The development of the scientific method is a precursor to modern research which has caused the logical empiricist paradigm to become the preeminent method for theory construction in marketing. If we follow Bagozzi's (1984) and Arndt's (1985) call for the use of alternative paradigms, then we must pay attention to what precursors are needed to generate an environment tolerant of such multiple viewpoints—which, unfortunately, is not the case at the present time.

While a full explication of systems precursor theory is beyond the scope of this chapter, we present a model of marketing theory development (evolution) in precursor format. Given the purpose at hand, we have limited the approach to major antecedents, focal concepts, and consequences in theory development, thus integrating it with Bagozzi's work. Figure 8–3 presents the evolution of marketing theory in precursor format. The precursors (antecedents) are the disciplines (e.g., economics, sociology, psychology, mathematics) that contribute to the development of marketing. The environment would be external forces such as changes in political, economic, legal, technological, and/or social factors impinging on marketing. Notice that the causal structure is indicated by the time arrow and sequential nexus creating the future state of marketing theory. Furthermore, the structure is compatible with Bagozzi's construal and a subset of our more general construal. Specifically, there are antecedent conditions (precursors), a focal concept (marketing theory in period T_n, and consequences (the new state of the field in a future time period T_{n+1}). The rows are sequential in time; within rows, the columns are concurrent. A full model of the process would be more complex (and difficult to present visually). It should be apparent from the integration of the structure that the consequences of one process may be precursors of another. For example, in time period T_n, the current state of marketing is the intersection of two focal axes (*FF*), while, in the next period, it is a consequence and focal concept (*CF*). Other relationships are identified by matching the row and column symbols. The movement from antecedent to focal concept to consequence is the essence of causality in the first place. The problem is that the focus on precursors shows that once paradigmatic closure occurs, it tends to persist in perpetuity. To break the cycle becomes more difficult and (as suggested by the diagram) must come from outside. That is, method error generated from structural error locks in the bias. Hence, breakthroughs become more difficult and do not naturally evolve. In fact, the longer the situation cycles, the more dramatic the breakthrough (evolution) must be to generate a change; hence, the need for books such as *Philosophical and Radical Thought in Marketing*.

Our purpose in this section has been to point out that the causal model approach to theory development (via the holistic construal) is both appropriate and useful. In particular, the important message is that causally dynamic processes which are self-referential can become sterile closed systems. Hence,

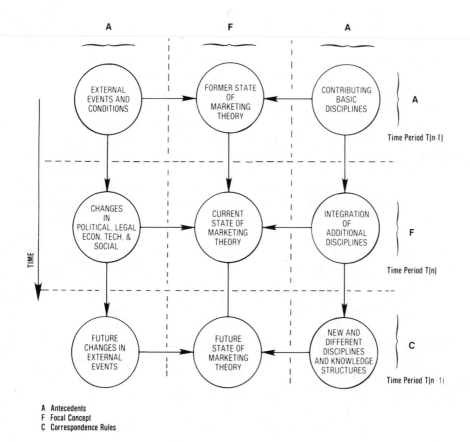

A   F   A

EXTERNAL EVENTS AND CONDITIONS

FORMER STATE OF MARKETING THEORY

CONTRIBUTING BASIC DISCIPLINES

A

Time Period T(n-1)

CHANGES IN POLITICAL, LEGAL ECON. TECH. & SOCIAL

CURRENT STATE OF MARKETING THEORY

INTEGRATION OF ADDITIONAL DISCIPLINES

F

Time Period T(n)

TIME

FUTURE CHANGES IN EXTERNAL EVENTS

FUTURE STATE OF MARKETING THEORY

NEW AND DIFFERENT DISCIPLINES AND KNOWLEDGE STRUCTURES

C

Time Period T(n-1)

A Antecedents
F Focal Concept
C Correspondence Rules

Figure 8–3. The Process of Theory Evolution in Marketing: System Precursors Joined to Bagozzi

there is an important need to keep such systems open to ensure that theory development has the requisite variety needed to deal with the evolving, diverse, and dynamic nature of marketing thought.

Extension 4: Limits

Bagozzi indicates that the canonical form of the received view of scientific theories would go far to improve theories in marketing (1984, pp. 13–15). We agree, but think that it should be extended in two different but related areas: one of which Bagozzi touches on, but does not explicitly include in the canonical form, the other of which is generally ignored in the marketing literature. One reason for using the construal approach is to recognize explicitly that errors are a virtual certainty. That is, the only thing we are sure of is that our current theorizations are probably incomplete. Bagozzi points out that the deviations between l_t and l_e are a function of measurement problems. Every data point is a system of charactics. Some of these are artifacts of the measurement process, and some of these are not in the same observation plane as the researcher. The observer can only see those that are in the same observation plane. In figure 8–4, the marketing phenomenon under study is represented as a pyramid in three-dimensional space. Actually, it should show a different face to all three axial planes. (However, we could not draw the required figure adequately.) A researcher looking at the figure from perspective 1 (left plane) sees only a triangle, while another using perspective 2 (the bottom

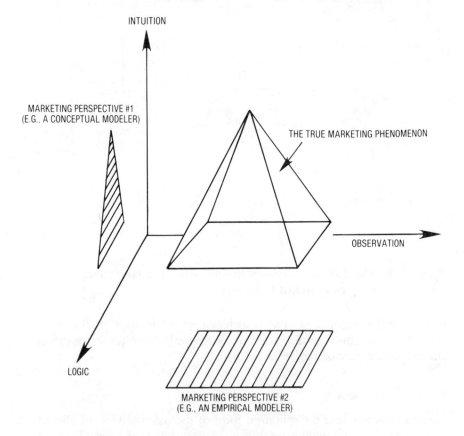

NOTE! The axes represent the three fundamental ways of knowing

Figure 8–4. A Depiction of Dimensional Bonding

plane) sees only a square. Two researchers discussing the object would only agree that the marketing phenomenon was a closed figure with no more than four sides and was symmetric. Each would have a piece of the truth. Only an observer who can integrate (view) both perspectives (all three dimensions) can really see the whole thing.

In the example, there is a dimensional limit which bounds knowledge. That is, if each of these researchers is limited to only two of the dimensions because they are dominated by their paradigmatic viewpoints, then they can, at best, only infer the nature of the true object as shown. But should the object exist in an even higher space, then the dimensional limit is a fundamental bound which cannot be exceeded with current ways of knowledge acquisition. Notice that in the diagram, each axis represents one of the three major ways of gaining knowledge: observation, logic, and intuition. The axial planes represent major paradigmatic approaches. For example, the logical empiricist plane results from the interaction of observation and logic. Similarly, the empirical intuitionist (IE) and intuitional logicist (LI) planes are generated. The least used in marketing is the LI approach (mostly found among those with a philosophy of science orientation), which has generated some major breakthroughs in mathematics and theoretical physics. The search for more extensive and precise measuring devices is an attempt to increase an observational space's dimensions, as the development of radio telescopes, electronic microscopes, cyclotrons, and various scaling techniques has done in astronomy, biology, physics, and marketing, respectively. Note that these extensions are *not* new means of knowledge acquisition. They are means of increasing the resolution of a particular knowledge axis. Unfortunately, there are limits to the amount of extension that can be accomplished. The lower limit to empirical testing is implied by the consequence of the Heisenberg uncertainty relations. (See Nagel 1979.) Essentially, this implies that the measurement process interacts with the object being measured at very fundamental levels. Objects being measured may, therefore, be artifacts of the measurement process, which can add and/or ignore various characteristics of the object.

Another consequence of Heisenberg deals with its effect on the concept of causality. In simple terms, the principle states that the position and momentum of elementary particles cannot be determined at the same time. This has been viewed at philosophical levels as support for the Humeian (1963) position against cause and effect. Nagel (1979) and Popper (1981) take issue with overextending the implications of Heisenberg indeterminancy to the concept of causality. As stated earlier, our point here is not to focus on issues of causality, but rather on the fact that there is a lower limit to our ability to make accurate observations. That this is bound up with issues of causality and the dimensional bounding that may exist suggests that those who argue for hard-core empiricism as the way to truth are like alchemists searching for a way to turn lead into gold.

If there is a limit to the observational side of the canonical form, is there also a theoretical bound (limit to logic)? The answer is yes (Bartley 1962). In fact, Gödel's theorems (Nagel 1979; Nagel and Newman 1958; Popper 1981; Hofstadter 1979) formally detail such a limit. While it is beyond the scope of this chapter to detail the theorems or otherwise explicate axiomatic systems, the following overview is given. Stated simply, Gödel showed that axiomatic systems (Blanche 1966) can never be fully axiomatized (i.e., they are incomplete). Furthermore, he demonstrated that internal logical consistency for a very large class of mathematical systems is indeterminate. The implications are that since mathematical systems (our best logical efforts) are flawed, virtually all other theoretical attempts are subject to one or both of these limitations in varying degrees. The upshot of this for marketing is that its theories will always be in some sense unfinished (incomplete). From a different vantage point, it can be argued that a "complete" theory is probaby tautological, hence, of little value (Weimer 1979). Given the dynamic and evolving nature of marketing, even without Gödel, it should be realized that theories in marketing are generally going to be incomplete until society becomes static and "well behaved"—a very unlikely event. Given the foregoing, widely recognized contributions such as those by Howard and Sheth (1969) and Bass (1974), to name a couple, are truly impressive.

We have not talked about intuition, the third means of knowledge acquisition represented in figure 8–4. The reason for this is that, to some extent, it is a philosophically difficult subject to deal with, a subject on which there is not much general agreement. What is agreed upon is that, when we speak of intuition, we mean some sort of direct and immediate knowledge of the object under study without using the other means of knowledge acquisition. Key results along this dimension are generally characterized as "intuitive leaps." Limits to intuitions clearly exist, but a description of them is acutely dependent on the source and nature one ascribes to intuition. Finally, since it seems to have less importance in empirically grounded phenomena, such as marketing, as a planned mode of research (hence, the dominance of the scientific method), we have limited the discussion of this knowledge axis. We do reiterate that the IL approach (axial plane) has produced significant results in disciplines such as mathematics. Non-Euclidean geometries are a result of this paradigmatic method.

Considering the above limitations to knowledge acquisition, we feel that the canonical form should be modified as shown in figure 8–5, with the corresponding remodification of the representation of the effects of source credibility on attitudes as shown in figure 8–6. Notice that in our conceptualization, the rules to correspondence link the world of theory with the world of observation. Each of these in turn is linked imperfectly to the world of pure logic (plane of completeness and consistency) and pure fact (plane of reality),

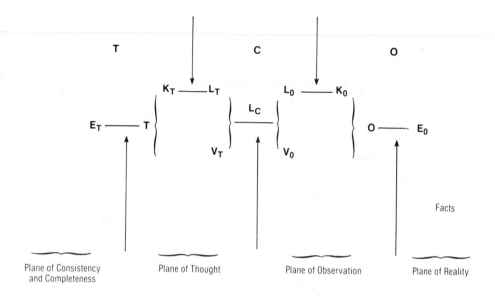

T Theory
C Correspondence Rules
O Observation
K Calculus
L Language
V Terms
E Error

Figure 8–5. The Canonical Form Revised

respectively. The imperfections are the two limits given earlier and symbolized as follows:

E_t = limits to logic
E_o = limits to observation

Since T is connected to O by C, this should be specified in Bagozzi's figures. This means that the plane of observation should intersect the rules of correspondence (symbolized as a language L_c). The interaction at this point sets up the world that we perceive. It is the interplay between our thinking processes and our sensory apparatus that creates our reality (Hayek 1969). This explains why both empirical and theoretical approaches are needed or, similarly, why both approaches can be used as starting points. Outside the plane of observation is the world of facts (plane of reality). The greater our improvements in measuring devices, the greater our ability to push back the world of facts. Beyond the plane of thought lies the world of perfect logic (plane of consistency

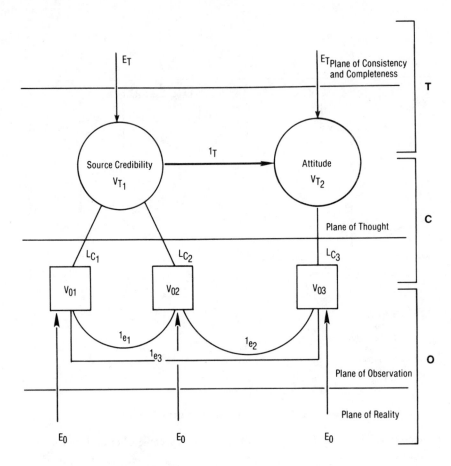

Key: Symbols are the same as in the previous diagram
with the exception of the additions noted below:
1_e = Empirical Propositions
1_t = Theoretical Propositions

**Figure 8–6. Effects of Source Credibility on Attitudes Under the Revised
Canonical Formulation**

and completeness). Extending the plane of thought comes from increasing the
number of perspectives used. The more viewpoints are used, the more likely it
is that the linkages of concepts and/or facts will mirror reality.

Finally, there is an overlap: extensions in one area are tied to progress in the
other. Thus, as our ability to "see" improves, our thinking becomes more
precise. This is implied by the fact that an increase in ability along one
knowledge-acquisition axis increases the area of the axial plane, and, therefore,
knowledge. In a two-dimensional representation, the overlap is difficult to

present. Also, a more precise description of the revised canonical form would show the figure folding in on itself, intersecting at the limits. (Imagine making a tin can, but instead of joining it at the seam, having it pass through itself.) Furthermore, intuition would have to be represented as a horizontal plane slicing the cylinder created by the folding. This arrangement would neatly allow for the proper placement of such fields of study as cosmology, and theoretical physics, whose domains operate along the seam at the limits to knowledge.

Extension 5: Concept Linkages

One thing that should be evident from Bagozzi's analysis and the comments presented so far is that concept linkages must play a large role in theory development. Going back to our generalized construal, it is how the elements are linked that is critical in distinguishing between different theories (models) of marketing phenomena. This means that the relation set $\{R\}$ is an important object of study in theory building. The essence of the situation is summed up by Blaise Pascal: "Let no man say that I have said nothing new; the arrangement of the material is new. Just as the same words differently arranged form different thoughts."

Unfortunately, in marketing, very little research has focused on such issues. Our view is that linkage structures are prime determinants of theory. This is consistent with our position that marketing phenomena can be viewed as related wholes made up of elements and relationships. By way of analogy, if we view the cogs in a Tinker Toy set as elements $\{E\}$ and the dowels as relationships $\{R\}$, then the differences in the systems built are defined by the ways the cogs are related to one another. A bridge differs from a house by the way the cogs are related. The same is true, in large part, for theory building. For example, Bagozzi's cannonical form is a linkage structure whose element set is L, T, O, K, V, and C. Studying the nature of linkage structures as an object of analysis requires metatheoretic approaches (Nagel and Newman 1958). This is, as indicated above, not usually done in the social sciences. Yet, it is interesting that causal modeling (Bagozzi 1980) is a linkage structure analysis. What we are referring to, however, are approaches that use marketing concepts as the element set across the entire discipline. Most of the current work of the type has been carried out in systems theory and more esoterically, yet fruitfully, in mathematics and philosophy. Three pragmatic approaches worth note are by Troncale (1978), Jain (1981), and Robbins and Oliva (1982, 1984). In marketing, the most formalized approach of this type has been accomplished by Oliva and Reidenbach (1985). Using an iterative partitioning technique developed by Warfield (1979), they develop a tentative concept linkage structure of marketing based on a sample of 172 *Journal of Marketing* articles. Their list of key terms and major categories is presented in table 8–1. While the

Table 8–1
A Concept Linkage Structure of Some Key Terms in the Literature

Control analysis	*Organizational analysis*
Cost control	Job satisfaction
Budgeting	Directing
Decision analysis	Planning
Controlling	Values
Social process analysis	*Information analysis*
Conflict	Information
Group theory	Content analysis
Adaptation	Mass media
Cognitive psychology	Quantitative analysis
Staffing	Theory
Humanity	Educational psychology
Industrial psychology	*Regulatory analysis*
Advertising	Governement
Regulation	Ethics
International	*Systems analysis*
Buyers	Systems
Statistics	Complexity
Resources	Feedback
Power	Operations research
Market structure analysis	*Marketing dynamics analysis*
Econometrics	Exchange theory
Demand analysis	Interaction theory
Pricing	Logistics
Market segmentation	Location
Marketing mix	Innovation
Models	Calculus
Demographics	Levels
Forecasting	Information theory
Products	Marketing models
Laws	Physical laws
Algebra	
Modeling	
Process	
Markets	
Strategic planning	

Source: Adapted from: Oliva and Reidenbach (1985).

Note: The terms within the categories are linked together in the sample literature used to develop this list. What appear to be anomalous inclusions are probably due to the small sample size used.

sample and scope of their study prevents generalization beyond the domain of the sample, the structure is interesting and suggests a possible new categorization scheme for marketing research, as well as providing limited support for Hunt's (1976) three-dichotomy taxonomy. Notice that instead of consumer behavior, channels, advertising, and so forth, they have categories such as social processes, marketing dynamics, market structure, and information processing. These are not simply nominal changes in category titles; rather, they are different underlying structures. This can be seen by looking at the intra-categorical elements in the table. Such empirically developed studies may eventually tell us more about the nature and direction of theory development than standard content analyses. Our point is not to suggest that Oliva and Reidenbach have found the "true" structure of the discipline, but, rather, to point out their structure makes sense in terms of how marketing researchers should probably characterize their own efforts. Beyond this, our point is to indicate that there is a need for more work on concept linkages, which should become an important and integral part of theory development in marketing.

Summary

We feel Bagozzi's prospectus is an important step in the right direction for analyzing theory development in marketing. One hopes that it indicates a new maturity in the discipline, which it has not previously had. His article, along with Arndt's (1985) paper, helps to fill the void of neglect that exists in the philosophy of science area of marketing. We applaud those efforts and hope our own extensions contribute to and enhance Bagozzi's fine starting point. It is also our hope that others join in the dialogue started here. The actuation of the theory development process requires ongoing critical evaluation and refinement. Hence, it is imperative that others add to, modify, and criticize what has been presented here. Our fear is that the dominance of the LE paradigm and the consequent power it provides to empirical methodologists may create a uni-dimensional intellectual approach that will stultify the development of marketing. There is some evidence that this is already the case. And, while so-called data grubbing can provide us with insights, we cannot build a complete theory of marketing on it. The gatekeepers to knowledge generation in the field (primarily journal editors and reviewers) must avoid provincial and conservative approaches which reduce intellectual variety. Radical thought in marketing must be integrated, formalized, and accepted as an appropriate and valuable means of developing contributions to marketing theory.

References

Arndt, J. (1985), "On Making Marketing Science More Scientific: Role of Orientation, Paradigms, Metaphors, and Puzzle Solving," *Journal of Marketing* 49 (Winter): 11–23.

Bagozzi, R. (1980), *Causal Models in Marketing*. New York: John Wiley & Sons.

———, (1984), "A Prospectus for Theory Construction in Marketing," *Journal of Marketing* 48 (Winter): 11–29.

Bartley, W. (1962), *The Retreat to Commitment*. New York: A.A. Knopf.

Bass, F. (1974). "The Theory of Stochastic Preference and Brand Switching," *Journal of Marketing Research*. 11 (February): 1–20.

Blanche, R. (1966), *Axiomatics*, translated by G.B. Keene. London: Routledge & Kegan Paul.

Bridgman, P. (1927), *The Logic of Modern Physics*. New York: Macmillan.

Bunge, M. (1959), *Causality: The Place of the Causal Principle in Modern Science*. Cambridge, Mass.: Harvard University Press.

Carnap, R. (1956), "The Methodological Character of Theoretical Concepts," in *Minnesota Studies in the Philosophy of Science*, vol. 1, Feigl and Scriven, eds. Minneapolis: University of Minnesota Press, 33–76.

Chomsky, N. (1963), "Formal Properties of Grammars," in *Handbook of Mathematical Psychology*, vol. 2, Luce, Bush, and Galanter, eds. New York: Wiley, 323–418.

Gray, W. (1977), *General System Formation Precursor Theory*. Cambridge, Mass: Aristocrat.

Harary, F., R. Norman, and D. Cartwright (1965), *Structural Models: An Introduction to the Theory of Diagraphs*. New York: John Wiley & Sons.

Hayek, F. (1952), *The Sensory Order*. Chicago: University of Chicago Press.

——— , (1969), "The Primacy of the Abstract," *Beyond Reductionism*, Koestler and Smythies, eds. New York: Macmillan.

Hofstadter, D. (1979), *Gödel, Escher, Bach: An Eternal Golden Braid*. New York: Basic Books.

Howard, J., and J. Sheth (1969), *The Theory of Buyer Behavior*, New York: John Wiley & Sons.

Hume, D. (1963), *The Philosophy of David Hume*, V.C. Chappell, ed. New York: Random House.

Hunt, S. (1976), "The Nature and Scope of Marketing," *Journal of Marketing*, 40 (July): 17–28.

——— , (1983), "General Theories and the Fundamental Explananda of Marketing," *Journal of Marketing* 47 (Fall): 9–17.

Jain, V. (1981), "Structural Analyses of General Systems Theory," *Behavioral Science* 26: 51–62.

Leap, T., and T. Oliva (1981), "General Systems Precursor Theory as a Supplement to Wren's Framework for Studying Management History: The Case of Human Resource/Personnel Management," *Human Relations* 36: 627–40.

Lewis, C. (1929), *Mind and the World Order*. Cambridge, Mass.: Harvard University Press.

Marchal, J. (1971), "On the Concept of a System," *Philosophy of Science* 42: 448–68.

McLuhan, M. (1964), *Understanding Media*. New York: McGraw-Hill.

Miller, J. (1978), *Living Systems*. New York: McGraw-Hill.

Murdick, R., and J. Ross (1975), *Information Systems for Modern Management*, 2nd ed. Englewood Cliffs, N.J.: Prentice-Hall.

Nagel, E. (1979), *The Structure of Science*. Indianapolis, Ind.: Hackett.

Nagel, E., and J. Newman (1958) *Gödel's Proof*. New York: New York University Press.

Oliva, T. (1976), "Laszlo, Semantics, and Systems Definitions: A Critique," *Behavioral Science* 21 (May): 196–99.

Oliva, T., and T. Leap (1981), "A Typology of Metamodels in Collective Bargaining," *Behavioral Science* 26: 337–45.

Oliva, T., and R. Reidenbach (1985), "Iterative Partitioning Methods: The Use of Mapping Theory as a Clustering Technique," *Journal of Marketing Research* 22 (February): 81–85.

Popper, K. (1959), *The Logic of Scientific Discovery*. New York: Harper.

———, (1981), *Objective Knowledge: An Evolutionary Approach*, rev. ed. Oxford, England: Clarendon.

Robbins, S., and T. Oliva (1982), "The Empirical Identification of Fifty-one Core General Systems Theory Vocabulary Components," *Behavioral Science* 27: 377–86.

Robbins, S., and T. Oliva (1984), "Usage of General Systems Theory Core Concepts by Discipline Type, Time Period, and Publication Category," *Behavioral Science* 29: 28–39.

Skvoretz, J. (1984), "Languages and Grammars of Action and Interaction: Some Further Results," *Behavioral Science* 29: 81–97.

Stoll, R. (1963), *Set Theory and Logic*. San Francisco: W.H. Freeman.

Troncale, L. (1978), "Linkage Propositions between Fifty Principal Systems Concepts," *Applied General Systems Research*, G. Klir, ed. New York: Plenum.

Warfield, J. (1979), "Some Principles of Knowledge Organization," *IEEE Transactions on Systems, Man, and Cybernetics* 9: 317–25.

Weimer, W. (1979), *Notes on the Methodology of Scientific Research*. Hillside, N.J.: Lawrence Erlbaum Associates.

Whitehead, A. (1929), *The Function of Reason*. Princeton: Princeton University Press.

Part III
Marketing, Society, and the Consumer

Figure 9–1. Koko and All Ball

9

O, Consumer, How You've Changed: Some Radical Reflections on the Roots of Consumption

Morris B. Holbrook

> Man need not be surprised that animals have animal instincts that are so much like his own. . . . Man may learn from the animals, for they are his parents.
>
> —Paracelsus (1493–1541)

> Novelists, dramatists and biographers had always been satisfied to exhibit people's motives, thoughts, perturbations and habits by describing their doings, sayings, and imaginings, their grimaces, gestures and tones of voice. In concentrating on what Jane Austen concentrated on, psychologists began to find that these were, after all, the stuff and not the mere trappings of their subjects. . . . Man need not be degraded to a machine. . . . He might, after all, be a sort of animal, namely, a higher mammal.
>
> —Gilbert Ryle (1949, p. 328)

Consuming Animals

Koko and All Ball

Once upon a time, in the state of California at the Gorilla Foundation during the year 1985, there lived a 13-year-old, 230-pound ape named Koko—surely one of the world's best educated and most celebrated pongids (Patterson and Linden 1981). Koko spoke to her trainers in American Sign Language (ASL), using her hands to encode a vocabulary of over 500 words. Having become quite sophisticated in her capacity to communicate in this manner, this talented primate one day greeted her keepers with the announcement that she wanted

The author thanks Russ Belk, Steve Bell, Dave Brinberg, Geraldine Fennell, Beth Hirschman, Sally Holbrook, John Howard, John O'Shaughnessy, and Francoise Simon-Miller for their helpful comments on an earlier draft of this chapter. He also gratefully acknowledges the support of the Columbia Business School's Faculty Research Fund.

them to bring her something to play with, namely a cat (Patterson 1985). Koko's trainers responded by giving their intelligent anthropoid a small kitten without a tail, whom Koko named All Ball and spoke about in such phrases as "Koko love visit Ball." As shown in figure 9–1, the gorilla and kitten played together long and happily, with Koko displaying highly developed qualities of tenderness and affection (Vessels 1985).

This playful friendship ended prematurely, however, when All Ball was killed by a car. When Koko's keepers broke the news that All Ball was dead, Koko showed obvious and painful symptoms of extreme grief, mourning her loss in an anguished expression of the most profound sadness (Hackett 1985). As described by Patterson: "I went to Koko at once. I told her that Ball had been hit by a car; she would not see him again. . . . Ten minutes later, I heard Koko cry. It was her distress call—a loud, long series of high-pitched hoots" (1985, p. 24).

Actually, in spite of this touching tale, good reasons exist for remaining skeptical on the question of whether animals in general and apes in particular can learn a human language (Sebeok 1981; Sebeok and Umiker-Sebeok 1981; Terrace 1985). However, such issues appear largely irrelevant to my present purposes. For one thing, no one questions that animals can communicate with people via the interspecies use of signs (Sebeok). Further, what they communicate in this fashion is a wide range of wants and emotions, many of which we can also recognize in ourselves without fear of the "pathetic fallacy" that results from excessive anthropomorphism: "Let us not be scared by the bogey of anthropomorphism into the arms of the spectre of Cartesian mechanism. It is not anthropomorphism to believe that man and the higher animals have much in common so far as instinct and emotion are concerned, but an acknowledgment of truth scientifically demonstrated" (Armstrong 1963, p. 195).

In other words, animals experience wants and feelings closely related to those found in human consumers. Not coincidentally, Koko's typical day (as described by Patterson and Linden 1981, chapter 8) is a veritable festival of consumption activities: breakfast, housecleaning, schoolwork, play, snack, more lessons, lunch, more play and instruction and snacks, dinner, dessert, entertainment, toothbrushing, bedtime. About the only difference between Koko and many human children in these respects is that Koko does not say her prayers (yet). Thus, Koko's activities closely parallel the experiences involved in human consumption. In that sense, Koko becomes a metaphor—a metaphor for consumer behavior.

In sum, I regard Koko as a metaphorical consumer—far more human in her thoughts, emotions, activities, and values than the reductionst, brand-choosing, decision-making automatons that most consumer researchers (myself included) have studied for the past two decades. Koko's story continues a movement begun when the gestaltists recognized insight in the behavior of their problem-solving apes (Køhler 1925) and declared that no atomistic, behaviorist, or other reductive explanation could adequately account for such displays of intelligence and primal creativity (Koestler 1964). Koko provides anecdotal evidence—often the most persuasive kind—that animals (at least semiotically sophisticated primates) engage in complex consumption experiences characterized by fantasies (imagining and requesting a cat), feelings (love for the kitten and grief over its death), and fun (the enjoyment of games and other playful activities). Clearly, Koko consumed the services provided by All Ball as a kind of living toy. Just as clearly, All Ball participated in a reciprocal consumption experience centered around those curious and sensuous proclivities for which cats are justly famous. Together, the kitten and gorilla remind us that animals display complex behaviors not easily explained by conventional learning models or other simplistic accounts.

If we grant this status to animals, then surely we must acknowledge that humans, too, pursue consumption experiences not well handled by any sort of reductionist formulation. If animals evince such apparent examples of fantasies, feelings, and fun in their consumption activities, we cannot plausibly deny these phenomena in the case of human consumers. Yet, it appears that much consumer research has verged on such denials and has thereby tolerated the existence of wide gaps in our understanding of the consumption experience.

The Consumption of Pets

In our prevailing model of the consumer as a cognitively guided decision maker who makes purchases based on choices among available brands, we often overlook elemental consumption phenomena of intuitively obvious importance. The flavor of this neglect appeared in our recent experience with a paper on evaluating household pets in general and dogs in particular (Moore and Holbrook 1982). In the lengthy review process preceding publication, we were surprised to learn that some colleagues do not regard pet ownership as a viable example of consumer behavior.

This denial flies in the face of well-established findings on the psychological importance of domestic animals as nearly full-fledged members of the family (Hickrod and Schmitt 1982; Horn and Meer 1984; Meer 1984; Tucker 1967). As in the case of Koko, a pet's death may create nearly unbearable emotional consequences for its owners: "Loss of a pet is often agonizing, akin to the loss of a close friend or relative. . . . Many people go through an agonizing separation when they lose a pet. . . . Characteristic symptoms include depression, anger, guilt, apathy, loss of appetite, loneliness, sleeplessness, numbness, periods of intense anxiety and episodes of crying" (Brody 1985, p. C8). Indeed, this phenomenon opens the way to expensive pet-loss counseling services (Brody) and $650 burial plots in pet cemeteries (Haitch 1985). These and other lucrative business opportunities have not escaped the attention of real-world marketers:

There are about 98 million dogs and cats in the United States, a number greater than the human population of all but seven nations. Well over half of America's households are home to a furred, finned or feathered friend of some kind. Those pets are the foundation of an $8.5 billion-a-year industry that translates peoples' love for animals into profits. . . . As Leslie B. Charm, president and chief executive officer of Docktor Pet Centers, puts it, "The company philosophy recognizes that its business is predicated on 'selling love,' but that does not obfuscate the profit motive." (Lefferts 1985, p. F15)

Indeed, pet supplies are the single largest product category in terms of shelf space in the average supermarket (Meer).

Yet, for reasons difficult to comprehend, our colleagues in consumer research have resisted the acknowledgment of such consumption phenomena. Apparently, the nature of consumption experiences that appear so obvious in the case of Koko may elude our grasp in the case of human consumers. Perhaps our decision-making models prevent us from recognizing such phenomena at our own level on the evolutionary ladder. Whatever the reason for their neglect, I wish to insist that such consumption experiences exist and deserve our full attention, but cannot be adequately represented by conventional cognitive, rational, decision-oriented buyer-behavior models (including, no doubt, those studied by Moore and Holbrook 1982).

A Think Piece

A vivid illustration, still couched within the framework of pet consumption, appeared in *A Think Piece* (a recent play by Jules Feiffer), whose characters and plot might almost have been designed to demonstrate the point argued here. In this play, Betty Castle (the female protagonist) appears as a person filled with feelings and governed by her rather volatile emotions, with a passion for shopping but an inveterate inability to make decisions about the trivia that crowd her daily life. By contrast, her husband Gordon (a teacher) maintains a cool rationality governed by logic and intellect, thereby embodying the conventional view of the consumer as an almost computerlike decision maker. When, in an emotional frenzy bordering on hysteria, Betty assassinates the beloved family dog (Zero) by dropping it from the window of the Castles' high-rise apartment, all Gordon can do is sadly repeat his stereotypical diagnosis: "Dumb, dumb, . . . , dumb."

Besides illustrating that humans (Feiffer's female protagonist Betty) can sometimes act with less gentleness and affection than gorillas (our own heroine Koko), *A Think Piece* represents a complex consumption experience (Betty's frantic anger at the hapless family pet) while satirizing the futile attempt of cognitively oriented rational decision models to explain such phenomena (Gordon's diagnostically inadequate "dumb, dumb, . . . , dumb"). Obviously, the wife's treatment of Zero is far worse than "dumb"; it is appalling and, on the night I saw the play, elicited a horrified gasp from the audience. But, however unsavory, it reminds us how much happens in consumer behavior that eludes our conventional models and methods. Our job is to try to recapture some of those missing ingredients of the consumption experience.

Toward a Radical View of Consumption

The Radical Premise

I wish to propose a view of consumer behavior that is "radical" in the same sense that a radish is a "radical" plant. Specifically, it has roots. The first dictionary definition of *radical* is "of, relating to, or proceeding from a root" (*Webster's Ninth New Collegiate Dictionary* 1984, p. 970). The second is "of or relating to the origin: *fundamental*." Only when we arrive at the third definition do we encounter the meaning "marked by a considerable departure from the usual. . . . *extreme*."

Similarly, my proposal for revisions in our approach to consumer research strikes me as radical in the senses (1) that it returns to the roots and (2) that it explores the fundamentals of consumer behavior. It is extreme only in the sense that it does depart from the current conventional wisdom by getting back to basics.

As our intellectual forebears in consumer research fully recognized, consumer behavior rests on value, and all customer value inheres in the consumption experience (Holbrook 1985a). For example, in an early book on consumer behavior, Norris anticipated the appropriate conclusion concerning the nature of consumption and its dependence on the experiences that goods provide:

> The emphasis . . . is upon the *services* of goods, not upon the goods themselves. Wants should be thought of not as desires for goods—but rather for the events which the possession of them makes possible. . . . Goods are wanted because they are capable of performing services—favorable events which occur at a point in time. (1941, pp. 136–37)

Abbott extended the implications of this view:

> The thesis . . . may be stated quite simply. What people really desire are not products but satisfying experiences. Experiences are attained through activities. In order that activities may be carried out, physical objects or the services of human beings are usually needed. Here lies the connecting link between man's inner world and the outer world of economic activity. People want products because they want the experience-bringing services which they hope the products will render. (1955, p. 40)

Thus, an emphasis on the consumption experience is not something new and esoteric, but rather something quite old and fundamental. In advocating fuller recognition of the experiential aspects of consumption (Holbrook and Hirschman 1982), I return to the roots of our discipline and try to revive a focus that used to seem obvious but that has recently disappeared behind the miasma of the decision-oriented buyer-behavior perspective.

The Importance of Consumption

The urgency of this enterprise appears with particular force if we pause to ponder the importance of consumption in our daily lives. Hampshire's (1982) *Thought and Action* begins with some difficult passages that, carefully read, establish consumption as central to our apprehension of reality. Specifically, Hampshire argues (1) that our apprehension of reality depends on language and (2) that language reflects the nature of consumption:

> A language is always a means of singling out . . . certain elements of experience and reality as subjects which can be referred to again and again. . . . Reality and experience cannot be thought about unless we have rules that correlate particular groups of signs with particular recurrent elements in reality and experience. (p. 11)

> In any natural language, the objects of reference primitively chosen will be persisting things, differentiated into kinds, at least in part, by their usefulness in serving different but constant, human needs . . . that is, anything that can be used to serve exactly the same human need will count as the same kind of thing. (p. 21)

In other words, our needs as consumers and their gratification in consumption shape the language that, in a Whorfian fashion, mediates our experience of reality. (For related points, see Coward and Ellis 1977, p. 79; Eco 1976, p. 316; Harman 1973, p. 84; Silverman 1983, p. 180.) Perhaps this is why Koko seems such a prototypical consumer. At least figuratively, Koko has learned to talk in her prehensile sign vocabulary and now speaks the language of consumption by which we define our own reality. Clearly, we must construct the language of consumer research—that is, the theories by which we study consumption phenomena—to reflect that reality and not vice versa.

Shortcomings of the Recent Conventional Wisdom

Yet, when we turn to the psychological, sociological, and philosophical principles generally taken to account for consumer behavior, we find a rather narrow view of the web of life that pervades consumption phenomena. From psychology, we have borrowed rational cognitive decision-making models typified by the expectancy-value framework which assumes that beliefs about probabilistic means-ends relations (E) can be weighed by the evaluation of ends (V) and summed or otherwise aggregated to explain the intentions (I) that guide behavior (B): $\Sigma E \cdot V \to I \to B$ (e.g., Fishbein and Ajzen 1975). The analogous sociological approach to studying action systems adopts a similar viewpoint (e.g., Parsons 1937). In philosophy, we find parallel concepts in the theory of action, which holds that beliefs and wants provide reasons to explain the intentions that shape purposive rule-following behavior (e.g., Anscombe 1957; Davis 1979; Goldman 1970; Hampshire 1982).

Though seldom juxtaposed in explicit comparisons, these perspectives share a focus on rational rule-following purposive action. They thereby explain much that is important in consumer behavior, while leaving much else that is equally important unexplained or even unexamined. Probably, a fair assessment might conclude that the conventional decision-oriented models do an excellent job of accounting for that part of consumer behavior that is (1) easiest to explain (e.g., brand choice as opposed to product usage), (2) most important to practical marketing applications (e.g., the firm's market share as opposed to society's quality of life), and (3) most trivial in terms of human happiness (e.g., buying as opposed to consuming). When we contemplate using such logically tight analytic schemes to address consumption phenomena as broad as loving a pet cat or dog, admiring a charismatic political leader, or appreciating the awesome beauty of the Sistine Chapel, we wonder which model better represents the consumption experience:

$$\sum_{i=1}^{I} E_i \cdot V_i \qquad \text{or} \qquad$$

Some Lessons from Our Pets

I suggest that Koko and Zero have much to teach us in this respect. They speak—eloquently if metaphorically—for the fundamental importance of consumption experiences in the lives of consumers. Let us, therefore, pause to take stock of ten lessons extracted from the two anecdotal stories about pet consumption.

First, both Koko and Betty Castle in Feiffer's play engage in *consuming as opposed to buying behavior* (Alderson 1957). This realization reinforces the call for more work on consumption activities versus purchasing decisions (Belk 1984; Bristor 1984; Granzin 1984; Holbrook 1984a, 1985c; Holbrook and Hirschman 1982). For example, Jacoby (1978) and Sheth (1985) have distinguished among acquisition, consumption, and disposition phenomena and have suggested that we ignore the latter two categories only at our peril. The fact that both All Ball and Zero represent particularly unfortunate examples of product disposal only serves to reinforce this point.

Second, both anecdotes indicate that consumption is an *experience rather than a decision*. They thereby remind us that our psychological, sociological, and philosophical theories of rational, purposive, goal-directed, rule-following action may represent only a small subsection in the relevant spectrum of consumption experience. For example, Koko's feelings of love and grief or Betty's expression of discontent and rage are intimately bound up with consumption-related phenomena that can never be captured by a decision-making framework.

Third, both Koko and Betty engage in *product usage rather than brand choice*. In both cases, the primary selective process concerns the allocation of resources (money, time, ability, effort) among products rather than among brands. Betty chooses walking the family dog versus cooking dinner; Koko chooses playing with the kitten versus eating a banana. I have argued elsewhere that too little consumer research involves macrolevel analysis across products as opposed to microlevel analysis across brands (Holbrook, Lehmann, and O'Shaughnessy 1986). The former across-products perspective appears more central to questions about how people organize the activities that shape their lives as consumers.

Fourth, both stories about pet consumption focus our attention on consuming *intangible services as opposed to tangible goods*. Pet kittens and dogs provide value via the services that they render. But the same truth applies to all instances of consumption—whether of tangible or intangible products, whether in fact or in imagination. As previously mentioned, nothing can yield value except through experience of its services (Abbott 1955; Holbrook 1985a; Norris 1941). The only difference (in this respect) between a kitten and a banana lies in the durability of the services available therefrom.

Thus, fifth, both anecdotes call our attention to products that lasted more briefly than expected and thereby remind us of *the distinction between durables and nondurables*. *Durability* might be defined as the length of time over which a product (a good, service, or idea) yields its characteristic value. This perspective uncovers two important points that appear to have attracted little notice (Holbrook 1986c). First, the distinction between nondurable and durable goods (e.g., a candy bar versus a lawn mower) mirrors analogous but seldom drawn contrasts between nondurable and durable services (e.g., dry cleaning versus cosmetic surgery) and between nondurable and durable ideas (e.g., a political campaign speech versus an artistic masterpiece). These distinctions refer to the temporal span of a consumer-product interaction that produces value-conferring benefits in the form of consumption experiences. These experiences vary in longevity for services and ideas, just as they do for more tangible goods. Second, durability in goods, services, and ideas implies a relevant range far broader than that normally considered.

For example, we might define levels of durability on a logarithmic scale as (1) under one year (subdurables), (2) under ten years (quasi-durables), (3) under one hundred years (mere durables), (4) under one thousand years (ultradurables), (5) under ten thousand years (maxidurables), (6) under one hundred thousand years (superdurables), (7) under one million years (hyperdurables), and (8) millions of years (megadurables). Yet, oblivious to this range of durability, most available research has dealt with the subdurables in category 1 (e.g., light bulbs), the quasi-durables in category 2 (e.g., automobiles or household appliances), or the mere durables in category 3 (e.g., houses and furniture). I suggest (Holbrook 1986c) that we might learn more about the consumption of durables by studying the more paradigmatic cases of durability that occur among the ultra-, maxi-, super-, hyper-, and even megadurables in categories 4 through 8 in which the goods, services, and ideas in question render their value over a period of hundreds, thousands, or even millions of years (e.g., The Statue of Liberty, a Stradivarius violin, the *Declaration of Independence*, *Hamlet*, Greek sculpture, the *Bible*, the Grand Canyon, the Sun). Elsewhere (Holbrook 1986e) I have argued that, figuratively speaking, marketers often emulate Polaroid by trying to sell consumers a "piece of the sun." The marketing of Halley's comet offers a spectacular case in point. Telescope sales recently doubled in a single year (Geist 1985). Similar phenomena surround the consumption of artworks, whose appreciation may endure for centuries and beyond. Yet, we lack an adequate understanding of these consumption events. Hence, a closer examination of such paradigmatic examples of true durability may shed light on the importance of less dramatic differences in longevity at the lower end of the durability continuum.

Sixth, in terms of resource allocation, both Koko and Betty Castle engage primarily in *the investment of time, effort, and ability* (animate resources) *as opposed to money* (inanimate resources) in their respective consumption experiences (cf. Alderson 1957, p. 286). Recently, progress has been made toward treating time, effort, and ability as key animate resources allocated by consumers among consumption activities (Holbrook et al. 1984; Holbrook and Hirschman 1982; Holbrook and Lehmann 1981). For example, Becker (1976) regards time as a key input into the household's production/consumption function. More generally, when we consume, we expend part of our life force or psychic energy (Csikszentmihalyi and Rochberg-Halton 1981). The resources that we allocate among different consumption experiences are alive. This point appears clearly in the activities of the penniless Koko, whose time, effort, and ability are all she has to spend.

Seventh, both Koko and Betty Castle remind us that the consumption experience contains *multifaceted emotional components that extend far be-*

yond simple affect. Traditionally, consumer researchers have treated affect as a unidimensional continuum that extends from positive to negative, from pro to con, from favorable to unfavorable, or from liking to disliking. Yet, this conception of affect appears unnecessarily restrictive. Thus, I have argued for replacing our unidimensional concept of affect narrowly conceived with a broader concept of emotion (Holbrook 1986b; Holbrook and O'Shaughnessy 1984). Specifically, I have pointed out that consumer emotions range over a wide variety of types (joy, sadness, love, hate, anger, fear, pleasure, arousal, surprise, disgust, and so on) and have suggested that emotional responses involve at least four mutually interdependent components: physiological responses, cognitive interpretations, subjective feelings, and behavioral expressions. These aspects of responding, interpreting, feeling, and expressing appear to interact in a reverberating network of interrelationships with no necessary causal priority among its constituent parts (Denzin 1984; Giorgi 1970). Thus, all subcomponents are equally important to the overall emotional experience. The most visible to the external observer, however, is the expressive component that involves such overt behavioral manifestations as body postures, nonverbal gestures, and facial mien (Cacioppo et al. 1986). Behavioral expression performs an important communicative function that, as in the case of artistic creativity, may itself serve as a purpose for the consumption experience (Holbrook and Zirlin 1985). Such expressive consumption reaches its apotheosis in the dance (Highwater 1981, chapter 6; Ruesch and Keese 1956). At a recent performance in honor of Bishop Desmond M. Tutu, for example, I saw Welcome Msomi and the Izulu Dance Theatre execute an ecstatic outpouring of physical movement which could not be seen anything other than an exultant expression *and* consumption of pure joy. King and Straub offer an apposite description of classically trained ballet dancers practicing in a studio:

> Their faces ran with sweat. Their leotards were wet with sweat. The room, as large and airy as it was, stank of sweat. . . . Most of all he remembered their expressions—all that exhausted concentration, all that pain . . . but transcending the pain . . . he had seen joy. Joy was unmistakenly what that look was . . . . *Joy* . . . *Joy*, he thought again . . . . *Joy*—damn, but that's a cheerful little word . . . . And . . . that feeling of joy remained, like a rainbow inside his head. (1984, pp. 192–193)

Eighth, our animal examples reflect the fact that many behavioral expressions of emotion or other consumer activities fall outside the bounds of conventional personal or social norms and are therefore labeled as aberrant cases of *misbehavior as opposed to behavior.* In a recent paper on consumer *mis*behavior, I distinguish among irregular, irrational, illegal, and immoral types of consumption (Holbrook 1986a). These distinctions are less important than the broader recognition that such forms of deviant, foolish, unlawful, and unethical consumer behavior exist widely but receive scant notice from our discipline. For example, transvestites, gamblers, burglars, and drug addicts represent exaggerated forms of extremely common consumer misbehaviors—namely, dressing out of fashion, taking chances unwisely, cheating, and over-indulging. Yet, we grant them very little systematic attention. Why do we turn our backs on such important and widespread phenomena? I suspect it is because we think that consumer misbehavior is not very nice. It makes us rather uncomfortable. For example, the acknowledgement that robbing banks is just one more type of consumption might seem to degrade our discipline a bit. In other words, we respond to consumer misbehavior with an almost prissy aversion—as if in the hope that, by ignoring it, we can make it go away. I received a brief taste of this bias in the reactions of some academic friends who reviewed an earlier draft of this chapter and found fault with my picture of Koko in figure 9–1: "The . . . sketch of Koko is technically good, and I recognize the news photo pose, but at a quick glance it looks like the gorilla is masturbating."

Besides attesting to the sex-obsessed nature of my esteemed colleagues, this comment suggests a deep reluctance to accept and deal with the masturbatory activities even of animals, let alone people. Apparently, we think that masturbation is not nice and, like other forms of consumer misbehavior, should therefore be avoided. To this, I have two responses. First, as anyone who has ever played with a kitten will immediately recognize, Koko is *not* masturbating. All Ball has grabbed Koko's hand with all four paws, thereby making it impossible for the gorilla to masturbate even if she wanted to. Second, if Koko *were* masturbating, this would serve as an excellent opportunity to illustrate one important type of consumer misbehavior that deserves greater attention — namely, socially proscribed sexual enjoyment. Thus, fortuitously, Koko's example again indicates a neglected area of consumption that invites further exploration.

Ninth, by recalling the work in gestalt psychology, Koko evokes an awareness of the mutual interdependency among consumption phenomena. Like any gestalt, the consumption experience is *a complex whole that cannot meaningfully be decomposed into isolated parts.* Thus, we may define the consumption experience as *an emergent property that results from a complex system of mutually overlapping interrelationships in constant reciprocal interaction with personal, environmental, and situational inputs* (Hirschman and Holbrook 1986). We distinguish among four components of the experience: thought, emotion, activity, and value. However, we borrow from Lewin's (1936, 1951) field theory to suggest that these components may best be regarded as interdependent regions of the life-space and may be represented most clearly by a Venn diagram showing all possible intersections of thought, emotion, activity, and value as overlapping subregions of the psychological field into which a person can move at any time. Among other things, this view questions our ability to construct a well-identified causal model of the consumption experience. Rather, "like other aspects of human behavior, the consumption experience is a complex concatenation, a network, a web, an organic whole, a dynamic unity, a reverberating system of mutually overlapping interdependencies" (Hirschman and Holbrook 1986, p. 215).

Tenth and finally, I can find virtually no managerial relevance to marketing or other practical implications in the stories of Koko and All Ball or Betty and Zero. Rather, in both anecdotes, *the criteria of relevance spring from the interests of the consumers themselves and not from those of any managers* who might wish to benefit from, improve upon, or otherwise alter the nature of their consumption experiences. This nonpragmatic aspect of my animal stories coincides with my predilection for viewing consumer research as an end in itself apart from any benefits that it might confer upon marketing practitioners or other users. Though I find this orientation salutary and recommend it to all who will listen, I shall not dwell on it here. Elsewhere, I have argued the case for impracticality in a manner with which a predictably large number of presumably reasonable and rational colleagues appear to disagree (Holbrook 1985b, 1985c, 1986e).

Telling Stories

Conceptual Humanism

The ten preceding lessons from our pets suggest the need for a radically revised view of the consumption experience. Together, these ten proposed departures from the current orthodoxy imply reorientations relevant to both substantive and methodological issues. Substantively, they move us toward a theoretical stance different in kind from that which characterizes the conventional decision-oriented models of consumer behavior. Specifically, they suggest that consumption experiences result from the investment of living resources in the usage of products and involve complex reverberating networks of such components as thought, emotion, activity, and value. Further, methodologically, the development and validation of theory regarding such processes must proceed in a manner that departs from the positivist approach which has thus far characterized most consumer-research efforts. In particular, I sense the need for more eclectic, creative, diverse, or even deviant pathways to theory development (Holbrook 1984b) and anticipate making room for more introspective, phenomenological, qualitative, or self-expressive approaches to validation (Fennell 1985; Holbrook 1986d).

Drawing on work by Mitroff and Kilmann (1978), Hirschman (1985) has recently characterized four styles of consumer research. Each has its place in the creation and validation of theory. To advance the development (though not necessarily the testing) of theory on the consumption experience (especially its emotional components), I incline increasingly toward the style known as *conceptual humanism* or what Hirschman and Holbrook (1986) later called "introspective self-cultivation."

Conceptual humanism involves the extensive use of subjective, personal, introspective material and often proceeds via the construction of anecdotes, analogies, or metaphors. In short, conceptual humanism relies heavily on telling stores—stories rich in personal and metaphorical content (Mitroff and Kilmann 1978). This focus accords with the increased interest in the role of metaphor in science (Jones 1982) and philosophy (Lakoff and Johnson 1980). It sees stories as one potential path toward knowledge. For example, Hunter suggests:

> When we wish to communicate . . . , we tell a story of some sort. These are revelatory stories which disclose to us the meaning of our existence and experience in new and regenerative ways. Story is the language of the spirit. If we are to escape both sterile positivism and solipsistic subjectivism we must address ourselves to the issues of the *truth* and the *effectiveness* . . . of revelatory stories. (1983, p. 3)

Lewin agrees that narrative accounts can often reveal otherwise inaccessible complexities of mutually interdependent psychological processes:

> The most complete and concrete descriptions of situations are those which writers such as Dostoevski have given us. These descriptions have attained what the statistical characterizations have most notably lacked, namely, a picture that shows in a definite way how the different facts in an inidividual's environment are related to each other and to the individual himself. (1936, p. 13)

Though Hirschman (1985) offers some pertinent examples in her provocative essay (see also Hirschman and Holbrook 1986; Mitchell 1983; Tucker 1967), it is not easy to explain the use of stories in consumer research. Rather than attempting an explication, I shall provide a brief illustration and leave its exegesis to others. Specifically, I shall record a story that I wrote one sunny morning in May 1984. It is called "I Awake."

I Awake

I awake. My first conscious thoughts concern the double ugliness of the rough sound emanating from the Sony clock radio purposely placed on the other side of the nearby bookcase so as to force me eventually to leave my warm bed to turn it off—once ugly because that sound has shattered the peaceful tranquility of my gentle slumber and twice ugly because the Sony now plays Willie

Nelson's unconscionably syrupy version of "Stardust" embellished by harsh sibilant scratching noises that the *High Fidelity* I was reading last night attributes to multipath distortion caused by reflections of the FM signal off New York's high-rise buildings. One such edifice looms above me, and, as if by divine calculation, bright rays from the newly risen sun strike one of its windows at precisely the right angle to glint cruelly into my half-cracked eyes while I inwardly gather my strength in preparation for the aural assault soon to be mounted by the Sunbeam electric clock also positioned beyond my arm's reach and carefully set to lag five minutes behind the radio. Willie has stopped singing by now, thank God, and the comparatively cheerful sounds of Roberta Flack and Peabo Bryson have just started when the buzzer itself begins to wail. Sally moans in dormant rebellion from her fetal position on the wrinkled sheets beside me, pulling the softly odored comforter even more tightly around her face until only her nose pokes through.

I summon the courage necessary for my most heroic deed of the day. Suddenly, in one well-practiced and nearly continuous motion, I leap from the covers, press the switch that silences the Sunbeam's grating alarm, shuffle my feet into a pair of leather slippers which I have been cultivating since the seventh grade, click off the loud fan which we run all night to drown out street noises, flip the button that mercifully relieves Roberta, Peabo, and the Sony of their multipath burden, and appear before my own eyes stark naked in the mirror over the bathroom sink.

Here, I commence the rituals that members of my family refer to as my "ablutions." Their execution requires only a few moments, but they proceed according to a fixed routine so rigid that Sally, a psychotherapist, labels them "compulsive" and almost clinically "obsessive." Once begun, my ceremonial cleansing and anointment deviates from its ineluctable course for no force on earth, save perhaps an insufficient supply of Crest or Mennen. First, I splash warm water on my bristly cheeks and chin, wincing when the temperature suddenly changes from warm to scalding and making my two thousand six hundred and eighty-third mental note to ask the super to fix the faucet. Next, I apply a liberal quantity of lime-scented–and–flavored Edge shaving gel, congratulating myself on the discovery of this miraculous face-preserving ointment that daily saves me from the painful blood letting suffered with urbane equanimity by Cary Grant in Monday night's rerun of *Mr. Blandings Builds His Dream House*. In contrast to Cary's ordeal, my slippery face slides uneventfully under the smooth strokes of my Gillette Atra until I note with satisfaction the almost babylike perfection of the finished results. Still moist from rinsing off the Edge, I squeeze a generous dollop of mint-flavored Crest onto my medium-hard Colgate toothbrush and then let my mechanical wrist-flicking and arm-bending technique take over while I inspect with disapproval the sparse patch of straggling growth that barely adorns the top of my high and shining forehead. After automatically slurping, swishing, spitting, and drying,

I brush these forlorn locks in a few brisk getures which manage to impose order on every pathetic one of them with the expenditure of only a few seconds' time and energy. Finally, I come to the cherished moment in which I wipe a little squirt of Mennen Afta on my newly razored skin, rejoicing in its balmlike powers.

Now is the time to dress. I march to my closet, and since I shall work at home today, I abandon my process of sartorial choice to whim and reckless impulse. Of course, I do not deviate from my standard practice of pulling on size 32 jockey shorts and grey cotton socks since I long ago discovered, first, my acute sensitivity to even the tiniest variations in underwear design, and second, the happy maxim that virtually any combination of shoes and pants interacts harmoniously with charcoal-colored hosiery. Capitalizing on this reassuring principle, I force my way into a tight pair of faded Levi's (which I momentarily suspect of belonging to my slender fifteen-year-old son), climb into a lavender polo shirt (which for some reason features a blue pig standing on the very spot where an alligator is supposed to reside), and slip into my trusted Weejuns (acquired in high school and now so nicked and scuffed that they rival my ancient slippers in venerability).

I barely avoid stepping on Quarter, the cat, who lolls playfully on his back in the foyer (specifically, on that narrow portion of the hardwood floor through which all traffic must pass). I plod into the kitchen where, with practiced expertise, I fill the kettle with cool water, set the gas burner ablaze under it, and dole out Zabar's coffee grounds into the filter paper at the top of an incriminatingly stained Mehlita pot. In this enterprise, I maintain an incorruptible compromise exactly halfway between the amount of grounds preferred by Sally and by me (as gauged by my Prufrockian coffee measure); like Solomon, I believe that fairness must decide all such questions. Justice must also prevail in issues concerning the morning juice, a matter toward which I now direct my full concentration. Through careful experimentation and empirical study, I have determined (1) that orange juice is too sour, (2) that apple juice is too sweet, (3) that Chris, my growing son, can consume either beverage with approximately twice the speed empowered to me, and (4) that Sally's consumption of fruit juice cannot be detected by even the most unobtrusive measurement (though she does occasionally eat a kiwi fruit or two). Careful balancing of the scales of justice therefore demands that I purchase huge quantities of both orange and apple juice, that I mix small amounts of each into a combined potion (which I call "orple" juice and which, thankfully, my son would not touch with a broom handle even if such life-and-death concerns as his next Genesis record were at stake), and that I consign the remainder of the Tropicana and Mott's to Chris for purposes of immediate disposal in huge Herculean gulps while I take dainty sips of my special concoction.

The first such sip of orple washes down my daily vitamin pill, which I rather casually select as the most general-purpose specimen to be found in the three-tiered array of bottles reflecting Sally's $70-a-month vitamin habit. Such monetary thoughts even now flood my mind as she bustles cheerfully into the kitchen and announces with enormous enthusiasm her discovery that, before 7:00 a.m. on weekdays, one can call Italy for only $1.85 for the first three minutes and, further, that she has just put this telephonic privilege to excellent use by direct-dialing Porto Venere and locating a hotel room that we can inhabit next summer for only 280,000 lire per night (meals included). I suppress my reflex question concerning the exchange rate between lire and dollars and opt instead for imploring her to stop using her fingers to remove the surface raisins from the box of Raisin Bran before passing it to me. After finally securing what is left of the Kellogg's, I pour some rather flaky cereal into a small plastic bowl and flood it in a bath of low-fat milk. My use of this dairy product represents still one more compromise that attains nearly rabbinical wisdom in its careful balance of equity and fairness. I prefer skimmed; Chris prefers homogenized; so we all drink 2 percent low-fat—except, of course, Sally, who hates all milk, as reflected perhaps by her small-boned stature. I infer her disproportionately dainty size from the impression that her body seems too tiny to contain her huge spirit—particularly, this morning, her boundless enthusiasm for travel to such places as Italy and (I now learn with growing financial apprehension) Switzerland.

Carrying my freshly brewed cup of mocha/Colombian blend, I stumble toward my study. I execute one more precarious pirouette around Quarter (still spread across the foyer floor) and, finally, sit before my big, white, glass-topped desk. I reach for a piece of Kleenex and blow my nose lustily (for the cat exacerbates my aching allergies). I switch on the 100-watt G.E. bulk in my yellow-shaded antique brass lamp (for the sky has grown dark and it has begun to rain). I remove my Sheaffer fine-tipped fountain pen and two pieces of Eaton's Berkshire Bond from my drawer and place them on the desk in front of me (for I think I should write something about consumer behavior today).

The blank expanse of white pages on white desk stares up at me expectantly. I wait for a profound thought about consumer behavior to occur to me. Suddenly, it comes.

Like everyone else in this world, I am a consumer. I climbed out of bed exactly one half-hour ago, and already I have spent twenty-nine minutes and thirty-six seconds engaged in various consumption experiences. Allowing six hours for sleep (during which consumption is reduced, though not altogether stopped), I shall spend about eighteen hours consuming today. In my forty years, this kind of behavior has added up to about 262,800 hours of consumption experiences. Surely, I should by now be an expert on consumption. If I had one lira for every hour I have spent consuming, we could spend a night in the Italian hotel to which Sally at this moment busily writes a letter requesting a reservation.

Then why do I feel so ignorant about consumer behavior? Perhaps it is because consumer researchers seem to ignore the experiential phenomena through which I have been living. I glance nervously at my shelves of periodicals and journals, all neatly arranged in chronological order. A pale brown section containing forty issues of *Journal of Consumer Research* nestles among the other multicolored bindings. I notice absentmindedly how the lettering changed from black to brown in 1977 and the cover from tan to beige in 1983. I ponder the mystery of these alterations. I think about all the models of brand choice and buying behavior that these wise pages contain. I wonder dreamily where the flesh-and-blood consumer hides amidst all this talk of product adoption and purchasing decisions.

This thought seizes me now. My demon has called me. My muse has spoken. I begin to write. I am awake.

Conclusion

This chapter advocates a radical shift in consumer research away from the conventional wisdom and back to the roots of consumption. In sum, conventional consumer research tends to focus on buying decisions that result in brand choices in some product class of tangible, relatively nondurable goods on which the buyer spends money on the basis of a rational linear progression from cognition to affect to behavioral intention that can be studied positivistically in a manner useful to marketing managers. If this summary statement appears unconscionably stereotypical, at least it embodies the ten lessons mentioned in the preceding discussion. Our reflections on those issues, as inspired by two stories about pet consumption, have suggested that the conventional models and methods cannot adequately encompass the full range of phenomena relevant to the consumption experience. They cannot represent the grief-stricken misery of our poor whimpering gorilla or the hysterical cruelty of the dog owner in Feiffer's play.

I therefore propose an expansion of consumer research to reflect a fuller treatment of (1) consuming (versus buying), (2) experiencing (versus deciding), (3) using products (versus choosing brands), (4) intangible services and ideas (versus tangible goods), (5) more (versus fewer) durable products, (6) expenditures of time, effort, and ability (versus money), (7) emotional components (versus narrowly defined affect), (8) consumer misbehavior (versus behavior), (9) mutually interdependent wholes (versus their parts), and (10) concern with consumption for its own sake (versus managerial relevance). Further, I suggest the greater reliance on story telling and other aspects of conceptual humanism (as opposed to the various positivist dictates of the hypothetico-deductive approach).

As I write this conclusion, on the coldest day in New York City since the 1880s, the wind howls outside my window, blowing freezing gusts against the trembling panes and leaving a solid crust of white ice crystals on the inside. This picture evokes an image of the cold analytic light under which consumer researchers have so often scrutinized their subject. In attempting to meet the positivist prescriptions imposed by the hypothetico-deductive method, we often work in the name of dispassionate detachment to shed a chilly illumination on the phenomena we wish to study, but we too seldom admire the rainbow of feelings and the sunny appreciative responses that pervade all consumption experience.

My title says, colloquially, that the consumer has changed. I realize, of course, that it is we consumer reseachers who must change and not the consumer, but I adopt the same poetic license that we grant to astronomers when they talk about changes in the position of the sun in the sky even though they know full well that it is we who move and not the sun. This image of the sun is a comfort on this cold day. It connotes the warm roots of consumption and contrasts vividly with the cold decision-oriented perspective adopted by conventional consumer research. Through the frost that blurs the icy scrutiny under which we generally regard the consumer, we now search for a glimpse of the consumption experience in our vision of Koko in her cage. We seek the variegated, warmy suggestive spectacle of this massive but gentle gorilla who tenderly tickles the tummy of her tiny playful kitten. O, Koko, how you consume! O, consumer, how you have changed!

References

Abbott, Lawrence (1955), *Quality and Competition*. New York: Columbia University Press.

Alderson, Wroe (1957), *Marketing Behavior and Executive Action*. Homewood, Il.: Richard D. Irwin.

Anscombe, G.E.M. (1957), *Intention*. Ithaca, N.Y.: Cornell University Press.

Armstrong, Edward A. (1963), *A Study of Bird Song*. London: Oxford University Press.

Becker, Gary S. (1976), *The Economic Approach to Human Behavior*. Chicago: University of Chicago Press.

Belk, Russell W. (1984), "Manifesto for a Consumer Behavior of Consumer Behavior," in *Proceedings*, 1984 AMA Winter Educators' Conference, Paul F. Anderson and Michael J. Ryan, eds. Chicago: American Marketing Association, 163–167.

Bristor, Julia (1984), "Organizing Consumer Behavior: A Paradigmatic Perspective," in *Proceedings*, 1984 AMA Winter Educators' Conference, Paul F. Anderson and Michael J. Ryan, eds. Chicago: American Marketing Association, 173–176.

Brody, Jane E. (1985), "Strategies for Coping with a Pet's Death, Which Can Be as Painful as That of a Friend," *New York Times* (October 16): C8.

Cacioppo, John T., Mary E. Losch, Louis G. Tassinary, and Richard E. Petty (1986),

"Properties of Affect and Affect-Laden Information Processing," in *The Role of Affect in Consumer Behavior: Emerging Theories and Applications*, Robert A. Peterson, Wayne D. Hoyer, and William R. Wilson, eds. Lexington, Mass.: Lexington Books.

Coward, Rosalind, and John Ellis (1977), *Language and Materialism: Developments in Semiology and the Theory of the Subject*. Boston: Routledge & Kegan Paul.

Csikszentmihalyi, Mihaly, and Eugene Rochberg-Halton (1981), *The Meaning of Things: Domestic Symbols and the Self*. Cambridge, England: Cambridge University Press.

Davis, Lawrence H. (1979), *Theory of Action*. Englewood Cliffs, N.J.: Prentice-Hall.

Denzin, Norman K. (1984), *On Understanding Emotion*. San Francisco: Jossey-Bass.

Eco, Umberto (1976), *A Theory of Semiotics*. Bloomington: Indiana University Press.

Fennell, Geraldine (1985), "Things of Heaven and Earth: Phenomenology, Marketing, and Consumer Research," in *Advances in Consumer Research*, vol. 12, Elizabeth C. Hirschman and Morris B. Holbrook, eds. Provo, Utah: Association for Consumer Research, 544–49.

Fishbein, Martin and Icek Ajzen (1975), *Belief, Attitude, Intention and Behavior*. Reading, Mass.: Addison-Wesley.

Geist, William E. (1985), "The Selling of the Comet, 1985," *New York Times* (October 16): B3.

Giorgi, Amedeo (1970), *Psychology as a Human Science: A Phenomenologically Based Approach*. New York: Harper & Row.

Goldman, Alvin I. (1970), *A Theory of Human Action*. Princeton, N.J.: Princeton University Press.

Goodall, Jane (1971), *In the Shadow of Man*. Boston: Houghton Mifflin.

Granzin, Kent L. (1984), "Consumer Logistics: A Characterization of the Field by Means of General Living Systems Theory," in *Proceedings*, 1984 Winter Educators' Conference, Paul F. Anderson and Michael J. Ryan, eds. Chicago: American Marketing Association, 168–172.

Hackett, George (1985), "Newsmakers," *Newsweek* (January 21): 48.

Haitch, Richard (1985), "Burying Pets," *New York Times* (October 13): B1.

Hampshire, Stuart (1982), *Thought and Action*. Notre Dame, Ind.: University of Notre Dame Press.

Harman, Gilbert (1973), *Thought*. Princeton, N.J.: Princeton University Press.

Hickrod, Lucy Jen Huang, and Raymond L. Schmitt (1982), "A Naturalistic Study of Interaction and Frame: The Pet as 'Family Member'," *Urban Life* 11 (April): 55–77.

Highwater, Jamake (1981), *The Primal Mind*. New York: Harper & Row.

Hirschman, Elizabeth C. (1985), "Scientific Style and the Conduct of Consumer Research," *Journal of Consumer Research* 12 (September): 225–39.

Hirschman, Elizabeth C., and Morris B. Holbrook (1986), "Expanding the Ontology and Methodology of Research on the Consumption Experience," in *Perspectives on Methodology in Consumer Research*, David Brinberg and Richard Lutz, eds. New York: Springer-Verlag, 213–251.

Holbrook, Morris B. (1984a), "Belk, Granzin, Bristor, and the Three Bears," in *Proceedings*, 1984 AMA Winter Educators' Conference, Paul F. Anderson and Michael J. Ryan, eds. Chicago: American Marketing Association, 177–78.

———, (1984b), "Theory Development Is a Jazz Solo: Bird Lives," in *Proceedings, 1984 AMA Winter Educators' Conference*, Paul F. Anderson and Michael J. Ryan, eds. Chicago: American Marketing Association, 48–52.

———, (1985a), "Axiology in Consumer Research: The Nature of Value in the Consumption Experience," working paper. New York: Graduate School of Business, Columbia University.

———, (1985b), "The Consumer Researcher Visits Radio City: Dancing in the Dark," in *Advances in Consumer Research*, vol. 12, Elizabeth C. Hirschman and Morris B. Holbrook, eds. Provo, Utah: Association for Consumer Research, 28–31.

———, (1985c), "Why Business Is Bad for Consumer Research: The Three Bears Revisited," in *Advances in Consumer Research*, vol. 12, Elizabeth C. Hirschman and Morris B. Holbrook, eds. Provo, Utah: Association for Consumer Research, 145–56.

———, (1986a), "Consumer Misbehavior: The Nature of Irregular, Irrational, Illegal, and Immoral Consumption," working paper. New York: Columbia University.

———, (1986b), "Emotion in the Consumption Experience: Toward a New Model of the Human Consumer," in *The Role of Affect in Consumer Behavior: Emerging Theories and Applications*, Robert A. Peterson, Wayne D. Hoyer, and William R. Wilson, eds. Lexington, Mass.: Lexington Books.

———, (1986c), "Greatness in Consumption," working paper. New York: Columbia University.

———, (1986d), "I'm Hip: An Autobiographical Account of Some Musical Consumption Experiences," in *Advances in Consumer Research*, vol. 13, Richard J. Lutz, ed. Provo, Utah: Association for Consumer Research, 614–18.

———, (1986e), "Whither ACR?" *Advances in Consumer Research*, vol. 13, Richard J. Lutz, ed. Provo, Utah: Association for Consumer Research, 145–56.

Holbrook, Morris B., Robert W. Chestnut, Terence A. Oliva, and Eric A. Greenleaf (1984), "Play as a Consumption Experience: The Roles of Emotions, Performance and Personality in the Enjoyment of Games," *Journal of Consumer Research* 11 (September): 728–39.

Holbrook, Morris B., and Elizabeth C. Hirschman (1982), "The Experiential Aspects of Consumption: Consumer Fantasies, Feelings, and Fun," *Journal of Consumer Research* 9 (September): 132–40.

Holbrook, Morris B., and Donald R. Lehmann (1981), "Allocating Discretionary Time: Complementarity among Activities," *Journal of Consumer Research* 7 (March): 395–406.

Holbrook, Morris B., Donald R. Lehmann, and John O'Shaughnessy (1986), "Using versus Choosing: The Relationship of the Consumption Experience to Reasons for Purchasing," *European Journal of Marketing* 20 (8): 49–62.

Holbrook, Morris B., and John O'Shaughnessy (1984), "The Role of Emotion in Advertising," *Psychology & Marketing* 1(2): 45–64.

Holbrook, Morris B., and Robert B. Zirlin (1985), "Artistic Creation, Artworks, and Esthetic Appreciation: Some Philosophical Contributions to Nonprofit Marketing," in *Advances in Nonprofit Marketing*, vol. 1, Russell W. Belk, ed. Greenwich, Conn.: JAI Press, 1–54.

Horn, Jack C., and Jeff Meer (1984), "The Pleasure of Their Company," *Psychology Today* 18 (August): 52–58.

Hunter, James (1983), "Truth and Effectiveness in Revelatory Stories," *ReVision* 6 (Fall): 3–15.

Jacoby, Jacob (1978), "Consumer Research: A State of the Art Review," *Journal of Marketing* 42 (April): 87–96.

Jones, Roger S. (1982), *Physics as Metaphor*. New York: New American Library.

King, Stephen, and Peter Straub (1984), *The Talisman*. New York: Viking.

Koestler, Arthur (1964), *The Act of Creation*. New York: Dell.

Køhler, Wolfgang (1925), *The Mentality of Apes*. New York: Harcourt, Brace.

Lakoff, George, and Mark Johnson (1980), *Metaphors We Live By*. Chicago: University of Chicago Press.

Lefferts, Nicholas E. (1985), "What's New in the Pet Business," *New York Times* (July 28): F15.

Lewin, Kurt (1936), *Principles of Topological Psychology*, translated by Fritz Heider and Grace M. Heider. New York: McGraw-Hill.

———, (1951), *Field Theory in Social Science: Selected Theoretical Papers*, Dorwin Cartwright, ed. Chicago: University of Chicago Press.

Meer, Jeff (1984), "Pet Theories," *Psychology Today*, 18 (August): 60–67.

Mitchell, Arnold (1983), *The Nine American Lifestyles*. New York: Warner.

Mitroff, Ian I., and Ralph H. Kilmann (1978), *Methodological Approaches to Social Science*. San Francisco: Jossey-Bass.

Moore, William L., and Morris B. Holbrook (1982), "On the Predictive Validity of Joint-Space Models in Consumer Evaluations of New Concepts," *Journal of Consumer Research* 9 (September): 206–10.

Norris, Ruby Turner (1941), *The Theory of Consumer's Demand*. New Haven: Yale University Press.

Parsons, Talcott (1937), *The Structure of Social Action*. New York: Free Press.

Patterson, Francine (1985), *Koko's Kitten*. New York: Scholastic.

Patterson, Francine, and Eugene Linden (1981), *The Education of Koko*. New York: Holt, Rinehart and Winston.

Ruesch, Jurgen, and Weldon Kees (1956), *Nonverbal Communication*. Berkeley: University of California Press.

Ryle, Gilbert (1949), *The Concept of Mind*. New York: Barnes & Noble.

Sebeok, Thomas A. (1981), *The Play of Musement*. Bloomington: Indiana University Press.

Sebeok, Thomas A., and Jean Umiker-Sebeok (1981), "Smart Simians: The Self-Fulfilling Prophecy and Kindred Methodological Pitfalls," in *The Play of Musement*, Thomas A. Sebeok, ed. Bloomington: Indiana University Press, 134–209.

Sheth, Jagdish N. (1985), "Presidential Address: Broadening the Horizon of ACR and Consumer Behavior," in *Advances in Consumer Research*, vol. 12, Elizabeth C. Hirschman and Morris B. Holbrook, eds. Provo, Utah: Association for Consumer Research, 1–2.

Silverman, Kaja (1983), *The Subject of Semiotics*. New York: Oxford University Press.

Terrace, H.S. (1985), "In the Beginning Was the 'Name'," working paper. New York: Columbia University.

Tucker, W.T. (1967), *Foundations For a Theory of Consumer Behavior*. New York: Holt, Rinehart and Winston.

Vessels, Jane (1985), "Koko's Kitten," *National Geographic* 167 (January): 110–13.

10

Cultural Propriety in a Global Marketplace

John F. Sherry, Jr.

As an exercise in cultural criticism, the biases of this chapter should be quite evident. The chapter springs from an anthropological interest in marketing and consumer behavior, but pretends to be neither social scientific nor managerial in its perspective. Historian Jean-Christophe Agnew (1984) has proclaimed that to demand a "thick" description of the symbolic world of goods "is to open vistas of interpretation that are almost vertiginous in their potential complexity" and to "threaten the classic linear movement of historical narrative" (p. 69). Following Ulin's (1984) hermeneutically inspired insight, I have drawn my comments from the encounter between consumer and analyst that represents a commonly neglected, culturally communicative frame in its own right. The multivocal richness of "consumption" and "culture" is explored in this chapter, while marketing is examined as an intervention strategy promoting a particular idea system.

Marketing: A Culture-Critical View

Keegan and MacMaster (1983) advise us that there are three major paradigms for approaching world markets: assumptions about the nature of world markets, orientations toward international business, and planning and execution of designs. It seems to me that these first two models are often implicit and infrequently examined in any truly reflective way. The third paradigm is more readily discernible in practice, and provides us with the data from which the first two models of an individual, a company, or a country can be inferred. It is from my experience of this third model, as a consumer, a marketing analyst, and a social scientist, that my remarks about the first two paradigms derive.

Elsewhere (Sherry 1987a), I have described marketing as perhaps the most potent force of cultural stability and cultural change at work in the contemporary world. This potency stems from the same dynamic tension that animates the old saw deciphering the Chinese ideogram for "crisis" into its components of "opportunity" and "danger." Without forcing the metaphor, a critical correspondence between "marketing" and "crisis" can be discerned at the level of culture. Marketing has alternately been praised for averting and damned for creating many of the crises plaguing humanity. Marketing strategies that are bold and successful are often charted along the fine line between opportunity and danger. It is this fine line to which we must turn in any discussion of cultural propriety. Without scratching too deeply beneath the multivocal surface of his profound observation, we can resonate with Gerard Manley Hopkins' insight:

Generations have trod, have trod, have trod;
And all is seared with trade; bleared, smeared with toil;
And wears man's smudge and shares man's smell: the soil
Is bare now, nor can foot feel, being shod.

Whether or not we will witness the same hopeful outcome of such searing that Hopkins affirms:

And for all this, nature is never spent

depends upon our ability to harness the forces of hyperindustrial society to humane ends. The cultural consequences of and marketing responses to this searing are explored in this chapter.

Levy (1976) has written eloquently of the "fallacy of composition"—a phenomenon he has detailed as the synechdochic mechanism—by which marketing has become stigmatized. The nature of the degradation has its roots in antiquity and is intimately bound up with the ambiguity of the enterprise (the opportunity/danger complex, if you will) as reflected in Levy's foray into etymology: neutral or positive root ideas such as *mercari, mereri,* and *merere* are used to form words such as mercenary and meretricious. In her ideological defense of commerce, Vlahos (1985) treats us to historical and cross-cultural descriptions of the ways in which merchants are villified even as they are valued. She cites the Reformation as a sort of watershed, wherein businessmen could "come into their own," which they seem to have done by skillfully manipulating their ambivalent status. In his discussion of trade diasporas, Curtin (1984) views commerce as among the most important stimuli to cultural change, and merchants as privileged strangers, the point men of intercultural communication. In pressing for opportunity, merchants are at once dangerous and endangered.

In fascinating cognate studies, Brown (1947) and Agnew (1979) have explored the ways in which language, as a map of culture, can enhance our understanding of marketing behavior. Etymologically, the ancient marketplace is a *limen* or threshold. It was situated in the ambiguously neutral periphery between settlements and hedged about by ritual safeguards; the site could alternate between marketplace and battlefield (Agnew 1979). The market site was demarcated as sacred ground by boundary stones and was presided over by the god Hermes. The god of the boundary stone became the god of trade, as merchants became professional boundary crossers. Over time, Hermes became a trickster, a thief, and a herald, each a marginal identity under whose aegis the class marginal to society at large—merchants—plied its trade. For Brown (1947), Hermes symbolizes the new commercial culture and the ethic of acquisitive individualism. From the twelfth century, when the term *market* first entered the English language, to the late eighteenth century, we witnessed the gradual separation of the generality of the market process from the particularity of the market *place* "which accompanied the historical change in productive and distributive relations: the historical appearance of exchange-value as a perceived or half-perceived social form distinct from and alien to the natural form of the human artifact" (Agnew 1979, p. 109). In encouraging us to read beyond Marx's "mystifying language of commodities," Agnew draws our attention back to the "problematic threshold of exchange": the material and social geography of the market culture (p. 116).

The moral landscape of this geography is difficult to tend. As Macfarlane (1985) observes, the root of all evil in a Biblical sense is also the root of all good in Adam Smith's sense: the market principle. Market capitalism, in eliminating absolute moralities, ushered in a "world of moral confusion" in which "private vice, passions and interests have merged into public goods" (Macfarlane, pp. 73–74). Contemporary marketers have inherited this problematic geography, and have aggravated the paradox by uncritically exporting a culture they have in large part shaped. This culture of consumption may be inimical to the lifeways of its prospective consumers, an antagonist rather than a synergist to humane development. Both Douglas (1966) and Turner (1967) have alerted us to the social power with which boundaries are invested, and to the peril and promise inherent in crossing these boundaries. The greatest challenge currently facing marketers—the globalization crisis—is to transform the danger posed by consumption to the world's cultures into opportunity for cultural pluralism to thrive.

The Culture of Consumption

Through the confluence of a number of ecological, social structural, and ideological factors over the past five hundred years, contemporary Euro-American societies find themselves inhabiting and further elaborating a culture of consumption. This culture is characterized by a high-intensity market mechanism (Leiss 1976) and an insupportably high level of energy consumption (Bodley 1985). Within this culture, individuals are encouraged to interpret their needs exclusively as needs for commodities, which fosters the dynamic between expanding gratification and frustration that infuses everyday life with meaning (Leiss). Consumer culture has been characterized as an ethic, a standard of living, and a power structure, each of which encourages individuals to equate commodities with personal welfare and, ultimately, to conceive of themselves as commodities (Fox and Lears 1983). Consumerism, viewed here as a social pathology which has become the dominant worldview, is an improvised alternative to other traditional cultural forms that imparted aesthetic and moral meaning to everyday life (Bellah et al. 1985). The social construction of scarcity produces some profound dilemmas for individuals and societies guided by an ideology of insatiable want and unlimited growth (Leiss). The modern social idiom (Fox and Lears) is corporate and therapeutic: social control is achieved by an elite able to subordinate notions of "transcendence" to those of personal fulfillment and immediate gratification.

The idea systems of which culture is composed contain ideologies structuring our perceptions of the system as grounded in the essence of the universe, so that our cultural perceptions become natural perceptions (Wolf 1982). In our Euro-American business-cultural tradition, the shift from merely using goods as markers to create intelligibility and make stable the categories of culture (Douglas and Isherwood 1979), to the shaping of epistemology and praxis by commodity fetishism (Taussig 1980) has occurred virtually outside of our conscious awareness (Dholakia and Sherry 1987). Thus, we view as "natural" (and, therefore, beyond enlightened reflection) the creation and expansion of a system based upon ideologically and technologically ethnocentric factors. Further, "consumption" is viewed as therapeutic, curative, and, therefore, universally desirable. Traditional, positivist, "progress"-centered idea systems of the type espoused by Levitt (1983) become global "meta-products" of this culture. The consumption ethic driving this culture (indeed, overconsumption may be both the defining feature of and ultimate threat to the culture) accelerates the evolution of high-energy societies whose industrial adaptation is ecologically unstable at the expense of low-energy societies whose preindustrial adaptations have proven stable for half a million years (Bodley 1982, 1985). As Wolf (1982) has shown in his meticulous examination of world system dynamics, trade has rendered obsolete all conceptions of culture save that as process, while rendering all cultural boundaries permeable. Clearly, it is critical that we examine the processing we accept as natural for its impact upon ourselves and others.

Consumption has become a "hegemonic way of seeing" in Euro-American culture (Fox and Lears 1983, p. x). Consumption has become a form of social control cross-cutting culture, politics, personal and social identity, and the economy (Ulin 1984). Enlightened self-interest suggests that we must "free the processes for satisfaction of needs from their tendency to become exclusively oriented to the blandishments of the marketplace" (Leiss 1976, p. 126). Divesting ourselves of "theological attitudes" toward market mechanisms (Toffler 1983) is an apostasy not easily launched; proselytizing in its service is fraught with danger. Expressing his concern that a diverse environment is essential to human life, Dubos (1968) laments that "the creeping monotony of overorganized and overtechnicized life, of standardized patterns, will make it progressively more difficult to explore fully the biological richness of our species, and may handicap the further development of civilization" (p. 93). Berry's (1977) study of U.S. agriculture is only one timely validation of this concern.

The Consumption of Culture

Within the context of the culture of consumption, a trend of considerable significance may be discerned. This trend has been labeled the consumption of culture, and it appears to have two distinct dimensions which turn upon the multivocal richness of its major terms. The first dimension concerns "culture" and its complex penumbra of meanings (Worsley 1984). The manner in which culture has been transformed into a commodity, or experience into a product, is worthy of discussion. The second dimension concerns "consumption" as it is used to connote alternately a using (or a using up) of a product and a progressive wasting (in the sense of pathology or morbidity). Culture consuming warrants close consideration.

Culture as Product

Since the time that C.P. Snow (1959) recognized and lamented the gulf between the two cultures of science and the humanities, we have witnessed a disheart-eningly rapid balkanization of experience. Cultures and subcultures of every style and hue have proliferated despite the attempts of individuals to unify and aggregate traditions. Worsley (1984) remarks that all historic usages of the term *culture* constitute a "family of overlapping meanings which direct our attention to society as a whole and insist that it cannot be reduced to the economic or the political." For Worsley, culture is the realm of "those crucial institutions in which the ideas we live by are produced and through which they are communicated" (p. 59). Worsley has proposed four ideal type conceptions of culture which serve nicely the purposes of the present chapter. *Holistic* culture is the whole way of life of a people. *Elitist* culture is a superior set of values reserved for the few. *Hegemonic* culture is a set of behaviors imposed upon a majority by those who rule. *Pluralist* culture is a relativist construction encompassing distinctive behavior codes and value systems in communities within the same society. Each of these cultures is touched by the phenomenon of consumption.

Defamiliarization and decomposition plague holistic culture as the commodity form moves outside of its "traditionally designated enclaves" to become a complex material symbolic entity (Agnew 1984). In Agnew's phrase, commodified cultural symbols become infinitely polyvalent as the "fluid medium of the mass market dislodges the meanings we have always expressed through and attached to our artifacts" (p. 71). Advertising then must recontextualize and refamiliarize these attribute bundles in the commodity environment (Agnew 1984). This transmogrifying process has been referred to as "cultural commoditization" (Greenwood 1977) and "commodification" (Westbrook 1984); it is particularly apparent in the tourist industry. Its analog in the service sector has been called the commercialization of feeling (Hochschild 1983) or "emotion work." In his indictment of the promotion of "local color" as a part of tourist merchandising, Greenwood (1977) argues persuasively that local culture may be expropriated, and its bearers exploited, when activities are altered and evacuated of traditional meaning in the service of marketing. The destructive conversion of authentic, efficacious cultural forms into "local color" over which tourists have rights occurs worldwide, from Haight-Ashbury to Harajuku, from Baffin to Bali.

Cultural commodification abounds in advertising, where we may view Papuan chief Wopkaimin sport a Pentel pen in place of a nosebone, learn how one anthropologist's encounter with Central American natives resulted in Dr. Juice One Drop Fish Scent, or hear a black minstrel extol the virtues of Darkie Toothpaste. When market research revealed that Aussie-persona Paul Hogan would prove too popular with the Japanese, plans to launch a campaign to lure Japanese tourists to Australia were scrapped until the local infrastructure could be strengthened (*Advertising Age* 1985a). German-language posters advertising comic books by Walt Disney Productions, Inc., mistakenly placed in the town of Neuchatel, Switzerland, were defaced by the local French-speaking populace, whose city council in turn issued a formal protest to the offending agency (*Advertising Age* 1985b). Such anecdotes are legion.

Elitist culture has been a benefactor of the consumption ideology despite the perennial (and spurious) conflict between so-called high culture and popular culture (Gans 1974). Increasingly, individuals are devoting themselves to the consumption of experience, variously construed, in implicit affirmation of the bread-and-circus paradigm. It has been argued (Kelly 1984) that the phenomenon of conspicuous consumption has been displaced or rerouted from the orbit of goods to that of experience. Increasingly, status may accrue to those who "do" rather than to those who "have"; incorporeal property will become an even more significant marker. Products designed to capture or reify incorporeal property—photographic and video equipment, for example—might be expected to boom. The consumption of symbols in the form of arts (through galleries, theaters, symphony halls, etc.), sciences (through museums, institutes, seminars, etc.), nature (through park services, conservatories, expeditions, etc.) or human potential (through encounter groups of various incarnations), and the conversion of experience to commodity may be expected to accelerate. The *Chicago Tribune* runs a weekly "Culture" column featuring an art marketplace. Salvador Dali made his advertising debut in Spain in June 1985 with an outdoor board campaign promoting Spanish arts and an interview in which he claimed that the only truly outstanding admen in history were Jesus Christ and himself (Specht 1985).

Cultural Imperialism and Pluralism

Examining elitist culture in relativist perspective, we might best see it as one pole of a continuum of "expressive culture" bounded on the other end by "folk culture." In this perspective, specific experiences analogous to the ones cited for elitist culture may be discerned at every point along the continuum; while these experiences may be status-linked, we can divest them of any supposed intrinsic superiority or inferiority. Thus, so-called popular cultural phenomena—cinema, spectacle, sport, and any other medium of symbolic expression for mass consumption—qualify as examples of cultural consumption. The middle-aged exjock who pays to attend a baseball camp directed by his current and boyhood sports idols consumes experience at a level comparable to the season ticket holder enraptured by the New York Philharmonic Orchestra.

A discussion of hegemonic culture moves us into some of the darker dimensions of the ideology of consumption. Hegemony can be built into "the very mutual expectations and practices of material activity through which people produce and reproduce social life" (Ulin 1984, p. 165), as may be obvious from the conception of culture taken from Wolf (1982). The high-energy, high–market-intensity culture of consumption appears to institutionalize processes of cultural imperialism, homogenization, and degradation. We see increasing diffusion of products, life styles, values, and modes of production and consumption designed for and perfected in Western industrialized nations to societies where the social utility of these items is questionable (Kothari 1984; Kumar 1980). Whether "progress," "development," or "nation-building" are invoked as catalysts to this diffusion, the results are often unanticipated and harmful.

Cultural imperialism—or structural imperialism in Galtung's (1971) more precise phrase—is the label used by critics to describe the shaping of one culture to suit the ends of another. The consumption ideology is one form of cultural imperialism. The diffusion of American TV shows which allegedly glorify greed and immorality by local standards—"Dallas" or "Dynasty," for example—to Third World nations is one manifestation (Cote 1984). The South Korean government's protest of direct broadcasting signal spillover from Japan is another (*Advertising Age* 1984). Cultural homogenization appears crucial for the continued growth of the world capitalist system (Dagnino 1980), and cultural autonomy of communities is at odds with nation-building attempts where diversity is equated with disunity. The net impact is cultural degradation in the forms of desertification, deforestation, forced migration, and urbanization in the service of development as conceived by elites (Kothari 1984). The subversion of entire cultures, such as the Miskito of Nicaragua, through engagement with hegemonic cultures, is a tragically common occurrence (Bodley 1982). The transformation of our own in the face of contemporary business practices—the "malling" and "chaining" of America (Kowinski 1985; Luxenberg 1985)—is receiving renewed attention.

The effect of the consumption ideology on pluralist culture is difficult to gauge. It is tempting to discern a resurgence of individuation, of a form midway between reactance and revitalization, among cultures through which consumption ideology has diffused. Octavio Paz (1985) asks whether we are witnessing "the historical vengeance of particularisms" in the unrest of former colonies. Creative integration of Western products into local consumption use-systems indicates the ability of cultures to adapt and reframe their meaning-systems, permitting a kind of syncretism between "modern" and "traditional" to flourish. The rich cultural mix of nations such as Israel force alterations in the way the consumption ideology may be implemented (Brooks 1985). Domestic market fragmentation in the United States may shape and reflect the formation of subcultures seeking forms of satisfaction currently unavailable in the culture of consumption. The sheer bringing together of peoples of different traditions through such mass migrations as tourism or industrial relocation—themselves a function of consumption ideology—encourages pluralism.

The Future of Hyperindustrial Society

Polar perspectives of the future of culture are represented by the ethics of unfettered capitalism and entropy (Harris 1981). The former would fuel the ideology of consumption, the latter would attempt to smother it. Proponents of each viewpoint predict global disaster if their opponents' philosophy carries the day. Between utopian and dystopian visions is a projected practopia (Toffler 1980, 1983) to be achieved by some fusion of paramodern and paraprimitive solutions. How might such a practopia be realized?

We live less in a postindustrial society than in what Harris has termed a "hyperindustrial" society. In this society, the processes and dimensions undergirding industrial capitalism are intensified, accelerated, and translated into the service/information sector. The nascent self-care movement in which Toffler (1980) embeds the prosumer (i.e. the actively producing consumer) of his projected third and postindustrial wave, and which will alter the role of the market in social life, is perhaps an incipient revolt against the consumption ethic. However, the sociopolitical and technological support required to launch prosumption as a popular ethic and achieve the conversion from consumer to prosumer society will have to be massive; that the invisible hand will require considerable help is an understatement (Toffler 1983). The conversion will require the voluntary abdication of the ruling consumer elite, and the restructuring of all of the institutions of thought control in the culture of consumption. A more likely scenario is a gradual shift from a holistic consumer culture to a pluralist culture in which prosuming enclaves may be able to find a niche. Such small enclaves would resemble the societies of ethnographic record which epitomize Toffler's first (preindustrial) wave. Whether these enclaves will become millenarian movements or models of mazeway reconstruction is impossible to forecast. Whether or not the United States is returning to the values the prosumer never left remains to be seen. If republican democracy poses a threat to the culture of consumption (Westbrook 1984), how much more strongly will a first wave reaction be resisted?

In their "guided tour through the badlands of modern culture," Montagu and Madsen (1983, p. 215) have asserted that our fate hangs by the thread of moral recognition. They call for a countercultural remaking of society, claiming that sapience is insufficient to meet the challenge: the marriage of thought and feeling is required to break through to a new and higher consciousness recovering "the lost world of fellow feelings" (p. 220). This recovery implies a recognition and rejection of commodity fetishism plus a redefinition of consumer behavior. It is time for consumer researchers to explore the shapes that Toffler's projected transmarket civilization might take and for marketing practitioners to envision ways of implementing the fruits of that research.

Seeking Synergy through Syncretism: The Key to Cultural Propriety

Returning to our original notion of merchants as boundary crossers, it is apparent that marketers have much to contribute to the remaking of society. While they may make no pretensions of being social architects or engineers, they do deal in the very stuff of culture change: diffusion of innovation. Further, while people can be encouraged to borrow indiscriminantly, they are more likely to benefit from borrowing that which will mesh with their own cultural patterns. Arensberg and Niehoff (1964) have documented the reworking and reinterpreting of newly borrowed ideas, techniques, and products that enable them to be integrated into local cultural patterns. In their discussion of the rush to globalization—a trend apparently resolving a bit more rationally to regionalization (Sherry 1987b)—Dholakia and Sherry (1987) have advocated a more humane, decentralized approach to marketing intervention which is less reactive in responding to unanticipated consequences and more proactive in assessing holistically the potential impact of such intervention upon society. Marketers, as privileged strangers, are historically disposed toward local needs assessment and technology transfer (if we consider resources "tools"). Thus, if marketers can relearn literally and figuratively to step outside of the culture of consumption and identify culturally specific, culturally relevant needs, they will be better able to identify, develop, and promote solutions to these needs which are culturally appropriate. Resources that embody such solutions can be considered preadaptations in that they contain traits that can enable them to exploit new or changing environments and on which new adaptations can be built. This hidden advantage of advance preparation—structural, functional, or symbolic properties of a resource that suit it to more than one consumption-use system—is more likely to be discerned if the marketer recognizes that the flow of synergy is multidirectional and that syncretism is the key to synergy.

Syncretism is the grafting of a newly introduced cultural element to a currently recognized cultural element. This element may be as complex as an idea system or as straightforward as technology; in most marketing instances, these elements are fused. The elements to be united may be complementary or conflictual. While syncretism is often a long and serendipitous process and often as well a defensive local reaction to hegemonic culture which results in cryptobehavior and pseudoconformity, it can be a carefully planned and managed enterprise as well. Such care can only be exercised if the marketer has a thorough understanding of local principles of categorization and evaluation as they relate to the consumption-use system. Authentic synergy will result only when it is recognized that consumption innovations can also flow from South to North, from low-energy to high-energy cultures, from third world to first world, and from one product category, organizational structure, or research discipline to any other.

Marketing is more than a preeminent medium of intercultural communication. It is a program of directed intervention which must engage and overcome barriers at the cultural, social, psychological, and physical levels to provide a resource that is compatible with—in that it may complete or transform—a local consumption-use system. Too often, this directed intervention has been short-term and concerned primarily with purchase or repurchase behavior. It needs to become a longer-term proposition concerned more with social impact assessment, forecasting, and authentic synergy. The marketing concept we espouse domestically, which all too often assumes a production orientation internationally, must be transmitted to an ecological perspective with a global provenance.

Marketing, as popularly conceived and practiced, may well need to be demarketed. At the very least, its technology of influence must be channeled to the service of cultural pluralism. Berman has observed that industrial society—

capitalist and socialist—officially strives for homogeneity in thought and behavior. Hyperindustrial society has accelerated this monomania:

> Systems that are reduced in complexity lose options, become unstable and vulnerable. Flexibility in personality types and world views provides, instead, possibilities for change, evolution, and real survival. Imperialism, whether economic, psychological or personal (they tend to go together) seeks to wipe out native cultures, individual ways of life, and diverse ideas—eradicating them in order to substitute a global and homogeneous way of life. It sees variation as a threat. A holistic civilization, by contrast, would cherish variation, see it as a gift, a form of wealth or property. (Berman 1984, 264–65).

Social marketing, the bastard offspring of our dominant idea-system, must be legitimated as a first step in achieving cultural propriety and as a foundation upon which we can construct a more satisfying life.

Cultural propriety is the marketing of resources appropriate to the needs of a local culture. It is segmentation written large and cast in an ethical idiom. It is motivated by an intimate, locally rooted understanding of lifeways and a profound respect for the integrity of traditional social structures. The guiding rule of such a marketing strategy, as in any ethically invasive procedure, is *primum non nocere*: first do no harm. In the rush to globalization, the preservation of local culture has been considered primarily as an opportunity cost. If cultural integrity is epiphenomenal to business practice, splendid; if not, social disorganization is frequently the cost of progress. Clearly, this view must be drastically tempered. The preservation of boundaries, with its promise of continued diversity and a perpetual role for marketers, may be the most evolutionary significant contribution that marketing can make to cultural ecology.

The analogy with which I began this chapter has now come full circle. Cultural hegemony is the "danger" of our idea-system; cultural pluralism is the "opportunity." The vehicle I have advocated for mediating these dimensions of "crisis" is cultural propriety. Through carefully managed syncretism, the synergy required for a humane cultural evolution can be generated. Whether marketers can be persuaded to adopt this perspective remains to be seen.

References

Advertising Age (1984), "South Korea Protests DBS Japan Signal" (February 20, 1984): 42.

———, (1985a), "Australian Spots Too Good to Export" (June 17, 1984): 48.

———, (1985b), "International Briefs" (August 19, 1985).

Agnew, Jean-Christophe (1979), "The Threshold of Exchange," *Radical History Review* 21 (Fall): 99–118.

———, (1984), "The Consuming Vision of Henry James," in *The Culture of Consumption: Critical Essays in American History: 1880–1980*, R. Fox and T. Lears, eds. New York: Pantheon, 65–100.

Arensberg, Conrad, and Arthur Niehoff (1964), *Introducing Social Change*. Chicago: Aldine.

Bellah, Robert, Richard Madsen, William Sullivan, Ann Swidler, and Steven Tipton (1985), *Habits of the Heart: Individualism and Commitment in American Life*. Berkeley: University of California Press.

Berman, Morris (1984), *The Reenchantment of the World*. New York: Bantam.

Berry, Wendell (1977), *The Unsettling of America: Culture and Agriculture*. New York: Avon.

Bodley, John (1982), *Victims of Progress*. Palo Alto, Calif.: Mayfield.

———, (1985), *Anthropology and Contemporary Human Problems*. Palo Alto,Calif.: Mayfield.

Brown, Norman (1947), *Hermes the Thief: The Evolution of a Myth*. Madison: University of Wisconsin Press.

Brooks, Andree (1985), "Cultural Mix Sparking Israeli Ad Dilemma," *Advertising Age*, (May 27): 48–49.

Cote, Kevin (1984), "Hollywood Glitter May Hurt Global Marketers," *Advertising Age* (September 17, 1984): 48.

Curtin, Philip (1984), *Cross Cultural Trade in World History*. New York: Cambridge University Press.

Dagnino, Evelina (1980), "Cultural and Ideological Dependence: Building a Theoretical Framework," in *Transnational Enterprises: Their Impact on Third World Societies and Cultures*, K. Kumar, ed., Boulder, Col.: Westview, 297–322.

Dholakia, Nikhilesh, and John F. Sherry, Jr. (1987), "Marketing and Development: A Resynthesis of Knowledge," in *Research in Marketing*, vol. 9, J.N. Sheth, ed., Greenwich, Conn.: JAI Press, forthcoming.

Douglas, Mary (1966), *Purity and Danger*. London: Routledge & Kegan Paul.

———, and Baron Isherwood (1979), *The World of Goods*. New York: Norton.

Dubos, Rene (1968), *So Human an Animal*. New York: Scribner's.

Fox, Richard Wightman, and T.J. Jackson Lears, eds. (1983), *The Culture of Consumption: Critical Essays in American History: 1880–1980*. New York: Patheon.

Galtung, Johan (1971), "A Structural Theory of Imperialism," *Journal of Peace Research* 8 (2): 81.

Gans, Herbert (1974), *Popular Culture and High Culture*. New York: Basic Books.

Greenwood, Davydd (1977), "Culture by the Pound: An Anthropological Perspective on Tourism as Cultural Commoditization," in *Hosts and Guests: The Anthropology of Tourism*, Valene Smith, ed. Philadelphia: University of Pennsylvania Press, 129–138.

Harris, Marvin (1981), *America Now: The Anthropology of a Changing Culture*. New York: Simon and Schuster.

Hocschild, Arlie (1983), *The Managed Heart: Commercialization of Human Feeling*. Berkeley: University of California Press.

Hopkins, Gerard (1877), "God's Grandeur," in *The Norton Anthology of Poetry*, A. Eastman, ed. New York: Norton, p. 887.

Keegan, Warren, and Norman MacMaster (1983), "Global Strategic Marketing," in

International Marketing: Managerial Issues, Research and Opportunities, V. Kirpalani, ed. Chicago: American Marketing Association, 94–105.

Kelly, Robert (1984), "Museums as Status Symbols II: Attaining a State of Having Been." Unpublished manuscript. Vancouver: University of British Columbia.

Kothari, Rajni (1984), "Peace in an Age of Transformation," in *Culture, Ideology and World Order*, R.B.J. Walker, ed. Boulder, Colo.: Westview, 323–61.

Kowinski, William (1985), *The Malling of America*. New York: Morrow.

Kumar, Krishna (1980), *Transnational Enterprises: Their Impact on Third World Societies and Cultures*. Boulder, Colo.: Westview.

Leiss, William (1976), *The Limits of Satisfaction*. Toronto: University of Toronto Press.

Levitt, Theodore (1983), "The Globalization of Markets," *Harvard Business Review* 61(3): 92–102.

Levy, Sidney (1976), "Marcology 101, or the Domain of Marketing," in *Marketing 1776–1976 and Beyond*, Kenneth Bernhandt, ed. Chicago: American Marketing Association, 577–81.

Luxenberg, Stan (1985), *Roadside Empires: How The Chains Franchised America*. New York: Viking.

Macfarlane, Alan (1985), "The Root of All Evil," in *The Anthropology of Evil*, David Parkin, ed. New York: Basil Blackwell. 57–76.

Montagu, Ashley, and Floyd Madsen (1983), *The Dehumanization of Man*. New York: McGraw-Hill.

Paz, Octavio (1985), *One Earth, Four or Five Worlds*. San Diego: Harcourt Brace Jovanovich.

Sherry, John (1987a), "Advertising as a Cultural System," in *Marketing and Semiotics: New Direction in the Study of Signs for Sale*, Jean Umiker-Sebeok and Sidney Levy, eds. Berlin: Mouton de Gruyter.

———, (1987b), "What in the World Is Going On? Some Trends in International Advertising Issues," *Journal of Global Marketing* 1 (1–2).

Snow, C.P. (1959), *The Two Cultures*. New York: Cambridge University Press.

Specht, Marina (1985), "Reclusive Salvador Dali Enters Spain's Ad World," *Advertising Age* (June 17, 1985): 47.

Taussig, Michael (1980), *The Devil and Commodity Fetishism in South America*. Chapel Hill: University of North Carolina Press.

Toffler, Alvin (1980),*The Third Wave*. New York: William Morrow.

———, (1983), *Previews and Premises*. New York: William Morrow.

Turner, Victor (1967), *The Forest of Symbols*, Ithaca: Cornell University Press.

Ulin, Robert (1984), *Understanding Cultures: Perspectives in Anthropology and Social Theory*. Austin: University of Texas Press.

Vlahos, Olivia (1985), *Doing Business: The Anthropology of Striving, Thriving, and Beating Out the Competition*. New York: Franklin Watts.

Westbrook, Robert (1984), "Politics as Consumption: Managing the Modern American Election," in *The Culture of Consumption: Critical Essays in American History: 1880–1980*, T. Fox and T.J. Lears, eds. New York: Pantheon, 143–173.

Wolf, Eric (1982), *Europe and the People without History*. Berkeley: University of California Press.

Worsley, Peter (1984), *The Three Worlds: Culture and World Development*. Chicago: University of Chicago Press.

11
Marketing as Technique: The Influence of Marketing on the Meanings of Consumption

Christine Moorman

Numerous social thinkers have worried about the influence of what Jacques Ellul has called "technique" on forms of social organization and human consciousness. Technique can be thought of as more than mere technology; instead, it is an epistemology that guides the development and use of the methods, procedures, sets of assumptions, ways of thinking, and outcomes that characterize virtually any field of modern human endeavor. Marketing professionals (both academicians and practitioners) have not tended to think of their discipline as an application of technique, in Ellul's overarching sense, yet they often find themselves caught in an ill-defined tension between the abstract repercussions of their activity and its pragmatic, results-oriented component. Many marketers, I suspect, would not consider themselves to be agents of social change, but upon analyzing marketing as technique, we discover that pragmatic results and the methods that drive them have their own unexpected and far-reaching consequences.

This chapter conceptualizes marketing practices and their outcomes as technique, thus establishing a unique framework for analyzing the broad social change aspects of marketing. This conceptualization describes technique both at the general level and at the level of selected marketing mix variables. The influence of marketing technique is then investigated in one particularly interesting and neglected way—in terms of its impact on the meanings consumers derive from their consumption experiences. Consumption meanings are traced to the assumptions preceding them, illustrating how consumers derive meaning. Following this, several changes in consumption assumptions resulting

The author would like to acknowledge and thank Russell Belk, Morris Holbrook, Linda Price, James A. Wilson, Donna J. Wood, Gerald Zaltman and the editors of this book for comments on an earlier version of this chapter.

from the application of marketing technique are explored to illustrate how consumption experiences have acquired new meaning. Finally, the framework explicitly links marketing technique to these changes as part of the total influence that technique has upon the values and assumptions underlying consumer decisions and, ultimately, the meanings ascribed to those decisions. Finally, several important questions are raised for future research.

The Character and Implications of Technique

Technique has been discussed by many social thinkers in the past century (Mumford 1956; Junger 1956). This chapter draws primarily from Ellul (1964). His thesis is that technique has always existed among human beings and that its practice and essence are the same over time. However, although all techniques are structurally similar, a change has occurred in the relation between technique and society (p. 63). Early technique was developed to relate individuals to their environment (tools, gathering techniques); technique was subordinate to people and was easily adapted because it was firmly enmeshed in the framework of life and culture. Technique, from the eighteenth century on, however, has tended to divorce people from the ecological, reticulated nature of the environment. It has become superordinate, artificial, and no longer a cultural artifact. People no longer adapt technique to their needs; instead technique causes people to adapt to *its* demands. Technique is uniform and its universal application takes no account of the extreme diversity of the operational environment. Simon identifies two ethics explaining the difference between early and later technique. He claims that later technique has "an ethic that rests on man's apartness from the rest of nature." The alternative ethic views "man as a part of nature, governed by natural law" (1977, p. 195).

Technique is results-oriented.   At the simplest level, Ellul describes technique as a method or process for achieving some predetermined objective or result. From Ellul's perspective, results are overemphasized. He explains that a preoccupation with results fixates the performer on achieving the result to the near exclusion of recognizing other benefits and problems derived from the process itself. Furthermore, a preoccupation with results tends to limit the scope of the problem. That is, how to achieve the desired results becomes the important question and not whether these results have other far-reaching implications or are "appropriate" results to be pursued.

Although Ellul points out that the purpose of technique is to achieve results, he also notes that the preoccupation with results forces a central focus on the method. Simply, if results are to be achieved, then another goal becomes making the method more efficient or effective. Thus, the preoccupation with results creates a preoccupation with finding the "one best way" to achieve them. Furthurmore, Ellul argues that the preoccupation with results and the search for the one best way reduce method to its logical dimension alone (p. 79). He cites the specialization of labor and the standardization of modern factories as the most obvious examples of this reduction. The term *logical*, as used by Ellul, is results-driven; one works backward from the desired result in order to derive the steps that will achieve it. Therefore, a logically derived method or process has little concern for anything other than achieving the result. The method is unidimensional and largely isolated from the environment in which it operates except as the two narrowly interact to achieve the designated objectives.

Technique is amoral.   As noted above, technique's concern with results in turn focuses effort upon improving the methods or means for achieving those results.[1] Ellul extends this argument by claiming that, ironically, the ends are forgotten eventually and the method itself becomes the end. Frederick W. Taylor's view of the industrial plant as a "closed organism" or an end in itself (1911, p. 133) perfectly expresses this complete separation of the goal from the mechanism. Numerous thinkers decry this separation of means from ends and seek ways to rejoin them but Ellul sees this occurrence as the natural progression of technique. Robert K. Merton notes in the introduction to Ellul's book that "in the economic sphere, technical economic analysis is substituted for the older political economy included in which was a major concern with the moral structure of economic activity; in the political sphere, doctrine becomes based on what is useful and not what is good, purposeful or the common will of the people" (p. vii). In these examples, the original ends have been subsumed by the methods originally developed to achieve them. Moreover, there emerged a shift from a concern with what is right or what ought to be to a concern with what is or what will work. Fundamentally, the separation seems to lie in the distinction between positive and normative questions. Ellul argues that the perpetuation of technique (and its attendant results-oriented and logical dimensions) divorces the normative questions from their proper sphere and focuses questions on what is and the feasibility of what is. As a result, technique tends to be amoral; it exists outside of questions of its appropriateness. Ellul argues that "the principal characteristic to technique is its refusal to tolerate moral judgements; it is absolutely independent from them and eliminates them from its domain; techique never observes the distinction between moral and immoral. It tends, on the contrary, to create a completely independent technical morality" (p. 95). This "technical morality" is instrumental in nature and is unconcerned with seeking truth, upholding values beyond its own, or answering to any other moral or ethical questions.

Technique is self-augmenting.   Ellul further argues that technique is self-augmenting—it is progressive in its development, creating whole new fields for its application and generating previously nonexistent problems that can only be solved by further development and application of technique. In other words, technique engenders itself. When one technical form appears, it makes possible and even inevitable a number of others (p. 87). To take a simple example, the production of the internal-combustion engine engendered the techniques of the automobile, submarine, and airplane. To cite a more disturbing example, an offshoot of the NASA space program was a technique for producing styrofoam. Companies soon adopted this technique for the mass production of disposable cups, plates, and coolers. However, these same objects became environmental hazards because of their nonbiodegradable construction; hence, technique spawned a potential crisis which only it can hope to answer.

Technique is universal. This characteristic has two important applications. First, technique's essential features are identical wherever it is introduced. Ellul notes that the details of technique's development may be different because of climate, population, or country, but its course is uniform in essence, operation, and effect once these variable factors have been weakened or overcome. Vogt (1948) shows that, in the area of agriculture, the most-up-to-date techniques have become universal. The techniques of mass production are also becoming increasingly homogeneous in such widely disparate cultures as China and Brazil. Second, in correspondence with the first application, the effects on the societies that technique enters are universal. Sociologists today recognize that the impact of techniques is destroying non-Western civilizations. This involves the collapse of cultural and economic forms as well as traditional psychological structures. Ellul argues this point, noting: "Technical invasion does not involve the simple addition of new values to old ones. It does not put new wine into old bottles; it does not introduce new content into old forms. The old bottles are all being broken. The old civilizations collapse on contact with the new" (p. 121). The multinational corporation of today represents a vehicle for spreading technique's universality and culture-shaping power, strewing the earth with the broken bottles of lost cultures, as nation after nation seek the benefits of industrial technique and ignore the possible social costs.

This section described the character and implications of technique. Technique was shown to be results-oriented, seeking the "one best way" to achieve those results; to reduce method to its logical dimension alone and, thus, be amoral or autonomous; and, finally, to be self-augmenting in its development and universal in its form and effects upon culture and people. The following section defines marketing as it is currently conceptualized. This discussion sets the stage for the subsequent development of a framework for analyzing the technique-oriented aspects of marketing and the influences they have on human behavior and culture.

Marketing: a Definition

Since the mid 1960s, the marketing discipline has been arguing the question: "What is marketing?" This debate has settled little, yet has expanded and enriched the view of the field both on the inside and the outside. Over the years, one obvious trend has been the use of marketing in widely differentiated domains (politics, health care, charitable organizations) with a wide range of purposes (elect a candidate, fill a hospital bed, raise nonprofit monies). Marketing, in a sense, has been broadened (Kotler and Levy 1969; Kotler and Zaltman 1972; Kotler 1972). And although the field is without unanimity on the value of this change, the extent of it, and marketer responsibility in these developments (Luck 1969; Arndt 1978), the discipline generally acknowledges this movement.

Recently, the American Marketing Association adopted a definition of marketing that shows the wide-ranging dimensions of the activity. The group agreed that marketing is "the process of planning and executing the conception, pricing, promotion, and distribution of ideas, goods, and services to create exchanges that satisfy individual and organizational objectives" (Atac 1985, p. 2).

Marketing has evolved from an era where production was the focus, to an era where sales and selling were central, to the current era where the marketing concept is the theoretical goal. The marketing concept suggests that marketers attempt to find out what the consumer wants/needs and then attempt to meet those needs and wants in the form of products and services.

Marketing is also conceptualized as consisting of the four P's (product, price, promotion, and place or distribution) as the definition above clearly illustrates. The configuration of these four components, commonly called the marketing mix, results in a successful marketing effort. Using these definitional properties of marketing, the following sections argue that there are technique-oriented aspects of marketing, in Ellul's sense, that affect individuals' consumption meanings and, thus, drive human desires to adapt to the necessities of marketing technique.

Technique-Oriented Aspects of Marketing

Before beginning this examination, it is important to make the following note. Marketing is a part of society and, thus, has been developing as a part of the historical evolution of human beings and their world. As Ellul notes, technique has infiltrated every aspect of human activity and has perpetuated its own need and use. Marketing, as such, has been a step in the progression of technique. This is not to discount marketing's role in this perpetuation. However, we must be careful not to place the responsibility for this progression solely in the hands of marketing. As Fırat notes, "the characteristics primarily attributable to marketing have developed as a result of societal necessities created by capitalist growth and developments" (which are also links in the progression of technique) (1984, p. 5). With this warning in mind, technique-oriented aspects of marketing are characterized at the general level and among select marketing mix variables.

One aspect of technique to which marketing is akin is the concern with results. Largely because marketing is an organizational effort (profit or nonprofit), this fact is self-evident. Whether it be meeting customer needs, filling sales quotas, penetrating markets, decreasing viewer miscomprehension, achieving organizational objectives, filling hospital beds, or increasing capital productivity (human or monetary), results are clearly articulated by the marketing process. One outcome of this concern with results, Ellul notes, is the tendency to fixate on results to the near exclusion of learning from the process itself. Park and Smith (1985) note this occurrence in marketing by pointing out that many managers focus on market share as the goal of their efforts to such an extent that they fail to learn from competitors' mistakes and innovative ideas. In the area of market research information, Desphande and Zaltman (1982) discovered that research performed for previous market studies goes virtually unused, when, in fact, it may be quite appropriate to the questions currently being asked. In this case, the results have driven the process to the extent that previous learning is overlooked.

The fact that marketers operate in an environment where there is overemphasis on achieving results may in fact lead them to neglect the consequences of their acts. Most important is the tendency to ignore the implications of results. Marketing practitioners have been criticized for this tendency by pursuing short-term results without considering the repercussions of such results on the environment (Sirgy, Samlı, and Meadow 1983), social organization (Reisman 1950), and values (Baier and Rescher 1969). Often the exigencies of organization life prompt behaviors that segments of broader society find unacceptable. This concern for immediate results prompted Kotler to state that "the sensitive marketer has to take responsibility for the totality of outputs created" (1980, p. 16). Such a marketer would worry about not only achieving results but also the effects of doing so. Marketing scholars are also subject to the same tendency, but with an interesting difference. In the push to publish or to meet the "scientific" criteria of the discipline (the desired results for scholars), theories and empirical research remain far from practitioner's needs. Researchers seem to have little concern for the real-world implications of their ideas. The repercussions of this divergence are practically unusable research and an increased likelihood for misunderstood or misapplied ideas.

The reduction of marketing technique to its logical dimension alone is indicated by the virtual absence of other important dimensions, (for example, social, moral, and ethical ones). This logical dimension demands that tasks be accomplished in a way that will achieve results most efficiently. As a result, marketing technique can be shown to be amoral or autonomous of social and ethical standards. The marketing definition discussed above either ignores or presumes a normative dimension in these areas. It seems to have left out the fact that marketing is a process that must be carried out within a society and, therefore, must operate within the social parameters of justice, ethics, and morality. Tawney argues otherwise, stating that "business exists to promote the ends of society, whereas hitherto society has been regarded in the world of business as existing to promote them" (1920, p. 26).

The absence of other dimensions in technique-oriented aspects of marketing has had the effect of replacing human values with exchange values (Fromm 1955). Activities, objects, and human beings themselves are experienced in a manner that emphasizes their exchange values; they are evaluated with an abstract and quantifying attitude. Exchange values tend to extract life from its human dimensions. Human values, on the other hand, rely on concrete experience of objects, activities, and individuals outside of questions of their manageability and exchange value. An exclusive focus on exchange values alienates individuals from their acts and the effects of their acts upon objects and others. Ellul would argue, and I would agree, that technique has the potential to do totally away with human values (e.g., natural rights, political rights, intrinsic human worth) even to the extent that some commonly accepted "truths" are discarded. Technique-oriented aspects of marketing have similar potential. Fromm cites a hard-hitting example of this distinction. He notes that the same people who would probably be incapable of even slapping, not to speak of killing, a helpless person could push the button of a nuclear warhead and cause the destruction of hundreds of thousands of men, women, and children because the button and the deaths have no "real" or meaningful connection to them.

Technique-oriented aspects of marketing provide for similar opportunities. Marketers' ideas of "the consumer" or "a segment" are constructed by abstracting and quantifying human beings, looking at their perceptions, desires, and values in a very mechanized and exchange-oriented fashion without considering their human dimensions (except as they relate to exchange). Marketing academicians have also perpetuated this process. By adhering to logical empiricism, researchers approach human behavior searching for empirical support for theoretical generalizations. This paradigm suggests that humans are merely instruments and science is not concerned with making value statements about their welfare or betterment (Arndt 1985, p. 13). McGuire (1973) supports this assault, stating that scientists contemplate data, not life.

Increasing commercialization provides another example of technique's propensity for displacing—even consuming—human values.[2] Product and brand proliferation is only one tangible aspect of this phenomenon; commercialization is, in addition, a way of thinking. Consistent with exchange values, modern commercialization promotes the idea that everything—love, sex, friendship, beauty, approval, status, respect—can be bought and sold in almost any situation. As one aspect of marketing technique, this expanded notion of commercialization promotes life's intangible essences in bottles, tubes, and cans. We try to buy the satisfactions of life that formerly were earned or given freely.

Related to increased commercialization is the perpetuation of the use of material resources for nonmaterial needs. This activity is called compensation. In this case, the individual substitutes an artificial need for the real need (artificial needs may be created and stimulated by means of marketing activities) (Grønmo 1984). For example, a young woman views herself as a social misfit and feels a need to make friends. This real need is overlaid with an artificial need which might say something such as "I need to dress more fashionably or wear more make-up." Foa's (1971) experiments validated his hypothesis that attempts to meet such needs through the use of "compensatory behavior" are rather unsuccessful and frustrating.[3] Furthermore, Leiss (1974) develops the idea that human desires are insatiable because people always generate new wants as soon as the old are satisfied. However, individuals continue to try to meet such needs because marketing and especially advertising use such suggestions and promises to increase the appeal of their products and services. An equally important question that has gone unasked is whether people who forgo such a product or service are led to believe that they must also forgo the promise as well. If consumers decide they do not want to wear make-up or dress fashionably, are they therefore socially unacceptable? Is the nonbuyer without, merely because the buyer is with? Such a possibility could do much to alter the way consumers assign meaning to their consumption experiences or lack of consumption experiences.

The use of commercialization in the above sense is very results-oriented and tends to be logical at the expense of thoughtfulness or concern with the effects of such uses. Roszak explains that the reason for the use of technique in this manner is that it (technocracy, as he calls it) has promulgated its own secret success. It has convinced us that:

> The vital needs of man are (contrary to everything the great souls of history have told us) purely technical in character. Meaning: the requirements of our humanity yield wholly to some manner of formal analysis which can be carried out by specialists possessing certain impenetrable skills and which can then be translated by them directly into a congeries of social and economic programs, personnel management procedures, merchandise, and mechanical gadgetry. If a problem does not have such a technical solution, it must not be a *real* problem. It is but an illusion . . . a figment born of some regressive cultural tendency. (1969, p. 10)

In that sense, consumers may find satisfaction for their needs because they expect it and other vital needs may be overlooked because they are not addressed by commercialized products.

One outcome of the results-oriented and self-augmentative nature of marketing technique is the increasing complexity of products and the rate of technological innovation introduction. As Atac notes, "Many products and processes are invented long before a consumer need has been established— sometimes the products are so futuristic that consumers can't even assess potential need; these conditions challenge the abilities of marketing researchers and their techniques" (1985, p. 2). Atac claims that finding *product* needs is now the job of marketing researchers. One can clearly see the distinction between this and the marketing concept, which starts with looking at consumer needs and aims to build profits through integrating marketing efforts to satisfy consumers.

This new role of marketing technique also lends itself to the universality characteristic. In the article discussed above, Atac asserts that as a result of businesses being internationalized, they are "marketing products in countries where consumer needs are not of primary importance." Atac cites Kotler's comment, "I now believe that marketers can influence the environment in which the firm operates and do not simply have to accept and adapt to it" (p. 2). Atac suggests that the use of marketing tools such as public relations and government lobbying "may turn buyer's markets into seller's markets where consumers' needs lose priority" (p. 2). And although he notes that it is getting more difficult for researchers to justify their actions from the perspective of the marketing concept, he contends that (quite in line with the characteristics of marketing technique) "if the job of the marketing executive is to find a satisfactory market, the job of the researcher is to supply the information to achieve that goal and whether the researcher does so by finding a need for a product or finding a product for a need is of secondary concern" (p. 2). Putting the ethics of this situation aside, the application of marketing techniques in this way clearly lends itself to the character of technique—that means evolve into ends.

Advertising is the most powerful of marketing's promotion methods and certainly contains characteristics of technique. First, advertising is results-oriented—it is designed to prompt attention, interest, search, and, ultimately, consumption. If a particular ad does not provide the desired response, it is replaced or redesigned. The preoccupation with results has prompted advertisers to search for the most efficient way to achieve their objectives. Pollay notes the extent of this orientation in applied behavioral technologies for consumer behavior and advertising research. He states that these techniques "like most technologies today, have grown increasingly sophisticated and elaborate. This gives at least the major advertiser a large arsenal of information and the technique with which to fine tune a message, aided by an army of experienced professionals running market research surveys, focus groups, copy testing procedures, recall and awareness tests and test markets" (1986, p. 18).

Qualter (1962) notes some of the repercussions of this preoccupation with results. He states:

> As advertising became increasingly significant, closer and more specialized attention was given to the study of technique and method. Advertisers discovered the power of the nonrational, the appeal of novelty, the force of repetition and the need for simplicity. Necessity compelled advertisers to develop the most effective process for presenting an idea in a form in which it would be seen, understood, remembered and acted upon. They tended thereby to overemphasize the irrational and the spectacular. (1962, p. 45–46)

The fascinating and ironic feature of this transformation is that the technique of advertising acknowledges and incorporates irrationality and incomprehensible human motivations into its processes in a thoroughly logical fashion. The logic of this irrationality lies in the systematic use of "repetitive, fantastic, one-sided, often exhortative rhetorical styles of advertising [which] blur the distinction between reality and fantasy" (Pollay 1986, p. 26.)

Advertising has also taken on a reality quite distinct from the society to which it is delivered. Belk and Pollay note that the images used in advertising are not very reality-based (1985, p. 888). These images blur occupational realities, income realities, suffering realities, and life-style (material possession) realities, tending to perpetuate a stereotype of the "good life." The images used in marketing have several distinct attributes lending themselves to the character of technique. In *The Image*, Boorstin describes the attributes of image use as:

1. *Synthetic.* They are planned and created especially for a purpose, to make a certain kind of impression (trademark, brand name). Often they can disguise what actually exists.
2. *Believable.* They serve no purpose unless they are believable. ("Ivory soap is 99.44 percent pure.")
3. *Passive.* Images act as invitations to behavior; they invite individuals to passively fit themselves to images rather than individuating. "Products have become props for images into which sellers assume consumers will try to passively fit themselves."
4. *Vivid and concrete.* They often appeal to the senses; they must be more graspable than any specific list of objectives.
5. *Simplified.* They must be simpler than the objects they represent, yet not so handy as to seem the natural symbol for the whole class of objects they describe (Kleenex, Xerox, Band-aid).
6. *Ambiguous.* They float somewhere between the imagination and the senses, between expectation and reality. (The use of fuzzy outlines was designed to make it easier for the viewer to see whatever he wished to see.) (1982, p. 183–194.)

Advertising's use of images reflects these attributes and has led to a shift from an emphasis on "truth" to an emphasis on "credibility." The real has been replaced by the image—it has become the real (Boorstin 1982; Boulding 1956). Boorstin argues that we have lost our sense of reality because of the use of images. These images in return homogenize our experience, perpetuating the illusion. These repercussions are not normally considered by marketers as they seek to improve their methods and achieve their goals.

Marketing technique is also self-augmenting—it is progressive in its development, creating whole new fields for its application. The "generic concept of marketing" put forth by Kotler (1972) holds that marketing is a relevant subject for all organizations in their relations with all their publics, not only their customers. Today, all types of organizations apply marketing techniques—even health care organizations, educational institutions, charitable organizations, and political parties. Independent professionals such as doctors and lawyers have also been applying these techniques. The advent of social marketing (Kotler and Zaltman 1972; Kotler and Levy 1969) illustrates the augmenting effect of marketing. Social marketing has been defined as "the design, implementation and control of programs calculated to influence the acceptability of social ideas involving considerations of product, pricing, planning, communication, distribution, and marketing research" (Kotler and Zaltman 1972). Therefore, marketing now considers social change within its domain. This author would not argue that these developments are inherently bad; however, it is important to point out that it is the technique that drives these applications. Marketing has been used very successfully in all of these domains, and yet both practitioners and academicians must be alert to these technique-driven applications and use great care and foresight so that new and different problems do not arise. For example, a great deal of discomfort rippled through the discipline when the discussion of marketing abortion services began a few years ago.

Other examples of marketing's self-augmenting nature are found in most consumer goods industries. In the computer industry, consumers face an increasing number of "extras" that solve "problems" of time, knowledge, money, and comfort. Cosmetics are another example. Many companies are moving to the "full facial care treatment" and establishing complete product lines of cleansers, toners, day and night moisturizers, astringents, masks, powders, bases, and blushes. In addition, the customer is led to believe that each product's success depends upon using the "system" of products. For example, Clinique's facial care system engenders itself—when one product is used, it conditions the use of a number of other Clinique products.

Finally, marketing technique is universal. In the past twenty years, we have witnessed the application of marketing technique all over the world. Lately, we have seen marketers calling for the refinement of this technique as markets become more developed and competitive (Wind, Douglas, and Perlmutter

1973; Walters 1975; Lauter and Dixie 1975). As with the techniques, there are differences in the form of marketing techniques found in all parts of the world because of basic differences in population, climate, and country (culture, values, and language). However, Ellul notes, as these differences diminish or are overcome (and he predicts this will occur because of the application of technique), marketing techniques too will become more and more similar. Even now, we find that marketing techniques are uniform in essence, operation, and effect in the areas of franchise systems (Walker and Etzel 1973) and food retailing (Goldman 1974).

However, to date, marketers have shown little concern for the effects of their efforts upon the cultures they enter. This is not to say that advancements have not been made and societies improved, but, again, the important point is that technique drives these applications. Marketers must be sensitive to the diversity of cultures and the repercussions of their activities. As yet, this sensitivity has not been reflected in the literature or in the work of practitioners. Marketing technique continues to shape cultures in line with its universal characteristic. Levitt agrees that world differences will be overcome, noting "Everywhere everything gets more and more like everything else as the world's preference structure is relentlessly homogenized" (1983, p. 93). In fact, Levitt supports this change by advocating a global marketing strategy that does not account for cultural differences. Dholakia and Sherry (1986) interpret this advocation as an explicit championing of marketing as a global acculturating agent. Alternatively, Sherry (1985) advocates the adoption of a cultural perspective in marketing and consumer research, pointing to the fact that the global marketplace is comprised of a myriad of cultural systems, each with its own meaning systems and material flows. Hirschman (1985) also suggests the importance of looking at the needs of different cultural systems and the potential for dysfunctional consequences of marketing. Specifically, she notes that marketing's role as a social agent often creates unnecessary and harmful demand, population displacement, unemployment, and an intensified social structure.

The Influence of Technique-Oriented Aspects of Marketing Consumption

Consumption activities have been conceptualized as falling into three general classes: buying, using, and disposing (Nicosia and Mayer 1976). These consumption activities are void of meaning. They are general and neutral classes of activity. It is a particular consumer with particular motives and goals in a particular time and space who assigns meaning to these activities. There are many different perspectives on what that meaning is and the processes by which we derive or assign it. Hirschman (1979) traces these different perspectives and their respective contributions toward understanding the meaning of consumption experiences. As her review of the literature suggests, researchers have done much to conceptualize *how* individuals derive meaning in addition to noting the salience of these issues.

Hirschman states, "Until we understand more fully from where these subjective attributes arise and what cognitive and affective processes are involved in their association with a particular product stimulus, we will remain largely ignorant of a vast and important facet of consumption" (1979, p. 7). We are, no doubt, in need of "how it works" type answers to consumption meaning. However, we are also in need of yet another kind of probing and speculation: Why is the experience meaningful to consumers and how do consumers use this meaning in their lives? This line of questioning reveals the influence of marketing technique in a new and interesting way.

The Nature of Consumption Meanings

Before exploring the nature of consumption meanings, it is important to consider the more general question of what is meaning. This question pries into important domains of thought involving philosophy, psychology, sociology, politics, and economics. This section focuses primarily on the individual level of analysis although it is acknowledged that many sources influence and interpret meaning as it is subsumed in the individual human being.

One profound and important work addressing this issue is Viktor Frankl's *Man's Search for Meaning* (1959), which delves into such questions as "What is meaning?" and "How do individuals acquire it?" In brief, his approach describes "man's search for meaning as a primary force in his life and not just a 'secondary rationalization' of instinctual drives" (p. 154). He describes meaning as unique in that it must and can be fulfilled by the individual alone. Meaning is not something that is derived from specific acts, things, or experiences. It is not a commodity that can be bought and sold. Frankl notes a distinction between meaning as an expression of the self and the will to meaning. The expressive type of meaning has been studied extensively by consumer researchers and value researchers. It depicts humans as emerging into existence, defining themselves through expression of their values and needs, and finding meaning through these thoughts, things, and activities. In contrast, Frankl notes:

> The will to meaning is not only an emergence from existence itself (through self-expression), but rather something confronting existence. If meaning that is waiting to be fulfilled by man were nothing but a mere expression of self, or no more than a projection of his wishful thinking, it would immediately lose its demanding and challenging character; it could no longer summon him. (p. 156)

Frankl's thought is displayed powerfully in the words of Nietzsche: "He who has a *why* to live can bear any *how*." Frankl's experiences as a prisoner at Auschwitz led him to note that meaning lies in the *why*, not the *how*, the fundamental distinction being that human beings' lives have meaning because there is some purpose or significance to their continuation, not because of how they package that life or express it.

How do meanings derived from consumption experiences fit into Frankl's discourse? By answering this question, I hope to illuminate one of the many ways that technique has influenced consumption meanings. Consumption experiences have been shown to have meaning merely because they occur within a larger cultural system. This system identifies, organizes, and relates its components to one another through systems of meaning (McCracken 1985a; Sherry 1985). Culture's defining categories and principles provide material objects, activities, and, hence, consumption experiences, with different levels and types of meanings. Individuals (within that system) can derive varying degrees of "how" and "why" meanings from these experiences.

Consumption meanings, in line with Frankl's thinking, should ideally help human beings answer the "why" question in life. And yet, the meaning derived from and linked to consumption experiences has been argued as supporting and furthering primarily the "how" question (Veblen 1899; Slater 1980; Fromm 1968). That is to say, the meaning derived from consumption experiences focuses the individual on "how" the person is to live rather than on "why." Fromm supports this contention in his argument that "the act of consumption should be a meaningful human productive experience. In our culture, there is little of that. Consuming is essentially the satisfaction of artificially stimulated phantasies; a phantasy performance alienated from our concrete real selves" (1955, p. 122).

Consumption meanings have been argued to have lost their link to the deeper question of the why of meaning and have evolved into ends in their own right. This focus is the result of the "technologizing" of consumption meanings. The remainder of this chapter investigates this technologizing process and marketing's role in its promulgation.

Consumption Assumptions

As I have stated, consumption experiences are void of meaning aside from their situational particulars. Meaning is derived in each situation from the application and operation of individuals "consumption assumptions." These assumptions suggest that certain outcomes will result or certain values will be realized through products, services, and consuming behaviors. These assumptions come from many sources—family, history, peer groups, institutions in society, media, and advertising, to name just a few. In almost all product categories and classes and among consuming behaviors, one can find a set of assumptions used to provide the consumption experience with particular meaning(s). Consumption assumptions operate in two important places. First, consumption assumptions are made about the product's or service's ability to meet the consumer's desired consequences. For instance, a consumer perceives that a new line of automobiles is high quality, luxurious, and very expensive. Consumers frame these perceived product attributes with a set of assumptions that relate the product to the outcomes or consequences they expect. For example, the consumption assumption a consumer might use implies that "high-quality, new, expensive, and luxurious cars make people (purchasers, users) more visible to others." This assumption provides the consumption experience with meaning. The meaning, of course, will be different across consumers as different assumptions are evoked. In this case, meaning exists not in the attributes or the bundles of attributes, but in the ideas or assumptions according to which these and other phenomena are organized and evaluated (McCracken 1985a).

A second set of consumption assumptions is made about the consequences of using the product or service or of performing the consuming behavior. These assumptions relate to the consequences' ability to meet the individual's values. Gutman (1982) notes the relationship between consequences and values, but does not acknowledge the operation of consumption assumptions. It is this author's contention that assumptions provide consumers with some reason to believe that their values can be met by the consequences that result from the consumption experience. Referring to the earlier example, consumers have assumed that a certain expensive, luxurious car will make them more visible. The consequence of increased visibility may be related to the realization of a value (for example, social recognition) as a result of the consumption assumption evoked. This assumption may imply, "People who are more visible are socially esteemed." This assumption provides the consumption experience with meaning as a result of its linking values and consequences. McCracken explains similarly, "Goods represent tangible objects of the phenomenal world in which principles can be invested and which can then serve as the tangible representation of intangible values" (1985a, p. 22). Again, it should be noted that these assumptions vary across consumers.

The Influence of Technique-Oriented Aspects of Marketing on Consumption Meanings via Consumption Assumptions

Technique-oriented aspects of marketing have had a profound influence on the meanings individuals attach to consumption experiences. Marketing's increasingly results-oriented, logical, autonomous, amoral, self-augmentative, and universal character has played a fundamental role in changing consumption assumptions. How has this occurred specifically? Recall from the preceding discussion that one set of consumption assumptions is made about how the product or service will provide for certain consequences. Marketing technique has strengthened this set of assumptions considerably. First, as discussed earlier, the widespread use of commercialization to sell such things as beauty, love, sex, and friendship has led the consumer to believe that certain products or services will lead to certain outcomes or consequences. This use of commercialization has been supported by the extensive use of images and symbols in marketing, especially in advertising. These images and symbols are imbued with meaning which consumers transfer to the product and what it can do for them (Levy 1959; Grubb and Grathwohl 1967; Reynolds and Gutman 1984). Some critics believe this so much that one was prompted to ask the question, "Do television commercials make people behave like Pavlov's dogs?" (*Wall Street Journal* 1984). Roszak questions the use of symbols and images in this way, claiming an "eclipse of meaning" has occurred. He explains:

> Symbols also find their technological expression. Things go wrong when a culture cuts symbols away from their transcendent correspondence and so allows them to densify; then our sense of reality diminishes. We begin to think of the experience as being uniquely *in* this material object; the object becomes the real thing. A symbol that has become dense carries no enduring meaning into life. It has become only an opaque object before the senses; it cannot transcend itself. They leave ungratified that dimension of the self which reaches out into the world for enduring purpose, undying value. (1969, p. 346–48)

The second set of consumption assumptions relates the consequences of product or service use to the achievement of values. The influence of marketing technique on this set of assumptions parallels the influences noted above— images, symbols, and commercialization are used to suggest that the consequences of consuming result in value acquisition. Consumption assumptions are also strengthened by changes in values that occur as a result of marketing technique. Thus, the effect on consumption assumptions is indirect but nevertheless important to note, as it is these assumptions that ultimately link products/services and values.

Deflecting the Success Ethic

There are two important changes in values that can be traced to technique. The first has been termed the "deflection of the success ethic from the sphere of production to that of consumption" (Nicosia and Mayer 1976, p. 23). For example, Mills (1951) and Bell (1960) point out that if status aspirations are frustrated at work, these aspirations are likely to be more strongly emphasized off the job. Coleman and Rainwater suggest that occupational status may no longer be a useful indicator of social standing as in the past. They cite a typical response to support that view: "If you can afford to live in a nice neighborhood, no one really cares what you do for a living" (1978, p. 25). Belk notes a similar deflection among yuppies (young, urban professionals) because they must endure slow job mobility relative to their aspirations and, therefore, have little reward to justify their work effort and lives. This group has seemingly turned to consumption for their gratifications (1985, p. 516).

Galbraith sees such a deflection as a natural progression of our industrial-ized (technological) society. He states, "Because the society sets great store by its ability to produce a high standard of living, it evaluates people by the products they possess. The urge to consume is fathered by the value system which emphasizes the ability of the society to produce" (1958, p. 155). Veblen notes a similar consequence in the evolution of an industrial society: "The basis on which good repute in any highly organized industrial community ultimately rests is pecuniary strength; and the means of showing a pecuniary strength, and so of gaining or retaining a good name, are leisure and conspicuous consump-tion of goods" (1899, p. 7). The deflection of the success ethic from the production sphere to the consumption sphere changes the values of individuals as well as the assumptions they make about consumption experience to meet those values, thus altering the relationship between the two. This deflection strengthens the relationship and provides the consumption experience with new meanings and uses.

Focus on the Self

Another fundamental shift in values and consumption assumptions is the present focus on "the self" rather than on "others" or "the social community" (Yankelovich 1981; Lasch 1978; Fromm 1955; Slater 1980). Rokeach (1968) describes how values can have either a social (interpersonal, society-centered) focus or a personal (intrapersonal, self-centered) focus. These two focuses seem to be proportional to one another; in other words, an increase in a social focus involves some trade-offs in terms of a personal focus and vice versa. Clearly, the trend toward a preoccupation with the self and personal matters has implica-tions for consumption assumptions as well.

Yankelovich (1981) empirically documents this trend toward a preoccu-pation with the self in *New Rules*. Therein he describes how "personal fulfill-ment is at the center of many of our lives" (p. 70) and the new moral principle of our era is "I have a duty to myself" (p. xviii). Simply stated, Americans have latched on to a new "giving and getting compact." The old compact was built on the belief that self-denial, sacrifice, obeying the rules, and subordinating the self to the institution all made sense (p. 231). The new compact denies this historically derived set of beliefs. The new giving and getting compact is primarily intrapersonal in nature, focusing on the many things the individual deserves at the expense of interpersonal obligations. Returning to Rokeach, the trade-off becomes clear—historians note the increasing weakening of a social contract (Bell 1976). Carmen (1979) suggests that societal norms are being replaced by consumption efforts with the goal of being "right" with one's self. Individual values do seem to be narrowing in scope, focusing more pointedly on "the self." The trade-off between individualism and a sense of community seems to be an important part of our culture today (Bellah et al. 1985). As Lasch says, "To live for the moment is the prevailing passion—to live for yourself, not for your predecessors or posterity" (1978, p. 5).

Marketing technique perpetuates the alienation of individuals from one another by supporting the values and consumption assumptions that do so. For example, this shift in values could have the following effects on the consumption assumptions an individual makes: (1) Product/service purchase and use are imbued with more meaning if they promise to provide self-fulfillment and "the duty to oneself." (2) Consumption for personal ends is more meaningful than consumption for societal ends. These hypotheses are meant to provoke attention to the effects of this value change on consumption assumptions.

Closing the Loop: The Relationship of Consumption Meanings to Life Meanings

Consumption meanings fit into life meanings in a complicated way. Belk asks the question, "What role does consumption satisfaction play in life satisfaction?" (1983, p. 518). This author puts forth the question, "What role do consumption meanings play in life meanings?" and promotes it as a viable and important research question that needs to be answered. If marketing academicians and practitioners are truly to understand the nature of consumption and its relationship to life meanings, they need to investigate the relationship of the two in a more systematic and effective manner.

An important contention of this chapter is that technique-oriented aspects of marketing tend to focus on answering the "how" question instead of the "why" question. Some critics argue that this focus results in individuals perceiving the "how" as the "why" of meaning. That is, individuals have begun to regard consumption experiences and meanings as an end in themselves and not as the means to chosen ends or "whys" (Fromm 1955; Slater 1980; Csikszentmihalyi and Rochberg-Halton 1981). The effect of this confusion of means and ends and hows and whys on life meanings is a critical issue to be dealt with. Have humans lost sight of their true ends? Have they been reduced to Fromm's depiction of "homo consumers?"

One researcher speculates that consumers displace "why" meanings because they are confronted with the recognition that reality is impervious to their personal ideals (McCracken 1985b). Furthermore, he notes that consumers then try to recover this lost meaning by acquiring objects that act as a bridge to this idealized version of life (p. 18). I would argue that marketing technique has two roles in this process that are worthy of investigation. First, marketing technique may affect the way that consumers form "why" meanings. For example, the use of images and the enlarged sphere of commercialization may encourage people to develop "why" meanings (those that point their significance or purpose) that are unrealistic or unattainable by most humans. On the other hand, marketing technique may have the effect of trivializing human purpose. For either case, consumers may respond by displacing "why" meanings and attempting to recover the lost meaning in their lives through "how" meanings.

Another direction for future research may be in empirically documenting changes in the consumption assumptions consumers hold. Such research would be an invaluable tool for tracking the extent to which marketing technique influences the assignment of meaning. Furthermore, such documentation may provide the impetus for marketing to take some responsibility for its role in this change. Finally, as mentioned earlier in the chapter, marketing technique is only one of the many types of technique. Understanding the relationship between marketing technique and other forms of technique (political, social, scientific) may also shed some light on the overall effects of technique. Is there a synergistic effect between different forms of technique? How are consumers, consumption meanings, and life meanings affected by the combined influence of these techniques? The importance of thinking about such issues cannot be understated.

Conclusion

Technique-oriented aspects of marketing are but one aspect of technique in general. There exist many other forms of technique which influence our lives and meanings. Political, social, and economic techniques also impact our values and consumption assumptions. However, this chapter has sought to expose only one aspect of the manner in which technique has influenced our lives—primarily, to show how marketing at both the general and specific levels has taken on the attributes of technique described by Ellul (1964). It is in this character that one important and interesting area of consumption has been discussed—meaning. Consumption experiences were shown to have meaning because of the consumption assumptions made about the experiences. These meanings have been altered over time due to fundamental changes in the consumption assumptions used by consumers. Technique-oriented aspects of marketing were shown to have influenced these assumptions and, as a result, consumption meanings were shown to have been altered. Finally, the relationship between consumption meanings and life meanings was discussed and important questions were posed for future thinking on this topic of concern.

If Ellul is correct on the nature of technique, then marketing scholars and practitioners are indeed, however unwittingly, crucial agents of social change. The existence of marketing technique that drives itself, that ignores and overrides the richness of cultural diversity, that turns away from ethical issues, may be an endless source of positive, productive change. But it may also foster new and more terrible problems, and it may radically alter the nature of human consciousness and the search for meaning in ways as yet undreamed of. To the extent that marketing professionals can give careful consideration to these issues, many of the undesirable consequences of the application of technique may yet be avoided.

Notes

1. Technique, notes Ellul, is autonomous. Individuals and societies no longer determine which techniques will be operative. Accompanying technique is a technical mentality and morality which preconditions the selection and continuation of technical solutions to problems. This notion is explored in the sections that follow.

2. Commercialization is the process of making something a commodity, of putting it on the market for sale and profit (Guralnik 1978).

3. However, if the young woman's attempts result in the acquisition of more friends and admirers, the situation may still be viewed as dysfunctional. The accepted reality cannot be fully integrated into the young woman if she does not have an accompanying psychic change. Moreover, the precedent of overlaying real needs with artificial needs may alienate the woman from herself, regardless of how successful she is in meeting her social needs in this manner.

References

"AMA Board Approves New Marketing Definition," (1985) *Marketing News* (February): 1.

Arndt, Johan (1978), "How Broad Should the Marketing Concept Be," *Journal of Marketing* 42(1): 101–3.

———, (1985), "On Making Marketing Science More Scientific: Role Orientations, Paradigms, Metaphors, and Puzzle Solving," *Journal of Marketing* 49 (Summer): 110–23.

Atac, Osman Ata (1985), "Finding New Product Needs: A New Job for Researchers," *Marketing News* (January 4).

Baier, Kurt, and Nicholas Rescher, eds. (1969), *Values and the Future*. New York: Free Press.

Belk, Russell W. (1983), "Worldly Possessions: Issues and Criticisms," in *Advances in Consumer Research*, vol. 10, Richard P. Bagozzi and Alice M. Tybout, eds. Ann Arbor Mich.: Association for Consumer Research, 514–18.

————, (1985), "Yuppies as Arbitrators of the Emerging Consumption Style," in *Advances in Consumer Research*, vol. 13, Richard J. Lutz, ed. Provo, Utah: Association for Consumer Research, 514–19

Belk, Russell W., and Richard W. Pollay (1985), "Images of Ourselves: The Good Life in Twentieth Century Advertising," *Journal of Consumer Research* 11 (March): 887–97.

Bell, Daniel (1960), *The End of Ideology*. New York: Free Press.

————, (1976), *The Cultural Contradictions of Capitalism*. New York: Basic Books.

Bellah, Robert N., Richard Madsen, William M. Sullivan, Ann Swidler, and Steven M. Tipton (1985), *Habits of the Heart: Individualism and Commitment in American Life*. Berkeley: University of California Press.

Boorstin, Daniel J. (1982), *The Image: A Guide to Pseudo-Events in America*. New York: Basic Books.

Boulding, Kenneth E. (1956), *The Image*. Ann Arbor: University of Michigan Press.

Carmen, James M. (1979), "Values and Consumption Patterns: A Closed Loop," in *Advances in Consumer Research*, vol. 5, H. Keith Hunt, ed. Atlanta, Ga.: Association for Consumer Research, 403–07.

"Coca-Cola Turns to Pavlov . . ." (1984), *Wall Street Journal* (January 19): 31.

Coleman, Richard, and Lee Rainwater (1978), *Social Standing in America: New Dimensions of Class*. New York: Basic Books.

Csiklszentmihalyi, Mihaly, and Eugene Rochberg-Halton (1981), *The Meaning of Things: Domestic Symbols and the Self*. Cambridge, England: Cambridge University Press.

Desphande, Rohit, and Gerald Zaltman (1982), "Factors Affecting the Use of Market Research Information: A Path Analysis," *Journal of Marketing Research* 19 (February): 14–31.

Dholakia, Nikhilesh, and John F. Sherry (1986), "Marketing and Development: A Re-Synthesis of Knowledge," working paper. Evanston, Ill.: Northwestern University.

Ellul, Jacques (1964), *The Technological Society*. New York: Vintage.

Fırat, A. Fuat (1984), "A Critique of the Orientations in Theory Development in Consumer Behavior: Suggestions for the Future," in *Advances in Consumer Research*, vol. 12, E. Hirschman and M.B. Holbrook, eds. Provo, Utah: Association for Consumer Research, 3–6.

Foa, Uriel D. (1971), "Interpersonal and Economic Resources," *Science* (171): 345–51.

Frankl, Viktor (1959), *Man's Search for Meaning*. Boston: Beacon.

Fromm, Eric (1955), *The Sane Society*. New York: Rinehart.

————, (1968), *The Revolution of Hope*. New York: Harper & Row.

Galbraith, John Kenneth (1958), *The Affluent Society*. Boston: Houghton Mifflin.

Goldman, Arien (1974), "Outreach of Consumers and the Modernization of Urban Food and Retailing in Developing Countries," *Journal of Marketing* 38 (October): 8–16.

Grønmo, Sigmund (1984), "Compensatory Consumer Behavior: Theoretical Perspectives, Empirical Examples and Methodological Challenges," in *AMA Winter Educators' Conference: Scientific Method in Marketing*, P.F. Anderson and M.J. Ryan, eds. Chicago, Ill.: American Marketing Association, 184–88.

Grubb, Edward L., and Harrison L. Grathwohl (1967), "Consumer Self-Concept, Symbolism and Market Behavior: A Theoretical Approach," *Journal of Marketing* 31 (October): 22–27.

Guralnik, David B. ed. (1978), *Webster's New World Dictionary*. World Publishing.

Gutman, Jonathan (1982), "A Means-End Chain Model Based on Consumer Categorization Processes," *Journal of Marketing* 46 (Spring): 60–72.

Hirschman, Elizabeth (1979), "Attributes of Attributes and Layers of Meaning," in *Advances in Consumer Research*, vol. 7, Jerry C. Olsen, ed. Ann Arbor, Mich.: Association for Consumer Research, 7–12.

———, (1985), "Marketing as an Agent of Change in Subsistence Cultures: Some Dysfunctional Consumption Consequences," in *Advances in Consumer Research*, vol. 13, Richard J. Lutz, ed. Provo, Utah: Association for Consumer Research, 99–104.

Junger, Fredrich George (1956), *The Failure of Technology: Perfection without Purpose*. Chicago, Il.: Gateway.

Kotler, Philip (1972), "The Generic Concept of Marketing," *Journal of Marketing* 36(2): 46–59.

———, (1980), *Marketing Management: Analysis, Planning, and Control*. Englewood Cliffs, N.J.: Prentice-Hall.

Kotler, Philip, and Sidney J. Levy (1969), "Broadening the Concept of Marketing," *Journal of Marketing* 33(1): 10–15.

Kotler, Philip, and Gerald Zaltman (1972), "Social Marketing: An Approach to Planned Social Change," *Journal of Marketing* 35(3): 3–12.

Lasch, Christopher (1978), *The Culture of Narcissism: American Life in an Age of Diminishing Expectations*. New York: W.W. Norton.

Lauter, G. Peter, and P.M. Dixie (1975), "Multinational Corporation in European Socialist Countries," *Journal of Marketing* 39 (March): 40–46.

Leiss, William (1974), "The Imperialism of Human Needs, "*North American Review* 259(4): 27–34.

Levitt, Theodore (1983), "The Globalization of Markets," *Harvard Business Review* 61(3): 92–102.

Levy, Sidney J. (1959), "Symbols for Sale," *Harvard Business Review* 37 (July-August): 117–24.

Luck, David J. (1969), "Broadening the Concept of Marketing Too Far," *Journal of Marketing* 33(3): 40–50.

McCracken, Grant (1985a), "Culture and Consumption I: A Theoretical Account of the Structure and Content of the Cultural Meaning of Consumer Goods," working paper 85–102. Guelph, Ontario: University of Guelph.

———, (1985b), "The Evocative Power of Things: Consumer Goods and the Recovery of Displaced Cultural Meaning," working paper 85–105, Guelph, Ontario: University of Guelph.

McGuire, William J. (1973), "The Yin and Yang of Progress in Social Psychology," *Journal of Personality and Social Psychology* 26 (June): 446–56.

McLuhan, Marshall (1964), *Understanding Media: The Extensions of Man*. New York: McGraw-Hill.

Mills, C. Wright (1951), *White Collar: The American Middle Class*. New York: Oxford University Press.

Mumford, Lewis (1956), *The Transformations of Man*. New York: Collier.

Nicosia, Francesco M., and Robert N. Mayer (1976), "Toward a Sociology of Consumption," *Journal of Consumer Research* 3 (September): 65–75.

Park C. Whan, and Daniel Smith (1985), "Managing Competition: The Learning Perspective," working paper. Pittsburgh, Penn.: University of Pittsburgh.

Pollay, Richard W. (1986), "The Distorted Mirror: Reflections on the Unintended Consequences of Advertising," *Journal of Marketing* 50 (April): 18–36.

Qualter, Terence H. (1962), *Propaganda and Psychological Warfare*. New York: Random House.

Reisman, David (1950), *The Lonely Crowd*. New Haven, Conn.: Yale University Press.

Reynolds, Thomas J., and Jonathan Gutman (1984), "Advertising is Image Management," *Journal of Advertising Research* 24 (February/March): 28–37.

Rokeach, M.J. (1968), *Beliefs, Attitudes and Values*. San Francisco: Jossey-Bass.

——— , (1973), *The Nature of Human Values*. New York: Free Press.

Roszak, Theodore (1969), *The Making of a Counterculture*. Garden City, N.Y.: Doubleday.

——— , (1972), *Where the Wasteland Ends*. Garden City, N.Y.: Doubleday.

Sherry, John F. (1985), "The Cultural Perspective in Consumer Research," in *Advances in Consumer Research*, vol. 13, Richard J. Lutz, ed. Provo, Utah: Association for Consumer Research, 573–75.

Sirgy, M.J., A.C. Samlı, and H.L. Meadow (1982), "The Interface between Quality of Life and Marketing: A Theoretical Approach," *Journal of Marketing and Public Policy* 1: 69–84.

Simon, Herbert (1977), "What Computers Mean for Man and Society," *Science*, 195 (March): 1186–91.

Slater, Philip (1970), *The Pursuit of Loneliness*. Boston: Beacon.

——— , (1980), *Wealth Addiction*. New York: E.P. Dutton.

Tawney, R.H. (1920), *The Acquisitive Society*. New York: Harcourt, Brace & World.

Taylor, Frederick W. (1911), *The Principles of Scientific Management*. New York: Norton.

Veblen, Thorstein (1899), *The Theory of the Leisure Class*. Boston: Houghton Mifflin.

Vogt, William (1948), *Road to Survival*. New York: W. Sloane Associates.

Walker, B.J., and M.J. Etzel (1973), "The Internationalization of U.S. Franchise Systems: Progress and Procedures," *Journal of Marketing* 37 (April): 38–46.

Walters, J. Hart, Jr. (1975), "Marketing in Poland in the 1970's," *Journal of Marketing* 4 (October): 47–51.

Wind, Yorman, S.P. Douglas, and H.V. Perlmutter (1973), "Guidelines for Developing International Marketing Strategies," *Journal of Marketing* 37 (April): 14–23.

Yankelovich, D. (1981), *New Rules*. New York: Random House.

12

Self-Actualization and the Consumption Process: Can You Get There from Here?

William E. Kilbourne

In Maslow's (1954) theory of motivation, the individual is postulated to progress through a hierarchy of five need levels. The levels, from lowest to highest, are physiological, safety, belongingness, self-esteem, and self-actualization. Maslow argues that higher-order needs only become prepotent as the lower-order needs are reasonably met. Though lower-order needs may never completely disappear, they assume less importance to the individual as the higher-order needs come to dominate motivation.

My purpose in this chapter is to establish the relationship between Maslow's hierarchy of needs and the consumption process in Western industrialized society. Though Maslow and others have addressed part of this issue in the production process, the relationship between the consumption process and Maslow's hierarchy has been relatively neglected. It is this aspect of the industrial society that I will focus upon. The first step will be to demonstrate that needs hierarchies are not unique to Maslow and have, in fact, been developed by philosophers at least as far back as Aristotle, who recognized the influence of the consumption process in the development of the self. Then it will be shown that, in the more contemporary theories, the role of culture in individual development has been assigned a role of substantial significance. Finally, it will be demonstrated that those philosophies concerned with ontology all believe that "being" is something greater than the sum of the physical parts making up the body and that one's perception of self is not independent of consumption.

It is understood at the outset that the study of values, the primary focus of the chapter, has presented major difficulties in the past; this effort will find no exception. Nevertheless, what follows is not amenable, as yet, to "scientific" inquiry (experimentation). This, of course, has been one of the prevailing criticisms of Maslow's theory of motivation. Despite numerous attempts to validate the theory empirically, there has been no substantial success as yet. This should not be interpreted as a negation of Maslow's theory, however, since as Churchman (1961) suggests, we have not yet developed a science of values that allows us to examine values in the same manner that physical phenomena are examined. It is a deficiency that must be tolerated at this point in the development of scientific method.

The Hierarchy of Needs in History

"The 'better' culture gratifies all basic human needs and permits self-actualization. The 'poorer' cultures do not" (Maslow 1962, p. 197). Thus is stated Maslow's view of what cultures *ought* to do. This is, of course, a purely normative statement whose relevance might be called to question by the reader. Though objective verification of the validity of the statement is not possible, it should be noted that the ultimate objective in Western conceptions of freedom and individualism is the development of human dignity that flows from individuals' right (if not obligation) to choose their life path. It should be noted that neither Maslow nor his predecessors prescribed the direction of individual development. Only individuals can determine this with the express proviso that their choices be their own and not the shibboleths of the *status quo*. This aspects of personal growth has been developed by Marcuse (1964) and Skinner (1972). Each of these authors has been devout in his insistence that individuals choose their own directions for growth without interference from prevailing societal attitudes. That this is consistent with Maslow's conception of self-actualization will be demonstrated in the remainder of this chapter.

Huxley (1945) further demonstrates that both Eastern and Western philosophies have focused upon an ultimate end in human existence for thousands of years and, further, that the ends professed by both bodies of philosophy are remarkably similar. The role of culture in the attainment of these ends has also received substantial attention in Western philosophy. Philosophers from Marx to Jefferson have included the role of societies and their structures in the development of the individual as a major focus of their works. However, it is not implied in these works that culture should direct growth, only promote it.

Although the specifics of Maslow's system have been criticized, it is not without substantial precedent; similar types of systems have frequently been developed (Mathes 1981; Alderfer 1972; James 1962). Historically, related needs paradigms were developed at least as far back as Aristotle, who hypothesized three levels of goods—external goods, goods of the body, and goods of the soul—and speculated upon their interrelationships. Of the relationship between external goods and goods of the soul, for example, Aristotle concluded that an excess of the former detracts from the development of the latter (Barker 1946).

Plato and Aristotle both saw the fully developed individual as the ultimate goal of a social organization. These traditional philosophers were, of course, referring to normative conditions (what societies should do). Here, too, is historical precedent for the normative content of Maslow's theory. Though his hierarchy suggests a positive framework for human development, Maslow recognized the role of culture in the individual's progress through the hierarchy. What cultures should do, then, becomes an integral part of Maslow's theory.

The role of society or its institutions in individual development was initially recognized by Rousseau and later developed more fully by Hegel. Such conceptualization of the role of society in individual development ensured that this role could not be omitted from any developmental paradigm. As stated by Diggs, "On Hegel's view, each individual lives most of his life in roles and stations that laws and institutions make available to him; his potentialities are both relative to and actualized in different forms of institutional life" (1974, p. 154). Thus, for Hegel, the value of an institution lies in its contribution to the rational development of individual potential, and since institutions are themselves culture-bound, it necessarily follows that individual development must be culture-bound.

Marx developed the notion of the fully developed "species-man" in which he includes his own hierarchy of needs. He included a "realm of physical necessity" which must be satisfied with a minimum expenditure of energy in a dignified fashion. Beyond this realm of necessity lay the true realm of freedom, the development of human energy (Marx 1967; Fromm 1961). Fromm equates the concept of human energy with "productivity" as a process of actively producing one's self in relating actively to the "world outside of himself." Thus, for Marx, there are both the hierarchy of needs and the cultural determination (historical materialism) of individual ascendancy, both of which are contained within Maslow's theory as well.

As can be readily seen, Maslow's hierarchy of needs is not without precedent and, as will be shown later, he has not ignored the role of culture in his system. The idea is, in fact, quite old and its expression throughout the centuries has been quite consistent. Whether it be Aristotle's "goods of the soul," Hegel's "rational self-determination," Marx's "fully developed species-being," or Maslow's "self-actualization," each system has as its end the full development of the individual.

The purpose of this introduction has been to establish that, historically, the development of the "self" has been a major focus of philosophers. For more recent philosophers, the role of culture (or institutions in cultures) has assumed increasing importance in its potential to promote or inhibit the attainment of self-realization or, to use Maslow's term, self-actualization.

Conceptions of Self

Since the focus of this chapter is on the development of the "self," a brief discussion of the different conceptions of self seems in order. For purposes of this chapter, the different conceptions will be considered to fall on a continuum with the "biological" self on one end and the "spiritual" self on the other. The biological self is the most obvious conception and, from the present perspective, the easiest to define. It is the physical manifestation of self, including the body, organs, and senses.

The spiritual self is, however, not so easily comprehended since its most elaborate development is based on Eastern, nondualist philosophy. Though there are certainly many variations among the different Eastern philosophies, it is the commonalities that are most relevant here. Primary among these is their basis in monism, the belief that all of reality forms a unified whole. Further, the common goal of Indian philosophies, both Hindu and Buddhist, is liberation from the material world (Kim 1981). To attain liberation, all that is "ego" (the identification of the true self with the physical body) must be extinguished. So long as the "ego-sense" remains intact, true realization cannot be achieved. This is a most difficult concept for Western minds to grasp since it cannot be explained adequately by scientific methods. However, since the extreme points on the continuum of self are not at issue here, a thorough description of "self-realization" as professed in these philosophies is unnecessary. What is at issue is the location of the self in Western industrialized society; most readers would agree that it lies somewhere between the biological and the spiritual self.

Characterizing the self in Western societies has received a great deal of attention in recent years and it is to this task that I now turn. To be consistent with the "organic" theories of society which view the lives of individuals as growing out of the society in which they live, it is within the major institutions that the development of self in contemporary society should be sought. Among those interrelated institutions that are considered to be most relevant, one of the most influential has been the industrial system itself. For present purposes, this system will be divided into two separate but interacting parts, production and consumption. Of these two functions, the role of consumption in individual development will be the major concern throughout the remainder of the chapter. The role of production has, of course, been fully developed by Marx and discussed at length by many authors, so it will not be addressed here. To examine the relationship between Maslow's hierarchy of needs and the consumption process in industrial societies, the discussion will now turn to an examination of the elements of Maslow's theory that relate to consumption.

Maslow's Conception of Needs

Maslow adopts an existential framework in his analysis suggesting a twofold nature of individuals. We are essentially a combination of actuality (what we are) and potentially (what we could be) coexisting within each of us. Unlike the Eastern purist, however, Maslow suggests that self-development results from a synthesis of both facets of the individual and not a repudiation or a negation of one, as suggested by Eastern philosophies. Maslow's disillusionment with the prevailing psychological theories regarding self-conceptions is evidenced by the statement: "Certainly it seems more and more clear that what we call 'normal' in psychology is really a psychopathology of the average, so undramatic and so widely spread that we don't even notice it ordinarily" (Maslow 1962, p. 15). Fromm (1955) addresses the same issue in suggesting that failure to achieve freedom and spontaneity (aliveness) should be considered a defect in the individual if we accept that freedom and spontaneity are valid human goals. So long as few achieve these goals, the deficiency will remain hidden by pathological normality. This is, of course, the concept of a socially patterned defect. When a particular defect is shared by all, it is not recognized as a defect.

Though the major focus of the works of Maslow and Fromm differ, with the former being most concerned with how individuals develop and the latter most concerned with the conditions that inhibit individual development, they share the view that individual potential is far less developed than it could be. Much of Maslow's study involved particular individuals who did transcend the "averageness" of society; he used them as evidence that there is a higher plane in which individuals can exist, and that the plane is achievable, albeit by a very few under current cultural conditions.

It is to the nature of this higher plane that Maslow devoted a great deal of his research. So that a clearer understanding of the relationship between Maslow's hierarchy of needs and the consumption process can be attained, it is necessary, at this point, to examine the nature of the hierarchy itself. Though most readers are probably familiar with the basic pyramidal structure generally ascribed to it, some explanation of Maslow's theory regarding progress through the structure might be in order.

First, it is necessary to distinguish between two basic types of needs as hypothesized by Maslow. The two types of needs are referred to as deficiency needs and growth needs. Of deficiency needs Maslow states:

> It is these needs which are essentially deficits in the organism, empty holes, so to speak, which must be filled up for health's sake, and furthermore must be filled up from without by human beings other than the subject, that I shall call deficits or deficiency needs for purposes of this exposition to set them in contrast to another and very different kind of motivation. (1962, p. 21)

In contrast to, but not in contradiction with, deficiency needs (or basic needs as they are sometimes termed), Maslow developed the conception of "growth needs," which are of an essentially different character than deficiency needs. Growth needs are those that develop or materialize after basic needs have been gratified. As stated by Maslow, "Growth is seen then not only as progressive gratification of basic needs to the point where they 'disappear,' but also in the form of specific growth motivations over and above these basic needs, e.g., talents, capacities, creative tendencies, constitutional potentialities" (Maslow 1962, p. 24).

From the perspective of the hierarchy of needs, it has been hypothesized that the needs for safety, belongingness, love, and respect are essentially deficit in character, though the nature of self-respect is uncertain. The important point is that individuals who are functioning at the motivational level of growth needs are different than other people. And further, as expressed by Maslow, there are perceived "qualitative differences between the motivational lives of self-actualizers and other people." The key phrase here is *qualitative differences*, which expresses a difference that is more than quantitative. "In any case, the psychological life of the person, in many of its aspects, is lived out differently when he is deficiency need gratification-bent and when he is growth-dominated or 'metamotivated' or growth-motivated or self-actualizing" (Maslow 1962, p. 25). Though Maslow himself was not completely satisfied with his definition of growth-motivation, it is clear that individuals who function at that level operate on an essentially different plane than do other people (Goble 1970). It should be emphasized here that self-actualizing individuals are not, as the pyramidal structure usually ascribed to the hierarchy implies, simply functioning at the next highest level. Whereas an individual who is, hypothetically, moving from the third level (love-belongingness) to the fourth (esteem–self-esteem) is essentially of the same basic character, the individual at the self-actualization stage is not. Such a person is, as suggested by Maslow, qualitatively different.

Maslow's Self-Actualizing Individual

Maslow took great pains to define the self-actualizing character on many different dimensions. The complete description will not be presented here. Only those dimensions that pertain directly to the consumption process will be examined. The three factors that most directly relate self-actualizing behavior to the consumption process are (1) perception of reality, (2) autonomy, and (3) discrimination between means and ends.

Perception of Reality. Maslow (1954) has derived a characterization of self-actualizing individuals relating their psychological state to their ability to correctly perceive reality. He characterizes self-actualizers as being especially adept at seeing through the stereotypes and facades that impair the perceptions of other individuals. They are able to correctly perceive what is "concrete and idiographic" in their environment and are thereby in better touch than other people with objective reality. Consequently, compared to others, the self-actualizers are more likely to see people and objects in their true character and be less influenced by the artificial, the impermanent, or the unnecessary.

Autonomy.   From the perspective of consumption, the most interesting of the characteristics ascribed to self-actualizing individuals is autonomy. Maslow maintains that these individuals are relatively free of social or cultural influence and are thereby free of the physical and social environment. They seek continued growth through their own capabilities and are not motivated by extrinsic satisfactions. Unlike other people, these few are unconcerned with others' opinions of them and do not require the types of gratifications that are provided by external sources, be they from other people or from objects in the environment. Whereas deficiency-motivated individuals are compelled to seek external satisfactions, growth-motivated individuals can survive and grow on inner satisfaction. This certainly must set them apart from the crowd, but not at all to their displeasure. This does not mean that they do not like other people or seek companionship. It simply means that, unlike others who still have belongingness as a deficiency need, self-actualizers, who are growth-motivated, have developed beyond these requirements.

Discrimination Between Means and Ends.   The final area for consideration here is the perceptions of self-actualizers regarding the relationship between means and ends. Maslow suggests that self-actualizing individuals are more likely than most not to confuse ends with means and, further, that they tend more often to concentrate on ends than means. Of course, it may be difficult to assess the nature of a particular action in terms of ends and means. For example, when constructing an article of furniture, the end may be the article or the process of construction. Self-actualizers are more likely to maintain the proper perspective throughout the process. The proper perspective would relate the individual to the act and the consequences of the action in such a manner that the relation between means and ends would be firmly established. This is not to imply an invidious characterization of means and ends, but only that the actors know how they are related to the process.

Thus, the essential character of the self-actualizing individuals is such that they are reality-oriented but maintain a clear perception of their place in the larger order of things. These individuals, through clearer perception, have a better grasp of their role in society and tend to subordinate that role to the role of human being. Of this idea, Maslow states:

> Practically every serious description of the "authentic" person extant implies that such a person, by virtue of what he has become, assumes a new relation to his society and indeed, to society in general. He not only transcends himself in various ways, he also transcends his culture. He resists enculturation. He becomes more detached from his culture and from his society. He becomes a

little more a member of his species and a little less a member of his local group. (1962, p. 11)

The Materialistic Self

Having characterized the self-actualized individual from the works of Maslow and others, I will now turn to the more difficult task of characterizing the individual in contemporary industrial society. Here, as with the preceding, the focus of the effort will be directed to the aspects of the consumption process that influence the development of the "marketing orientation." Though the bulk of the developmental work has been in the role of the production process in shaping our essential character and consciousness, it is my contention that this represents only part of the process and has been emphasized historically because it was the most evident aspect of the social reality of the times. Since mass consumption (the corequisite of mass production) has only come to fruition within this century, its effects are only now becoming apparent.

To develop this characterization, it was necessary to escape the mainstream of marketing thought which has, as yet, all but ignored the role of the consumption process as "agent" in defining the individual character. There are, of course, a few exceptions to this found among marketing scholars—the number appears to be growing—but the paucity of social analysis in the marketing literature is distressing to say the least. Marketers have simply left the role of social analysis to sociology, philosophy, political science, and psychology, despite the fact that they are the purveyors of probably the most ubiquitous, highly organized, and integrated social process heretofore developed. Most of what follows was of necessity drawn from many diverse sources, some directly and some indirectly related to the consumption process.

From the perspective of this chapter, there are two primary processes that converge in industrial society, leading inexorably to one of the predominant character traits ascribed to the majority of individuals in industrial societies. The marketing orientation and its relationship to the consumption process will be examined here as will its dual antecedents, abstraction and ubiquitous negotiated exchange.

Abstraction

The process of abstraction is neither new nor unique to industrial societies. It is a process which, when engaged in rationally, produces results that could be obtained by no other mode of expression. No rational being, including the purveyor of Eastern philosophy, would deny the benefits to humanity resulting from abstractions in science and medicine. The difficulty only arises when abstraction becomes the predominant mode of expression excluding from the matrix of relations that which is real and concrete. In his discussion of the relationship between the concrete and the abstract, Fromm (1955) expresses the view that a full, productive relatedness to an object requires its being seen in both its uniqueness (concreteness) and its generality (abstractness). The lack of this potential for relatedness can be seen in everyday consumption. The products one buys carry the abstract qualities so generally ascribed to them, but they are completely lacking in uniqueness. Each is a carbon copy of the next, made so by the exigencies of technological efficiency. A recent advertisement for an Oldsmobile Toronado characterizes this *ersatz* uniqueness. The main caption directs us to "Set yourself apart from the crowd. Buy an Olds Toronado." Set yourself apart by buying a product identical to what everyone else is buying to express their uniqueness.

Pirsig (1974) expresses the same philosophy in *Zen and the Art of Motorcycle Maintenance* in his description of an "a priori" motorcycle as both a product of the mind and of sense data: abstract and concrete. He further expresses the difficulties in relating to the motorcycle when it is not viewed in its completeness, as both abstract and concrete.

That the essence of abstraction can be seen clearly, an example of the process can be drawn from the realm of the quintessential abstracter, the economist. Among the many problems that must be dealt with on a personal level by individuals is the prospect of unemployment. However, in the unemployment level, the economist has a unique way of dealing with this highly personal phenomenon which removes it from the realm of the real and places it firmly in abstraction. By dealing with so many human data, the economist can proceed with the calculating precision of a machine working out "solutions" to human problems without a thought of human feelings. The economist need not consider the fact that beyond the realm of abstraction is a real world of real people to whom there are only two levels of unemployment: 0 percent if they have a job and 100 percent if they do not. Fromm might well have had this example in mind when he stated: "The concrete reality of people and things to which we can relate with the reality of our person, is replaced by abstractions, by ghosts that embody different quantities, but not different qualities" (Fromm 1955, p. 114).

Although the process of abstraction would seem to apply in many areas of industrial society, only those areas relating it to the consumption process will be considered here. The focal points of the relationship are considered to be the two fundamental dimensions of the process (products and people); it is these that will be dealt with here. Though the direction of the process relating products to people is, in contemporary marketing, generally considered to be people creating products, there is substantial historic and contemporary precedent for considering the logical flow to be bidirectional, with products also contributing to the development of people. It is this latter relationship, products contributing to the development of people, that I will now consider.

A product exists as a thing to be used for satisfaction of needs that exist in the user. This is, of course, referred to as its use value and presents no major characterization difficulties. Products, however, undergo an enigmatic transcendence when the realm of value is expanded to include exchange value when products become commodities. Fischer states, "A motor-car as use-value has nothing enigmatic about it but as a commodity it is so capricious and unaccountable that not only the buyer, but also, and especially, the producer is confronted with new riddles at every step" (1970, p. 55). Marx referred to this enigmatic process through his description of a table constructed of wood. Though, once constructed, it is still wood, it also has use value to its owner. It is a table. Once it assumes the abstract value of a commodity, however, it transcends its original nature to become much more. To the producer, its essence is profits; to the merchant, it has exchange value; and to the owner, it might well be the essence of social status.

This example captures the essence of the abstraction process as the almost mystical transformation of a physical thing, a product, into a social thing, contributing to and sometimes governing social relationships between people. The product develops, through abstraction, exchange value (*vis-a`-vis* other products) and the quality of abstract expressiveness within the social relationships of its agents. Marx's table can be either subject or object in one's relationship to it. When it is being used as a table, the user is the subject and the table is the object. Conversely, when abstract expressiveness of the table is operational, the table confers social status on the owner. The table is the subject and the owner is the object. The status conferred by the table (subject) to the owner (object) then serves to govern social relations of the owner by virtue of the status message it presents (abstract expressiveness) to others.

Thus, the essence of abstract expressiveness is the degree to which the product means more than its professed use value to its owner or seller. The character of abstract expressiveness is so well accepted in society today that it hardly requires explanation here. As for exchange value, it can be reasonably stated that the process has been abstracted one step further to the common denominator of all exchange values, money.

In advanced industrial societies in which the exchange process is most fully developed, the quality of abstract expressiveness in products has achieved its most complete development. Bredemeier and Toby (1960) suggest that among the governing principles in the pursuit of success in American society can be found the materialist orientation. As testament to the full development of the process of abstract expressiveness in commodities and the role it plays in society, they state that Americans have made a religion out of things (materialism) and, more importantly, that they are far more interested in the symbolic aspects of products than the physical aspects. They further state, "Americans are materialistic by default—because they try to use 'things' to express their search for the meaning of existence" (p. 77).

As can be seen from the interpretations of "product" presented here, the traditional view of product as object is considered to be insufficient from the perspective of the consumption process as a whole. Product as subject, operating on the individual consciousness, provides a more meaningful framework in determining the relationship between the consumption process and the social relations it develops. This becomes particularly acute when determining the role of abstraction of products on perceptions of self in societies in which the principle of negotiated exchange is one of the dominant forces in social relations.

Negotiated Exchange

Bredemeier and Toby suggest that this principle is so potent in American society that it even supersedes that of competition. They state, "American society has gone far in institutionalizing a market mentality" (1960, p. 124). The ultimate expression of this quid pro quo philosophy is in the principle of negotiated exchange which has become the dominant force in society today. This is neither unusual nor necessarily bad so long as the domain of application remains the marketplace for goods and services, as in lesser industrialized societies. As with the abstraction of products, however, the difficulties arise when this domain is transcended.

The intrusion of negotiated exchange into the personal experience of individuals has evolved to the point where the negotiated exchange mentality pervades even the most private of exchanges (those between individuals) and the most public (the democratic process itself). Casual observation reveals this process in all areas of experience. Bredemeier and Toby (1960) emphasize this with numerous examples from dating relationships, political relationships, and education.

Negotiated exchange has transcended the product domain to become a way of life in contemporary industrialized societies. It is a consequence of this development, combined with abstraction of products, that prompts the type of characterization of the transcendent nature of the process of negotiated exchange provided by Bredemeier and Toby. They state that this principle is institutionalized in American society and, more importantly, that it has become a principle of self-assessment—it has transcended the domain of products to enter the domain of personal relations. The pursuit of material things has become so relentless that it has been characterized by Slater (1980) as an addiction to wealth which is highly analogous to drug addiction. Even more recently, Dholakia and Venkatesh (1986) characterized this fetish for consumption as a "pathology of consumption" which can render the individual socially dysfunctional and/or alienated.

Effects on Individuals in Industrial Society

The resultant of the parallelogram of forces—abstraction of products and a ubiquitous process of negotiated exchange—leads inexorably to the transcendence of product as object to the domain of product as subject. Through the contemporary exchange process, the relationship between individuals and the product of their efforts is transformed from the historical relationship in which individuals assumed a dominant role in both the production and sale of "their" product to "their" customer, to the obscure relationship in which the individual as either producer or seller assumes a subordinate position conforming to the needs of the product. The product presents itself as pure exchange value in the impersonal market of abstract expressiveness; through this process, the transformation of the individual from subject to object in juxtaposition to the product as subject begins to take shape.

The nature of the process has been described variously by Marx (1906), Fischer (1970), Marcuse (1964), and Fromm (1955). The results of the transformation of a human into an expression of the product have received literary attention by Ibsen (1935), Tolstoy (1960), Hesse (1957), and Emerson:

> 'Tis the day of the chattel,
> Web to weave, and corn to grind;
> Things are in the saddle,
> And ride mankind.
> (Van Doren 1946)

Numerous other expressions could be easily called to mind. Suffice to say that the idea is not new or unique. Fromm expresses the concept succinctly in the following passage:

> The market concept of value, the emphasis on exchange value rather than on use value, has led to a similar concept with regard to people and particularly to oneself. The character orientation which is rooted in the experience of oneself as a commodity and of one's value as exchange value I call the marketing orientation. (1947, p. 68)

With the transformation of individuals as the subject of their activity to individuals as the object (commodity), only one step remains in the complete transformation. Here again enters the abstract expressionism of products. In their search for identity, individuals in the marketing orientation (focused as it is on the salability of the "person commodity") must of necessity rely on the opinion of others, since it is through others' actions that their true exchange value is determined. Since others' experience of the individual, as with the individual's of them, is through the marketing orientation, each is reduced to the status of product by the other. With the mutuality of experience being that of product to product, in the impersonal market mechanism of negotiated exchange, the aberrant logic of the exchange mentality dictates the extension of abstract expressionism from the domain of things to the domain of individuals. With this, the transformation of the individual as subject to the individual as object is completed in the exchange process. From the productive orientation in which individuals experience themselves as the subject of their actions described by the statement, "I am what I do," their identity is reduced to one characterized by the statement, "I am what I have," thus providing the direct link between the search for self and the consumption process in industrial societies. The impact of the process through which individuals seek identity through possessions has been examined for many decades through such classic works as Veblen's (1899) *The Theory of the Leisure Class*, Josephson's (1934) *The Robber Barons*, Tawney's (1920) *The Acquisitive Society*, and scores of others with which we are only too familiar.

The nature of individuals as evidenced in a society oriented around the production-marketing dyad, in which consumption assumes such a dominant role, is described most clearly in Fromm's (1976) characterization of the having mode of self-expression. Within industrial societies, the having mode predominates and is an indirect result of the two processes previously described, abstraction of products and abstract expressionism in individuals. In the having mode, the product (consumption) becomes the means through which individuals seek identity, in effect, expressing themselves through the outward manifestations of their possessions. The clothes one wears, the car one drives, and the house one lives in become the means of self-assessment in the most invidious of comparative appraisals, those between individuals. That this process operates in consumption-oriented societies is practically beyond dispute. The only question that arises is the degree to which it manifests itself in particular individuals. Though the nature of the process through which the having mode develops in industrial societies is an important one, it is not the focus of this chapter. The most complete analysis of this is found in the works of Eric Fromm. What is important here is the effect of the having orientation on the development of self or, more specifically, on the development of self-actualization as described by Maslow.

For the sake of clarity, it should be pointed out that "having" as used here does not de facto condemn individuals to meaningless, unproductive lives. Having, as with the other concepts upon which this chapter is based, is not, in and of itself, bad. Rather, it is viewed as a two-dimensional construct. There are what Fromm refers to as *existential having* and *characterological having* (the having mode). The former refers to having that is necessary for existence, that is the product of rational behavior, and that carries with it other types of behavior relating the individual to the product. This includes behaviors related to acquisition, protection, and maintenance of existentially related products. The having mode is a qualitatively different form, related much more to passion than to need in the existential sense. It is this type of having that Fromm (1976) suggests prevails in industrial societies in which the consumption process is fully developed. It should be made clear that it is not the act of consumption that precipitates the having mode, but rather one's relationship to what is consumed and to the process of consumption. The act of consumption is essential to the maintenance of life and one can consume in great quantity without falling victim to the having mode of existence.

When the individual's relationship to the things consumed and the process of consumption becomes distorted, as through the processes previously discussed, the having mode develops. When individuals identify with and through the things consumed, they are in the having mode. When consumption becomes the end in itself (consumption for its own sake), rather than assuming its natural role as a means to an end, the individual is in the having mode. Such distortions in the consumption process have characterized Western industrial societies with highly integrated marketing processes to the point that individuals are often considered to be caricatures of themselves. Critics of the market process such as Veblen (1899) and Huxley (1946) saw clearly the signs of things to come with the full development of the new consumption morality. More recently, Scitovsky (1976) and Slater (1980) indicate that the consumption morality was not a temporary aberration, but is flourishing yet today. Ewen (1976) provides a description of the process through which the new morality was engendered through the industrial-marketing process.

Self-Actualizing Self versus Materialistic Self

Having characterized the self-actualizing self of Maslow and the materialistic self in industrial-marketing societies, the task remaining is to compare the two to determine the degree to which individuals in contemporary society are capable of achieving self-actualization as described by Maslow. To do this, each of the three traits described previously as being related to the consumption process and attributed to self-actualizing individuals will be briefly reexamined and compared to the same trait as attributed to the materialistic self. The traits discussed were autonomy, reality orientation, and perception of means and ends.

The self-actualizing individual was described by Maslow as being autonomous. By this he meant that the individual was relatively free from social and cultural forces and did not rely on external judgments regarding development and growth satisfactions. The individual was predominantly growth-motivated rather than deficiency-motivated. The characteristics ascribed to individuals in contemporary society were predominantly those relating to the having mode, which has external judgment as its sine qua non. The individual in this orientation requires and is dependent upon social and cultural forces for direction in self-development, which is attained through the consumption process. These two character types, autonomy and the having mode, appear to be virtually incompatible.

The second trait ascribed to self-actualizing individuals was a clearer perception of reality (seeing things and people as they are, not as they would like them to be or as someone else says they should be). This is clearly not independent of what preceded nor will it be independent of what follows. What it suggests in the context of this chapter is that the reality of the consumption process is understood more clearly by the self-actualizing individual as existential consumption rather than identity seeking. The reality of consumption is that it is necessary and that certain patterns make life easier or more comfortable. Beyond that level, consumption can become dysfunctional and detract from growth pursuits. The materialistically oriented individuals of contemporary industrial society have a dramatically different conception of the reality of the consumption process. They seek identity through it and allow its domain to be expanded to include the most personal of relationships. It becomes for them, not a way to a better life, but a way of life precluding many other personal growth opportunities. This leads directly to the last of Maslow's attributes, perception of ends and means.

Maslow suggests that, for the self-actualizing individual, the relationship between ends and means remains in clearer perspective than it does for other individuals. For the self-actualizing individual, the consumption process would simply be a means to the end of personal development. Consumption is, in fact, absolutely necessary if growth motivations are to ascend within the individual, as it is the means through which deficiency motivations are satisfied. As Maslow states clearly, deficiency motivations must be satisfied before growth motivations can ascend. Thus the self-actualizing individual would not take the process lightly, but would keep it in its proper perspective as a means to a higher end.

For the individual in the having mode, the perception of the consumption process is drastically different. As suggested in the discussions of autonomy and reality orientation, the process takes on an expanded expression. The literature cited suggests that consumption in contemporary society has become the end in itself rather than a means to a higher end. This distortion of means and ends results from what has been referred to as a "false consciousness" inured to its falseness (Laing 1967). The materialistic individual comes to believe that consumption represents the solution to personal development when, in fact, it detracts from it when pursued as the end rather than a means to an end. Thus, the distortion of means and ends in the consumption process tends to move individuals away from personal development while giving the false impression that they are moving toward it.

Thus, it can be seen that Maslow's conception of where individuals should be going is diametrically opposed to where the consumption process in contemporary industrial society seems to be taking them. If the literature describing the individual in contemporary society is even remotely accurate, it is not surprising that Maslow's estimate of the number of individuals who actualize is so small. He felt that the number was as small as one-half of 1 percent. However, considering the literature on individuals in industrial society, one might reflect on why his estimate was so high. Maslow was, of course, an optimist.

Implications for Marketing

Though it is not the intent of this chapter to determine the full impact of self-actualization on marketing, a few comments are in order. If self-actualization were to become the dominant mode in society, it seems likely that dramatic changes in the marketing process would materialize. The nature of the product offering would be the most dramatically affected. Since many products now offered relate to satisfaction of deficiency needs which would tend to disappear, these products and their promotion methods would also tend to disappear to the extent that they do not satisfy real needs. They would be replaced with a new set targeted at growth needs. Though some may question marketing's ability to survive under such conditions, it should be pointed out that growth needs are relatively unlimited whereas deficiency needs are not. In addition, lower-order needs only remain unimportant to the extent that they continue to be satisfied. It is my contention that fears of failure in the marketplace are unwarranted. A complete reorientation of marketing practices would be required, but, in the end, both the consumer and the system as a whole would benefit. Marketing would assume its appropriate role in society. It is a means to the end of individual growth and, as such, could not be an end in itself as it so frequently is today. In the well-ordered society envisioned by Maslow, consumption would not distract us from our goals or decrease our potential for achieving them.

Conclusions

The purpose of this chapter was to examine the nature of self-actualizing individuals as described by Maslow and to compare the individual character to that which appears to develop through the consumption process in industrial societies with highly integrated marketing systems. The result of this analysis is an apparent inconsistency between what we say individuals should be and what they appear to become. The essence of this incompatibility lies in the relation of the individual to consumption. As was suggested, existential consumption with a minimum of toil is necessary for self-actualization to develop.

However, when one's relation to the consumption process is transformed from existential having to the having mode, the result is a fundamental inconsistency with self-actualization. The process of consumption becomes the end in itself rather than a means to the end of self-actualization. When this occurs, individuals assume that they are enhancing the self through consumption, thus precluding truly self-actualizing experiences and yielding an *ersatz* self-development inured to its own inconsistencies. The result is perpetuation of the status quo and continued pursuit of self through increased consumption.

It would seem, then, that enhancement of opportunities for self-actualization in industrial society would require a return to a rational consumption process in which the proper ordering of means and ends is reestablished. An efficiently functioning consumption process is the sine qua non of self-actualization. By a rational consumption process is meant one in which the proper relation of consumer is reestablished to its historic position (individual as subject/product as object). Though many critics of the consumption process admonish us to consume less (saying the problem is overconsumption), the conclusion of this chapter suggests that it is not the quantity of consumption that detracts from self-actualization, but one's relation to the process of consumption. Though overconsumption is certainly a problem that needs resolution in contemporary industrial society, it only represents a symptom of a deeper problem. To allow individuals to pursue a path toward self-actualization, the quality of consumption and one's relationship to the process require redress.

References

Alderfer, F.P. (1972), *Existence, Relatedness and Growth*. New York: Free Press.

Barker, E., translator (1946), *The Politics of Aristotle*. Oxford, England: Clarendon Press.

Bredemeier, H., and J. Toby (1960), *Social Problems in America*. New York: John Wiley & Sons.

Churchman, C.W. (1961), *Prediction and Optimal Decision*. Englewood Cliffs, N.J.: Prentice-Hall.

Dholakia, N., and A. Venkatesh (1986), "The Cycle of Consumption in the Post-Industrial Age," working paper Kingston: Dept. of Marketing, University of Rhode Island.

Diggs, B.J. (1961), *Prediction and Optimal Decision*. Englewood Cliffs, N.J.: Prentice-Hall.

Emerson, R.W. (1946), "Ode," in *The Portable Emerson*, M. Van Doren, ed. New York: Viking, 322–25.

Ewen, S. (1976), *Captains of Consciousness*. New York: McGraw-Hill.

Fischer, E. (1970), *The Essential Marx*. New York: Seabury.

Fromm, E. (1947), *Man for Himself*. New York: Rinehart.

———— (1955), *The Sane Society*. New York: Holt, Rinehart and Winston.

———— (1961), *Marx's Concept of Man*. New York: Frederick Unger.

———— (1976), *To Have or to Be*. New York: Bantam.

Goble, F. (1970), *The Third Force*. New York: Grossman.

Hesse, H. (1957), *Siddhartha*. New York: Bantam.

Huxley, A. (1945), *The Perennial Philosophy*. New York: Harper.

———— (1946), *Brave New World*. New York: Harper.

Ibsen, H. (1935), *Eleven Plays of Henrik Ibsen*. New York: Random House.

James. W. (1962), *Psychology: A Briefer Course*. New York: Collier.

Josephson, M. (1934), *The Robber Barons*. New York: Harcourt Brace Jovanovich.

Kim, Y.C. (1981), *Oriental Thought*. Totowa, N.J.: Littlefield, Adams.

Laing, R.D. (1967), *The Politics of Experience*. New York: Ballantine.

Marcuse, H. (1964), *One Dimensional Man*. Boston: Beacon.

Marx, K. (1906), *Capital*, vol. 1. Chicago: Charles W. Kerr.

———— (1967), *Capital*, vol. 3. New York: International.

Maslow, A.H. (1954), Motivation and Personality. New York: Harper & Row.

———— (1962), *Toward a Psychology of Being*. Princeton: D. von Nostrand.

Mathes, E.W. (1981), "Maslow's Hierarchy of Needs as a Guide for Living," *Journal of Humanistic Psychology* 21 (Winter): 69–73.

Pirsig, R. (1974), *Zen and the Art of Motorcycle Maintenance*. New York: Morrow.

Scitovsky, T. (1976). *The Joyless Economy*. Oxford, England: Oxford University Press.

Skinner, B.F. (1972), *Beyond Freedom and Dignity*. New York: Bantam/Vintage.

Slater, P. (1980), *Wealth Addiction*. New York: E.P. Dutton.

Tawney, R.H. (1920), *The Acquisitive Society*. New York: Harcourt, Brace.

Tolstoy, L. (1960), *The Death of Ivan Ilych*. New York: New American Library.

Veblen, T. (1899), *The Theory of the Leisure Class*. New York: Macmillan.

13

Work, Consumption, and the Joyless Consumer

Raymond Benton, Jr.

> Consumerism is only the other side of the degradation of work—the elimination of playfulness and craftsmanship from the process of production.
>
> —Christopher Lasch (1984, p. 27)

W hen the hot discussions in marketing were concerned with broadening the marketing concept, Thaddeus H. Spratlen pointed out that such interest was largely confined to extending its application rather than expanding its orientation. "That is," Spratlen wrote, "its operational domain is being extended, not its philosophical domain" (1972, p. 403). In the years since Spratlen wrote, the operational domain of marketing has indeed expanded, so much so that Nikhilesh Dholakia (1985) recently questioned whether the marketing wave is even stoppable.

During this period of expansion, however, few marketers bothered to investigate, scrutinize, or criticize marketing's philosophical base. Consequently, marketing has not been significantly broadened in the philosophical sense. It is time to stop and look into, or behind, that philosophical base, to question it, and perhaps to criticize it. There is, after all, sufficient evidence, both empirical and anecdotal, to suggest that economic growth and goods consumption is not necessarily correlated with the feeling of well-being by the people who participate in the process.

Empirically, research suggests that there has been "no marked and significant increase in the self-perceived happiness of Americans to accompany the

An earlier version of this chapter was presented at the Eleventh Macromarketing Seminar, August 7-10, 1986, in Boulder, Colorado. The research and writing was made possible, in part, by a grant from the May Stores Foundation. Helpful comments and criticism from Professor A.R. Gini, Loyola University of Chicago, are acknowledged.

very substantial rise in the standard of living that has been achieved in the postwar period" (Rescher 1980, p. 7; see also Easterlin 1973, 1974; Leiss 1984). Anecdotally, on a recent morning commuter train ride, a perfect stranger—a young, well-dressed man in a gray three-piece suit (a lawyer?)— voluntarily commented, in response to a conversation I was having with the person sitting next to me, "My wife and I both work and we make lots of money. We have the house, the BMW, and the Mercedes, and we take the trips. Generally we buy anything we want. But you know what? This yuppie trip has got to be the most unfulfilling thing we have ever experienced."

Similarly, on *Nightline* on December 25, 1985—Christmas night, of all nights—Ben Wattenberg of the American Enterprise Institute commented, in response to the suggestion that maybe the baby-boomers are spending more (which they are and which Wattenberg presented as evidence that things are getting better) but might be finding that they cannot buy happiness,

> Well, you know, money can never buy happiness. The only thing that anyone intelligent would say that money can buy is the absence of specific miseries. It can prevent you from having clothes with holes in it [sic] or leaky windows, or it can give you a nice car. It can prevent certain unhappinesses but it doesn't buy happiness. No one ever said it does.

Indeed, despite widespread agreement among traditionalists that we must "get the economy moving again," Paul Wachtel might very well turn out to be correct in saying that "greater economic productivity is not what will relieve our distress and that the pursuit of economic growth may actually make things worse" (1983, p. 9). Explaining how this could be is part of the purpose of this chapter.

The question is not why we believe that consumption brings happiness— we believe it because we have taught ourselves to believe it—but—to borrow from Jeremy Seabrook's *What Went Wrong? Why Hasn't Having More Made People Happier?* (1977)—to understand contemporary patterns of consumer behavior, as well as contemporary patterns of consumer dissatisfaction and restlessness, one must understand consumer behavior in its relation to other domains of human experience (in this case, in its relationship to work and working). In brief, the argument is that much of contemporary consumption is a form of compensation for the lack of meaningful work. Consequently, the origins of our culture of consumption, as well as of contemporary patterns of consumer behavior, cannot be understood apart from an understanding of the progressive degradation of work during the twentieth century.

On Work and Consumption: The Theoretic

We need a theoretical understanding that will correct and compensate for the traditional understanding that work is merely something we do to obtain the means (money) to acquire consumption goods. We need to understand that, as Hannah Arendt expressed it, "the things of the world . . . are of a very different nature and produced by quite different kinds of activities" (1958, p. 94).

The Activities and the Products

Every European language, ancient and modern, contains two etymologically unrelated words for what we have come to think of as the same activity, and retains them in the face of their persistently synonymous usage. To illustrate, Arendt considered several languages and their respective words: Ancient Greek —*ponein* and *ergazesthai*; Latin—*laborare* and *facere* or *fabricari*; French— *travailler* and *ouvrer*; German—*arbeiten* and *werken*; English—*labor* and *work*. The distinction between them is the distinction between "the Labour of Our Body and the Work of Our Hands," a phrase Arendt borrows from John Locke's *Second Treatise of Civil Government*. It is a distinction reminiscent of that made by the ancient Greeks between the *cheirotechnes* (the craftsman, to whom the German *Handwerker* corresponds) and those who, like "slaves and tame animals with their bodies minister to the necessities of life."

In all cases, only the equivalents for *labor* have an unequivocal connotation of pain and trouble. The German *arbeit* applied originally only to farm labor executed by serfs and not to the work of the craftsman, which was called *werk*. The French *travailler* replaced the older *labourer* and is derived from *tripalium*, a kind of torture. In classical Greek, *ponein* connoted labor; in modern Greek, its derivative, *ponei*, simply connotes pain and hurt. The words for *work*, on the other hand, unequivocally connote creativity. These distinctions are maintained, as well, in popular idiomatic expressions. Consider the difference in implied meaning between the idioms "a labor of love" and "a work of art."

Just as we can distinguish between kinds of activities, between labor and work, so, too, can we distinguish between the things of the world, between consumption products and use products. In English, *consumption* is etymologically derived from the Laton *consumere* (to use up, eat, waste) and has the unmistakable connotation of destroying, doing away with, or devouring. Similarly, *use* is derived from the Latin *uti* (to use) and, while more general than *consume*, it connotes a sense of *using* as in employing or employing for a given purpose without the connotation of destroying, wasting, or devouring the thing used even though it may, in the process, be "used up."

The Relationships

The distinction between labor and work was ignored in classical antiquity and has been ignored in the modern age as well. There is not a single theory in which *animal laborans* and *homo faber* are clearly distinguished (Arendt 1958, p. 85). The distinction between productive and unproductive labor made by the classical economists, however, goes to the heart of the matter because it embodies the fundamental distinction between work and labor. The mark of all laboring is that it leaves nothing behind. The results of its effort are almost as quickly consumed as the effort is spent, because labor produces those things destined for consumption. Despite the apparent futility of this effort, "it is born of a great urgency and motivated by a more powerful drive than anything else, because life itself depends upon it" (Arendt, p. 87). For that reason, it cannot be escaped.

The mark of work, on the other hand, is that it creates permanence, stability, and durability. The products of work provide the permanent and durable world within which we find the consumption goods by which life assures the means of its own survival. "Needed by our bodies and produced by its laboring, but without stability of their own, these things for incessant consumption appear and disappear in an environment of things that are not consumed but used, and to which as we use them, we become used and accustomed" (Arendt 1958, p. 94).

The ideals of *Homo faber* are the creation of permanence, stability, and durability. The ideal of *animal laborans* is the production of abundance, the dream of growing wealth, "the happiness of the greatest number." The age-old dream of the poor and the destitute is the dream of the modern era: to emancipate people from that which is necessary. Indeed, the contempt for laboring originally arose out of a passionate striving for freedom from necessity (Arendt 1958, p. 81).

For the ancients, the way to achieve the dream was through the enslavement of others. They felt it necessary to possess slaves because of the slavish nature of all occupations that served the needs for the maintenance of life. What people share with all other forms of animal life was not considered to be human; slaves were not, consequently, considered human. It was not, however, their capacity to be human that was denied, but only their humanity when they were totally subjected to necessity. Indeed, peasants, who were not slaves but did provide the necessities of life, were classified by Plato as well as Aristotle as natural slaves. To be a master of slaves was the human way to master necessity (Arendt 1958, pp. 82–83).

The modern era has striven to eliminate the realm of necessity, that of labor, through the *mechanization* of the productive process, thereby relieving people of the necessity of producing what necessarily must be produced, while at the same time producing an abundance of it. It is in part that dream, the dream of liberation from the realm of necessity through the production of abundance, that lies behind the hope "that scientific and technological progress would result in enhanced human satisfaction/contentment/happiness" (Rescher 1980, p. 4).

The hope was that the division of labor, the breakdown of operations into their simple constituent motions, and their consequential reintegration through "teamwork," together with the application of machine technology, would deliver people from their human condition, from the necessity to "labor." What actually happened, and this is one of the ironies of the modern world, is that by dividing, subdividing, and mechanizing the tasks at hand (always with an eye toward greater productivity), what work existed was effectively eliminated, leaving only labor to be done. And while the tools and instruments employed may ease the pain and the effort involved, they do not change the necessity itself, but only hide it from our senses.

Part of the liberal philosophy that is our modern heritage is the assumption that if labor power is not spent and exhausted in the drudgery of life, it will automatically nourish other, "higher" activities. Freed from labor, people will pursue higher goals and ends. This was an assumption put forth as a policy by Adam Smith and a hope by Karl Marx; it lies behind contemporary concerns over what people will do with their leisure once they achieve it. Two hundred years after Smith and a hundred years after Marx, we intuitively know the fallacy of this reasoning:

> The spare time of the *animal laborans* is never spent in anything but consumption, and the more time left to him, the greedier and more craving his appetites. That these appetites become more sophisticated, so that consumption is no longer restricted to the necessities but, on the contrary, mainly concentrates on the superfluities of life, does not change the character of this society, but harbors the grave danger that eventually no object of the world will be safe from consumption and annihilation through consumption. (Arendt 1958, p. 133.)

We claim, proudly, that we live in a consumer society, in an "economy of abundance." Inasmuch as labor and consumption are but two stages of the same process, imposed upon people by the necessity of life, to proclaim that we live in a consumer society is to proclaim at the same time that we live in a society of laborers (Arendt 1958, p. 126). Hence, a society that does not work, labors, and a laboring society *is* a consuming society.

Not inconsequentially, we treat all use objects (the rightful products of work) as though they were consumer goods, so that a chair or a table is consumed as rapidly as a dress, and a dress is used up almost as quickly as food. We no longer use the worldly things around us, respecting and preserving their inherent durability, but "consume, devour, as it were, our houses and furniture and cars as though they were the "good things" of nature which spoilt uselessly if they are not drawn swiftly into the never-ending cycle of man's metabolism with nature" (Arendt, pp. 125–26). This mode of intercourse with the things of the world is perfectly adequate to the way they are produced. As the industrial revolution progressively replaced workmanship with labor, the things of the modern world have become products of labor. It is the natural fate of labor products to be consumed, unlike work products, which are there to be used.

The Primacy of Work over Consumption

There is no need to deny our zoological status, that we share something with the rest of the animal kingdom. Neither is there need to deny that there is a deep gulf between us and the rest of the animal kingdom. What we share with the rest of the animal kingdom is the necessity to be metabolically united with the rest of nature—we must consume. Where we are different, at least potentially, is in our need and capacity for work. Those systems of human activities that we call *work* are what define and determine the circle of humanity. No other animal *works*.

This duality was recognized by Milton Friedman when he noted that "Each of us is a producer and also a consumer" (1962, p. 143). Nevertheless, as Adina Schwartz has pointed out, the classical liberal/neoconservative tradition essentially holds that we "should not care about what persons do at work" (1982, p. 635). There is always a great deal of concern for the consumer's welfare, but not much for that of the worker. All social and political policy is, in the last resort, measured and gauged against its ultimate effect on "the consuming public." The concept of work is not even in the marketer's lexicon except in the form of "occupation" and then it is as a variable for segmenting consumer markets. Advertisers have recently discovered, however, that people generally dislike and even hate their work and that this can be exploited for commercial purposes just as "the striving for superiority and the needs for love, security and escape from loneliness" have been exploited "to sell toothpaste, deodorants, cigarettes, and even detergents" (Kassarjian and Sheffet 1981, p. 162).

Why, if each of us is "a producer and also a consumer," has the producer in each of us been given a back seat to the consumer in each of us, particularly if it is our patterns of work that define and determine the circle of humanity. How is it "obvious," as John Maynard Keynes wrote, that "the sole end and object of all economic activity" is consumption (1936, p. 104)? How could Adam Smith write that "Consumption is the sole end and purpose of all production" (1776/1937, p. 625). What decree authorized that social and psychological priority be given to consumption and that "sovereignty" (the right to rule, direct, and control a sociopolitical body) be vested in the consuming side of our selves? Why are social tensions analyzed and economic policies justified by recourse to the welfare of *animal laborans* rather than *Homo faber*?

Within the Western social science tradition, Karl Marx was the only writer to break with the liberal tradition to focus on work and to be concerned about what people do at work and what work does to people. Although a great many sociologists, anthropologists, and psychologists share these concerns today (without being Marxists in a strict sense of the word), it is still true that our contemporary social scientific understandings of what constitutes the degradation of work owe much to Marx. The Marxian tradition is not the only tradition that places primacy of concern on work and the conditions of work rather than on consumption. All religious traditions place primacy of importance on work over consumption. It is only the liberal tradition of the West that has reversed the ordering and given pride of place to consumption over work.

Protestantism

The United States is overwhelmingly a Protestant country. Protestant doctrine, primarily in the form of the Puritan formulations, significantly informs our beliefs, institutions, and sense of righteousness. When we speak of the Protestant ethic, however, it must be realized that there are two sides to it. One side is generally identified as the Protestant work ethic, the other as the Puritan consumption ethic. They are, however, two sides of the same coin.

In the Puritan/Protestant conception, God calls every person to serve Him by serving society and oneself in some useful, productive occupation. The emphasis is always on productivity for the benefit of society. In the Protestant formulation, work is not something done for itself or even for "the self," but for others, for society, for the community, for one's neighborhood, and—perhaps most importantly—for reasons of religious sanction. Work has primarily an extrinsic source of meaning as the satisfactions from work are gained in the knowledge that one is helping others, doing for others, and, thus, serving God. Every Christian has a "general calling" to serve God and a "personal calling," in the words of Cotton Mather, "by which his Usefulness, in his Neighborhood, is distinguished."

As an ethic, the Puritan/Protestant prescription is two-pronged—it is good to produce, but bad to consume any more than necessary. How much is necessary? Enough, but no more than needed, to maintain one's social position and to perform one's social duty. Indeed, the original condemnation of debt, which is very much a part of the ethic, was not that it threatened or revealed anything negative about the character of the individual borrowing the money, but that it left that much less for the person loaning the money to use in performing his social duty. As regards possessions accumulated, people are but the stewards of those possessions. If a person indulges in luxurious living, that much less will be available with which to support the church and society. People who needlessly consume their substance, either from carelessness or from sensuality, demonstrate failure to honor the God who furnished it. That is why the Puritan/Protestant temperament was and is uncomfortable with the prosperity that diligent effort produces (Morgan 1967; Shi 1985, chapter 1). God gives prosperity, but can use it as temptation, leading to idleness, sloth, and extravagance. Indeed, in Calvin's idea of predestination, it was God's will that everyone must work, but it was not God's will that one should lust after the fruits even of one's own labor. For the Puritans, a godly man worked diligently at his calling, not in order to accumulate personal wealth, but to add to the comfort and convenience of the community.

On Human Work

Pope John Paul II's recent encyclical *On Human Work* clearly states that *work* is a perennial topic because it is a fundamental aspect of human existence.[1] As a topic, it is always relevant and constantly demands renewed attention and decisive witness. It is, he wrote, a "basic dimension of human existence." The source of the Catholic Church's conviction that work is a, if not *the*, fundamental dimension of human experience is the Bible. The Book of Genesis states that man has been created "in the image of God," in the image of his "creator," the "Creator" of the Universe. It is God the Creator, not God the Consumer.[2]

The Pope makes an important distinction between work in the objective sense and work in the subjective sense. The *object* of work is to gain dominion over the earth so as to produce those things that people need. This is, indeed, the point of emphasis in liberal thought. But there is also a *subject* of work. In a subjective sense, the meaning of work is the person: "*the proper subject of work continues to be man*" (p. 378). And again, "*As a person, man is therefore the subject of work*" (p. 379). The entire encyclical is concerned with the subject, not the object, of work.

As people work, they perform various actions belonging to the work process. Independently of their objective content, these actions must all serve "to realize his humanity, to fulfill the calling to be a person that is his by reason of his very humanity" (p. 379). The value of work is not in the kind of work being done, not even in the results of that work, but in the fact that the one who is doing it is a person. The primary value of work lies with people, themselves, as the subjects of work, not with the object of it. Overall, one must recognize the preeminence of the subjective meaning of work over the objective one because "in the final analysis, it is man who is *the purpose of the work*" because "through work man . . . *achieves fulfillment* as a human being and indeed, in a sense, becomes 'more of a human being' " (pp. 380, 383).

When people work, they would like the fruit of that work to be used by themselves and by others. People like to feel useful; they like what they produce to be useful and to be used by others. People also like to handle the materials, to see them take shape as imagined because work has a creative aspect to it. It is, indeed, the only means of extending the human personality into nature. That is why people like to take part in the work process as sharers in responsibility as well as sharers in creativity. What is wanted is not only due remuneration for their work, but also to *know* that in their work, even on something that is owned in common, they are working "for themselves," are "producing" the self, and are developing their capacities as creative human beings to the fullest.

The Pope is unequivocal: "The church's teaching has always expressed the strong and deep conviction that man's work concerns not only the economy but also, and especially, personal values" (p. 386). While he does allude to the goods that result from the production process, he insists that human beings are also part of the result of the production process and that is why *work* has the priority: "work is 'for man' and not man 'for work' " (p. 380).

The American Work Ethic

The American work ethic has always included the "other-worldly" work-as-a-duty orientation of Protestantism. But it has always included conceptions of personal independence, self-regulation, and individual creativity (Gutman 1977; Rodgers 1978). These latter elements are generally considered to be derived from the Renaissance view of work, but they are strikingly similar to those understandings that motivate the encyclical *On Human Work*.

Americans generally view work as something that can be and should be intrinsically meaningful even if productive work is, at the moment, what most ordinary people dislike. The meaning of work is considered to lie, in part, in the work itself and not only in an ulterior realm or consequence. Not income, not salvation, not status, not power over other people, but the work process itself is seen as at least potentially gratifying. This has been described as the work-as-craftsmanship model (Mills 1956, pp. 215–38).

What is necessary for work-as-craftsmanship is that some tie between product and producer exist at the psychological level. It is less important that the producer actually own the product than that it be "owned" in the sense of knowing what goes into it by way of skill, sweat, and material and that the skill and sweat be visible in the result.

Craftspeople have an image of the completed product. Even though they may not make it all themselves, they see their place and their part in the whole, thereby understanding the meaning of their exertion in terms of that whole. Satisfaction, indeed fulfillment, is derived from the sense of accomplishment, of having achieved or reproduced that "image." The inner relation between the craftsperson and the thing made, from the image first formed of it through its completion, goes beyond the mere legal relations of property and makes the craftsperson's will to work spontaneous, even exuberant. All human activities have an element of travail and vexation because they involve the expenditure of physical and mental energy. The craftsperson is carried over it, not by the feeling of need, but by the feeling of keen anticipation.

Craftspeople have control—they can begin work according to their own plan and are free to modify its form and the manner of its creation as they go along. Craftspeople are the masters of the activity and of themselves in the process. The craftsperson's work is thus a means of developing skills as well as a means of developing oneself as a person. Self-development might be a motive, but it is also the cumulative result of devoting oneself to and practicing one's skills.

On Work and Consumption: The Historic

It is understandable how early Protestantism, particularly in the United States, could omit concern with the intrinsic aspects of the meaning of work. As late as 1840, the United States was largely preindustrial in its manufacturing processes. Except for the textile industries, manufacturing was conducted, not in the factory, but in the workshop, and was organized along the traditional model of masters and journeymen. It was, indeed, a society of yeoman farmers, small businesspeople, and self-supporting craftspeople.

In such a social economy, the aesthetic satisfaction of creating things, as well as the satisfaction of knowing that one has served others through what one has created and has distinguished oneself "in his Neighborhood," could be directly experienced. In this and all previous societies, the work of artisans and even that of the immense mass of the population engaged in crop or animal husbandry as farmers, peasants, and serfs was, as a rule, conducted autonomously. So far as the direct processes of work and labor are concerned, artisans and peasants, even in slave and feudal societies, worked according to traditional methods generally under their own control. This contrasts with contemporary industrial societies where many people work at jobs in which they are hired to perform specific series of actions such as assembly line work, keypunching, or clerking on an automated checkout line. These jobs provide almost no opportunity to formulate aims, decide on means, or adjust goals and methods in the light of experience. As Adina Schwarz expresses it:

> Instead of being hired to achieve certain goals and left to select and pursue adequate means, workers are employed to perform precisely specified action. Even the order in which they perform those operations, the pace at which they work, and the particular bodily movements they employ are largely determined by others' decisions. When the entire job consists of such mechanical activity, workers are in effect paid for blindly pursuing ends that others have chosen, by means that they judge adequate. (1982, pp. 634–35).

The "masters" take over the entire process, repeatedly reshaping it and reorganizing it, parceling it out as tasks to laborers for whom the process as a whole is now lost. The ownership of the tools and instruments of production is transferred to others, the ownership of the product is transferred to others, and the ownership of the proceeds from the sale of the product is transferred to others. First the capitalist and today "management" controls these things.

Everything about the productive process has become foreign to the workers in the sense that everything is outside their interests, claim, and/or control. It amounts to nothing less than the mass degradation of work (Braverman 1974; Terkel 1974).

Consumerism and the Degradation of Work

There is a distinct connection between consumerism (the acceptance of consumption as the way to self-development, self-realization, and self-fulfillment) and the degradation of work. If meaningful work is systematically denied to a people, then obviously they must seek their meanings elsewhere. It should be no surprise that the search was directed into the realm of consumption. As T.J. Jackson Lears expressed it, "A quest for self-realization through consumption [has] compensated for a loss of autonomy on the job" (1983, p. 29). But we all realize that no matter how much we try to convince ourselves to the contrary, the satisfaction derived from consumption is not the same as the sense of accomplishment, joy, and fulfillment that producing something engenders. Surrogate satisfiers are always inferior.

With the introduction and application of scientific management to the division of labor plus the mechanization of the productive process, work was reduced to an industrial labor routine. Two situations followed. First, as Loren Baritz (1960) has discussed, new forms of labor discipline had to be found or devised in order to deal with the problems of "motivation" and "morale" that arose when workers lost control of the design and rhythm of work. Second, the laboring middle class had to be encouraged to find in consumption that satisfaction and fulfillment that could no longer be found in work.

The second problem required a multifold attack. What was left of the original Protestant ethic's emphasis on frugal living had to be eradicated. The Puritan consumption ethic guided people to find satisfaction in work, not in consumption. The country had been flooded with a welter of goods that threatened to cause havoc unless people accelerated their spending. A newspaper editorial at the time proclaimed that the American's "first importance to his country [was] no longer that of citizen but that of consumer. Consumption is a new necessity" (as quoted in Shi 1985, p. 219). Consequently, the public had to be taught the joys of consumerism; the springs of impulse buying had to be uncoiled. This was largely the role of advertising. Writing in the *Encyclopedia of the Social Sciences* (1922), Leverett S. Lyon claimed that "Advertising is the greatest force at work against the traditional economy . . . [and] almost the only force at work against puritanism in consumption" (as quoted in Ewen 1976, p. 57).

This meant, however, that *use* goods, the proper products of work, had to be treated as *consumption* goods. Writing in *Printer's Ink* in 1930, Earnest Elmo Calkins declared, "consumption engineering must see to it that we use up the kinds of goods we now merely use" (as quoted in Salgo 1973, p. 31). Similarly, Leon Kelley wrote in *Printer's Ink* (1936):

> It grows more and more apparent that the modern cycle of over-production and market-glutting leaves practically no room for mankind's old ideas about long lasting products . . . Above all, we face the task of selling the whole public away from the deep-rooted idea of durability (as quoted in Salgo, pp. 31–32).

This also was the role of advertising. As an executive of General Motors proclaimed in 1929: "Advertising is in the business of making people healthily dissatisfied with what they have in favor of something better. The old factors of wear and tear can no longer be depended upon to create a demand. They are too slow" (as quoted in Salgo, p. 31).

What was needed, as Otis Pease noted in *The Responsibility of American Advertising* (1958), was for advertisements to "create in their middle class readers a frame of mind that constantly sought new acquisitions" (as quoted by Salgo, p. 27). Articles that did not wear out or were not consumed were thought of as business tragedies; one common approach, articulated by silver and watch manufacturers, was to ridicule the past from which the use goods came, those "ancestral heirlooms 'woefully outmoded' " then being used rather than used up (as quoted in Salgo, p. 27).

It was also realized, as *Printer's Ink* editorialized in 1919, that "if we encourage Gusseppi, the track laborer, to wear silken pajamas we must not complain when he strikes for more pay" (as quoted in Salgo, p. 27). The solution here was not so much to provide those higher wages (although real wages were rising) as to provide—at interest—the funds for the purchase of those silken pajamas.

Nothing is more obvious yet more overlooked than the simple fact that mass production, which (whether or not it invariably included a tremendous degradation of work) required mass consumption for ultimate success. Daniel Bell points out that while a number of technological revolutions made mass production possible, mass consumption was made possible by several specific social inventions, including the development of marketing, "which rationalized the art of identifying different kinds of buying groups and whetting consumer appetites," and the spread of installment buying, which, more than any other social device, "broke down the old Protestant fear of debt" (1976, pp. 66–72). American capitalism changed its nature in the 1920s, Bell wrote, "by encouraging the consumers to go into debt, and to live with debt as a way of life" (pp. 242, 69).

The tremendous increase in indebtedness in our time is widely viewed as reflecting a change in popular attitudes and behavior. Indeed it does. But the increase in indebtedness can only be understood for what it is if it is seen as an integral part of the whole. An increase in consumer debt, as Galbraith has pointed out (1976, chapter 13), is implicit in the process by which consumer appetites are whetted. Any society prepared to spend billions of dollars to persuade people of their wants must also find ways to finance those wants. That largely means that it must be prepared to persuade consumers of the ease and desirability of incurring debt to realize their wants.

The old value pattern that defined achievement as doing and making, and in which people displayed their character in the quality of their work, was intentionally and systematically replaced by a value pattern in which achievement was redefined to emphasize status and taste. The importance of *doing* was replaced by the importance of having as the citizen-craftsperson was replaced by the citizen-consumer. In a very real sense, a culture of production and creation was replaced by a culture of consumption (Ostreicher 1981).

Conclusion

We are at a point, then, where marketers must realize that if they sincerely want to contribute to a better and a higher quality of life, they must broaden their philosophical domain (their area of concern) and embrace much more than what has hitherto been embraced within the rubric of "marketing." They will have to realize that much consumption is necessary, but much of it today is part of a larger pattern of dependence, disorientation, and loss of control (Daun 1983). Consequently, there is little that marketing can do to enhance the quality of life as long as it is primarily concerned with maximizing the market's consumption of goods and services. Indeed, marketing might be expected to decrease, rather than increase, the quality of life in direct proportion to the vigor with which it pursues that traditional purpose.

Such a stance, however, would ally marketing with traditional social critics against the mainstream of the liberal tradition. It would also ally marketing with the women's movement, the ecology movement, and any number of other contemporary social change movements. These movements have a very different worldview than either traditional management or traditional labor as they embody or prefigure the sense that it is possible to live better by working differently and/or consuming less (Gorz 1980, 1982). To ally with such movements may pit marketers against those for whom they have traditionally worked, but it may also put marketing on the side of the future (Milbrath 1984).

Macromarketing researchers who want to understand consumption behavior in contemporary United States must move beyond the study of consumption by itself. Particularly, any attempt to understand prevailing patterns of consumption must have a historical perspective, one with a broader domain and embrace than the simple sphere of consumption by itself. Historians are beginning to understand the ways in which industrialization altered the daily lives of nineteenth century workers and the resulting evolution of working class culture (Dawley 1976; Edwards 1979; Nelson 1975). They are discovering that the process of industrialization took place within an atmosphere of deep ambivalence, not only among workers, but also among those who have previously been characterized as uncritical supporters of modernization. We have yet to fully confront the psychological reorientation that accompanied this development, although some progress is being made here, too (Fox and Lears 1983). That psychological reorientation is what the culture of consumption is all about. It would seem to be properly part of marketing as a discipline since it is related to marketing as a professional activity and to one of the central areas of marketing's concern—consumer behavior. Marketers must understand that it cannot be really understood without an equally detailed understanding of the entire process, including what happened to work.

Finally, those macromarketers who see themselves as change agents concerned with transforming our society and economy into one that serves life, rather than just living, might take their cue from Eric Fromm when he wrote:

> The transformation of our society into one which serves life must change the consumption and thereby change, indirectly, the production pattern of present industrial society. Such a change would obviously not come as a result of bureaucratic orders but of studies, information, discussion, and decision making on the part of the population, educated to become aware of the difference between life-furthering and life-hindering kinds of needs. (1968, p. 120)

Fromm, however, had things backward in that the transformation of our society into one which serves life must start by changing the patterns of work and thereby change, indirectly, the patterns of consumption. But he was correct that it cannot be the result of bureaucratic orders handed down from above but the result of studies, information, discussion, and decision making on the part of everybody. And in this, marketing educators can play a significant role.

But what of marketing as management technology? It will occupy the same role it occupies now, however much changed in scope and importance. Marketing as management technology will still be concerned with, as Kotler expresses it, "*influencing the level, timing, and composition of demand in a way that will help the organization achieve its objectives.* Simply put, marketing management [will still be] *demand management*" (1984, p. 15, emphasis in original). The objectives of the organization, however, will not lie solely with the expansion of capital and thereby serving the needs, wants, desires, hopes, dreams, and philosophies of "management." It will also lie with the expansion and creation of meaningful work for all, thereby serving the needs, wants, desires, hopes, and dreams of all people as workers, citizens, family members, community members, and consumers.

Notes

1. All page references to the encyclical are to the excerpted version in Williamson, Evans, and Rustad (1985, pp. 375–89).

2. This expression is mine and is not similarly expressed in the encyclical *On Human Work*.

References

Arendt, Hannah (1958), *The Human Condition.* Chicago: University of Chicago Press.

Baritz, Loren (1960), *The Servants of Power: A History of the Use of Social Science in American Industry.* Middletown, Conn.: Wesleyan University Press.

Bell, Daniel (1976), *The Cultural Contradictions of Capitalism.* New York: Basic Books.

Braverman, Harry (1974), *Labor and Monopoly Capital.* New York: Monthly Review.

Daun, Ake (1983), "The Materialistic Life-Style: Some Socio-Psychological Aspects," in *Consumer Behavior and Environmental Quality: Trends and Prospects in the Ways of Life.* Lissa Uusitalo, ed. New York: St. Martin's, 6–16.

Dawley, Alan (1976), *Class and Community: The Industrial Revolution in Lynn.* Cambridge, Mass.: Harvard University Press.

Dholakia, Nikhilesh (1985), "Is the Marketing Wave Stoppable? Kotler, Hirschman, and the Ever-Breaching Dykes," unpublished manuscript.

Easterlin, Richard A. (1973), "Does Money Buy Happiness?" *The Public Interest* 30 (Winter): 3–10.

――― , (1974), "Does Economic Growth Improve the Human Lot? Some Empirical Evidence," in *Nations and Households in Economic Growth: Essays in Honor of Moses Abramovitz,* Paul A. David and Melvin W. Reder, eds. New York: Academic Press.

Edwards, Richard (1979), *Contested Terrain: The Transformation of the Workplace in the Twentieth Century.* New York: Basic Books.

Ewen, Stuart (1976), *Captains of Consciousness: Advertising and the Social Roots of the Consumer Culture.* New York: McGraw-Hill.

Fox, Richard Wrightman, and T.J. Jackson Lears, eds. (1983), *The Culture of Consumption: Critical Essays in American History: 1880–1980.* New York: Pantheon.

Friedman, Milton (1962), *Capitalism and Freedom.* Chicago: University of Chicago Press.

Fromm, Eric (1968), *The Revolution of Hope.* New York: Harper & Row.

Galbraith, John Kenneth (1976), *The Affluent Society,* 3rd ed. Boston: Houghton Mifflin.

Glenn, Evelyn, and Roslyn Feldberg (1977), "Degraded and Deskilled: the Proletarianization of Clerical Work," *Social Problems* 25 (October): 52–64.

Gorz, Andre (1980), *Ecology as Politics.* Boston: South End.

――― , (1982), *Farewell to the Working Class: An Essay on Post-Industrial Society.* Boston: South End.

Gutman, Herbert G. (1977), *Work, Culture, and Society in Industrializing America.* New York: Alfred A. Knopf.

Kassarjian, Harold H., and Mary Jane Sheffet (1981), "Personality and Consumer Behavior: An Update," in *Perspectives in Consumer Behavior*, 3rd ed., Harold H. Kassarjian and Thomas S. Robertson, eds. Glenview, Ill.: Scott, Foresman.

Keynes, John Maynard (1936), *The General Theory*. New York: Harcourt, Brace & World.

Kotler, Philip (1984), *Marketing Management*, 5th ed. Englewood Cliffs, N.J.: Prentice-Hall.

Lasch, Christopher (1984), *The Minimal Self: Psychic Survival in Troubled Times*. New York: Norton.

Lears, T.J. Jackson (1983), "From Salvation to Self-Realization: Advertising and the Therapeutic Roots of the Consumer Culture, 1880–1930," in *The Culture of Consumption: Critical Essays in American History: 1880–1980*, Richard Wrightman Fox and T.J. Jackson Lears, eds. New York: Pantheon, 3–38.

Leiss, William (1984), "Economic Life as Symbolic Activity," in *Economic Growth and the Role of Science*, Soren Bergstrom, ed. Stockholm: Publishing House of the Swedish Research Councils.

Milbrath, Lester (1984), *Environmentalists: Vanguard for a New Society*. Albany, N.Y.: SUNY Press.

Mills, C. Wright (1956), *White Collar: The American Middle Classes*. New York: Oxford University Press.

Morgan, E.S. (1967), "The Puritan Ethic and the American Revolution," *William and Mary Quarterly*, 3rd series, 24: 3–43.

Nelson, Daniel (1975), *Managers and Workers: Origins of the New Factory System in the United States, 1880–1920*. Madison: University of Wisconsin Press.

Ostreicher, Richard (1981), "From Artisan to Consumer: Images of Workers 1840–1920," *Journal of American Culture* 4 (Spring): 47–64.

Rescher, Nicholas (1980), "Technological Progress and Human Happiness," in *Unpopular Essays on Technological Progress*. Pittsburgh: University of Pittsburgh Press, 3–22.

Rodgers, Daniel T. (1978), *The Work Ethic in Industrial America, 1850–1920*. Chicago: University of Chicago Press.

Salgo, Harvey (1973), "The Obsolescence of Growth." *The Review of Radical Political Economics* 5(3): 26–45.

Schwartz, Adina (1982), "Meaningful Work," *Ethics* 92 (July): 634–46.

Seabrook, Jeremy (1977), *What Went Wrong? Why Hasn't Having More Made People Happier?* New York: Pantheon.

Shi, David E. (1985), *The Simple Life: Plain Living and High Thinking in American Culture*. New York: Oxford University Press.

Smith, Adam (1937/1776), *The Wealth of Nations*. New York: Modern Library.

Spratlen, Thaddeus H. (1972), "The Challenge of Humanistic Value Orientation in Marketing," in *Society and Marketing: An Unconventional View*, Norman Kangun, ed. New York: Harper & Row, 403–13.

Terkel, Studs (1974), *Working*. New York: Pantheon.

Wachtel, Paul (1983), *The Poverty of Affluence: A Psychological Portrait of the American Way of Life*. New York: Free Press.

Williamson, John B., Linda Evans, and Michael Rustad (1985), *Social Problems: The Contemporary Debates*, 4th ed. Boston: Little, Brown.

14

The Social Construction of Consumption Patterns: Understanding Macro Consumption Phenomena

A. Fuat Fırat

The Questions

By 1974 (the last year for which ownership statistics were published in the *U.S. Statistical Abstract, 1978*), 83.8 percent of all households in the United States owned automobiles. The proportion of ownership in the same year for television sets was 96.6 percent. For refrigerators, it was 98.9 percent, and for washing machines, it was 71.9 percent.

Why have these products become so diffused among households, and so universally purchased and consumed in advanced market economies? Why is there no interest within marketing and consumer behavior disciplines in explaining this phenomenon? What are the forces behind the growing universality of consumption of certain products in the First World and increasingly in the Third World? Does this have anything to do with the "irrational" choices made by the poor and disadvantaged consumers in society?

The theoretical framework presented briefly in this chapter was developed to try and answer such questions. While to some, the large proportions of ownership reproduced above may be sufficient reason to believe that such products are indispensable in human life, such brushing aside of the issue is neither scientific nor pragmatic. However, such large proportions may partially explain the reason why, in the models of behavior in marketing, the need for a certain product (for example, a car or a television set) is taken for granted and the product features/brand choice process is studied.

Consumption choices, it must be recognized, take place at different levels. For example, there is the consumption mode choice: car versus public transportation. Then, there is choice among product groups or features: small truck versus automobile, family car versus sports car. Then, there is brand choice: Chevrolet versus Ford. For a consumer, these choices may be simultaneous or ordered. Further, some choices may be socially rather than individually made, and the consumer may be highly constrained.

As the above ownership statistics attest, there are some products that have become predominant in U.S. society, and a keen observer will realize that they are becoming so in many other societies in the capitalist world. A study of the reasons why this is so may provide an understanding of consumption and society, which may then enhance our explanations of the phenomena that marketing people have been studying for so long.

Consumption Pattern Dimensions

Why have certain products become so diffused and dominant? My argument is that there are some dimensions found in all of these commodities, and these dimensions have become sought by consumers due to some sociohistorical phenomena. Therefore, when consumers choose certain modes of consumption, they are selecting products representative of a pattern along these dimensions. Thus, the products may not be significant per se, but only as long as they represent a certain consumption pattern (CP).

Indeed, when a historical survey is made of the changes in consumption of consumers in advanced capitalist economies, certain transformations can be observed. These transformations can best be described along certain dimensions (Fırat and Dholakia 1977, 1982). These dimensions and their ranges are shown in figure 14–1. Since these dimensions have been discussed at some length elsewhere (Fırat and Dholakia 1982; Fırat 1986), I shall only introduce them briefly here. This brief introduction will show that the products for which proportions were given above, along with similar other products (e.g., clothes dryers, TV dinners, air conditioners, music systems, single homes, and dishwashers), do represent a pattern along these dimensions.

As figure 14–1 shows, the four dimensions are the social relationship dimension, the domain of availability dimension, the level of participation dimension, and the human activity dimension. The social relationship dimension defines a consumer's relationship with other consumers during the act of consumption, ranging from collective to individual consumption. Consumption is individual when relations with other consumers do not exist or are minimal. An example is someone eating a TV dinner alone. A picnic planned together with neighbors where cooking and transportation are shared is an example of a somewhat collective consumption. The kibbutz is an example of a highly collective CP (Reuven 1972).

The domain of availability dimension defines the availability of a product

Dimension	Range		
Social Relationship	Individual	———————————	Collective
Domain of Availability	Private	———————————	Public
Level of Participation	Alienated	———————————	Synergistic
Human Activity	Passive	———————————	Active

Adapted from Firat and Dholakia (1982)

Figure 14–1. Dimensions of Consumption Patterns

to the members of society. It ranges from private to public consumption. For example, an automobile is privately owned by one household and is generally not available to others. Public transportation vehicles and telephone booths, on the other hand, are available to many (the public). The difference between individual and private consumption could be pointed out by noting that while, for example, a telephone booth is public, its consumption is generally individual.

The level of participation dimension defines a consumer's level of participation in the development and production of a product and ranges from alienated to synergistic. Consumption is synergistic when the consumer is directly involved in the planning, development, and production of what is to be consumed. An example of synergistic consumption is a household planning and building its own dwelling from scratch. Alienated consumption occurs when the rules of consumption are developed and dictated without the participation of the individual consumer. This occurs in the case of products produced for the market. When a consumer buys, for example, a home video game system, the consumer is involved in alienated consumption since the games, as well as the technology and rules of the games, are developed without the direct participation of the consumer.

Finally, the human activity dimension defines the level of physical activity the consumer is involved in during the act of consumption. It ranges from passive to active consumption. Examples of passive consumption are watching television or using a washing machine or dishwasher. Active consumption examples are participant sports and hobbies.

From these examples of the dimensions of CPs, it can be discerned that the products highly diffused in North American markets represent a trend toward an *individual-private-alienated-passive* CP (Fırat 1986). As I will explain, it is because they represent such patterns of relationships which are dominating life in advanced market economies that these products have become so diffused in society.

Theory of the Social Construction of Consumption Patterns

The concept of a dominating CP, as used in this chapter carries two meanings. One is that the pattern of life expected and induced by the CP is consistent with, and in fact, an integral part of the socioeconomic order that prevails in society. As such, consumption values and norms represented by the dominant CP are ones that reign in the ideology that controls social choices. Consequently, consumers, whether or not they possess the products required to adopt the CP, aspire to it. The second meaning, a natural extension of the first, is that a growing majority of the population of consumers in society conform to the CP. This correspondence with the prevailing socioeconomic order and diffusion to a growing majority of consumers render this CP dominant.

The logical question that follows, given the purposes of this chapter, is whether this conformity is based upon total free choice by consumers or if this choice is determined by factors beyond the control of consumers. If there are factors beyond consumers' control, to what extent does this determination limit free choice by individual consumers?

Consider a family moving from Montreal, Canada, to Dallas, Texas. Since in Montreal, there is a fairly efficient public transportation system, this family did not own a car. When they move to Dallas, they realize that there is no public transportation to many parts of the metropolitan area, and they cannot even get taxis to or from certain areas. They recognize that they either own a car or they cannot even do their grocery shopping very well. Does this family now have a choice? Whatever choice is left to this family is greatly limited: They own a car or they become an isolated unit in society. Isolation, however, has great social, psychological, and economic costs. Thus events will make the choice situation so skewed that they will probably not even consider not buying a car. Their choice will basically be limited to what type and brand of car to buy.

The Structure of Available Alternatives for Consumption

The brief anecdote above exhibits well how the structure of society limits choice by individual consumers. From a consumption perspective, the structure that is important in determining choice is the *structure of available alternatives for consumption* (SAAC). The concept of the SAAC includes, by the presence of the term *structure*, the relations of available alternatives for consumption to each other in terms of importance, visibility, complementarity, and advantageousness; it does not just imply simple availability of products. One needs to understand the processes of the formation and transformation of the SAAC in society to understand choice at the level of CPs.

For any product to be present within the SAAC, it must be produced and made socially available. The question is, therefore: Which products get to be produced and made socially available? Why and how are they produced and made available? Which consumers, if any, participate in the decisions made to produce them, and to what extent do they participate?

The classical political economy paradigm finds the answer to the above question in the entrepreneurship of the investor. This is the commonly accepted view in marketing also. The entrepreneur with the right antennae feels the needs of the consumers in the market and provides the product(s) that will satisfy these needs. This, in fact, is the marketing concept. However, in a capitalist market economy, the entrepreneur is taking a risk by investing capital and expects a return that will make this risk justified. Therefore, for the entrepreneur, sensing a need is not sufficient, there must be effective demand (buying power) behind this need. Thus, the needs most likely to be satisfied in a market economy are the needs of those consumers who have buying power. The concept of the Pareto optima within the classical economy paradigm points out this fact (Pareto 1971). This means that not all consumers will satisfy all their needs, for within the SAAC, products to satisfy some of their needs will not be available due to insufficient effective demand. Resources will be preferentially allocated to those needs backed by buying power. If one assumes independence of needs, as is the case in classical political economy, this conclusion does not have any major implications. However, if the existing SAAC does influence the need perceptions of individual consumers (if needs and consumption behaviors of consumer units are *interdependent*) as argued by several scholars (Duessenberry 1949; Veblen 1899), the implication is that consumption choices by consumers with high buying power will influence those with low buying power. Some empirical support for this conclusion exists (Brady 1952). However, a full explanation of the process requires an understanding of how the preferences of consumers with high buying power are formed.

Critics of the classical political economy paradigm (Baran 1957; Galbraith 1971; Marx 1967; Sweezy 1947) have argued that need perceptions of consumer units are dependent on the social productive organization and/or the social structure, as well as being a function of interactions among consumers. Another deviation from the classical model (what could be called the consumerist model) argues that there is a power differential in the market between producers and consumers (Nader and Green 1973). The consumerist model, however, makes no distinction among consumers as being more or less powerful. It basically asserts the classical philosophical assumption of consumer sovereignty and only blames imperfect competitive conditions that give corporations great power in the market and impede the ability of consumers to communicate their needs to producers. The Galbraith model goes one step further to argue that the producers of goods and services deliberately manipulate the need perceptions of consumers, especially through their marketing practices.

The Role of the Powerful

A major common flaw in the consumerist and Galbraith models seems to be the somewhat arbitrary division of society into producers and consumers. Although one can separate the functions of production and consumption for purposes of theoretical discussion and analysis of some phenomena, society is not rigidly divided along these lines in reality. Every person who participates in production is also a consumer. What individuals do within the productive organization is an important part of their lives and will influence their values, worldviews, need perceptions, preference patterns, and consumption. In fact, productive activities are a major way by which people come in contact with and learn from the objective environment (Berger and Luckmann 1966). Moreover, social stratification is based fundamentally on the relations of the members of society to the productive forces, particularly the relative position of the individual within the productive organization (Bendix 1974; Tumin 1967; Weber 1964). Finally, those who own or control the means of production also participate actively in the decisions affecting the social, economic, and political environment (Bennett and Klecka 1970; Domhoff 1978; Dye 1979; Miliband 1973; Mills 1971; Zeitlin 1974). Political and social circumstances may lead to sporadic and limited participation by the less powerful or the underprivileged, but such participation has been found to have negligible impact on societal decision-making processes and their overall outcomes (Nadel 1971).

The overlap between those who control decisions within the productive organization and those who have the buying power in the market (Wright and Perrone 1977; Wright 1978) creates a certain consumption choice pattern. Because of their relations and interests in the productive units, the preferences of the powerful consumers are biased toward the CP that satisfies the needs and efficiency criteria of the productive organization. This is not a planned, purposive behavior, but rather a natural tendency resulting from everyday social interactions. In a capitalist society, the basic criteria of production are profitability and return on investment. These criteria can be continuously met through the expansion and extension of the markets. The greater the expansion of the market, the greater the impetus for production, for development of technologies, and for entepreneurship.

In a capitalist market economy, value systems that regard the market as the most free and democratic means for supplying the needs of consumers reinforce the requirements of the productive organization to expand the markets. In such societies, those who are in decision-making positions within the production units are influenced by these values that correspond well with the imperatives of success in their organizations. Therefore, they will encourage marketing of those products that enlarge the markets. As consumers, they appreciate these products; as producers, they develop a deep regard for the technologies that enable production of such products (Weber 1964).

Processes Reinforcing the SAAC

Such overlap of values, decision making, and consumers who can support development of novel products that impact on life patterns assures that in capitalist market economies, changes in CPs will be largely determined by the production technology and the need perceptions created by it—need perceptions first and forcefully felt by the powerful.

The model of the societal process sketched above is further supported by the historical observations made by scholars (cf. Tucker 1964) regarding the diffusion of products that were novel and represented a change in CPs and life patterns of consumers at the time they were first introduced. For such products, a definite trickle-down process is observed. One can find the proportions of ownership in different income groups for products such as automobiles, television sets, washing machines, dishwashers, microwave ovens, and refrigerators over the years in the *U.S. Statistical Yearbooks* (e.g., 1969 through 1978). A review of these proportions will be sufficient to recognize the presence of a trickle-down process. The higher-income and higher-social-status consumers (especially those who have large holdings in corporations, high-level managers, and some high-income professionals) have adopted such products first. The same result is supported by a review of the diffusion of innovations literature (Ostlund 1973). While diffusion of novelties in *brands* and in differentiated features of existing products shows no association with demographic characteristics of consumers, when new *products* are concerned, such associations are found.

However, this process is not the only one that confirms the influence of the productive organization on the formation of CPs, although it is probably the most significant. Production units (the corporations) themselves are major consumers in society. Corporations—which in theory and historically have developed to service the needs of the people in society, and have, as their reason for existence, such a responsibility—become social units themselves. They develop needs that require satisfaction, and they end up being the largest consumers in society. By any measure, they are the largest consumers of energy, transportation systems, and construction, for example. As the top managers of corporations make decisions regarding consumption of these production units, they use the criterion of economic efficiency, thus influencing the SAAC in society in a certain direction. For example, a major factor in the development of the automotive industry, highways, and electrical energy has been the consumption choices of these corporations as the major initial consumers of such products. Their lobbying activities as consumers and producers in favor of government investments in such areas have also had effects in the development of these products.

The allocation of state incomes among different programs also affects the formation of the SAAC. Whether the states encourage spending on highway transportation or suburban housing systems, say, is important because such decisions influence the socioeconomic structures of the housing and transportation subsystems directly and other subsystems (e.g., shopping and recreation) indirectly. When resource allocation by the enterprises and the state are controlled by the same criteria (e.g., capital accumulation and industrial growth) and the upper socioeconomic strata adopt and internalize the CPs that fit these criteria through their control of the productive organizations, it can be said that the SAAC is largely determined, not by innate needs of human beings, but by the necessities of the productive organization. The influence that enterprises have over government policies is also receiving close scrutiny; more and more examples that support this control are gaining public awareness (Dye 1979; Domhoff 1978; Edwards, Reich, and Weisskopf 1978; Therborn 1980; Wright 1979).

SAAC and the Consumer

The SAAC is, then, largely determined by the necessities of the productive organization of the society in a capitalist market economy. Consumers with higher incomes (especially those who control the enterprises) are instrumental in the societal acceptance of products that will satisfy the necessities of productive organizations. The choices for consumption by the productive enterprises, as well as public consumption advocated by state policies, along with the working of the market, determine both the social choices made in society and the SAAC.

When novel products that are enabled by the newly developed technologies are introduced, often it is only those consumers with high discretionary incomes who can afford them. Products that fit into new life patterns and which require, therefore, consumption of other supporting and related products present high-risk investments for consumers. Consumers with less discretionary incomes and less familiarity with these products—since they are not the ones who use prototypes first adopted by corporations (personal computers and new communication systems are cases in point)—are not the ones who can afford such risk. Thus, the further reason for the trickle-down process.

Consumers who have high discretionary incomes, mostly because they hold significant positions in productive units or professional business (Edwards, Reich, and Weisskopf 1978; Miliband 1973; Morgello 1974; Wright and Perrone 1977; Wright 1978; Zeitlin 1974), are in the best position to have knowledge of potential alternatives for consumption and to judge which ones will have the better potential for profitability and marketing. Their relations to and positions within the productive organizations largely determine their values, preferences, and appreciation for the new life patterns and products that further the success of these organizations. Adoption of products that extend these values and preferences to the consumption sphere by the socially more visible, affluent strata influences both the SAAC and the aspirations of other consumers who generally learn to follow the affluent life-styles in awe.

Implications for the Poor Consumer

The implication of such formation of the SAAC for the poor and the powerless consumers is that they are confronted with societal structures and subsystems of consumption which transform without their participation. This SAAC and the related subsystems (housing, transportation, shopping, health, etc.), then, largely determine what these consumers will perceive as "needs" and what consumption items they will value as acceptable, normal, and parts of standard CPs. If their income enables satisfaction of such needs and conformity to the CP without major problems, they will easily adapt to the transformation in the SAAC. If their resources run short, they will aspire and struggle to achieve this new CP. In this vein, they will get involved in "irrational" consumption practices as defined by the normative scientific and meliorative discourse (Irelan 1967). These consumers will either exhibit imbalance in their satisfaction of basic needs (malnutrition or inadequate sanitation, housing, or medical care) or they will overspend, going into debt and financial dependency.

Systemic Logic for the Contemporary CP

The formation and transformation of the SAAC and, consequently, of CPs is schematized in figure 14–2. The marketing system has been a major factor in the socialization of consumers into the dominating CP in market economies.

Marketing fosters the diffusion of this pattern through its product and price differentiation policies and also through its promotion capabilities (Moorman, Chapter 11, *Supra*; Schudson 1984). Differentiation enables purchase of products representing the dominating CP by consumers with income constraints and different cultural backgrounds. While the same CP has diffused among a majority of consumers, becoming uniform across households, within the same CP there has occurred an abundance of product and brand differentiation, creating a great variety of consumer choice within this

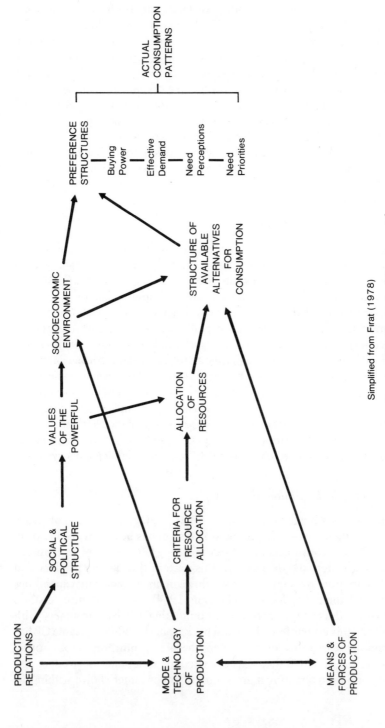

Simplified from Firat (1978)

Figure 14–2. Proposed Theoretical Framework

limited sphere. Examples include automobiles, television sets, designer jeans, and washing machines. While almost every household in the United States has one or more cars for going to work and shopping, for some households, it is a Dodge van that serves the purpose, for others, a Nissan sedan. Consumers feel a false sense of individuality in driving a brand that millions of others drive, doing the same things with their vehicle that others do using different brands. While product and brand differentiation help this diffusion phenomenon, promotion makes the powerful consumers' life-styles more visible as common reference points to all consumers, reinforcing the dominant CP.

Why *individual-private-alienated-passive* consumption? Do human beings have a natural tendency or need to withdraw from social relationships? In human nature, is there a desire to own things and protect them from others' use? Is it innate to be passive and expect to follow instructions rather than be active and have control over the method of consumption? The psychological findings show that, if anything, the transformation into individual-private-alienated-passive life patterns seems to create problems for many individuals—problems of personal identification, feelings of loneliness and dependency, and failed efforts of compensating for various dissatisfactions through possession of products, among others. The evidence is strong that human beings are forced into the contemporary CPs rather than freely select them. Indeed, this has much to do with choicelessness (Dholakia and Dholakia 1985; Dholakia, Dholakia, and Fırat 1983) at a fundamental level of consumption, that of consumption patterns, while there is much choice at the level of brands.

The reasons for the individual-private-alienated-passive CP are to be found in the character of capitalism. Economies of capital realization and accumulation require that market exchange expands in all facets of life and society. Only through consumers' willingness to exchange money for products in the market can the enterprises realize their criteria for existence, prosperity, and growth. The more products are bought and consumed *individually* and *privately* by consumers, the more markets will grow and expand, whereas *collective* and *public* consumption would limit this expansion. In order to enter all facets of life to expand markets, products will have to substitute more and more human labor in the household and elsewhere; thus, the trend toward *passive* consumption. The economies of scale, mass production technology, and mass market exchange require standardization and satisfaction of socialized (or common) needs. Furthermore, expansion of the markets requires that production be removed from households to organized productive systems; thus, the trend toward *alienated* consumption.

Implications for Marketing

Problems in the Literature

Marketing literature has successfully avoided attempts at a true understanding of the forces behind the growing uniformity in what and how consumers consume in advanced market economies or around the world. I find four reasons for this:

1. *The assumptions that dominate the marketing discipline.* A major assumption is one of consumer sovereignty. While it is usually understood that consumer choices occur under constraints, the unshakable faith is that the consumers, nevertheless, make their minds up about what and how they will consume independently, given their own needs and priorities. The rhetoric of freedom and free choice is so interwoven into the ideas of the market system and the workings of a free market, that it is thoroughly inconceivable, a taboo, in fact, to imagine and, certainly, to express anything otherwise. In step with the orientation of the method of positivism/logical empiricism that the marketing discipline has embraced, marketing scholars tend to get caught up with the appearances in the market. Exceptions to this rule are grimly rare and hardly visible in the literature. And, the appearance in the market is, after all, that each consumer voluntarily spends money on things to buy; there is no apparent physical or other kind of coercion. But, could need perceptions, wants, priorities, and preferences of consumers be controlled and determined by sociopolitical and economic phenomena without any apparent coercion? This chapter is partially an investigation into this issue.

2. *The demands of the primary audience and customers of the marketing discipline.* Historically, business organizations have been the primary audience of the discipline and the customers for the discipline's products: theories, methods, and market information. For this audience, why and how needs originate and transform—and, as an extension of the quest, why certain needs become perceived uniformly by so many in certain historical periods—have never been of interest. For these customers of the discipline, the important issues have been to recognize and identify the perceived needs, to know the decision-making processes of the consumers, and to apply the most effective techniques and methods for influencing consumer choices (brand choice in particular). As long as the consumers perceive the needs for the products and effectively demand them by using their purchasing power, no problem exists for the business marketer. Rather important problems may exist, however, for the consumers, especially for the poor, the disadvantaged, and the underprivileged. Yet, consumers have not been marketing discipline's customers, only its subjects.

3. *The predominantly micro orientation of the marketing discipline.* In line with the first two attributes, the marketing discipline has a predominantly micro orientation. Recently, there has been some interest in macro phenomena, but a truly macro theory in marketing has not yet been presented or widely heard. Macro theory seeks to explain the relationships between the society as a whole and its institutions or individuals (its social units). In marketing, the main interest in this relationship is in terms of reference group influence on individual consumer decision making. Connections between elements of the macro system (the sociopolitico-economic whole), the system itself, or the interactions between consumers in terms of structural relationships are basically not studied. Again, the system is assumed as a given.

4. *The managerial/technological character dominant in the marketing discipline.* The history of its ideology, its audience, and its micro orientation have given the discipline a managerial/technological character. There is little, if any, interest in understanding and explanation. What is crucial is prediction of success of the actions and practices within the given environment and system. Marketing, as the name of the discipline itself connotes, is interested in *action*, in *doing*, and not so much in reflection, contemplation, or investigation for the mere purpose of understanding.

Requirements for Relevance in Marketing

A discipline needs to provide information for more than just one or a few audiences in society to be socially relevant. In this respect, marketing is at a crossroad today. If the marketing discipline does want such relevance, it has to abdicate its advocacy role for business and take on a social scientific perspective. An almost exclusive interest in predictive frameworks and studies must be enlarged to include explanatory approaches. An orientation of seeking techniques that will be successful from a business/managerial perspective, given the present system, must be changed to include efforts to understand the system and its effects on the individual units.

In this respect, development of macro theories is essential and useful. Specifically, I maintain that macro theories are needed because:

1. Theories that are at a lower level of aggregation need to be put into a holistic (total) perspective. Unless this is achieved, micro theories will most probably be piecemeal and often contradictory in their predictions when compared across time, marketing systems, or societies.

2. There is a need to analyze the interrelations among the individuals' attitudinal and behavioral characteristics, actions of society's institutions, and the society at large. Without such analysis, it will become both impossible to understand consumption phenomena in their entirety and easy to fall into the trap of naive empiricism (Jacoby 1978).

3. Macro theories are essential to better understand and implement policies designed to further social goals. Without an understanding of the interface between society and its component units, it is not possible to predict the impact of social, political, or economic programs on society and on individual consumers.

In marketing, macro theoretical models or frameworks can enable explanation and understanding of some rather central phenomena and variables that are presently either ignored or considered as givens. One obvious reason for not making these phenomena and variables subject of study in marketing has been that their understanding did require macro theories, and the discipline did not provide such theories. Other reasons for this tendency were that (1) understanding these phenomena was considered to be the domain of other social science disciplines and (2) the phenomena were premises assumed to be true and given rather than variables to be studied. A typical example of such variables in the marketing discipline is the *need* or *need perception* for product classes. Macro theory can shed light in this area and put to test some of the major assumptions in marketing in this respect.

It is the consumption of certain products that are becoming so universal that seems to cause much of what is called "irrational" consumption on the part of poor consumers. While the scientific and meliorative knowledge that has been accumulated indicates that there are basic needs that ought to be satisfied (e.g., food and sanitation) for consumers to have a minimum acceptable standard of living and life expectancy, poor consumers are found to forgo such necessities, at the same time using their resources to consume products such as cars, television sets, washing machines and other time-saving household appliances, and designer clothes that do not satisfy basic needs, but "conspicuous" or "luxury" needs (Irelan 1967).

Since marketing scholars and practitioners are mostly interested in consumption at the individual consumer level, the differences among behaviors in different market segments and among choices for brands by consumers become the main subjects for inquiry. However, when a macro and societal perspective is acquired, the similarities rather than the differences in consumption can become more striking.

Conclusion

Marketing, as we know it, is part of a socioeconomic system where the necessities of the system determine human needs and forms of their satisfaction. The approach to facts that dominate contemporary social science is one that emphasizes method rather than philosophy. This is a condition that is naturally consistent with the technological orientation in society. Furthermore, the contemporary approach is cross-sectional rather than historical. It is positivist/logical empiricist. Such an approach that tends to generalize from temporal and contextual truths and relationships, rather than try to understand these truths and relationships, within the historical process (Fırat 1985), can easily gloss over the reality of the determination of human needs and forms of their satisfaction. When one looks at facts cross-sectionally and temporally, one observes the need for products so prevalent in society today. But this is merely a restatement, a description of what is. Understanding the phenomenon, on the other hand, requires an explanation of the causes for the changes that occur. Why does transformation take place and how does it occur? From where does the change come? In the case of consumption, why did consumers begin perceiving needs for a certain CP and products that represent it, and what initiated the transformation from earlier CPs to the one presently dominant? Answering such questions, as the theory presented in this chapter attempts, is an initiation toward understanding. Once the need perceptions for a certain CP and its representative products are established in society, the perceived needs and the system's dynamic will simply reinforce each other. Just repeating this reinforcement in our factual descriptions is almost tautological: "the phenomenon is because it is!" To *understand*, we must look at the forces behind the changes that creep in or sometimes seem to suddenly take over, and we must try to capture the processes that underlie these changes. We need to break away from just identifying needs and must try to understand them (Dholakia, Fırat, and Bagozzi 1980).

Many times, appearances of phenomena blind our visions into the essences of the phenomena. The reflections may create illusions or myths. We can easily get taken by certain facets of events and other facets may go unnoticed. This is especially the case if there are ideological, economic, and psychological barriers built into the system that tend to further blur certain aspects of reality. In marketing, the assumptions about the market system and its workings have blurred the choicelessness, the standardization, and uniformity behind the mist of enormous choice at the brand level. In many ways, this is an illusion of choice, however. Our lives are shaped, not by the brands we consume, but by the patterns of consumption these products create and impose on our lives. The time has come for those involved in marketing, as either academicians or practitioners, to lift the veil from the eyes and critically investigate the phenomena that concern not only the marketing organizations but other sectors of society as well, among them different classes of consumers. For the academicians, this is the step toward becoming social scientists rather than advocates of a certain system and technology.

References

Baran, Paul A. (1957), *The Political Economy of Growth*. New York: Modern Reader.
Bendix, Reinhard (1974), "Inequality and Social Structure: A Comparison of Marx and Weber," *American Sociological Review* 39: 149–61.

Bennett, S.E., and W.R. Klecka (1970), "Social Status and Social Participation: A Multivariate Analysis of Predictive Power," *Midwest Journal of Political Science* 14: 355–82.

Berger, Peter L., and Thomas Luckmann (1966), *The Social Construction of Reality*. New York: Anchor.

Brady, D.S. (1952), "Family Saving in Relation to Changes in the Level and Distribution of Income," in *Studies in Income and Wealth*, vol. 15. New York: National Bureau of Economic Research.

Dholakia, Nikhilesh, A. Fuat Fırat, and Richard P. Bagozzi (1980), "The Deamericanization of Marketing: In Search of a Universal Basis," in *Theoretical Developments in Marketing*, C.W. Lambe and P.M. Dunne, eds. Chicago: American Marketing Association.

Dholakia, Nikhilesh, and Ruby Roy Dholakia (1985), "Choice and Choicelessness in the Paradigm of Marketing," in *Changing the Course of Marketing: Alternative Paradigms for Widening Marketing Theory*, N. Dholakia and J. Arndt, eds. Greenwich, Conn.: JAI Press.

Dholakia, Ruby Roy, Nikhilesh Dholakia, and A. Fuat Fırat (1983), "From Social Psychology to Political Economy: A Model of Energy Use Behavior," *Journal of Economic Psychology* 3: 231–47.

Domhoff, G. Williams (1978), *Who Really Rules?* Santa Monica, Calif.: Goodyear.

Duessenberry, James S. (1949), *Income, Saving and the Theory of Consumer Behavior*. Cambridge, Mass.: Harvard University Press.

Dye, Thomas R. (1979), *Who's Running America?* Englewood Cliffs, N.J.: Prentice-Hall.

Edwards, Richard C., Michael Reich, and Thomas E. Weisskopf (1978), *The Capitalist System*. Englewood Cliffs, N.J.: Prentice-Hall.

Fırat, A. Fuat (1978), *The Social Construction of Consumption Patterns*, unpublished Ph.D dissertation. Evanston, Ill.: Northwestern University.

———, (1985), "Ideology vs. Science in Marketing," in *Changing the Course of Marketing: Alternative Paradigms for Widening Marketing Theory*, N. Dholakia and J. Arndt, eds. Greenwich, Conn.: JAI Press.

———, (1986), Towards a Deeper Understanding of Consumption Experiences: The Underlying Dimensions," in *Advances in Consumer Research*, vol. 14. M. Wallendorf and P.F. Anderson, eds. Provo, Utah: Association for Consumer Research.

Fırat, A. Fuat, and Nikhilesh Dholakia (1977), "Consumption Patterns and Macromarketing: A Radical Perspective," *European Journal of Marketing* 11: 291–98.

Fırat, A. Fuat, and Nikhilesh Dholakia (1982), "Consumption Choices at the Macro Level," *Journal of Macromarketing* 2: 6–15.

Galbraith, John K. (1971), "The Management of Specific Demand," in *The New Industrial State*. New York: Mentor.

Irelan, L.M., ed. (1967), *Low Income Life Styles*. Washington, D.C.: U.S. Dept. of Health, Education and Welfare.

Jacoby, Jacob (1978), "Consumer Research: A State of the Art Review," *Journal of Marketing* 42: 87–96.

Marx, Karl (1967), *Capital*. New York: International Publishers.

Miliband, Ralph (1973), "Economic Elites and Dominant Class," in *Crisis in American Institutions*, J.H. Skolnick and E. Currie, eds. Boston: Little, Brown.

Mills, C. Wright (1971), "The Corporate Rich," in *Radical Sociology: An Introduction*, D. Horowitz, ed. New York: Harper & Row.

Morgello, C. (1974), "Wall Street: Who Owns What," *Newsweek* (December 23): 68.

Nadel, M. (1971), "Economic Power and Public Policy: The Case of Consumer Protection," *Politics and Society* 1: 313–26.

Nader, Ralph, and Mark J. Green (1973), "*Corporate Power in America*. New York: Grossman.

Ostlund, L.E. (1973), "Diffusion: A Dynamic View of Buyer Behavior," in *Buyer Behavior*, J.H. Howard and L.E. Ostlund, eds. New York: Alfred A. Knopf.

Pareto, Vilfredo (1971), *Manual of Political Economy*. A.S. Schwier, translator. New York: Augustus M. Kelley.

Reuven, C. (1972), *The Kibbutz Settlement*, Translated by H. Statman. Tel Aviv: Hakibbutz Hameuchad.

Schudson, Michael (1984), *Advertising, The Uneasy Persuasion: Its Dubious Impact on American Society*. New York: Basic Books.

Sweezy, Paul M. (1947), *The Theory of Capitalist Development*, New York: Monthly Review.

Therborn, Göran (1980), *What Does the Ruling Class Do When It Rules?* London: Verso.

Tucker, W.T. (1964), *The Social Context of Economic Behavior*. New York: Holt, Rinehart and Winston.

Tumin, M.M. (1967), *Social Stratification: The Forms and Functions of Inequality*. Englewood Cliffs: N.J.: Prentice-Hall.

Veblen, Thorstein (1899), *The Theory of the Leisure Class*. New York: Macmillan.

Weber, Max (1964), *The Theory of Social and Economic Organization*. New York: Free Press.

Wright, Erik Olin (1978), "Race, Class and Income Inequality," *American Journal of Sociology* 83: 1368–97.

———, (1979), *Class, Crisis and the State*. London: Verso.

Wright, Erik Olin, and Luca Perrone (1977), "Marxist Class Categories and Income Inequality," *American Sociological Review* 42: 32–55.

Zeitlin, Maurice (1974), "Corporate Ownership and Control: The Large Corporation and the Capitalist Class," *American Journal of Sociology* 79: 1073–119.

Part IV
New Orientations and Conceptualizations

15

Humanistic Marketing: Beyond the Marketing Concept

Philip Kotler

A growing number of companies are professing to practice a customer orientation. Consider these ads: "Have it your way" (Burger King), "You deserve a break today" (McDonald's), "No dissatisfied customers" (Ford), "People helping people" (Commonwealth Edison).

Today's corporations seem intent on creating loyal customers, not just racking up one-time sales. They avow practicing the *marketing concept*: making what customers want to buy, rather than selling what the company wants to make. This marketing philosophy has been adopted by IBM, McDonald's, Sears, Procter & Gamble, and many other successful companies. It is hard to argue with their success.

But something is still missing. If corporations are so skilled at the marketing concept, why are there many dissatisfied consumers? Why are consumers still distrustful of business? Several explanations have been offered:

1. Many companies still act like robber barons and give the rest of business a bad name.

2. Many companies only put up a front of customer orientation to snare the customer into thinking they would find a friendly company or better values. After they buy, they realize they have been taken, and become distrustful of business.

3. Many companies have adopted the marketing concept as a principle, but they have not successfully implemented it in practice.

4. Although many companies practice the marketing concept, some errors in product quality or service inevitably creep in. Some consumers fall victim to unintentional company slipups.

Each explanation has some grain of truth. There are antisocial firms; there are firms that preach but don't practice the marketing concept; and there are customer-oriented firms that make errors. We are interested, however, in a fourth possible explanation, that the marketing concept is not the whole answer to serving consumers' interests. Peter Drucker hinted at this when he said:

> We have asked ourselves where in the marketing concept consumerism fits or belongs. I have come to the conclusion that, so far, the only way one can really define it within the total marketing concept is as the shame of the total marketing concept. It is essentially a mark of failure of the concept. . . .
>
> Consumerism means that the consumer looks upon the manufacturer as somebody who is interested, but who really does not know what the consumer's realities are. He regards the manufacturer as somebody who has not made the effort to find out, who does not understand the world in which the consumer lives, and who expects the consumer to make distinctions which the consumer is neither able nor willing to make[1]

I will argue that there is a further possible evolution in customer philosophy that will offer attractive opportunities to the first companies that are able to grasp and implement it. I call this philosophy *humanistic marketing*. It promises to be as important a guiding philosophy for business in the future as the marketing concept was in the past. The marketing concept emphasizes the view that companies should study what customers need and want and the companies should meet these specific needs and wants. Humanistic marketing goes further and says that companies should consider their customers' lives. I would define humanistic marketing as follows:

> Humanistic marketing is a management philosophy that takes as its central objective the earning of profit through the enhancement of the customers' long-run well-being. It assumes that: the customer is active and intelligent; seeks satisfaction of both immediate needs and larger interests; and favors companies that develop products, services, and communications that enrich the customer's life possibilities.

Humanistic marketing is an attempt to apply humanistic philosophy to the practice of marketing. Humanism is an ethical philosophy that attaches primary importance to human beings and the creation of conditions under which individuals can realize and perfect their potentialities. Humanism emphasizes the values of human freedom, progress, altruism, and community. Its chief enemies are reductionist philosophies such as determinism, fatalism, behaviorism, and authoritarianism. Humanism's credo was stated by Protagoras over two thousand years ago: "Man is the measure."

To develop the concept of humanistic marketing, we will begin by examining the range of ways in which sellers view buyers and buyers view sellers.

How Sellers View Buyers

Businesspeople differ greatly in the way they view and treat their customers. Four different seller orientations toward customers can be distinguished.

At one extreme are sellers who view customers as *prey*, people to entrap into purchase. Customers are seen as creatures of wants and whims who are easy to influence and manipulate. They are not as bright as the seller. The seller's main interest is to figure out how to separate customers from their money. This customer attitude may be found in oriental bazaars, port cities, auto dealerships, telemarketing calls from strangers touting oil investment opportunities, and many other situations. It is the mark of the quacks, fly-by-night operators, and rip-off artists. The attitude has existed throughout history in many countries and in many industries. The only thing that saves customers from full victimization is that they learn the lesson of "buyer beware" after getting burned a few times.

A second seller attitude views customers as essentially *strangers* to be treated with normal civility. Customers enter the premises, look over the merchandise, and buy or do not buy. The seller does not know the customers, does not particularly like or dislike them, and does not have a strong interest in their lives. The seller is interested in the customers' needs only to the extent of having something to sell them. The seller's interaction with the buyer is straightforward, mostly involving answering questions and discussing prices and terms. The seller is not trying to take advantage of customers, but simply is trying to make sales. This seller attitude is found in many large department stores and supermarkets because these establishments deal with so many customers that they cannot take the time to personalize their service. This attitude is also found in some small establishments and simply reflects the owner's or manager's attitude.

A third seller attitude views customers as *neighbors*. The seller wants customers to feel welcome and to come back often. The seller takes an interest in their lives beyond the immediate transaction and tries to interpret their changing needs over time. The "neighbor model" of the customer is typified in the general store of the nineteenth century in which customers would sit around and gossip with the merchant. It is found today in banks that have a "personal banker" arrangement for their customers, in stock brokerage businesses, in accounting and law firms, and in other professions.

A fourth seller attitude, one that is rare in practice, is to view customers as *friends*. Here, the seller exhibits warm and friendly feelings toward the customers. They are people whom the seller wants to serve and enrich through and beyond the commercial relationship. The seller would not think of hurting, being indifferent, or even being superficially friendly to the customer. The seller strains to be fair in setting prices, to give quality merchandise and service, and to inquire afterward about customer satisfaction. The seller always thinks: "Would I sell this way to members of my family?" This seller attitude is found among certain merchants, salespeople, doctors, and lawyers who are very wrapped up in the lives of their customers.

We can find all four seller attitudes in the area of industrial selling. Some salespeople see industrial customers as persons to ensnare; they will talk fast, build excitement, and try to make a quick sale. Other salespeople will proceed more coolly; they will describe their merchandise and hope that the customer will buy. Still others will listen carefully to their customers to determine whether they have anything of real benefit to offer. Finally, some salespeople will want to become real friends with the customer in a way that goes beyond their business relationship.

Although each seller has a general orientation toward customers, the seller's attitude will vary with respect to particular types of customers. The seller will be friendly to some customers, neighborly to others, indifferent to still others, and downright hostile to some. This is influenced by the personal characteristics and chemistry of the two parties; it does not refute the existence of distinct customer orientations.

What Do Buyers Want from Sellers?

Turning the question around, we can ask: What are the different ways in which buyers can view sellers? Here, too, we can distinguish four attitudes.

At one extreme are customers who view sellers as *foes*. They must protect themselves against seller machinations and even take advantage of the sellers if possible. These customers will bargain hard and, in extreme cases, abuse customer privileges or even steal from the seller. The seller is someone to outwit in the game of business.

The second customer attitude views sellers as *strangers*. The customers would prefer to be invisible in the buying situation, just wandering around looking at the goods, selecting what they want, paying, and leaving. They do not need or want help or any other interest shown in them as customers. They are self-service buyers. They prefer to deal with *impersonal sellers*.

The third customer attitude wants the seller to be a *helper*. The customer would like to enter the buying situation, get the sales person's attention, ask questions, and receive helpful and courteous answers. Thus, an investor says: "I want my stock broker to understand my financial goals and come up with creative suggestions that will build my income." These buyers want the seller's help in solving problems.

Finally, the fourth customer attitude wants the seller to be a *friend*. The customer does not want to be treated just with perfunctory courtesy. The customer wants signs of personal interest that transcend the strictly business relationship. They want the seller to be interested in them as people. Recently, a woman complained of her physician: "He is competent and attentive, but I do not feel he really cares about me. He never asks anything outside of the strict medical issues. He relates to me as a one-dimensional person." Buyers such as this woman are looking for a "humanized" relationship with the seller.

Although each buyer will have a general orientation toward most sellers, buyers may vary in their attitudes toward specific sellers or in specific situations. A buyer might prefer impersonal service in the supermarket, helpful service in the appliance store, and friendly service from the hairdresser.

One of the main causes of consumer dissatisfaction in the marketplace is that the wrong buyers end up transacting with the wrong sellers. A buyer seeking friendly employees walks into a "cold" store; a buyer seeking impersonal service is approached by a gushing salesperson; a buyer seeking help gets only courteous service. Sellers would find it easier if all buyers wanted the same treatment. Or they would find it easier if they could adjust their selling style to each buyer's preference. But the fact is that sellers have to develop a style appropriate to buyers in their target segment; their assumption about these buyers will influence their sales training program, their marketing communications, their store layout, and so on. Inevitably, this will result in not meeting the wants of buyers from other segments who have different needs and expectations.

Theory *X* versus Theory *Y* Views of the Buyer

Sellers, indeed, make assumptions about the buyers in planning their marketing program. We can collapse the previous seller views of buyers into two broad orientations which we shall call theory *X* (buyer as prey or stranger) and theory *Y* (buyer as neighbor or friend)[2] Theory *X* holds a *reductive view* of the customer:

1. The average customer is lazy and makes purchases without much thought or research.
2. The average customer is interested only in the product, not in the seller.
3. The average customer is self-centered and suspicious.
4. The average customer resists new products, services, and selling methods.
5. The average customer is not very bright and is easy to persuade.

Using theory *X*, the customer looks like a very limited person, one absorbed in gratifying lower-order needs, while behaving passively and naively in the marketplace. If the customer is a woman, she is thought to spend all her time worrying about her looks, clothes, and sexual attractiveness. If the customer is a man, he is seen as essentially interested in sitting in an easy chair and watching a football game, while drinking beer. Buyers are seen more as grown-up children than as adults. Many commercials show them as silly, complaining, pampered people. They are suckers for games, premiums, and inane jingles.

In contrast, theory Y holds a *humanistic view* of the customer:

1. The average customer is active and interested in learning about product differences and benefits.
2. The average customer is not just buying a product, but trying to meet a larger set of needs, including needs for information and reliable, courteous service.
3. The average customer is other-centered as well as self-centered, and interested in the organization as well as the product.
4. The average customer is responsive to new products, services, and selling methods.
5. The average customer knows how to select goods and vendors in a way that will serve long-run interests.

Using theory Y, the customer is seen as a capable and self-directed person. The customer wants quality products and adequate information on which to base decisions. The customer favors companies that continuously improve their products and show social responsibility. The customer wants communications that are adult-to-adult-oriented. Toothpaste should be sold on its power to clean, not its power to attract the opposite sex. Cars should be sold on their power to deliver comfortable and efficient transportation, not on their power to create envy in others. The customer resents marketing communications that promise love, money, or power by buying one brand of soap or cereal over another.

The contrast between theory X and theory Y views of the customer is being debated today within professional service industries such as medicine and law. In medical circles, some physicians are moving away from the traditional theory X view of the patient-as-child. Fink has distinguished five models of the physician-patient relationship. (See figure 15–1.)[3]

1. In the activity/passivity relationship (point A in the figure) patients are more or less helpless and the physician or other provider does something to them. The treatment takes place regardless of the patient's contribution. The relationship of the physician to the patient is similar to that of the parent to the helpless infant.
2. In the guidance/cooperation relationship (point B in the figure) the ill patient is aware of what is going on and capable of following directions and exercising some judgment. However, the patient is expected to follow

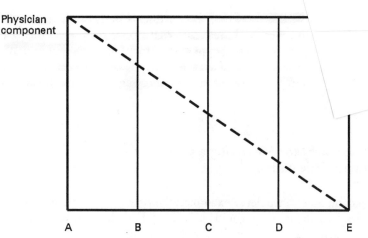

A = Activity/passivity

B = Guidance/cooperation

C = Mutual participation

D = Patient as primary provider

E = Self-care

Figure 15–1. Range of Physician–Patient Relationships

the physician's advice. The relationship is similar to that of a parent and preadolescent child.

3. In the mutual participation model (point C), the physician helps the patients to help themselves. This prototype is the adult-adult relationship, with one having specialized knowledge that the other needs.

4. In the patient as primary provider model (point D), responsibility clearly lies with the patient, who is recognized as the healer. The physician is the assistant, providing counsel and technical assistance.

5. In the self-care model (point E), patients are seen as both the source and resource for improving their health. In this case, no provider is necessary.

Thus, theory Y for the health professions views the patient as a competent adult who wants to be informed of alternative treatments of an illness, participate in the decision, and bear responsibility for the outcome.

Any business sector can see customers in either theory X or Y terms. What is interesting is that the company's view of the customer will be self-fulfilling to a large extent. The company that sees customers in theory X terms will draw more of these customers and cause customers to see themselves this way.

This leads to an interesting opportunity for companies that switch from a theory X to a theory Y view of the customer. They will gain market share if there is a substantial segment of buyers who want better treatment from the sellers.

An Instrument for Measuring a Company's Customer Orientation

Many companies have never examined their basic view of customers. If they undertook to do this, they would likely find that their employees exhibit a wide range of attitudes. One division or department may be strongly customer-oriented, another quite insensitive to customers. Top management may take a "helper" view of customers, but the salesforce may look at the customers as prey. The company may not have formulated explicit customer principles such as "the customer is always right" or "satisfaction or your money back."

Companies need a tool for auditing how their employees view the customers. A proposed instrument is shown in table 15–1.

The instrument assumes that a company that is highly customer-oriented would exhibit four characteristics. First, the company would exhibit a high regard for the customer's capacities, interests, and maturity. The customer would be viewed as active, intelligent, and trying to satisfy several needs through the buying situation.

Second, the company would actively research customer needs and wants. It would take into account consumer welfare as well as customer preferences in designing its products and offers.

Third, the company would develop marketing communications that respect the customer as a buyer and person. Company advertising would view the customers as intelligent and knowing how to get the most value for their money. The company salesforce would view the customers as people whose interests are to be served in the best possible way.

Fourth, the company would show a high concern for customer satisfaction. It would monitor customer satisfaction and take systematic steps to remove sources of dissatisfaction.

A company that served its customers in the best possible way would get sixteen points on the instrument in table 15–1. A company's score on customer-orientation can range between zero and sixteen:

0–4: Poor orientation toward the customer

5–8: Fair orientation toward the customer

9–12: Good orientation toward the customer

13–16: Strong orientation toward the customer

The instrument will reveal the ways in which the company can improve its customer-orientation. A company may discover, for example, that it takes too narrow a view of what the customer is seeking, that it relies too much on sale gimmicks to create sales, or that it is failing to track customer satisfaction.

From a research standpoint, the instrument can be used to investigate whether companies with a strong customer-orientation perform better in terms of such measures as sales, market share, relative image, and profitability. If customer-orientation correlates closely with company performance, the case becomes stronger that humanistic marketing is not only societally desirable but also more profitable.

From a managerial standpoint, the instrument can be used to check the correspondence between management's intended or perceived view of the company's customer philosophy and the actual view customers hold. In one company, its executives gave a much higher customer-orientation rating than the customers gave, indicating that management had an inflated view of their customer-orientation. The lesson was sobering and the company took major steps to implement more effectively its intended customer-orientation.

Company Examples of Humanistic Marketing

Companies are not likely to move in the direction of more humanistic marketing unless two conditions are satisfied. The first is that they perceive that an increasing number of customers prefer to deal with theory Y sellers. The second is that they believe that greater customer-orientation will produce more profits. Management is not likely to advance the interest of customers at the expense of the stockholders.

Some well-known companies have recognized these conditions and have pioneered new ways to provide more satisfaction to customers. They are operating somewhere between a narrow view of the marketing concept and a fuller view of humanistic marketing. They foreshadow some of the possibilities that lie ahead in serving the customers' interests.

Avon Company

The Avon Company illustrates the profit potential from adopting a highly humanistic approach to the customer. A small company in the early 1950s, Avon sought to sell its cosmetics through normal distribution channels. It encountered resistance from department stores and drugstores and decided

Table 15–1
Customer-Orientation Index

Elevated customer image

Does the company view the customer as basically:
0. Passive, lazy, and gullible?
1. Emotional at times, but rational at other times?
2. Active and intelligent?

Does the company view the customer as:
0. Simply buying a product?
1. Seeking to satisfy a specific need?
2. Seeking to satisfy several needs?

Consumer-oriented product design

How does management determine consumer needs and preferences?
0. Management has intuitive ideas about what customers want.
1. Management conducts occasional consumer research to gather ideas about what consumers want.
2. Management conducts frequent consumer research and testing in order to fine-tune its understanding of customer wants.

Does management include consumer welfare criteria (safety, health, etc.) in designing its products?
0. The company pays little or no attention to consumer welfare criteria.
1. The company considers consumer welfare criteria as one of several inputs in designing its products.
2. The company places major weight on consumer welfare criteria in designing its products.

Humanistic communications mix

What view of the customer is implicit in the company's advertising?
0. The customer is seen as poorly informed, not interested in much information, and easily swayed by sales arguments and gimmicks.
1. The customer is thought to have some product knowledge but is also influenced by emotional appeals.
2. The customer is seen as a knowledgeable and intelligent buyer capable of recognizing quality and value.

What is the saleforce's view of the customer?
0. The salesforce see their job as cajoling the customer into making the purchase.
1. The salesforce see their job as listening to the customer and seeing if there is an effective way to link the company's products with the customer's expressed wants.
2. The salesforce see their job as helping customers achieve their objectives through finding the best solutions to their problems.

Customer satisfaction objective

For what level of customer satisfaction does the company aim?
0. The company seeks to deliver the same level of satisfaction that competitors deliver.
1. The company seeks to deliver better than average customer satisfaction.
2. The company seeks to deliver the highest level of customer satisfaction.

Does the company have a system for tracking and improving customer satisfaction?
0. The company does not measure customer satisfaction.
1. The company provides opportunities for customers to complain.
2. The company tracks consumer satisfaction through complaint forms and customer surveys and uses the results to improve its performance.

instead to use door-to-door selling. Door-to-door selling did not have a good image among customers at that time. But Avon formulated an approach that was credible to the customer. The company recruited attractive women who were willing to sell cosmetics to their neighbors. Each "Avon lady" received a territory, training, and good compensation package. Avon ladies saw themselves, not as selling cosmetics, but rather as helping homemakers look and feel better. The Avon lady was a beauty consultant who was interested in her customers' lives and ready to be a helper and a friend. This selling approach, along with excellent products and a readiness to serve new and emerging customer needs, propelled Avon into one of the fastest-growing, highest-profit companies in the 1960s.

Marks & Spencer

Marks & Spencer, a leading British department store chain, adopted an innovative retailing approach to serve customers better. Marks & Spencer, which began as a penny bazaar store in 1884, recognized that its customers wanted to buy good-quality merchandise at low prices. The chain store hired and trained a capable buying staff who could find or develop quality merchandise at a low cost. Marks & Spencer decided to carry only fast-moving items, to design their stores to be simple and functional, and to promote self-service so that fewer salespeople would be needed. These and other policies to reduce costs and pass on lower prices to customers created one of the most successful institutions in British retailing.

Marshall Field & Company

Marshall Field & Company, Chicago's leading department store, earned its growth and reputation through consistently serving its customers' interests. All of its employees are trained according to the following principles:

The customer is always right if she thinks she is right.

We are more interested in pleasing a customer than in making a sale.

Every sale of merchandise or services includes the obligation to accept the article for credit, refund, exchange, or adjustment promptly and courteously to the customer's satisfaction.

We sell only merchandise of the best quality obtainable at the price.

We offer merchandise in a broad assortment from lowest to the highest price at which the quality, fashion, and value measure up to our store's standards.

We strive to give completely satisfactory service to every customer[4]

Giant Food, Inc.

Giant Food, Inc., is a leading supermarket chain in the Washington, D.C., area. In the late 1960s, the company adopted, as a response to the growing consumer movement, a new concept of its business. The typical food chain is content to carry those food products that manufacturers want to sell and buyers want to buy, without making any judgments or offering consumers any advice. Giant, however, adopted a different view: "We are the customer's channel for food. We should strive to help the customer obtain the best value possible, not only in his pocketbook but also in his/her food intake. Our store should be an instrument to help the customer know how to buy good food value."

Giant Food implemented this customer-orientation through a series of specific measures:

1. The chain would not carry any rip-off foods.
2. The chain would try to carry low-, medium-, and high-priced versions of basic foods to give customers real choice.
3. The chain would occasionally point out that some food items are too expensive and that specific substitutes would save customers money.
4. The chain would post brand prices clearly and in unit terms (ounces, pints, etc.) so that consumers could make easy brand price comparisons.
5. The chain would date perishable products so that consumers would know their freshness.
6. The chain would employ full-time home economists to answer consumer questions in the store about food values, recipes, and other matters.
7. The chain would make it easy for consumers to register complaints.
8. The chain would appoint a highly respected consumer advocate to its board of directors to keep the customer view always before the board.

Through these measures, Giant moved from being a distributor acting in the sellers' interests to an agent acting in the customers' interests. Did the customer-orientation pay? According to a spokesman for the company, "These actions have improved Giant's goodwill immeasurably and have earned the admiration of leaders of the consumer movement."

Carrefours

Carrefours, the French hypermarché, took an innovative step some years ago to provide consumers with more value for their money. Carrefours's management asked: "Is there a way to offer consumers good-quality staples at lower prices so that they have price choice as well as brand choice?" They decided to launch a large number of generic house brands called Plain Bread, Plain Soup, and so on, sold in plain packaging at low prices. These generic brands were placed next to popular manufacturers' brands. Management assumed that the customers' confidence in Carrefours would carry over to the new generic brands. They were right. Many customers turned to the generic brands and appreciated the savings they represented.

Whirlpool Corporation

Whirlpool, a major appliance manufacturer, wanted to offer consumers more satisfaction in their buying of appliances. Buyers who encountered appliance problems were expected to work them out with their dealers. Not all dealers, however, would take responsibility; some said that the warranty did not cover the problem. This angered many customers. Whirlpool decided to set up and advertise a toll-free hotline so that dissatisfied customers could reach headquarters directly. As a further step, Whirlpool rewrote its product warranty statement in clearer English and larger print, underscoring the main points. What were the results? According to Stephen E. Upton, Whirlpool vice president, "Our rate of increase in sales has tripled that of the industry. Our interest in the consumer has to be one of the reasons."

Kundenkreditbank

Kundenkreditbank, a large and profitable chain of consumer banks in Germany, represents one of the most creative examples of customer-oriented marketing. The bank's chairman, Stefan Kaminsky, decided to target working class customers. The bank's mission was to help such customers increase their assets so that they could enjoy a higher standard of living. This led to the notion that the bank's staff had to be well trained and well acquainted with the customers. Kaminsky decided that his branches should never have more than six employees. When he hires the branch manager, Kaminsky says: "I want you to operate this branch for the next thirty years. The employees and customers are your family. You will be rewarded for good performance through salary increases and bonus participation in the income earned by your branch." The result is that all branch managers dig deep roots in the community. They are available to customers even after hours. The staff does everything possible to help customers save more intelligently and purchase more carefully. The bank carries consumer reports and cassettes to help consumers make better buying and saving decisions.

Procter & Gamble Company

Procter & Gamble is considered the most effective consumer packaged goods marketer in the United States. The company enjoys leading market shares in almost every one of its markets. Some people credit P&G's success to its spending substantial sums of money in advertising. The major factor, however, is that P&G tries to introduce new products that provide new benefits or higher quality to the market. P&G does not play the game of "me-too" marketing. Its Crest toothpaste was the first toothpaste to aid in reducing tooth decay. Its Head and Shoulders was the first "nonmedicinal" shampoo to provide dandruff control. Its Pampers was the first paper diaper to perform well. In all three cases, P&G developed a unique and substantial consumer benefit that contributed to the satisfaction and welfare of its customers.

McDonald's Corporation

McDonald's is the most successful food-franchising system to appear on the U.S. scene. McDonald's success is traceable to identifying and delivering what customers wanted from fast-food service. Consumers wanted inexpensively priced food served rapidly in clean surroundings by pleasant personnel. McDonald's trained its franchise operators and employees to deliver "QSCV" (quality, service, cleanliness, and value). McDonald's sponsors many public service programs to enhance the life quality of communities. The company has developed numerous educational materials to help schools teach nutrition (Nutrition Action Pack), ecology (Ecology Action Pack), and economics (Economy Action Pack).

Barat College

Barat College, a women's school in Lake Forest, Illinois, published a college catalog that is impressive in its consumer-orientation. Instead of the normal college catalog that paints an idealistic picture of the campus, courses, and faculty, they issued a publication that spelled out Barat College's strong and weak points. Consider the following excerpts:

1. An exceptionally talented student musician or mathematician . . . might be advised to look further for a college with top faculty and facilities in that field.
2. The full range of advanced specialized courses offered in a university will be absent; the effects of a faculty member leaving may be greater, and it will be harder to avoid a teacher with whom you might develop a personality conflict.
3. The library collection is average for a small college, but low in comparison with other high-quality institutions.[5]

These statements create institutional credibility. They help students develop realistic expectations about Barat College.

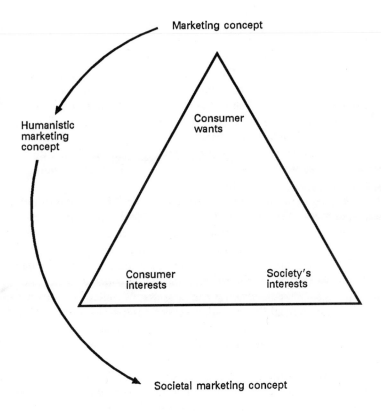

Figure 15–2. Factors in Consumer-Oriented Marketing

The Evolution of Marketing Orientations

Over the years, many companies have moved from a *product-orientation* to a *sales-orientation* to a *marketing-orientation*. They have moved from focusing on the product to focusing on customer wants. The marketing concept describes an orientation in which companies focus on researching and satisfying customer wants and preferences.

Now the marketing-orientation is itself evolving. We can distinguish two more stages in its evolution. They can be illustrated by recognizing three factors that companies can consider in developing their offers: customer wants, customer interests, and society's interests. These three factors are shown in figure 15–2 as the three vertices of a triangle.

The original marketing-orientation called for paying attention to what consumers want. The company marketer would make no judgments about the contribution of these consumer wants to consumer health or welfare. If consumers want cigarettes, alcohol, junk food, and so on, this is their business. Marketing is a responsive tool, not an educational tool.

The marketing concept has now evolved in some companies into the *humanistic marketing concept.* The humanistic marketing concept says that marketers should factor both consumer wants and consumer interests into their planning. The great English parliamentarian, Edmund Burke, once told the House of Commons, "I serve your interests, not your desires." While we recognize that some people act against their own interests, we still do not want someone else to decide what is in our interest. Humanistic marketers do not tell the people what they should have. They attempt to build better products and to educate the public to appreciate them.

A third evolution of the marketing concept is possible. Some products and marketing practices may serve customer wants and interests and yet hurt society's interests. Nonbiodegradable detergents work effectively in cleaning clothes, but ultimately harm the environment. Large cars may be more comfortable and safe than small cars, but they use up more fuel and make parking more difficult. At this point, the *societal marketing concept* enters and asks companies to consider society's long-run interests, as well as consumer wants and direct interests, in making their marketing decisions. As long as this is left up to companies and not enforced by arbitrary government edicts, we can agree that companies should consider the public interest in their marketing decision making.

How customer-oriented can companies be and still make a profit? Certainly, there are degrees of customer-orientation. An organization could be oriented toward narrow customer needs or broad consumer needs. It can be oriented toward the immediate needs of customers or their long-run interests. It can be oriented toward serving customers passively or creatively.

Our belief is that customers are becoming more educated and discriminating in their brand and vendor choices. They are demanding more value. We believe that the companies that move first and furthest in customer-orientation will lead the rest.

Each organization has to assess where it currently stands in customer-orientation, where it should go, what it will cost, and what benefits it will produce. Not every organization will come to the conclusion that the time is right to move ahead, but enough organizations will want to enhance their customer-orientation to make the next decade one of humanistic marketing.

Conclusion

This chapter has examined the range of attitudes that buyers can adopt toward sellers and sellers can adopt toward buyers. Either party can see the other as anything from someone to abuse all the way to someone to serve and enrich.

For many years, marketing professionals have advocated that companies should see their central mission as serving the needs and wants of buyers; this philosophy is known as the marketing concept. Centering the company's attention and action on serving customers well has been proposed as the way companies can survive and prosper in an intensely competitive marketplace.

But one can doubt whether the marketing concept is widely implemented by business. Too many customers are still dissatisfied with business practices. This chapter goes further and raises the question as to whether consumers would be fully satisfied even if the marketing concept were widely implemented. The marketing concept calls for meeting specific wants and needs of customers; it does not emphasize serving customers' total long-run well-being. The marketing concept is a philosophy of responding to what customers want rather than taking a larger view of the challenge of enhancing the person and enriching the society. This leads us to postulate that there is still a more enlightened concept of serving the buyer that goes beyond the marketing concept. We have called it humanistic marketing. We have described it as a management philosophy that takes as its central objective the earning of profit through the enhancement of the customers' long-run well-being. We have stressed that it rests on a theory Y view of customers, rather than the more traditional theory X view of customers.

An instrument has been proposed for measuring the degree to which a company practices humanistic marketing. One use of the instrument is to see whether companies that stand high on humanistic marketing also perform better in the marketplace. This underlying assumption needs to be tested, since it is not likely that companies would adopt humanistic marketing if it would hurt their profitability.

Several companies were described as moving in various degrees beyond the marketing concept into humanistic marketing. The distinction still needs further sharpening and calibration. Here is where researchers can make a contribution by helping us learn whether something better lies beyond the marketing concept and what its nature, contributions, and limitations might be.

Notes

1. Peter Drucker, "Consumerism: The Opportunity of Marketing," address before the National Association of Manufacturers, New York, April 10, 1969.

2. The theory X, theory Y framework was originally developed by Douglas McGregor in his study of company orientations toward their workforce. See Douglas Murray McGregor, "The Human Side of Enterprise," *Management Review* (November 1957): 22–28, 88–92.

3. Donald L. Fink, "Holistic Health: Implications for Health Planning," *American Journal of Health Planning* (July 1976): 23–31.

4. Taken from Marshall Field's employee manual.

5. Cited in "Barat College Grades Itself in Student Market," *Chicago Sun-Times* (November 20, 1976): 50.

16
A Radical Agenda for Marketing Science: Represent the Marketing Concept!

Geraldine Fennell

T
he agenda for marketing science that I discuss in this chapter is radical in two senses: It is rooted in marketing's essential contributions to society and to business, and it excludes from consideration—indeed, rejects as a legitimate part of marketing—what is probably the most prevalent notion of marketing outside the profession. Accordingly, this chapter is about two things: (1) marketing's essential function, contrasted where appropriate with popular misconceptions, and (2) implications of that function for marketing science.

Why Have Regard for Our Roots?

There are many different reasons why it is good from time to time to examine who we are, from whence we come, where we are going, and how what we are doing today may appear when viewed from some broader perspective. In the context of needed development in marketing theory, examining our roots may be especially fruitful by raising neglected issues that are, in fact, central to our very existence. More broadly, people return to their roots to refresh the spirit and then reenter the daily fray, renewed and invigorated.

The present chapter is motivated by such considerations and by one other. I want to express the perspective of a professional marketer who confronts the daily tasks of doing marketing in real-world organizations and, in particular, in the profit-making context of business enterprises. The pressures we face, or have faced in the past and may again, are not often reflected in the academic literature where, untouched by first-hand appreciation of our circumstances, authors discuss matters that concern us. Day-to-day, one's main function as a marketing practitioner is to represent the substantive, real-world, component of decision making. That means that if, in our professional opinion, the firm's information about the real world is seriously deficient, we recommend post-poning a decision until better information has been obtained. In any case, we make clear that the decision, if taken at that point, is not grounded in good information, but is a pure judgment call. As a practical matter, one never has all the information one wishes for, and the pressures on management to "do something" readily turn into pressures to "do anything." Political consider-ations (specifically, who in the firm's power structure is known to support what kinds of direction) may carry more weight than does the information we provide or recommend obtaining about the state of the relevant universe. Moreover, the time frame within which the wisdom (or lack thereof) of particular decisions becomes apparent may be quite distant, while in the meantime, rewards (in the form of being promoted out of the decision context or out of the firm) may go to those who simply "acted." In a word, the pressures in business today favoring short-term rather than long-term horizons are well known, but their implications for the status of the marketing function have not been articulated.

In those organizations where conditions are favorable for making our professional contribution, it is largely because top management is supportive as a matter of policy. It understands the stresses that arise in a competitive environment and it sees professional marketers as a positive counterforce, raising tough questions at the opportune time, namely, before productive resources are committed. The challenge that we face as professional marketers is a twofold one: In the short run, to extend the number of organizational environments where the significance of our professional contribution is appre-ciated and has become institutionalized; for the longer haul, to develop the conceptual and scientific underpinning of our discipline so that, in the difficult real-world circumstances that comprise, among other elements, interdepart-mental rivalries and personal ambitions, we are not as dependent as we now are on having been legitimated from above, but have in our professional toolkit concepts and data bases that help us to speak for ourselves as professionals. We search the literature of marketing and find little that is helpful to us in the circumstances we confront. In particular, marketing authors give little atten-tion to developing conceptualizations that flow from a clear statement of marketing's function in society and in business organizations. Accordingly, practitioners may seek in a book such as this on radical and philosophical thought in marketing a grounding for our discipline that furthers our profes-sional contribution.

Marketing's Function

The reasons for marketing's existence in society and in individual firms flow from two features of our current arrangements for the production of goods and services: The separation of the user and producer functions that occurred when society evolved a system of division of labor, and the producer's need for a strategy of survival in the competitive conditions of a free market.

The Societal View

Because it leads to more efficient production, division of labor creates a surplus but, in doing so, entails a difficulty that makes marketing an essential societal function. If I am the cobbler and you are the tailor, each of us may become efficient at our tasks. But if I do not make for you the shoes you would want to make for yourself and you do not make for me the coat I would want to make for myself, each of us is less well served than we wish.

When users and producers are in direct contact with each other, face-to-face communication may overcome the problem that flows from assigning the roles of user and producer to separate individuals. That problem must be addressed explicitly when mass manufacturing and mass media of communications result in impersonal exchange-at-a-distance between users and producers. Society needs an institution that returns to users control over what is produced, which they give up for the efficiency that results from specialization. When society opted for division of labor, it made marketing an essential function. Goods/services have no claim on existence except to serve the circumstances of prospective users, and society requires marketers to stand where users stand, appreciate the influences they experience, and act for them. It charges marketers with ensuring (1) that the productive enterprise reflects the influences, psychological and nonpsychological, that users experience, and (2) that the enterprise is made to be, in effect, an extension of the user's mind and body.

The Business View

Whether one has in mind a centrally planned economy or one that espouses free enterprise, division of labor means that individuals other than prospective users decide what is produced. In either case, if the productive enterprise is truly an extension of the user's mind and body, user-circumstances (the conditions that allocate people's resources to doing the things they do) are the conditions to which producers must be responsive. A centrally planned economy lacks a built-in mechanism for giving effect to user-circumstances. People may choose not to use some or all of the output that central planners provide but, in a closed economy, they have only two means of recourse—become their own producers or go without. Neither option is likely to bring pressure to bear that would make planners more responsive to users' wishes. In a closed system, to ensure a productive output that is responsive to users' wants, it would be necessary deliberately to design a mechanism that leads to unpleasant consequences for planners when users remain unsatisfied. In a free enterprise economy, the marketplace performs such a function by penalizing producers whose offerings users find to be less than desirable or useful, relative to the competition. A competitive market means that, for their survival, producers are dependent on users' finding their offerings valuable relative to the alternatives. Herein lies the rationale for the marketing concept: Do not sell what you happen to make; make what the customer wants to buy. Since producers must in any case choose the specifications of what they produce, why not guide that choice by information about the contexts of use for which the offerings are intended? In urging producers to take guidance from users' circumstances at the time when such information has value, namely, before deciding what to produce, the marketing concept capitalizes on what is a fact of competitive life in any case. Choosing the design and ingredients of your offering is directly under your control as producer. Making people buy what you "happen to make" is not, especially with your competitors bent on outsmarting you in pleasing your prospective customers.

The Essence of Marketing

In sum, the argument from division of labor shows that society must find a way to reestablish user–producer communication, which division of labor severs. The argument from competition sees reestablishing that communicative link as the producer's strategy for survival. The two arguments give similar direction to the marketing scientist. As intermediaries between users and producers, the essential exchange that interests marketers is an *interrole* exchange (one that occurs within an individual who is both user and producer, who recognizes that some adjustment must be made, and who exchanges resources for an improved state of being). Above all, marketers need to understand the natural process of want-occurrence and want-satisfaction; in particular, we need to be conversant with the kinds of condition that allocate an individual's resources to effecting change and with the means of making appropriate adjustments.

Considering micromarketing, then, the primary professional domain of marketers is to answer the question: What shall we produce or, more broadly, what shall we offer?[1] Since the 1950s, guided by the "marketing concept," practitioners have been directed to find the answer to that question in the use-contexts of their prospective users. Accordingly, in the substantive domains that are of interest to individual firms, it is marketers' task to speak for the wants of prospective users and to ensure that the firm's productive output is responsive to some specific subset of want-creating conditions. Various implications follow that run counter to popular wisdom: The marketing concept was never intended to be an altruistic doctrine. Selling is *not* a part of marketing. Marketers do not create demand. If, as some have suggested, the essential subject matter of our discipline is exchange or exchange relationships, marketing and selling implicate distinctly different models of exchange. Finally, the marketer's behavioral objective is different in nature from that which advocates of social causes hope to achieve. Marketers seek to participate in behavior that is underway; advocates of social causes seek to change behavioral direction as they find it.

Altruism a Nonissue

In light of marketing's groundings in the fact of division of labor and the exigencies of competition, it is unclear how some authors have come to construe the marketing concept as an "altruistic doctrine" (Houston 1986). Certainly, marketing practitioners are not likely to think of it in this way and the error seems to arise from confusing the notions of perspective and benefit (taking the customer's perspective versus considering what benefits the customer). Considerations of efficiency and competitive advantage are more than adequate to explain why producers would want to stand in the shoes of prospective users in order to appreciate the use-context from the customer's perspective. The notion of altruism is superfluous.

A different set of issues is raised by inquiring whether or not customers benefit from having goods/services produced that are responsive to their wants. The answer to that question is not an unqualified yes, particularly when—due to mass production, distribution, and media—want-satisfaction is the public and intrusive process we know it to be today. The negative aspects of our current arrangements for want-satisfaction warrant consideration in their own right, as an issue distinct from the reasons for according primacy to the use-context in deciding what to produce.

Adopting the customer's perspective is analogous to the value-free posture of the scientist. In each case, one is guided by what one finds and, within the law, follows wherever the trail may lead. In each case, critical reflection on the ethical implications of taking such a value-free posture is warranted and raises, among other thorny issues, the question of whose values are to prevail, should scientists or marketers abandon a value-free posture (Fennell 1986a, 1986b). Speculating about the altruism or otherwise of the individuals involved is of secondary interest.

Marketing is not selling.

The essential difference between marketing and selling is this: Marketers want to engage in exchanges (usually on an ongoing basis) and, within broad limits, are open-minded with regard to the specifications of their offering. Sellers have ready-made offerings for which they want something in exchange—tangible (for example, money or real goods/services) or intangible (in the case of social cause advocacy, for example, information that others have complied with their recommendations). Misusing the term *marketing* to refer to the activity of selling is a widespread practice which may be excusable among the general public but is regrettable, nonetheless. For a number of reasons, selling as an activity has a place in the public's consciousness, while marketing does not. Having something to sell and trying to sell it appears to be the prototypical case. As laypeople, we tend to accept existing goods and services as givens, forgetting that each is the result of human decision. Then, to the layperson's actual experience that goods/services arrive ready-made is added confusion from the widespread practice of sellers, persons, and organizations, who, anxious to avoid the negative connotations of "selling," describing themselves as marketers and use *to market* as a euphemism for *to sell*. In consequence, used as a verb, *to market* has acquired pejorative connotations similar to those associated with high-pressure sales tactics; more sinisterly, for some, it may even connote using a special expertise held within the profession to manipulate the trusting and the unsuspecting. It is worth noting that marketing practitioners and a very few authors who understand the marketing–selling distinction do not use *market* as a transitive verb, for the excellent reason that, once the object exists, the opportunity to engage in marketing is severely restricted. Moreover, many other words are available (e.g., *promote, advertise, publicize, sell*) to refer to activities that may occur when the characteristics of an offering are regarded as fixed.

In distinguishing marketing from selling, I have in mind two notions of "selling," from each of which marketing is distinguished. First, there is what I shall call the *strong* notion of selling. I refer to the stereotype of a high-pressure salesperson, including the enterprising youths who, uninvited, clean your windshield while you are stuck in traffic. There is a coercive element in strong selling. In contrast, *weak* selling is any noncoercive attempt to induce an individual to adapt to some ready-made offering—good, service, or idea. Much social cause advocacy belongs here (e.g., stop smoking, it is bad for you; start exercising, it is good for you). Contrary to popular misconception, the promotion of goods and services that is conducted under the aegis of professional marketers is distinguished from selling in either sense. Specifically, since marketers view the characteristics of the offering as variable, promoting for marketers is the targeted dissemination of relevant information (i.e., communicating to those prospective users selected as targets the availability of offerings designed for their use). In marketing, persuasion or behavioral influence is achieved by adapting the characteristics of offerings to those of the targets' use-context. Coercive measures and the suggestion that a prospective purchaser should adapt to fit the seller's specifications are foreign to the notion of marketing.

Potentially damaging to our discipline has been the practice of many contributors to the academic literature who have in mind a model of selling when they write about marketing. In a vast amount of "marketing" writing, examining the text leaves no doubt that the author assumes that an offering exists and that its attributes are no longer modifiable. When this happens, the key marketing question of what shall we make (and all its attendant issues) are assumed away. Discussion of structural rigidities arising, for example, from productive decisions at other levels or times (e.g., Dholakia, Dholakia, and Firat 1983) appear all too rarely.

Certain considerations may extenuate what would otherwise be an extraordinarily reprehensible example of dereliction by marketing scholars and scientists. Scholars trained in other disciplines, such as operations research and the social sciences, have contributed to our literature. Not having experienced the tasks and responsibilities of marketing practitioners, some of these scholars have brought their science and their scholarship to bear in regard to a misconception of marketing, which they hold as members of the general public. It is, of course, true that the marketing concept is prominently featured in most, probably all, textbooks in marketing and that it unambiguously distinguishes marketing and selling: "Do not sell what you happen to make; make what the customer wants to buy." It is similarly true that, having paid lip service to the marketing concept in their first chapters, textbook authors fail to follow up with systematic treatments of the marketing–selling distinction or with conceptualizations that marketing warrants. We may search the literature of marketing for representations of the marketing concept and find virtually none. "Make what the customer wants to buy" demands, above all, that marketing scientists represent the conditions that dispose people to exchange their resources for an improved state. It requires a model of marketing to include terms reflecting the influences on customers that occur outside the marketplace, which imbue a marketplace offering with value—the premarketplace elements that marketers must investigate in order to "make what the customer wants." When marketing's grounding in division of labor and competitive pressures is understood, it is unnecessary to *argue* the importance of the customer— the idea that is already embodied in the marketing concept—as Howard (1983) does, for example. His interesting conceptualization lacks, as does that of Wind and Robertson (1983), a representation of the premarketplace elements, personal and environmental, that it is marketing's function to investigate and serve.[2] As I discuss later, a marketing orientation influences the design of empirical research in characteristic ways, as yet seldom present in the literature.

Marketers do not create demand.

It follows that marketers do not "create demand." One must marvel that, in suggesting that marketers do create demand, otherwise reasonable people have come to accept a notion so alien to marketing thinking. The reason why such a notion has gained any currency appears to lie in the economist's use of the term *demand* to equal *goods/services sold*. In other words, demand in any year is equal to the goods/services sold in that year. One may, then, increase demand by increasing the goods/services sold. Doubtless, the convention of equating demand with goods/services sold is useful for the economist's purposes, but it is of no value to a marketer charged with the task of identifying the characteristics of goods/services that people will want to buy. Producers (and the marketers who assist them) are concerned with demand that *preexists* goods/services—the core notion of the marketing concept: Make what the customer wants to buy. Most assuredly, we are not doing our job if we produce goods/services at random and wait until year's end to learn if demand exists. Marketers need a concept of demand that is independent of the goods/services that satisfy demand. For us, demand is already there in the conditions that allocate people's resources to doing what they do, and it is marketers' task to describe it in a way that guides the production of saleable products.

Finding new uses for existing goods/services is sometimes mentioned as an example of creating demand—new uses for Arm & Hammer baking soda is a classic example. Except possibly in the economist's peculiar sense, this is not an example of creating demand. Smelly drains and refrigerators, reactions of distaste, and the expenditure of human resources of time and effort to eliminate these nasties all preexisted Arm & Hammer's identifying new uses for baking soda. Originally, Arm & Hammer erred in limiting its definition to baking, when it identified a focal behavioral domain corresponding to a product it could produce (baking soda). Some years later, it corrected that error when it included the activity of odor control as well as baking. Circumstances over which Arm & Hammer has no control (e.g., the conditions that lead to smelly refrigerators and drains plus reactions of disgust in humans) were already leading to human resource allocations in a particular way (i.e., to take countermeasures), thus laying the ground for Arm & Hammer to offer to participate in ongoing exchanges relating to odor control; belatedly, the firm took heed. Such behavioral demand preexists and is the basis for the economist's "demand."

Two Contexts for Exchange

The proper domain for our discipline may well be exchange relationships or transactions, as some have suggested (e.g., Bagozzi 1979; Kotler 1972), but we must distinguish at least two contexts for exchange: marketing and selling. In table 16–1, four main bases for distinguishing the two contexts are shown as row headings; the corresponding marketing or selling assumption is entered in the appropriate column. The entries in the marketing column follow readily from marketing's groundings in division of labor and competitive pressures. Claiming no expertise in selling, let me say that in constructing table 16–1, my entries in the selling column are somewhat tentative. As I will discuss, they suggest that the selling model runs into difficulties at the points indicated by

Table 16–1
Two Contexts for Exchange

	Marketing model	*Selling model*
Societal perspective		
Task regarding surplus	Create (surplus planned)	Dispose of (surplus given)
Origin of surplus	Within system, for example, produced by division of labor	Outside system, for example, bountiful nature
Role of exchange	Permit access to otherwise unavailable goods/services	Dispose of unplanned surplus
Productive task	Produce/offer what users would make for selves	Produce what you can (?)
Focus on	Context of use	Production and trade
Waste/unmet wants due to	Error in ascertaining/realizing users' wants	Poorly grounded (flawed) system (?)
Business perspective		
Entrepreneurial task	Engage repeatedly in exchanges	Dispose of goods/services
Strategic planning enters	Preproduction	Postproduction
Responsible for output	Marketing management	Production management
Entrepreneurial strategy	Make appropriate productive/purchasing decisions	Induce purchase
Behavioral implications		
Implicit model of exchange	Interrole—exchange resources for improved state of being	Interpersonal, for example, swapping, bartering, advocacy (?), inducing compliance (?)
Relevant dyad	User–producer	Seller–buyer
Persuasive task	Create/announce availability of instrumental offerings	Induce compliance/perception of value (?)
Persuasive strategy	"What are your circumstances?"	"This serves your purposes" (?)
Basic science		
Substance	Conditions of want-occurrence and satisfaction	Interpersonal influence
Discipline(s)	Behavioral, physical, biological sciences	Social science

question marks in the figure—it seems to have nothing of interest to say about the productive enterprise, and its behavioral underpinning is unclear.

Taking a societal perspective first, while *abundance* in some sense (a surplus over what you can use) is a prerequisite to engaging in exchange, the marketing and selling contexts differ in regard to whether the surplus is considered to be created and planned within the system (marketing) or to arise outside the system, a given to be disposed of (selling). Exchange may be viewed as providing access to goods/services one cannot make for oneself (marketing) or as a means of disposing of unplanned surpluses (selling). Society's charge to the productive enterprise is clear in marketing (make what people would make for themselves), but unclear in the context of selling. Absent explicit indication, the selling model seems to mandate: produce what you can. Society's locus of interest may be focused on using resources in a way that is responsive to the circumstances of people's lives (marketing) or on production and trade (selling). In marketing, wasted resources and unmet wants occur when producers err in ascertaining users' circumstances or in translating those circumstances into appropriate (kind, quantity, price) output; in selling, error results from a flawed system that permits goods/services to be produced without regard for the use contexts that are their justification and destination.

As regards business, in marketing, the entrepreneurial task is to engage repeatedly in exchanges; strategic planning enters before the point at which management decides what to produce (or order, in the case of retail outlets) and takes the form of trying to make productive/purchasing decisions that reflect the characteristics of contexts of use. In selling, strategic planning enters after deciding what to produce/order, when the task is to dispose of goods/services; strategy takes the form of trying to induce purchase.

Considering behavioral influence, in marketing, the implicit model of exchange is *interrole*, i.e., individuals (who are both producer and user) allocating resources to improving their current state; the relevant dyad is user-producer; and the persuasive task is to create and announce the availability of goods/services that are responsive to the circumstances of prospective users (the psychological and nonpsychological conditions that dispose people to spend their resources); the strategy for doing so is to investigate and understand those conditions. In selling, the implicit model of exchange is *interpersonal* and the relevant dyad is seller–buyer. There seems to have been some confusion about the way this dyadic exchange is to be construed. An economic perspective (one having regard to resource allocation) suggests the appropriate model is the activities of swapping or bartering, where individuals desire another's surplus and offer their surplus in exchange. A social psychological model (in the tradition of persuasion, advocacy, or attitude change) suggests the activity of trying to win acceptance for an offering that is promoted primarily because of its significance to the would-be persuader. In such an advocacy model, the task is to show that something whose existence is independent of a prospective buyer's circumstances is congruent with or even essential to the prospect's purposes. Alternatively, perhaps "mere compliance" is the appropriate model. (See, for example, much of Cialdini's 1985 discussion.) In the version of selling that permeates "marketing" writing, the economic model appears to have been overshadowed by the social psychological model.

Considering the domains of basic science to which students of exchange would turn for help, having regard to the conditions of want-occurrence and want-satisfaction, marketers would favor behavioral, physical, and biological sciences. It is not at all clear where sellers would turn for help. The activities of swapping or bartering may not be well simulated in advocacy or compliance models and appear to have been somewhat neglected by social scientists.[3]

Behavioral Objective: Participate versus Change

As the preceding analysis suggests, the behavioral implications of marketing are very different from those associated with attitude change or advocacy of social causes. The marketer's objective, which is to participate in behavior that is underway (e.g., "when you are thinking of controlling unpleasant odors, think of using our baking soda"), is readily distinguished from that of inducing behavioral change (e.g., "stop smoking," "start voting").

The differing behavioral objectives of marketers and advocates of social causes parallel discussions of the possible or proper sphere of strategic action by business firms (i.e., to achieve their ends business organizations may change themselves/their own actions or try to change their environments). There are at least three issues here that should be treated separately, namely, what aspect of the environment—prospective customers versus other aspects—is intended, the circumstances in which it may be efficient, and the extent to which it is possible to adapt to/try to change one's environment. The only environmental aspect at issue here is customer circumstances. By and large, it is going to be more efficient for a business firm, operating under competitive pressures, to adapt to, rather than try to change, customer circumstances as it finds them. For that reason, the experience of business firms is a poor parallel for those trying to change the direction of others' behavior (e.g., induce smokers to stop smoking; induce nonvoters to vote). Certainly, the success of business firms in adapting to their customers' circumstances is not evidence of the ease with which one may change one's environment. Marketers are in a position to offer some help to persons who want to promote social causes such as reducing littering, animal trapping, or smoking, or increasing voting, wearing seat belts, or fitness. We can be helpful by describing the dimensions of a persuasive task (i.e., characterizing a naturally occurring population in terms of the likely difficulty of securing the persuasive objective).[4] Practitioners do this all the time in the realm of goods/services. But note how management uses the information our analysis generates. We use our analysis to focus attention on those occasions of use for which our firm can offer a competitive brand. As marketers, we have no experience in effecting the kind of fundamental change that social cause advocates hope to realize. Moreover, consider the dismal record of a 20 percent success rate for new product entries, in a context where we are trying to adapt to our customers and not (as in the social advocates' more demanding persuasive task) trying to have people adapt to recommendations.

Let me be clear about what I am saying here. Consider the prototypical marketing case where, based on our study of prospects' circumstances, we have recommended the design of a new brand, which is being test-marketed. Consumer research has been conducted before, during, and after a thirteen- or twenty-six–week period during which the brand has been advertised and available for purchase. If the research shows among prospects/targets that predetermined levels of brand awareness, correct awareness of the brand's attributes, and actual brand trial have been achieved, but that repeat purchase of the brand is low, neither our science nor our practice permits us to claim that we know how to make that brand a winner, other than by identifying already-existing circumstances with which it is (competitively) compatible. Is there any formulation in social science that legitimately provides hope, let alone assurance, to mass marketers operating in a competitive environment, that they may bank on selling what they have produced in disregard of user circumstances? The main message found in the basic literature is that, with the possible exception of captive targets, little is known about changing behavior in fundamental ways.

Let me summarize to this point. When society opted for division of labor, it severed the natural connection between user and producer that is found when individuals play both roles—producing what they use or consume. It needed a mechanism by which users could control what is produced in their name. One such mechanism is the free-market economy, where people may choose among the offerings of competing producers. For the mechanism to do the job society intends, at least two things must happen: (1) The consequences of disregarding the circumstances of prospective users (e.g., competitive disadvantage, wasted resources, threat to one's survival) must be salient for producers as they answer the question: What shall we produce? (2) Given that a reason for committing society's resources to the production of goods/services is to help people make adjustments that their circumstances dictate, producers must understand those circumstances. In individual firms, it is marketers' responsibility to provide the information that leads to such understanding. It is the responsibility of marketing scientists to create the representations that help practitioners to do their job. Clearly, the confusion that has existed up to now between marketing and selling militates against giving effect to users' circumstances. Nothing is more likely to prevent producers from paying heed to users' circumstances than the mistaken notion that actions taken after the productive decision has been made can save the day for unwanted output.

Given the current state of the art, the best service marketing scientists and educators can perform in the short run is to help the public and emerging generations of business people to understand that producers' reason for existing and strategy for success involve becoming acquainted with the circumstances in which a proposed output will be used. Once offerings exist, marketers' contribution is limited. Relying on mass media of communications, we are not equipped to claim that we know how to engender reasons for using an offering where such reasons do not already exist in our prospects' circumstances.

Conceptual progress is impeded by failing to treat marketing and selling separately as two distinct and mutually incompatible forms of exchange. Whether one has regard to society's interest in ensuring that producers are responsive to users' circumstances or that the resources society allocates to the pursuit of knowledge are used to good advantage, keeping distinct the activities of marketing and selling and their attendant strengths, weaknesses, and ethical and political ramifications can only be beneficial. Within the profession and in the public at large, understanding of each activity is bound to grow if we succeed in disentangling them in our minds, writing, and client relations.

Implications for Marketing Science

What difference would it make were marketing scientists to adopt a thoroughgoing marketing perspective—one that is grounded in division of labor and competitive pressures and that clearly distinguishes marketing from selling? What would it look like—a science whose domain comprises phenomena relevant to using resources for human satisfaction, to facilitating producers' response to users' circumstances? I shall mention here just a few characteristics of the behavioral components of such a domain, which can be discussed at the levels of the universe as well as the individual. But first, I should mention an interesting feature of a science that would give formal expression to the marketing concept. When the marketing concept directs producers to adapt to the circumstances of prospective users, it merely extends to the behavioral domain the essential genius humans have shown in putting the natural world to work for their purposes. We have not put waterfalls to work by first requiring the water to reverse its direction; our windmills are designed to respond to the wind's characteristics. We have not learnt to use the sources of energy found in nature by first requiring them to change their ways. It has been the genius of the marketing concept to capture the same idea. It is time for marketing scientists to take the marketing concept seriously, see it as extending to the behavioral realm the tradition that has informed the natural sciences, and make its strategy explicit in a formal representational system.

Representing the Universe of Interest

With regard to marketing's grounding in division of labor, one implication is that we would view the productive enterprise as being systematically related to aspects of a naturally occurring population. It becomes apparent that a population is not optimally represented as a universe of individuals, but, minimally, must be viewed as a universe of occasions for all of the activities in which human beings engage. We must then find ways to represent the fact that individual producers do not try to respond to all the circumstances that allocate human resources. A first cut through a universe of activity-occasions is needed in order to exclude the portion for which a producer's domain of expertise is likely to be irrelevant (nonprospects). Within the remainder (prospects), circumstances are likely to be varied. (Behavioral demand is segmented.) From the totality of the producer's domain of expertise, only a portion may be deployed in producing an offering, which likely responds to a subset of the circumstances of prospective users (targeted circumstances).

In sum, marketing scientists must conceptualize populations in ways that reflect the systematic relationships between producers and the circumstances of prospective users. An immediate benefit will accrue in that the practitioner's two-stage analysis of naturally occurring populations will be recognized in marketing theory—a first cut that defines a market of interest (the portion of a universe of activity-occasions to which the producer's domain of expertise is likely to be relevant), followed by analysis of the nature of segmented demand within that market (market segmentation), leading to the producer's selecting some region of that demand to respond to (i.e. the positioning decision).

Representing Individual Processes of Interest

Having regard to marketing's grounding in division of labor, society assigns marketers the task of helping producers to participate in behavior that is underway. It follows that one of the first tasks that becomes the lot of marketing scientists is to represent the natural processes of want-occurrence and want-satisfaction—to develop, in fact, a general model of instrumental action with particular attention to representing the conditions that allocate people's resources. If the productive enterprise is helping users to do what they wish to do for themselves, then it must be possible to show how the attributes of individual goods/services are responsive to the conditions that allocate people's resources to making adjustments.

Characteristics of Marketing Studies

Authors who claim that their studies are relevant to the discipline of marketing are expected to ensure that their research designs embody elements that are characteristic of marketing. At present, academic authors appear to consider that the mere inclusion therein of something about goods/services qualifies a study as an example of work in marketing, even though the conceptualization and research design are otherwise indistinguishable from work in, say, psychology or sociology. Not only do such studies fail to do justice to marketing, but the authors miss an opportunity to develop marketing's distinctive contribution to behavioral science.

In contrast, in a thoroughgoing marketing study, authors would state the systematic status of audience members in relation (1) to the message domain (e.g., the audience comprises prospects and nonprospects) and (2) to the message (e.g., some—which?—or all prospects have been selected as targets). Similarly, one would expect that a characteristic of studies of reactions to product attributes would be the inclusion therein of operations and discussion relevant to the systematic relationship between the attributes and prospects' circumstances. Authors would be expected to state the considerations that led them to predict that some (which?) prospects would regard some (which?) attributes as possessing instrumental value.

Typically, such features are not found in studies that purport to be relevant to marketing. For example, much research that marketing authors conduct within the social psychological communications paradigm fails to qualify as appropriate to marketing. Specifically, the status of audience members as nonprospects, prospects, and targets is not stated. Similarly, research in the tradition of multiattribute attitude studies often begins, conceptually and empirically, with a set of attributes. Scholarly interest appears not to reach to the theoretical source of the attributes. In contrast, one would expect marketers to be interested in the model that represents the attributes' origins. Much academic research in the domain of conjoint analysis could be cited to illustrate both deficiencies. The systematic source of the attribute set is not a focus of concern and subjects are not characterized in a manner that permits studying systematic relations with utilities.

Science for Marketing

For too long now, our marketing scholars and scientists have neglected to do the basic science that society's charge to marketing requires. Moreover, failing to appreciate and act upon the distinction between marketing and selling, they have launched generations of students on "marketing" careers imbued with an orientation, concepts, and techniques appropriate to selling, to the neglect of concepts and techniques appropriate to marketing. Marketing scholars and scientists have abdicated their legitimate claim to the essential marketing question: What shall we produce? They have left marketing's proper domain of scholarship to the chance ministrations of other disciplines. They have left the real-world decisions to engineers, technocrats, and practitioners who, absent systematic treatment of marketing's core question, rely on common sense, trial and error, and professional practice.

In the world in which marketing scholars and scientists exist, there is no perceptible trace of the activity of marketing. Marketing academics have no direct responsibility for the existence of goods/services, as practitioners do. Collectively, we have not found a way to render marketing activity, properly understood, perceptible in the form of models and other representations; in a very real sense, the marketing concept is mere rhetoric to the marketing academic. It receives ritualist-acknowledgement at certain points in marketing textbooks and is, thereafter, ignored. Perhaps because it is thus imperceptible to them, marketing scientists have not realized their responsibility to create the conceptual devices that would make the marketer's task a perceptible presence in their world.

Aside from intellectual challenge and satisfaction for those who would undertake the task, let me mention a few other benefits that will follow from articulating marketing as a formal system. Marketing educators will be in a position to sensitize future marketers to the significance for their professional status of being handed some ready-made good, service, or idea and being asked (or told) to make a go of it. They will have provided them with diplomatic ways of educating their clients or bosses to the kind of contribution marketers are trained to provide. Marketing scientists will have equipped those same students with conceptualizations of the circumstances of prospective users so that, later, when the question of what to offer is on the table in some corporate conference room, they may take their proper leadership role as marketing professionals. No longer will their contribution be restricted to reacting to productive options that originate who knows where. Instead, they will lead the strategic planning team in reviewing the ramifications of responding to each of a series of systematically specified user-circumstances.

Moreover, notwithstanding the best efforts of our business schools to produce professional marketers, critics will still claim to observe opportunist actions or practices, and those concerned to advance the human condition will still have recommendations for marketers' ears. Marketing authors will be in a position to examine the charges and recommendations in the context of marketing science, properly understood. For example, analyzing the situation within a systematic framework, they can ask (1) How can it be that individuals, prompted by nothing more compelling than the words and images of one in a veritable blizzard of promotional claims (some from directly competing sources) would repeatedly execute a marketer's wishes rather than their own? (2) How can it be that competitive pressures appear not to exert their regulating effect? (3) By what mechanism can individual marketers, operating in a competitive environment, effect some recommended social policy? or (4) What are the details of realistic alternatives to, or modifications of, present arrangements for producing our goods and services?

Once our scientists address the task of representing the marketing concept, they will articulate a framework that permits us to consider such questions in a coherent and systematic manner. Then, we may both view aberrations as failures of a system and realistically review the feasibility of praiseworthy recommendations. Taking instruction from our failures and inspiration from those who would improve the human condition, we may extend our understanding and do better in the future. Such has always been the promise of science. It is time for marketing science to deliver.

Notes

1. Depending on whether one adopts a macro or micro marketing perspective, "we" may refer to society or to individual producers. My remarks herein refer exclusively to micromarketing, unless otherwise stated.

2. Some years ago, an academic colleague said to me, as though in confidence: "You know, of course, that the marketing concept is nothing more than rhetoric." His words were totally baffling to me at the time. The distinction between marketing and selling is plain in the daily experience of practitioners where retaining hegemony over one's proper domain as marketer is a significant issue of professional status. The professor's words were fruitful. Trying to understand how one so respected could be so mistaken, I came to realize that they are literally true, if one is a marketing academic.

3. From the present analysis of behavioral implications, I have excluded discussion of strong (i.e., coercive) selling. In doing so, I am following a practice in the literature on persuasion where authors may exclude coercion as, by definition, outside the scope of their subject. As noted, I am not offering a complete treatment of selling. I trust that those who find a selling model congenial will address the anomalies in its grounding suggested here.

4. In line with the present micromarketing perspective, the phrase *naturally occurring* refers to the state of the world as any one marketer finds it when studying whether or not to try to participate in some ongoing behavior.

References

Bagozzi, R.P. (1979), "Toward a Formal Theory of Marketing Exchanges," in *Conceptual and Theoretical Developments in Marketing*, O.C. Ferrell, S. Brown, and C. Lambert, eds. Chicago: American Marketing Association, 431–47.

Cialdini, R.B. (1985), *Influence: Science and Pratice*. Glenview, Il.: Scott, Foresman.

Dholakia, R.R., N. Dholakia, and A.F. Fırat (1983), "From Social Psychology to Political Economy: A Model of Energy Use Behavior," *Journal of Economic Psychology* 3: 231–47.

Fennell, G. (1986a), "Prolegomenon: Marketing, Ethics, and Quality of Life," in *Marketing and the Quality of Life*, A. Coskun Samlı, ed. Westport, Conn.: Greenwood.

———, (1986b), "Extending the Thinkable: Consumer Research for Marketing Practice," in *Advances in Consumer Research*, vol. 13, R. Lutz, ed. Provo, Utah: Association for Consumer Research.

Houston, F.S. (1986), "The Marketing Concept: What It Is and What It Is Not," *Journal of Marketing* 50 (April): 81–87.

Howard, John (1983), "Marketing Theory of the Firm," *Journal of Marketing* 47 (Fall): 90–100.

Kotler, P. (1972), "A Generic Concept of Marketing," *Journal of Marketing* 36 (April): 46–54.

Wind, Yoram, and Thomas S. Robertson (1983), "Marketing Strategy: New Directions for Theory and Research," in *Journal of Marketing* 47 (Spring): 12–25.

17
Entrepreneurial Behavior and Marketing Strategy

Ronald Savitt

Basics of Marketing Behavior

Marketing views the world as heterogeneous and actively pursues such differences. Alderson (1958) presented marketing as a sorting process in which buyers and sellers actively pursue their self-interest by the transformation of assortments. As the process unfolds, there are gaps to overcome in order for transactions to be completed. Want satisfaction is always partial, the gaps are only partially bridged, and there is always the opportunity to exploit the differences between offerings and wants. Some of these gaps exist because of the inequitable distribution of resources and demands; some are natural and permanent; others can be created by buyers and sellers in their search for differential advantage. The essence of marketing theory assumes *ab initio* that competition is the search for meaningful differentiation in discrepant markets (Reekie and Savitt 1982).

Marketing competition is the rivalry that takes place between sellers for the custom of consumers and between consumers for the access to suppliers. It takes place in the real world (which is fraught with uncertainty) and the process is entrepreneurial. That means that individuals and firms actively seek to mold and shape future environments by creating and exploiting market discrepancies and opportunities. Marketing competition is directed at the occupation of or claim to the use of resources, primarily time, space, and purchasing power. Participants seek to ensure their positions by searching for differential advantage. These take many characteristics including the form and function of goods

The author acknowledges the helpful comments of Dr. John A. Dawson (Fraser of Allander Professor of Distributive Studies, Department of Business Studies, University of Stirling, Stirling, Scotland), Professor E.T. Grether (School of Business Administration, University of California, Berkeley), and John C. Narver (School of Business Administration, University of Washington).

and services offered and assortments demanded, the time and space of transactions and their resultant positions, and the costs and benefits of exchanges.

Environmental Shaping

Before attempting to describe the concept of environmental shaping, it is necessary to define *environment*. Definitions in marketing have attempted to classify the elements that comprise the environment usually under two major categories, the physical environment and the social environment (Bartels 1970, pp. 261–62). Other definitions narrowed their emphasis to matters concerning the firm, such as: "The environment consists essentially of a series of input and output markets (for labor, capital, productive equipment, end products, etc.) in which the company must transact" (Thorelli 1981, p. 7).

There is no single definition of environment. Hence, "the best way to approach this problem is to ask what are the *relevant* elements in the environment for the operation of some system?" (Harvey 1969, p. 458). This approach relies not on what "the environment" is, but on what is perceived and how it is perceived. The environment varies greatly among individuals and the resultant behavior is affected only by the portion of the environment that is actually perceived. We do not absorb and retain the virtually infinite amount of information coming from the environment. "Our memory, far from holding every sensory impression from our environment, selects and retains only a small portion" (Gould and White 1984, p. 48). While lack of agreement and subjectivity regarding the environment appears troublesome at first, it is not. This characteristic adds richness because it offers opportunities to create and exploit market discrepancies.

Current thought in marketing does not fully recognize the ability of the firm to shape its environment, to affect the future of environment, and to more effectively shape supply and demand. The basic textual discussion assumes that the environment is uncontrollable (McCarthy and Perrault 1984, p. 59). Others suggest the effects of the environment are dynamic though most of the emphasis is placed upon how the "dynamic environment . . . influences business firms and populations of human beings alike" (Holloway and Hancock 1973, p. 20). Attention is paid to the potential effects of marketing on the environment; however, little if anything is said about how firms can manage the environment, let alone organize it. Even the most popular treatises on strategy take a passive approach (Porter 1979). In doing so, they not only ignore marketing practice, but limit the possibilities of competitive behavior.

Market participants have significant freedom to establish and shape present and future environments. This ability is perhaps no more clearly seen than in the areas of time and space. Both are plastic and their forms can be molded, an important point made by Edith Penrose, who described plasticity as "form giving." She argued this is what marketing is all about: "Firms not only alter the environment conditions necessary for their actions, but, more important, they know they can alter them and that the environment is not independent of their own activities" (1959, p. 42).

Recent discussions in the marketing literature have only begun to recognize this. Zeithaml and Zeithaml (1984) and Kotler (1986) have challenged the common wisdom "that the environment is uncontrollable." Kotler went so far as to say: "I now believe that marketers can influence the environment in which the firm operates and do not simply have to accept and adapt to it . . . The environment must be managed as well as the marketing mix" (Whalen 1984, p. 11). These are important developments; however, these authors have not gone far enough. Not only can the environment be managed, it can be shaped. This is an active role of creation for market participants rather than a passive role of managing. And, the environment must be shaped before it is managed.

Resource Occupation

Marketing transactions are examined in the context of the complete set of scarce resources. Historically, marketing (like economics) has concentrated on financial resources. Both time and space are necessary additions to the understanding of scarce resources. As transactions take place, buyers and sellers give up their rights to or access to scarce resources. To the extent that the future is unknown until conscious choice is made, market participants have the ability to affect their future resources. For example, a family purchasing furniture for a new house gives up present resources and possible future income by their purchase. They can purchase more or less now depending on how they view possibilities about future events. Similarly, the manufacturer can commit all of the firm's inventory of maple to present production or withhold part of it for future use. Marketing decisions are all about having and giving up rights to resources and about expectations about how resources might be renewed in the future.

Resource occupation goes beyond the traditional economic view that market participants give up scarce resources as the result of transactions. Market participants seek more than the gain from the transaction. They seek control over the scarce resources by preventing them from being used by competitors and by limiting the means by which the resources can be allocated and used in present and future periods. In these ways, they limit their rivals' abilities to engage in future transactions; resource occupation is forward-looking, that is, it is involved in organizing the future. Also, it is about occupying resources to limit or prevent transactions.

One of the most important resources in retailing is space. The presence or absence of good-selling space can make or break a retailer. Supermarket chains pursue space for their own needs as well as to deny space to competitors. Some chains have been known to lease, to take options on, and to purchase space as means of preventing direct competitors from having access to locations. Also, some have gone as far as preventing indirect competitors such as fast-food outlets from having access to such space.

Firms in competition with one another want to occupy the time of consumers both in terms of the results of immediate transactions and in terms of the availability of time remaining for other transactions and for the consumption of other goods and services. A firm pursuing time occupation betters its own chance for survival and diminishes the opportunities of its competitors. Competitive behavior takes on new dimensions as firm resources are reorganized around resource domination. Regional shopping centers provide a good example of this. As institutions, they have grown to serve concentrations of people. They are planned to draw customers from a wide area. By their size alone and the need for some customers to travel great distances to reach them, they occupy the time of these customers and, hence, prevent or restrict them from engaging in other shopping and consuming activities. Whether consumers purchase or not, resources have been taken by the shopping center. Centers may also be designed to maximize the time spent in shopping within them, as customers are required to cover large areas within each center. The competitive effects of regional shopping centers fall on all types of retail institutions, including traditional central business districts and even mom-and-pop corner grocery stores. They represent the widest example of full intertype competition when viewed in this perspective.

The role of environmental shaping through resource occupation as a basis for the development of marketing strategy is most clearly revealed in the context of entrepreneurial behavior. Before examining how the entrepreneur can shape the environment through the use of temporal and spatial elements, it is important to understand entrepreneurial behavior.

Entrepreneurial Behavior

Definition

There is some confusion as to what entrepreneurial behavior is. Many authors confuse entrepreneurial behavior with the function of management or define it as a combination of management and ownership. A common definition proceeds as follows: "The manager himself must then be employed and monitored by someone—ultimately, by the owner or owners themselves. Hence, an inescapable decision making aspect attaches to firm ownership; this combined function is traditionally called *entrepreneurship*" (Hirschleifer 1976, p. 228).

Even the wider definition of an entrepreneur as an individual who is "especially eager to profit from adjusting production to the expected changes in conditions, those who have more initiative, more venturesomeness, and a quicker eye than the pushing and promoting pioneers of economic improvement" is not totally satisfactory (von Mises 1963, pp. 264–65).

Entrepreneurial behavior or entrepreneurship in the context of Austrian economics has two distinct meanings. In both, the entrepreneur is found in dynamic conditions in which the premises of economic equilibrium are discarded. There is no perfect information; hence, the behavior of market participants cannot be predicted. In the real world of marketing, "economic systems function coherently, insofar as they do *because* of the bounds produced by imperfections of knowledge rather than, as in conventional theory, despite them" (Earl 1982, p. 7). What "equilibrium" provides is deterministic behavior. By that is meant that once conditions are stated and once assumptions are included, there is a single or limited set of alternatives open to decisions to be made. In such circumstances, events that cannot be easily dealt with are either ignored or viewed as fixed and, hence, uncontrollable. Equilibrium is an even-rotating system in which decision makers employ similar data in similar models which lead to similar results. It disregards the opportunities that come from diversity.

One definition of entrepreneurial behavior regards the entrepreneur as one who operates in the disparate market with the purpose of providing a corrective function. "Entrepreneur means man acting in regard to the changes in the market" (von Mises 1963, p. 54). Kirzner, for one, argues that: "We can see the entrepreneur as bringing into mutual adjustment those discordant elements that constitute the state of disequilibrium. His role is created by the states of disequilibrium and his activities ensure a tendency toward equilibrium" (1979, p. 111). The other definition of entrepreneur—the one adopted here—is the antithesis, namely, the entrepreneur works toward the disruption of any tendency toward equilibrium. This is akin to Schumpeter's entrepreneur working toward the destabilization of markets. Schumpeter argues that economic progress stems from the entrepreneur who pushes the economy away from the tendencies toward equilibrium (1934, p. 64). Entrepreneurs abhor the tendency toward equilibrium because it limits their opportunities. Also, they dislike equilibrium because it implies a situation in which independent decision making is given up to market forces, namely, competitors.

Entrepreneurs are faced with the double-sided challenge of disrupting markets for competitors and securing for themselves. They must, *at the same time*, shape the environment so as to build strong linkages with consumers and strong blockages for competitors. The entrepreneurial function is found in this process of environmental shaping; the managerial function is keeping the two in balance. An excellent example of entrepreneurial behavior in this context is

7-up with its "no caffeine, never has, never had" promotion. Management—entrepreneurs, to be sure—sought to destabilize the market by exploiting negative attitudes toward caffeine as well as to shape market preferences, build linkages to those who did not want caffeine, and create blockages for competitors who made their soft drinks with caffeine.

Further, it is important to recognize that entrepreneurial behavior is exhibited by buyers and sellers. Retail cooperatives in the United Kingdom in the nineteenth century were buyer-organized institutions pursuing market opportunities. They organized in ways that allowed them to shape markets so that they could exploit economies of size in purchasing food and other household items. "The fact that the retail cooperatives come to employ resources of land and have accumulated capital to purchase other forms of stocks and equipment may mean that some entrepreneurial acts in the modern consumer cooperative are inspired by resource owners such as managers or capitalists but the proximate entrepreneurship was undoubtedly that of consumers" (Reekie 1979, p. 114). Finally, entrepreneurial behavior is not limited to product markets, it is also applicable in the other markets of capital, information, labor, resources, and technology.

Entrepreneurial Behavior and Information

Entrepreneurial behavior operates on the premise that there is no knowledge (or, at best, limited knowledge) about the future. It varies from the general approach in marketing, which places great credibility on the availability of marketing information about future environments. A problem of this approach is that it conceives of the future as a series of probability distributions. Risk analysis assumes implicitly that, based on structural arrangements and past behavior, a list of all possible outcomes can be generated. The manager need only assign probability weights to the various outcomes and choose "the best." In reality, such a list does not exist. The state of the future is best described as a state of "partial ignorance." Knowledge about the future is limited; the number and variety of events that might take place are greater than the list of "risk analysis" (Loasby 1976, p. 6). While in the very short run, the manager will attempt to predict future outcomes, the longer run is more difficult to estimate. The long run can only be viewed as the summation of short-run periods if knowledge about the future or assumptions about the knowledge of the future are used.

True choice for market participants disappears when knowledge about the future has the characteristics previously mentioned and what we refer to as the logic of choice in such situations is no more than stimulus-response. Put in other terms: "We can choose only what is unactualized; we can choose only amongst imaginations and figments. Imagined actions and policies can only have imagined consequences, and it follows that we can choose only an action whose consequences we cannot directly know since we cannot be eyewitnesses of them" (Shackle 1970, p. 106). Choice is only genuine when it has the power to affect future events whose outcomes are not known and cannot be predicted. "Choice and determinancy are incompatible . . . If choice is real, the future cannot be certain; if the future is certain there can be no choice" (Loasby 1976, p. 5).

Entrepreneurs attempt to create expectations about the future by communicating information about the environments they are shaping to relevant audiences. This is provided to other market participants in order to influence their behavior. Information about the future is the means by which present environments are established and behavior is influenced. As Boulding stated, any decision is "a choice among alternative perceived images of the future" (1971, p. 28). Some marketers practice this. How many times are consumers encouraged to purchase items *now* because the seller either says or implies that they will not be available in the future?

The Time-Space Environment

The development of marketing strategy in the entrepreneurial framework is based on an understanding of the resource-laden environment which is to be shaped. The environment is the time-space domain. This concept developed by Professor Hägerstrand at the University of Lund "offers a contextual approach which views individuals' situations within their environments" (Johnston 1983, p. 134). His thesis is that human activities form environments having a hierarchical ordering to the extent that "those who have access to power in a superior domain frequently use this to restrict the set of possible actions permitted inside subordinate domains. Sometimes they can also oblige the subordinate domains to remove constraints or to arrange for certain activities against their will" (Hägerstrand 1977, pp. 16–17). The central focus of this analysis "is a respect for the conditions which space, time and environment impose on what the individual can do" (Thrift 1977, p. 4).

In order to shape future environments, substantial study of present conditions is required. This activity allows an understanding of where opportunities exist and the means for shaping future environments. The trend toward smaller houses, especially smaller kitchens, has made certain appliances such as coffee makers more difficult to use and store. As a reflection of these conditions, Black & Decker for one developed a line of "under-counter" and "under-shelf" appliances whose space-saving features have become well accepted, so much in fact that they are replacing the traditional large-size products.

Time and Space

Time is the transition from one event to another; it describes the transformation of one event into another (Shackle 1958, p. 15). Time is defined by the perceptions of the actors; they provide limitations on behavior. Time measures are conjectural and they are based on an individual's or organization's perceptions of events. Because of this perceptual nature, there will be differing definitions about the basic structural and behavioral elements, that is, cause and effect. For example, the same purchase of furniture may be defined as a simple stimulus-response process by one firm and as a continual inventory replenishment process by another. The first case might be viewed as a situation over which little influence besides traditional marketing activities can be exerted, while the second case may be one in which the seller can affect the environment so as to encourage the consumer to purchase more frequently. Understanding that time can be affected is a key part of entrepreneurial behavior.

Time is also a scarce resource; it can be described as a "fixed-budget commodity." Unlike money and space, no one is able to accumulate any more than a fixed quantity in any period and time must be spent or used even if there is no overt effort to do so. Time cannot be saved in general, though any individual can pack more events into a period if the time for each event is reduced (Wilson and Holman 1984, p. 29). It is this characteristic of time that opens the opportunity for strategic development. The temporal environment can be affected. Direct mail merchants such as L.L. Bean, Lands End, and Orvis base their strategies on affecting time by providing more time for shopping with their catalogs and twenty-four–hour ordering service.

Space represents the location at which events take place. Like time, space is also a perceptual phenomenon, though it is easier to define and measure. It is linked to time insofar that situations in transformation occupy space. Perceptions of space are affected by time and the information which flows in and out of the time process. The images that participants have of the spatial setting are known as mental maps (Gould and White 1974, p. 49). These maps are the result of perceptions and they can be influenced by experience and information. Not only do consumers have perceptual maps of where brands of beer are, they also have clear visions of where supplies are available in space. Location in space and its communication of it to users is part of environmental shaping. Fast-food operators advertise that they are just "around the corner" even though they may be miles away. Consumers asked to describe fast-food locations will show them closer than they really are.

In the absolute sense, only one item can occupy a particular space at a given moment. Space occupancy is a perceptual phenomenon. A marketer can affect the perception of the environment through the use of information and the creation of images. It can attempt to convince other market participants that space is occupied when in reality it is only partially occupied or even unoccupied. Where consumers or suppliers believe events will take place is more important than where they actually do.

The Domain

A domain is the "time-space" environment within which activities and events are under the control and/or influence of specific individuals or organizations. "Domains are intended to protect artificial or natural resources, to restrict population density, and to form an efficient arrangement of bundles" (Pred 1973, p. 42). Domains can be viewed as a perceptual phenomenon in which the members of the domain, as well as those attempting to affect the domain, play important roles in creating a definition. A domain in a simple sense can be thought of as a time period such as a day of twenty-four hours. Given a set of known processes, only certain activities can be accomplished in that time period; however, a change of the environment can be accomplished by extending or contracting the nature of the activities undertaken in the twenty-four hour period. The course of the day can be affected by rearranging and molding the activities that a person must perform to go through the period. The day can appear to have more time if onerous activities are shortened or changed; on the other hand, the day can be made to seem longer if such activities are increased in number or intensity. A good example of a domain in marketing is the marketing channel. An excellent example of the strategic management of this domain is the total order cycle concept (Lambert and Stock 1982). The underlying analysis comes from Bucklin's postponement and speculation proposition which describes the effects of temporal factors on distribution (1965).

In the case of the order cycle concept, the dimensions of time and space for the buyer have been defined in terms of a total process starting with awareness of the potential of product shortage through all of the various steps to implement an order, communication of other transaction information (such as credit), the shipment of goods, and, finally, evaluation of buyer satisfaction. The order cycle represents a purposefully constructed environment containing spatial and temporal elements whose purpose is the linkage of customers to a specific supplier. It is a domain that is a direct result of a firm's policies and programs "carefully carried out by instruments of product span, territorial expansion, temporal modes of operation and choice of customer groups" (Thorelli 1981, p. 9).

Basic Characteristics

The time-space domain can be described temporally in three ways. First, there is the historical statement. It is a description of what took place and can be viewed from the perspective of the participant or from the perspective of an observer. Second, there is the in-process statement which describes domains in which action is taking place and which contains some action of the immediate past, an ongoing activity, and a future set of activities whose limits are seen and defined. Third, there is the future domain which is constructed of expectations of how behavior will take place in the environment described by domain. It is the one to be shaped.

The three are related. Experience affects present behavior; to some extent, past and present behavior *may* point toward future behavior. It can be conditioned by affecting alternatives. In an entrepreneurial situation, past and present behavior do not predict future outcomes. If the environment were static, then future behavior in some significant way would be an extrapolation of the past. However, the environment itself, the domain, is shaped to affect future behaviors.

The ability of an organization or an individual to navigate through the domain is a function of constraints which limit action. Physical constraints such as product size, the location and size of facilities, and means of access to information affect passage through space and affect the consumption of time. Important are the perceptual constraints and beliefs that individuals hold about the possibilities of movement through time and space. There are three major classes of constraints.

1. *Capability constraints* define the amounts of time or space needed to perform basic functional activities. In intermodal competition, airlines promote flying time while railroads have promoted center city to center city travel time. Still (for other reasons, primarily frequency and cost), railroads have lost out to air travel. Each, however, has attempted to use capability constraints in building strategy.

2. *Coupling constraints* are those activities in which individuals must join other individuals and organizations must join other organizations in order to complete production, distribution, consumption, or other social activities. Marketing channels would not work without either external or internal coupling. Each coupling restricts others.

3. *Authority constraints* represent those general rules, laws, economic barriers, and power relations that determine who does or does not have access to specific domains at specific times to do specific things (Pred 1977, p. 208). Authority constraints arise as a result of the fact that it is difficult to pack more than one or several activities into a limited space.

There is a temporal hierarchy among domains. Certain activities must be performed before others. Each individual or firm has a multidimensional set of domains. These domains are also characterized by power or superiority as well as hierarchical order. The new result of this is that some individuals and firms will be able to affect the functions of others; "those who have access to power in a superior domain frequently use this to restrict the set of possible actions permitted inside subordinate domains" (Pred 1973, pp. 41–43).

Domains will vary from product to product and behavior to behavior. We all know of individuals who are thought to be provincial because their spatial boundaries are limited. The same is true for firms. The fact that all firms do not enter the same markets (points at which buyers are located in time and space) cannot be argued on the basis of economic factors alone. Some firms, like some countries, do not perceive opportunities over large areas. It is unrealistic to argue that cost functions alone set spatial boundaries. In international business, for example, some firms enter foreign markets because they have a comprehensive perception of space. In this context, we can easily identify the perceptual factors. For example, studies in export behavior hypothesize that size of firm, education of management, product type, and complexity of activity (exporting as innovative behavior) all affect perceptions of time and space (Axinn 1985). The behavioral environment represents that segment of the environment that is perceived by the individual or firm; it is that part of space from which information signals are received and interpreted by the perceptual mechanism of the decision maker. Only a small amount of the information emanating from the objective environment is received. "It is this [perceived information] that determines the nature of the individual's behavioral environment, and it is this and only this, that is relevant to purposive behavior" (Lloyd and Dicken 1972, p. 138).

Summary

Each individual or firm has a unique region, a relevant geographic market, for example. The domain, as we have seen, is an area having time and space dimensions; it is the arena in which all resource allocation decisions—including financial ones—are made. Decision makers operate in an environment defined by their perceptions of it. Hence "decision makers operating in an environment base their decisions on the environment as they perceive it, not as it is. The action resulting from a decision, on the other hand, is played out in the real environment" (Brookfield 1969, p. 53).

Every firm is surrounded by an environmental framework or pattern of resource and activity alternatives that must be dealt with if want satisfaction is to take place. These alternatives are unevenly distributed in the Aldersonian sense and they are known to the extent that information-seeking behavior takes place. They are relative to the individual; individual behavior can generally be characterized to the extent that it is either geocentric or ethnocentric (the degree to which the individual is outward-looking or inward-looking) (Perlmutter 1967). The extent of the behavior depends on the individual's perceptions, the availability of information (which in itself is dependent upon the outward or inward search behavior), and the available resources.

The Development of Marketing Strategy

The Essence of Strategy

The key to successful market participation is the development of a strategy. In the purest sense, a strategy is "a scheme or principal idea through which an objective would be achieved" (Luck and Farrell 1985, p. 2). The ultimate goal for the firm will be some individually stated objectives of want satisfaction which will incorporate a variety of factors including profitability and survival. Want satisfaction can be expressed in a similar fashion for consumers. The means to reach the specific want-satisfaction objectives are found in the shaping of future environments. Strategy for firms is about shaping the future by applying constraints so as to establish relationships with customers or suppliers and by restricting or limiting the opportunities of consumers, competitors, or suppliers to occupy and use resources in the future.

Strategies (or, more appropriately, strategic plans) are developed in light of expectations of future events. Both buyers and sellers prepare themselves for the future by mapping out plans as to how they will move forward in time. Whether formally or informally established, these plans are based on what is expected to happen. Expectations are based on assumptions about the relevance of past experiences and events as extrapolated into the future. As Shackle has clearly argued, there is a problem with this: "Estimation, judgment, inference, the exploitations of suggestions which the visible present and the records of the past supply, are worthy forms of language, but they must not be allowed to disguise the essential non-observability of the future" (1970, p. 111). Peter Drucker has recognized this point in more traditional managerial terms. "One cannot do marketing research for something genuinely new. One cannot do market research for something that is not yet in the market" (1985, p. 191). What this means is that the entrepreneurial firm must start out with assumptions that its offerings may find customers in markets that "no one thought of, for uses no one envisioned when the product or service was designed, and that it will be bought by customers outside its field of vision and even unknown to the new venture" (Drucker, pp. 191–92).

Entrepreneurship and Marketing Strategy

Entrepreneurship has been described as the creation and exploitation of environments by market participants. This is based on the premise that the environment is malleable and plastic and can be molded. Exploitation depends upon observation of market discrepancies and/or the potential for creating such discrepancies and the pursuit of them in such a fashion as to upset and affect the plans of other market participants. This type of activity is made possible because of the limited knowledge of future events. Entrepreneurship is an active rather than a passive process, and it requires a willingness to make guesses about outcomes. Entrepreneurs want to achieve continuity and stability for their operations through shaping activities and, at the same time, keeping competitors and other participants off guard by the application of various constraints. Being able to keep competitors surprised is part of shaping the environment (Shackle 1970, pp. 115–17). An excellent example of this was the 7-up campaign discussed earlier.

Basically, the objective of strategy is to occupy the spatial and temporal domains of market participants. This is carried out by purposeful molding or shaping of the environment based upon managerial perceptions of the state of future markets.

Environment-Shaping Strategy

Environment shaping takes place when the entrepreneur sets definitions for the three constraints previously discussed, namely, the capability constraint, the coupling constraint, and the authority constraints. In operational terms, these are: (1) to maximize the time involved in selection of the entrepreneur's offerings and to minimize the time involved in the selection of others' offerings, (2) to maximize the time involved in the consumption of the entrepreneur's offerings in contrast to others, (3) to maximize the blockages to other market participants to supplies and resources and to maximize the entrepreneur's access to those items, and (4) to maximize customer's access to the entrepreneur's offerings and minimize their access to those of others.

While there is no case that systematically incorporates strategic elements developed from the shaping constraints, there are many examples that, taken one at a time, provide insights into what a complete environment-shaping strategy might look like. Many retailers, regardless of absolute size, shape their environment to keep customers there for long periods by the use of complicated floorplans, large product assortments, and promotion activities. K Mart has used its flashing blue light as a means of keeping customers in the store on the expectation of new bargains. Manufacturers can maximize consumption time by offering larger sizes of items, products of greater quality, and products tied to service and warranty agreements as well as components for additional uses.

Blockages to prevent other market participants' access to resources include everything from long-run supply contracts to tying arrangements (Revzan 1961, p. 20). Other activities include the purchase of specific locations to keep them out of use by others, the purchase of patents to keep products from commercial activities and the hiring of people. Zayre, as part of a number of environment-shaping activities, has attempted to maximize consumers' access to the products by extending rain-check programs with a 10 percent-off policy for customers who actually purchase the merchandise ("Zayre Discusses . . . p. 18). At the same time, Zayre has instituted a "three-in-line" checkout policy in which if more than three people are waiting in a line, another checkout is opened. At first, this might seem to be inconsistent with the first proposition, but they view the spatial environment as having two parts, the selection segment and the checkout segment. While increasing selection opportunities, they minimize for the consumer the more onerous of the two, the checkout activity.

Within each of these practices, there are limits to which shaping can take place. However, the limits can only be discovered through experimentation. There are most likely limits on the amount of time consumers will spend in shopping or in consumption. In the case of some blockages, there are public policy limits.

A Final Observation

Environmental shaping is a necessary first step to environmental management. To the extent that entrepreneurs are able to shape the environment and occupy resources, they have the opportunity to manage the environment. Entrepreneurs are never satisfied with the status quo; they are intent on shaping the future, rather than being shaped by it. As Robert Onstead, CEO of Randall's Food and Drugs, said: "I don't want our competitors making decisions for us" (Berry 1986, p. 4).

References

Alderson, W. (1958), *Marketing Behavior and Executive Action*. Homewood, Ill.: Richard D. Irwin.

Axinn, C.N. (1985), "An Examination of Factors That Influence Export Involvement," unpublished Ph.D. dissertation. East Lansing: Graduate School of Business Administration, Michigan State University.

Bartels, R. (1970), *Marketing Theory and Metatheory*. Homewood, Ill.: Richard D. Irwin.

Berry, L.L. (1986), "Editor's Corner," *Retailing Issues Letter* 2 (April): 4.

Boulding, K.E. (1971), "The Economics of Knowledge and the Knowledge of Economics," in *Economics of Information and Knowledge*, D.M. Lamberton ed. Harmondsworth, England: Penguin, 21–36.

Brookfield, H.C. (1969), "On the Environment as Perceived," in *Progress in Geography*, C. Board et al., eds. London: Arnold, 51–80.

Bucklin, L.P. (1965), "Postponement, Speculation and the Structure of Distribution," *Journal of Marketing Reserach* 5 (February): 26–31.

Entrepreneurial Behavior and Marketing Strategy • 321

Drucker, P.F. (1985), *Innovation and Entrepreneurship, Practice and Principles*. New York: Harper & Row.

Earl, P.(1982), *The Economic Imagination: Towards a Behavioral Analysis of Choice*. Brighton, England: Wheatsheaf.

Gould, P., and R. White (1974), *Mental Maps*. Baltimore: Penguin.

Hägerstrand, T. (1970), "What about People in Regional Science?" *Papers of the Regional Science Association* 24: 7–21.

Harvey, D. (1969), *Explanation in Geography*. London: Edward Arnold.

Hirschleifer, J. (1976), *Price Theory and Applications*. Englewood Cliffs, N.J.: Prentice-Hall.

Holloway, R.J., and R.S. Hancock (1973), *Marketing in a Changing Environment*, 2nd ed. New York: John Wiley.

Johnston, R.L. (1983), *Geography and Geographers: Anglo-American Human Geography Since 1945*. London: Arnold.

Kirzner, I.M. (1979), *Perception, Opportunity, and Profit Studies in the Theory of Entrepreneurship*. Chicago: University of Chicago Press.

Kotler, P. (1986), "Megamarketing," *Harvard Business Review* 62 (March-April): 117–24.

Lambert, D.M., and J.R. Stock (1982), *Strategic Physical Distribution Management*. Homewood, Ill.: Richard D. Irwin.

Lloyd, P.E., and P. Dicken (1972), *Location in Space: A Theoretical Approach to Economic Geography*. New York: Harper & Row.

Loasby, B.J. (1976), *Choice Complexity and Ignorance*. Cambridge, England: Cambridge University Press.

Luck, D.J., and O.C. Farrell (1985), *Marketing Strategy and Plans*. Englewood Cliffs, N.J.: Prentice-Hall.

McCarthy, E.J., and W.D. Perrault, Jr. (1984), *Basic Marketing*, 8th ed. Homewood, Ill.: Richard D. Irwin.

von Mises, L. (1963), *Human Action*, Chicago: Regency.

Penrose, E.T. (1959), *The Theory of the Growth of the Firm*. Oxford, England: Basil Blackwell.

Perlmutter, V. (1967), "Social Architectural Problems of the Multinational Firm," *Quarterly Journal of AIESEC International* 3 (3): 33–44.

Porter, M.E. (1979), "How Competitive Forces Shape Strategy," *Harvard Business Review* 57 (March-April): 137–45.

Pred, A. (1973), "Urbanization, Domestic Planning Problems and Swedish Geographic Research," in *Progress in Geography*, C. Board et al., eds. London: Arnold, 1–77.

———, (1977), "The Choreography of Existence on Hägerstrand Time-Geography and Its Usefulness," *Economic Geography* 53: 207–21.

Reekie, W.D. (1979), *Industry, Prices and Markets*. Oxford, England: Philip Alan.

Reekie, W.D., and R. Savitt (1982), "Marketing Behaviour and Entrepreneurship: A Synthesis of Alderson and Austrian Economics," *European Journal of Marketing* 16 (7): 55–66.

Revzan, A. (1961), *Wholesaling in Marketing Organization*. New York: John Wiley & Sons.

Schumpeter, J.A. (1934), *The Theory of Economic Development*. Cambridge, England: Cambridge University Press.

Shackle, G.L.S. (1958), *Time in Economics.* Amsterdam: North-Holland.

———, (1970), *Expectation, Enterprise and Profit: The Theory of the Firm.* London: George Allen & Unwin.

Thorelli, H.B. (1981), "International Marketing: An Ecological View," in *International Marketing Strategy*, revised ed. H.B. Thorelli and H. Becker, eds. New York: Pergamon, 520.

Thrift, N. (1977), *An Introduction to Time-Geography.* Norwich, England: Geo Abstracts, University of East Anglia.

Whalen, B. (1984), "Kotler: Rethink the Marketing Concept," *Marketing News*, student ed. (October): 11, 15.

Wilson, R.D., and R.H. Holman (1984), "Time Allocation Dimensions of Shopping Behavior," in *Advances in Consumer Research 1984*, T. Kinnear, ed. Provo, Utah: Association for Consumer Research, 29–34.

"Zayre Discusses Urban-Suburban Split" (1985), *DM: the Discount Merchandiser* (February): 2, 18.

Zeithaml, P., and A. Zeithaml (1984), "Environmental Management: Revising the Marketing Perspective," *Journal of Marketing* 48 (Spring): 46–53.

18
Dichotomy of Issue-Specific and Overall Perceptions: A New Paradigm for Channel Conflict and Cooperation Research

Rajiv P. Dant
Kent B. Monroe

T he concept of "conflict" has attracted considerable research interest in sociology, psychology, economics, organizational behavior, and marketing. Over the past twenty years, several marketing scholars have investigated conflict within the context of channels of distribution. Perhaps due to the nature of the phenomenon, normative biases and value judgments are generally evident in conflict studies. Often, conflict has been perceived as indicating a relative absence of cooperation and, therefore, as undesirable. Although some theoretical writings suggest that the relationship between channel conflict and cooperation is more complex, little effort has been made to investigate this relationship (Ross and Lusch 1982), leaving a conceptual void in the development of a theory of channel behavior (Dant 1985a, 1985b).

Two broad perspectives regarding the relationship between "channel conflict" and "channel cooperation" can be isolated in the present literature: (1) cooperation conceived as absence of conflict and (2) conflict and cooperation viewed as distinct constructs. The key problem with either perspective is that neither one really corresponds with the behavioral nature of marketing channels. The chief contributing factors to this lack of correspondence have been (1) paradigmatic commitments from behavioral contexts not comparable or analogous to the channel context and (2) insufficient awareness of the peculiarities and uniqueness of the channel context.

After a brief discussion of the channel context and the dominant current conceptualizations of channel conflict and cooperation, a new paradigm is presented that offers a distinction between the issue-specific and the overall (or generalized) perceptions of conflict and cooperation. In addition to resolving several anomalies of earlier channel research, such a conceptualization draws the theory closer to the contextual realities of the channel framework.

The Behavioral Context of Channels

A channel of distribution is a system of institutions concerned with the process of making products available for use or consumption. This process entails several activities or functions. Although channels differ in the manner in which these functions are divided among specific constituent members, this division leads to inherent mutual interdependence, routinization of activities, and specialization. Hence, the creation of a channel implies a cooperative effort aimed at achieving superordinate common goals.

On the other hand, channel relationships are also typified by a legal-social setting, complexity, and disproportionate risktaking (Bowersox et al. 1980). Often, channel members find it in their interest to attempt to control the activities of other members. Such control attempts may be perceived to be goal impediments or infringements on individual autonomy and lead to disagreements and, possibly, conflict. Hence, the channel relationships can also be potentially conflictful.

Thus, the channels of distribution behaviorally represent a mixed-motive or a non-zero-sum-game context where independent firms work together in an interdependent system. While interdependence and superordinate goals are generally acknowledged, this very interdependence may lead to differences of opinion when the organizational interests of individual members clash among themselves or with the common goals. Simultaneously, though channel members frequently negotiate and disagree on a variety of business issues, the continued existence of these channels despite conflicts suggests the presence of an overriding cooperative bias in such systems. Behaviorally, then, the constructs of channel conflict and channel cooperation are bounded by and should be examined within such a mixed-motive context rather than in zero-sum-game contexts (where one party can gain only if the other loses) or unilateral dependence conditions.

Past Definitions and Operationalizations

Conflict

Within the channel literature on conflict, there has been little consensus on what conflict is or how it should be defined. Early conceptualizations, strongly influenced by an economic perspective, were limited to overt or manifest conflictful acts and the term was used as a synonym for competition (e.g., Palamountain 1967). More recently, the behavioral literature on channel conflict has generally recognized latent, perceived, and affective conflicts as additional states of the construct. The construct channel conflict has been further refined to mean *vertical* rather than horizontal conflict, *interorganizational* rather than intraorganizational conflict, *intertype* instead of intratype conflict, and *intrachannel* as opposed to interchannel conflict (Pearson and Monoky 1976). Within these limits, even though conflict often has been defined with reference to its antecedents and consequents rather than formally defined, the basic notion would appear to be that conflict occurs when the behavior of one member frustrates the goal attainment of others.

Fink (1968) and Raven and Kruglanski (1970) have provided comprehensive definitions of the construct. Both views hold incompatibility or incongruity of actual or desired states, and antagonism (Raven and Kruglanski use the term *tension*) to be the key characteristics of a conflict. As such, conflict can be defined as any social situation or process in which two or more entities are linked by either a form of an antagonistic psychological relationship or a form of antagonistic interaction caused by the incongruity or incompatibility between actual and/or desired states of the involved parties. Incompatibility or incongruity as the central cause of conflict is well documented in the literature (e.g., Brown and Frazier 1978; Brown and Day 1981; Eliashberg and Michie 1984: Hunger and Stern 1976; Ross and Lusch 1982).

The actual issues causing the incompatibility or the incongruity (e.g., goals, strategies, values, activities) have been considered to be of secondary importance by the scholars. At the current stage of theoretical understanding of channel conflict, such a position makes pragmatic sense. Conceivably, a host of issues can trigger this perception and the various issues are, therefore, primarily an operational or measurement problem.

Viewing conflict in terms of incompatibility is similar to the common definitions of dissatisfaction. However, dissatisfaction, though also arising from a discrepancy between the desired and actual states, does not imply antagonism. The term *antagonism*, though frequently used in defining conflict also, has not been formally defined (Fink 1968). *Antagonism* means hostility or opposition; an opposing force, principle, or tendency (*Random House College Dictionary* 1982, p. 56). In the proposed paradigm, the dictionary definition of *antagonism* has been accepted in the absence of theoretical definitions for this term. In other words, when a perception of incompatibility becomes directed and associated with a party, and the party is perceived as an adversary or an opponent, the resultant psychological state is no longer dissatisfaction, but conflict. The presence of antagonism has been considered essential to the evolution of conflict in the new paradigm.

Cooperation

Most current definitions of channel cooperation tend to define the construct in relationship to conflict.

Cooperation as Absense of Conflict. Mallen has suggested that the act of exchange indicates the elimination of conflict and implies a cooperative act (1963, 1967). As presented, this economic perspective was concerned primarily with issue-specific conflict and cooperation experienced in individual acts of exchange. Though some factors that could cause ongoing conflict have been enumerated, these did not become the focal points of channel conflict research. The behavioral conceptions of cooperation as representing the absense of conflict can be categorized into two perspectives attributable to Sherif (1958, 1979) and Pearson and Monoky (1976).

Sherif's theory postulates that in win/lose or zero-sum-game contexts, aggressive competition naturally brings about conflict that can be eliminated if the competing parties begin to pursue common or superordinate rather than mutually exclusive goals. Stern, Sternthal, and Craig (1973a, 1973b, 1975), and Hunger and Stern (1976) have implicitly subscribed to this conceptualization in testing the efficacy of superordinate goals as conflict-reducers. However, the empirical investigations of the efficacy of superordinate goals in channel context for reducing channel conflict have not replicated Sherif's findings.

This anomaly can be explained by contextual differences. A zero-sum-game setting is seldom found in channels. The very formulation of a channel represents a cooperative effort, and superordinate goals *definitionally exist*. In fact, in the vast majority of ongoing channel relationships, cooperation remains the modal behavior. For the same reason, then, conceptualizing cooperation as the absence of any conflict becomes questionable.

Pearson (1971, 1973) and Pearson and Monoky (1976) see cooperation and conflict to be the relative absences of each other. They propose that a channel relationship with a great amount of conflict would by definition have very little cooperation, and vice versa (Peabody and Monoky, p. 240). The ratio of the number of conflictful and cooperative issues therefore becomes the determinant of whether the channel relationship is characterized as cooperative or conflictful.

Several questionable unstated assumptions underlie the Pearson and Monoky conception. It is apparently assumed that channel members do not have any yardsticks for evaluating their relationships other than the relative frequencies of conflictful and cooperative issues, and that the importance of the various issues is disregarded. Such a relative tally would obviously only yield some measure of overall perceptions. This view not only ignores the history effects which can be expected to influence the way they perceive issues, but also does not recognize the possibility that a certain number of conflictful issues may have to occur before the mutually beneficial relationship is perceived as conflictful.

From a measurement perspective, this conceptualization is essentially tautological. A heightened measure of overall conflict would be obtained by combining responses across a number of issues members might disagree on (as has, indeed, been done so far in channel conflict research). One would expect, then, following the above conceptualization, that such a relationship will be characterized by absence of cooperation. However, whenever conflict and cooperation have been measured within the same study, they have been found to coexist (e.g., Pruden 1969; Schmidt and Kochan 1977; Whyte 1976).

Cooperation and Conflict as Distinct Constructs. Several researchers have conceptualized interorganizational cooperation as a distinct construct. However, these conceptualizations are theoretically insufficient in that the definitions used have described operational indicators of cooperation rather than the construct itself. Thus, they do not have constitutive meaning, or, in other words, it is not possible to relate cooperation and conflict at a theoretical level using these definitions (Torgerson 1958). Another deficiency of these definitions is that they have ignored the psychological state implicit in cooperation and have confined themselves to the manifest behavioral aspects of the construct.

Robicheaux and El-Ansary (1976) recognized the need to include the psychological component of cooperation when defining channel cooperation as members' *willingness* to coordinate their activities in an effort to help all channel members achieve superordinate goals. However, their definition fails to explain the construct in a context of simultaneous presence of issue-specific conflicts and cooperations. Recently, Childers and Ruekert (1982, p. 117) have defined channel cooperation as "the expectation of a balanced exchange of the resources required to achieve both intraorganizational and interorganizational goals through joint action among two or more actors." This definition has a psychological component captured in "the expectation of a balanced exchange," as well as a behavioral component specified in "through joint action among two or more actors." Childers and Ruekert have argued that both conflict and cooperation can be issue-specific and might be found *concurrently* among some of the exchanges that occur between channel members. The extent to which conflict would lead to a deterioration in the overall level of cooperation is hypothesized to depend on (1) saliency of the issues and (2) the duration of the negotiations.

Central to this conceptualization is the notion of "expectations." For example, assume that a manufacturer and a wholesaler are cooperating on an advertising campaign and are in conflict over the inventory levels the wholesaler should maintain. If such a situation does not diminish their expectations of being able to achieve a balanced exchange of resources, the inventory issue may generate only an issue-specific perception of conflict and not influence the overall perception of cooperation. That is, issue-specific perceived conflict ordinarily would not rule out an overall perception of cooperation. Only when conflictful issues decrease one's expectations of equitable relationships, would overall perceptions of cooperation be undermined. Such a situation may be expected when the issues are important and have been subject to negotiations for a duration of time.

However, the Childers and Ruekert conceptualization also fails to recognize the presence of any evaluation criteria or guiding expectations. They do not explain *how* "expectations" come to be formed—a conceptual missing link central to their theory. Relative salience of various conflictful or cooperative issues is a judgment predicated on organizational priorities that are reflected in the role-sets prescribed for the boundary personnel. In other words, an issue would be deemed salient by the interacting channel members if their firms determined them to be important. Similarly, any judgments on the durations of negotiations would be based on the past experiences of the boundary personnel. Hence, for instance, if the negotiator for the wholesaler firm knows from past experience that changing inventory level requirements takes approximately two months, then a duration of two months would not be deemed "long." Thus, it is not the duration of negotiations per se, but how the duration relates to the past experience on the issue that would determine evaluative judgments.

A New Paradigm

The new paradigm we introduce postulates a distinction between issue-specific and overall perceptions of channel conflict and cooperation. The dyadic theoretical framework of exchange theory (Thibaut and Kelley 1959) is employed to guide the deductive development. However, exchange theory remains an instrumental (Chalmers 1982, pp. 113–128) analogous framework, and the new conceptualization draws its deductive reasoning and plausibility directly from the concept and the context of channels.

Summary of Salient Features of Exchange Theory

Thibaut and Kelley's exchange theory suggests that all social interaction involves explicit or implicit exchange of rewards and costs. An assumption is made that rewards and costs can be measured on psychological scales, and that these psychological scales can be combined into a single scale of goodness of outcome, with states of high reward and low cost being given high-scale values. In other words, the goodness-of-outcome is an absolute bipolar scale that arrays various combinations of rewards and costs in terms of relative attractiveness. Outcome is a general term for rewards gained and costs incurred.

Specific outcomes are not judged directly by the goodness-of-outcome scale, but are evaluated with reference to two standards: (1) *comparison level*

(CL), the standard against which the member evaluates the "attractiveness" of the relationship, and (2) *comparison level for alternatives* (CL-alt), the standard the member uses in deciding whether to remain in or to leave the relationship. CL has been conceptualized as a kind of zero or neutral point on the goodness-of-outcome scale, whereas CL-alt has been conceived as the lowest level of outcomes a member will accept in the light of available alternative opportunities.

The key determinant of CL is held to be *past experiences* (either personal or vicarious). Hence, CL can alternatively be conceptualized as some salience-weighted average of past experiences. A person who has experienced superior outcomes will have a higher CL than a person who has only known mediocrity.

Salience influences the CL in two distinct ways. The salience associated with a certain outcome may be dependent upon the recency of experiencing that outcome. Hence, salience depends in part upon momentary cues which serve as reminders of certain relationships and alternatives: CL is subject to situation-to-situation and moment-to-moment variations; and CL tends to move to the level of outcomes currently being attained, implying a learning effect. On the other hand, there are outcomes whose salience is independent of the immediate situation; these outcomes are likely to be salient under almost all circumstances because of some special significance they have to the individual. In the channel context, certain outcomes may be perceived as salient if they are closely related to organizational priorities. The evaulation of outcomes may also depend upon the individuals' conceptions of their power. A perception of having more power may, then, serve to raise the exception levels, while, conversely, low power perceptions may lower them. The detailed determinants of CL-alt are not discussed because the conceptualization proposes relations between conflict and cooperation in the context of ongoing channel relationships—the channel is attractive enough for its members to preclude any intentions of opting out of the channel.

Assuming an ongoing dyadic relationship, exchange theory makes the following predictions about how individuals evaluate outcomes: (1) If the outcomes are superior to or above the CL (*positive incongruity*), the resultant psychological state is satisfaction. (2) On the other hand, if the actual outcomes are inferior to or below the CL (*negative incongruity*), the resulting psychological state is dissatisfaction. Moreover, the extent of satisfaction and dissatisfaction is determined by the magnitude of discrepancy between actual outcomes and CL, and the salience of the outcomes.

Exchange Theory and Channel Behavior

To assume that all social interactions involve exchange of rewards and costs captures the sense of channel interactions where boundary personnel usually meet to discuss such exchanges involving rewards and costs. The exchange theory formulation parallels the channel context in several other ways as well.

Applicability of Comparison Level. The notion of CL or an evaluative criterion for judging relationships on the basis of past experiences, salience, and recency is intuitively appealing within the channel context. Subjected to numerous dyadic interactions, channel members can develop reasonable expectations about channel relationships. Part of this experience base would also be an understanding of typical issues that cause disagreements and conflicts, and the kinds of issues and contingencies over which accord is quick and expected. Moreover, certain outcomes, issues, and experiences would stand out as salient because of their recent occurrence or because they are intrinsically important. All this together would constitute a kind of repertoire which a channel member can be expected to invoke as a yardstick or criterion for evaluating the issue-outcomes and, eventually, the satisfaction with the relationship itself. Indeed, it is tautological that an evaluation requires the use of some criterion for comparison. The theory merely specifies the determinants of such a criterion, which seem to fit the channel context rather well.

Dissatisfaction and Conflict. As presented, exchange theory suggests that negative incongruity would lead to dissatisfaction, and positive incongruity would result in satisfaction. Both dissatisfaction and conflict arise from perceptions of incompatibility; empirical investigations have shown the two constructs to covary strongly (Brown and Day 1981; Schul, Lamb, and Little 1981). A perception of dissatisfaction, it was argued earlier, becomes a perception of conflict when perceptions of antagonism also occur simultaneously. As such, dissatisfaction and conflict are closely related. It is possible that several negative incongruities may only result in dissatisfaction, while others could cause perceptions of conflict. However, conflict is most likely to occur when the issues are salient as well.

Satisfaction and Cooperation. Satisfaction in a channel context has been defined as (1) positive affective evaluations and attitudes concerning channel arrangements (Schul, Lamb, and Little 1981) and (2) the degree to which expectations about goals are met (Brown and Frazier 1978). It is easy to see how such experiences of satisfaction may enhance a channel member's expectations of a balanced exchange relationship (cooperation). The issue of the conceptual relationship between satisfaction and cooperation has not been addressed previously in the channel literature. When channel members evaluate the issue-outcomes, they may experience satisfaction if the outcomes please them. Hence, satisfaction is experienced first after positive issue-outcome evaluations. However, a perception of cooperation goes beyond satisfaction. Now the channel members are making inferences about how the satisfaction they have experienced has strengthened their expectations of balanced exchange relationships.

Positive and Negative Congruities.   Although exchange theory predicts satisfaction only in the event of positive incongruity, another scenario to consider would be a situation where issue-outcomes coincide with CL near the positive pole of the goodness-of-outcome scale (a condition of "positive congruity"). Would channel members experience cooperation and satisfaction? Since CL defines the expectations from the relationships, when positive congruity occurs, channel members will find their expectations met, leading to satisfaction, and an experience of balanced exchange relationships (cooperation) can be expected. The strength of the perceptions of satisfaction and cooperation arising out of positive congruity can be expected to be less than those arising out of positive incongruity where outcomes exceed the expectations.

Of course, this would not happen if the expectations defined by CL were not high enough. When CL is closer to the negative pole of the goodness-of-outcome scale, and the issue-outcome coincides with this low CL, then the outcome can be labeled "negative congruity." It is suggested that, as a first recourse to a relationship typified by negative congruities, the channel members would probably opt out of the channel. If there is only one existing channel for the product category or if the particular channel is indispensable, channel members may retain the relationship even though they experience dissatisfaction and possibly conflict in the relationship. The perceptions of dissatisfaction and conflict in the negative-congruity condition would be weaker than in the case of negative incongruity, since in the negative-congruity condition, the channel members have chosen to stay in the channel.

However, the conditions of positive congruity and negative congruity may not occur in certain circumstances depending on the placement of the CL along the goodness-of-outcome scale. Though certain ranges on this scale may be well defined in terms of desirability or undesirability (i.e., when the CL is close to poles), there may also be ranges on the scale that can be termed "ranges of indifference." If the CL is located in a range of indifference and one of the congruities occurs, neither satisfaction/cooperation nor dissatisfaction/conflict may occur. The notion of such ranges of indifference is consistent with social judgment theory and adaptation-level theory.

In summary, to the original two situations of positive incongruity and negative incongruity visualized by exchange theory, we have now added two supplemental conditions of positive congruity and negative congruity on the basis of alternate scenarios that may exist in channels. The four situations and related predictions are summarized in figure 18–1.

Issue-Specific Perceptions and Exchange Theory.   Theories of social learning suggest that people form evaluation criteria largely on the basis of personal and vicarious experiences. This proposition is equally applicable to global and particular criteria. The CL, however, is formulated on the basis of a number of past experiences over different over kinds of issues. Hence, when evaluating a particular issue-outcome, it is likely that channel members would invoke a criterion based on past experiences over *similar kinds of issues*. This CL used for assessing a single outcome would then be a subset of the CL used for evaluating overall relationships.

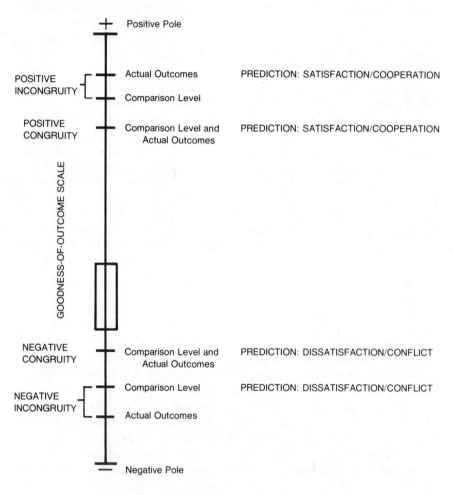

The Box Represents an Example of a Range of Indifference That May Exist

Figure 18–1. Predictions from Four Incongruity and Congruity Conditions

This notion of use of subsets of CL is implicit in exchange theory. CL is not conceived as a fixed criterion, but can change from situation to situation. The notion of certain experiences having lasting salience also implicitly suggests that outcomes belonging to this category will be evaluated differently than outcomes from categories not considered salient.

The argument can be best presented by an example. Consider a channel relationship where past experiences suggest to channel member *A* that (1) *A*'s representatives are courteously received by channel member *B* and (2) that *B* is very reasonable in negotiating markups allowed in light of cost justifications. Such perceptions and many others would be the building blocks of *A*'s CL. Let us further assume that there is an incident where *B* mistreats *A*'s representative. How would *A* evaluate the ongoing relationship with *B*? First of all, in light of all the other positive elements in the relationship, *A* might continue to characterize the overall relationship as satisfactory and cooperative. However, *A* would also have an evaluation of the unfortunate incident, consider how *B* had treated *A*'s representatives in the past (a subset of CL), and determine the particular incident to be dissatisfactory, perhaps even conflictful. In other words, *A* would experience issue-specific conflict even though the overall characteristics of the relationship is cooperative. What has been argued is an obvious issue: When we are evaluating a particular outcome, we recall our past experience over similar kinds of issues as the evaluation criterion. Hence, the exchange theory analogy holds for issue-specific perceptions also.

Overall Perceptions

Regarding the relationships between issue-specific perceptions and overall perceptions, the exchange theory postulates have two alternative sets of propositions to offer.

Situation 1. Mentzer and Hunt (1983) have proposed that in channels of distribution, each member is constantly evaluating the performance of the other channel members; and a dissatisfied channel member may start a search for alternative channel relationships. Specifically, such a recourse is thought to be dependent on variables such as degree of unacceptable performance and the nature of past relationships between the two channel members. Hence, if past relationships have been profitable and the extent of unacceptable performance is not great, the extreme step of channel dissolution is likely to be avoided. Moreover, the evaluation of other alternatives must take into account the substantial costs (economic and psychological) of a channel dissolution. Therefore, only when the alternative is sufficiently superior to overcome the costs of a changeover will the extreme step be taken.

Conceptually, the above arguments allude to exchange theory's second standard, CL-alt, used in deciding whether to terminate or continue a relationship. This standard takes into account the quality of alternatives available as compared to current relationships. Channel members are likely to consider alternatives when the performance levels become unacceptable, and not just because the situation is perceived to be cooperative or conflictful. Hence, a series of issue-specific conflict perceptions may lower the expectations of a balanced exchange required to achieve specific performance goals, and, ultimately may lead to a termination of the relationship. Although a cumulation of issue-specific conflict perceptions resulting in an overall perception of conflict is implied above, two important qualifiers need to be borne in mind.

Foremost, a threshold effect may be operative, i.e., a certain number of issue-specific conflict perceptions may be required before the cumulation of such perceptions translates into an overall conflict perception. Further, the conceptual links between perceptions of overall conflict and unacceptable performance are not clear, and the two may be related to each other through other mediating variables. This issue is not addressed further, as the relationships stemming from the above arguments are not examined in this chapter.

Situation 2. When past relationships have been profitable enough to remain in the channel, the issue is not unacceptable performance, but conflict over issues. In such a context, the comparison level for alternatives becomes irrelevant as channel members are not contemplating the possibility of channel dissolutions. In this setting, a series of issue-specific conflict perceptions, *if unmitigated* by a series of issue-specific perceptions of cooperation, may then lead toward overall conflict perception.

Hence, issue-specific conflict perceptions may get neutralized by issue-specific perceptions of cooperation, and the overall perception of a cooperative relationship may remain unchanged. Implicitly, it is being asserted in these arguments that the general bias in channel relationships is toward cooperation rather than conflict. This contention appears to be justified in light of actual channel realities. When such a neutralization does not occur, the channel members would again invoke the CL to evaluate *the overall* attractiveness of their relationships. Only when the preponderance of issue-specific conflict perceptions over issue-specific perceptions of cooperation is found to have destroyed the expectations of balanced exchange relationship, can an estimate of overall conflict be obtained *by combining measures* of issue-specific perceptions of conflict.

Conclusions and Contributions

The most fundamental contributions to the proposed paradigm fall into three broad categories.

Constitutive Meaning for Constructs

The new paradigm provides conceptual clarity to the widely studied but variously conceived phenomena of conflict, cooperation, dissatisfaction, and satisfaction. Moreover, this clarity is achieved in a fashion that simultaneously provides constitutive meanings to these constructs permitting one to unambiguously relate them to each other at a theoretical level within the channel context. In earlier channel literature, the distinctions between conflict and dissatisfaction and between cooperation and satisfaction have been either unclear or not even attempted. Indeed, the adopted operational definitions of conflict and cooperation in some studies have been almost identical to the operational definitions of dissatisfaction and satisfaction in other studies. This definitional difficulty has of course led to nebulous conceptualizations of these constructs which not only has encouraged a diversity of definitions, but also has prevented researchers from providing clear managerial implications of academic research.

The greatest conceptual problem has concerned the relationship between conflict and cooperation. Previously, cooperation often has been perceived as the relative absence of conflict leading to normative biases against conflict. In the interest of cooperation, it is considered to be important to understand the causes of conflict, its various forms, and means of reducing conflict. Although a general distinction is usually made between functional and dysfunctional conflict, the practical research orientation continues to be managing conflict through its reduction (Hunger and Stern 1976). This normative bias is also evident in managerial books (Bowersox et al. 1980; Stern and El-Ansary 1982). Conflict management and reduction by use of power or by getting cooperation are presented as a central task for effective channel management. Bowersox et al. point out that one plausible explanation for this bias may be the problem of determining levels of conflict that are functional.

Determining "correct" levels of conflict can be difficult and costly. Different industry channels, different channel relationships, and different channel segments may have different levels; the levels may change as personnel change; and, moreover, to determine such levels, they must be surpassed—an expensive exercise. Not surprisingly, then, after acknowledging the functional aspects of conflict, the normative literature reverts to conflict resolution. However, since conflict and cooperation can both be issue-specific and related to incongruity perceptions, salience, and antagonism, business executives can turn to assessing the behavioral expectations, the previous experience, and the importance attached to issues by the channel boundary personnel. Not only are these variables relatively easier to estimate, but they represent variables that can be managerially influenced. For instance, salience of issues can be redefined if needed; and the role-sets can be suitably altered by providing appropriate job descriptions. Such changes would further ensure that the boundary personnel perceive overall conflict or cooperation as well as issue-specific conflict or cooperation at appropriate times in consonance with the firm's priorities, thereby facilitating better performance.

Phenomenological Consistency

The new conceptualization consistently keeps the behavioral context of channels in focus in the course of theoretical development. Several of the present conceptualizations may be considered exemplars of how paradigms that once become accepted within a discipline tend to override the realities of the phenomena under scrutiny, and their all-important contextual confound. The offered paradigm, in some ways then, represents a modest proposal to break the tyranny of borrowed paradigms which has inhibited the researchers from letting the phenomenological realities dictate the research questions.

The observance of channel relations shows that channel members have conflicts over particular issues and yet continue to retain the overall cooperative relationships. This fundamental phenomenological reality has not been recognized in the dominant channel literature. Hence, a valid question of "so what?" arises as far as the business implications of current channel conflict research are concerned. In effect, the current literature base has not studied the theoretical underpinnings of normal cooperative channel behavior and has not recognized the distinction between issue-specific and overall perceptions in channels.

Comprehensive Instrumental Framework

Social researchers usually search for analogous instrumental theoretical frameworks to explain hypothesized theoretical relationships. To the extent that such a chosen framework makes predictions consistent with the phenomenological realities of the matter being studied, the choice of the framework can be considered justified. From this perspective, as argued throughout the chapter, exchange theory provides an exciting theoretical framework and, additionally, accommodates the dichotomy premise of issue-specific and overall conflict and cooperation perceptions.

However, another key consideration guiding the selection of theoretical frameworks is normatively proposed to be the ability of the chosen framework to resolve past anomalies in the discipline (Laudan 1977). Exchange theory framework makes an important contribution from this perspective as well.

The dichotomy conception explains several anomalies of earlier channel research, and it can serve as a superior alternative explanation for several behavioral channel relationships. For instance, though some channel conflict researchers have tended to see superordinate goals as a major answer to the conflict problem, empirical results have not substantiated this expectation.

Conceivably, the superordinate issues may have failed to reduce conflict because (1) the issues were not salient and (2) behavioral expectations and previous experiences led the parties to expect cooperation on such issues and, as such, they only caused issue-specific perceptions of cooperation that did not reduce the overall conflict perception. If the superordinate issues were important and typically bones of contention, their successful resolution could have had the desired effect. In fact, this may also be seen as an alternative explanation of Sherif's realistic group conflict theory (1958) that calls for a series of superordinate goals to reduce conflict.

Again, it is generally believed that conflict may be good or bad for channel performance. This belief has been reified in the form of the inverted-U-shaped curve (Rosenbloom 1973), which simply asserts that while conflict may initially stimulate performance, beyond a certain level it can be dysfunctional. The proposed conceptualization offers an alternative behavioral explanation for the same phenomenon. It may be that simple increases in conflict levels will not undermine performance if such conflict is expected on those issues and/or if they are unimportant issues. The latter situation may only cause issue-specific perceptions of conflict. On the other hand, performance levels may drop only when the overall relationships begin to be characterized as conflictful.

In summary, the conceptualization offered can be used to develop an alternative perspective to channel conflict theory that accommodates several behavioral constructs and unifies them within a single theoretical framework. This is achieved quite simply by shifting the focus from levels of conflict that are functional to the theoretical distinction between issue-specific and overall perceptions for both conflict and cooperation.

References

Bowersox, Donald H., M. Bixby Cooper, Douglas M. Lambert, and Donald A. Taylor (1980), *Management in Marketing Channels*. New York: McGraw-Hill.

Brown, James R., and Ralph L. Day (1981), "Measures of Manifest Conflict in Distribution Channels," *Journal of Marketing Research* 18 (August): 263–74.

Brown, James R. and Gary L. Frazier (1978), "The Application of Channel Power: Effects and Connotations," in *Research Frontiers in Marketing: Dialogues and Directions*, Subhash C. Jain, ed. Chicago: American Marketing Association, 266–70.

Chalmers, Alan F. (1982), *What Is This Thing Called Science?*, St. Lucia, Australia: University of Queensland Press.

Childers, Terry L., and Robert W. Ruekert (1982), "The Meaning and Determinants of Cooperation within an Interorganizational Marketing Network," in *Marketing Theory: Philosophy of Science Perspectives*, Ronald F. Bush and Shelby D. Hunt, eds. Chicago: American Marketing Association, 116–19.

Dant, Rajiv P. (1985a), "Behavioral Channel Conflict Research: Slave of Paradigms?"

in *Marketing in the Long Run*, Stanley C. Hollander and Terence Nevett, eds. Chicago: American Marketing Association, 441–55.

———, (1985b), "An Investigation of the Relationships between Issue-Specific Channel Conflict and Cooperation and Overall Channel Conflict and Cooperation," unpublished Ph.D. dissertation. Blacksburg: Virginia Polytechnic Institute and State University.

Eliashberg, Jehoshua, and Donald A. Michie (1984), "Multiple Business Goals Sets as Determinants of Marketing Channel Conflict: An Empirical Study," *Journal of Marketing Research* 21 (February): 75–88.

Fink, Clinton F. (1968), "Some Conceptual Difficulties in the Theory of Social Conflict," *Journal of Conflict Resolutions* 12 (December): 412–60.

Hunger, J. David, and Louis W. Stern (1976), "An Assessment of the Functionality of the Superordinate Goal in Reducing Conflict," *Academy of Management Journal* 19 (December): 591–605.

Laudan, Larry (1977), *Progress and Its Problems: Towards a Theory of Scientific Growth*. Berkeley: University of California Press.

Mallen, Bruce E. (1963), "A Theory of Retailer-Supplier Conflict, Control, and Cooperation," *Journal of Retailing* 39 (Summer): 24–51.

———, (1967), "Conflict and Cooperation in Marketing Channels," in *Marketing Channel: A Conceptual Viewpoint*, Bruce E. Mallen, ed. New York: John Wiley & Sons, 124–34.

Mentzer, John T., and Kenneth A. Hunt (1983), "The Use of Power: A Model of the Marketing Channel Behavioral Dimensions," unpublished working paper. Blacksburg: Virginia Polytechnic Institute and State University.

Palamountain, Joseph C., Jr. (1967), "Distribution: Its Economic Conflicts," in *Marketing Channel: A Conceptual Viewpoint*, Bruce E. Mallen, ed. New York: John Wiley & Sons, 114–18.

Pearson, Michael M. (1971), "An Empirical Study of the Operational Results Associated with Conflict and Cooperation in Channels of Distribution," unpublished Ph.D. dissertation. Boulder: University of Colorado.

———, (1973), "The Conflict-Performance Assumption," *Journal of Purchasing* 9 (February): 57–69.

Pearson, Michael M., and John F. Monoky (1976), "The Role of Conflict and Cooperation in Channel Performance," in *Marketing: 1776–1976 and Beyond*, K.L. Bernhardt, ed. Chicago: American Marketing Association, 240–44.

Pondy, Louis R. (1967), "Organizational Conflict: Concepts and Models," *Administrative Science Quarterly* 12 (September): 296–320.

Pruden, Henry O. (1969), "Interorganizational Conflict, Linkage, and Exchange: A Study of Industrial Salesmen." *Academy of Management Journal* 12 (September): 339–50.

Raven, Bertram H., and Arie W. Kruglanski (1970), "Conflict and Power," in *The Structure of Conflict*, Paul Swingle, ed. New York: Academic Press, 62–73.

Robicheaux, Robert A., and Adel El-Ansary (1976), "A General Model for Understanding Channel Market Behavior," *Journal of Retailing* 52 (Winter): 13–30, 93–94.

Rosenbloom, Bert (1973), "Conflict and Channel Efficiency: Some Conceptual Models for the Decision Maker," *Journal of Marketing* 37 (July): 26–30.

Ross, Robert H. and Robert F. Lusch (1982), "Similarities between Conflict and Cooperation in the Marketing Channel," *Journal of Business Research* 10: 237–50.

Schmidt, Stuart M., and Thomas A. Kochan (1977), "Interorganizational Relationships: Patterns and Motivations," *Administrative Science Quarterly* 22 (June): 220–34.

Schul, Patrick L., Charles W. Lamb, Jr., and Taylor E. Little, Jr. (1981), "A Path Analysis of the Interchannel Conflict Process," in *The Changing Market Environment: New Theories and Applications*, Kenneth Bernhardt, Thomas Kinnear, Ira Dolich, William Perreault, Michael Etzel, Kenneth Roering, and William Kehol, eds. Chicago: American Marketing Association, 39–42.

Sherif, Muzafer (1958), "Superordinate Goals in the Reduction of Intergroup Conflicts," *American Journal of Sociology* 63: 349–56.

———, (1979), "Superordinate Goals in the Reduction of Intergroup Conflict: An Experimental Evaluation," in *The Social Psychology of Intergroup Relations*, William G. Austin and Stephen Worchel, eds. Monterey, Calif.: Brooks/Cole, 257–61.

Stern, Louis W., and Adel El-Ansary (1982), *Marketing Channels*, 2nd ed. Englewood Cliffs, N.J.: Prentice-Hall.

Stern, Louis W., Brian Sternthal, and C. Samuel Craig (1973a), "Managing Conflict in Distribution Channels: A Laboratory Study," *Journal of Marketing Research* 10 (May): 169–79.

Stern, Louis W., Brian Sternthal, and C. Samuel Craig (1973b), "A Parasimulation of Interorganizational Conflict," *International Journal of Group Tensions* 3: 68–90.

Stern, Louis W., Brian Sternthal and C. Smauel Craig (1975), "Strategies for Managing Interorganizational Conflict: A Laboratory Paradigm," *Journal of Applied Psychology* 60: 472–82.

The Random House College Dictionary (1982), rev. ed. New York: Random House.

Thibaut, John W., and Harold H. Kelley (1959), *The Social Psychology of Groups*. New York: John Wiley & Sons.

Torgerson, W. (1958), *Theory and Methods of Scaling*. New York: John Wiley & Sons.

Whyte, William F. (1976), "Research Methods for the Study of Conflict and Cooperation," *The American Sociologist* 11 (November): 208–16.

19
Feminism and the New Home Economics: What Do They Mean for Marketing?

Ruby Roy Dholakia

According to economic theory and marketing philosophy, the target and justification for all productive activity is consumption. The locus of consumption activity is the household, and the major consumer representative of the household is still the adult female. Increased levels and individualization of consumption activity have been facilitated by the role of women as consumption managers. However, qualitatively different relationships are likely to emerge as a result of the changes in the role of women. This chapter will examine some of the significant changes taking place in the role of women and attempt to identify the implications of these changes.

The basic premise of the chapter is that while marketing has always tried to be adaptive and responsive to the changes in the market characteristics, it is really not prepared to deal with the fundamental implications of feminism and the new home economics. In order to explore this premise, the chapter will first examine the socioeconomic changes affecting the organization and performance of household activities. The concept of role overload will be used to integrate the forces and pressures that are transforming the household production function. The second part of the chapter will look at some of the responses being made by marketing managers as they adjust their offerings to the changing realities of the marketplace. It will be argued that most of the marketing responses are attempts to ameliorate the stress felt by the "overloaded" consumer. However, these responses are not enough. The new role of the woman in the household is sowing seeds of fundamental changes in the consumption experience. The final part of the chapter will examine the impact of these changes on core concepts such as consumption values, consumption volume, and consumer socialization.

Consumption in the Household

In preindustrial societies, the household was typically composed of many related and unrelated family members engaged in productive labor at or near home. Adults and children worked together to satisfy their consumption needs. However, with industrialization and urbanization, the household has been transformed. A distinct division of labor has been created between home and work which has now become a distinction of woman's and man's work. In the process, the self-sufficient, collaborative household has become a market-reliant, socially isolated, woman-run household, and the purchase and consumption of market goods and services has become a dominant theme in society.

Household consumption, as measured by ownership of various goods and services, has risen. It is obvious that the household today is more affluent than at any earlier time in history. What then are the problems?

Several questions are being raised. Linder (1970) has talked about the "harried leisure class" with the problem of consumption time as the scarce commodity. Feminists are concerned with a consumption standard built on women's wages and women's household work but supported by social norms and practices that underpay and undervalue women (Berk 1985; Bose 1985; Cowan 1983; Margolis 1984). There are also concerns about the continued substitution of market goods and services for home-produced ones—many of the newer goods and services pertain to activities (such as child rearing) that were excluded from market forces during the industrialization era and affect core societal concerns (such as socialization of children).

As the household and market systems attempt to adjust to these changes and pressures, the consumption experience is likely to be transformed. Insights into these problems and questions will be obtained by first examining the household itself.

Changes in Household Characteristics

A visible form of socioeconomic change is in the characteristics of households in affluent societies. Statistics indicate that the typical U.S. household is no longer the married family with two adults and 2.7 dependent children. Though the total number of households increased by 25 percent in the 1970s (Hu 1980), nonfamily as well as single-head (male and female) households are increasing at a faster rate.

One major consequence and cause as well of the changing household is the increased participation of women in the labor force. Social factors such as high divorce rates, economic factors such as inflation and consumption aspirations, as well as individual factors such as education are all having a positive influence on the participation of women in the labor force. The employed wife and role overload have thus become part of the current scene.

The Employed Wife

By 1980, over 50 percent of women aged 16 and over were engaged in market employment, constituting 42.5 percent of the total labor force. The most significant increases have been among married women with husband present and married women with preschool children. Analysis of data on the employment of women outside the home indicates a step-by-step movement of women in the market labor force: first, single women; then, married women with grown children; and, finally, married women with preschool children. In analyzing the trends, Chafe (1976) comments: "It was almost as though each step in the process was necessary to prepare the way for the next one until by the mid-1970s, there was a consistent departure from the traditional norm of mothers staying at home full time to care for children" (p. 25).

The tradition itself is neither universal nor ancient. Separation of mother and productive worker roles is an effect of industrialization and urbanization (Bernard 1974; Margolis 1984). The trends indicate that the employed wife is likely to persist in the labor force (Ferber and Birnbaum 1980). Econometric models of women's participation in the labor force indicate that dynamic labor supply equations for men and women are very similar. Rather than children, it is changes in the marital status that strongly affect women's participation in the labor force (Nakamura and Nakamura 1985). Figure 19–1 shows the impact of the employed wife.

Work Commitment and Role Overload

Along with increased participation of women in the labor force, there has been an occupational upgrading (Mott 1978). For the first time, there are more women than men in selected professional categories. These factors are facilitating greater commitment to market labor and likely role overload among women.

Work commitment is evidenced from the demographic shifts among the working force—not only are more women occupied, their interruptions from market labor due to factors such as childbirth are shorter. Surveys indicate that women are happy with their jobs (Mott 1978), the reasons including increases in security, status, privileges, and involvement (Marks 1977). Work commitment increases with education and marital problems; it is higher among blacks than whites (Mott). Increasing enrollment of women in postsecondary education and the rising divorce rate indicate that women's commitment to market labor is likely to continue and flourish.

Increased work commitment, however, sets up conditions for role overload. Role overload is "conflict that occurs when the sheer volume of behavior demanded by the positions in the position set exceeds available time and energy" (Reilly 1982, p. 408). One can expect role overload to be higher among

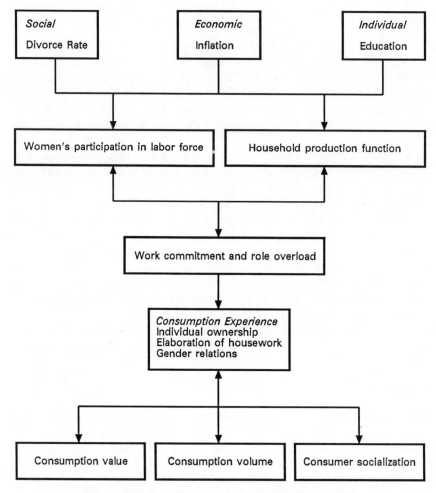

Figure 19–1. The Impact of the Employed Wife

employed wives than homemaker wives and to be positively related to work and family commitments. To examine the impact of role overload, one needs to examine the household production system and the organization of household activities.

The Household Production System

There are two views of the household. The old one emphasizes consumption and assumes that market goods and services produce utility directly to the household. The *new home economic* view treats the household as a production unit which buys and uses goods, materials, and time to produce useful commodities (Becker 1976; Pollak and Wachter 1975). It is the commodities produced in the household that provide the ultimate sources of satisfaction, not market goods directly (Berk 1980; Berk and Berk 1979).

The impact of the new home economics has been to encourage research on the black box between procurement and consumption in the household. Detailed studies reveal, for example, that with increased urbanization and industrialization, households shift from a task-related orientation to a time-related one (Nelson 1980): cooking by smell becomes cooking by time (Linder 1970). However, when household tasks and time are analyzed in developed economies, there is very little discretion regarding household tasks but relatively more discretion with respect to household time (Berk 1985).

The existence of role overload can be inferred from the way household activities are organized and performed. Although modern conveniences such as the electric iron and washing machine have eliminated the physical drudgery of home labor, they have not eliminated the labor itself. In fact, research indicates that modern machines have led to "elaboration of housework" which is being done by women alone, in social isolation, to meet higher demands of performance (Cowan 1983; Strasser 1982). So, instead of the one-pot stew, a meal has become a multipot process, and house cleaning has been transformed from an occasional spring event to a daily ritual.

The increasing participation of women in the labor force has not led to significant changes in the allocation of household tasks (Vanek 1974, 1980; Robinson 1980). There are still significant disparities between husbands' and wives' involvement in the household production system. Furthermore, there is very little evidence to support the idea that consumption of convenience goods (such as ownership of time-saving durables) is any higher among employed wives than homemaker wives (Reilly 1982; Strober and Weinberg 1980; Weinberg and Weiner 1983). Only some data exists to suggest that frequency of use of services such as eating out may be higher among employed wives than homemaking wives (Joag, Gentry, and Hopper 1985).

So far, employed wives have given up on their leisure time to manage their dual careers (Berk and Berk 1979; Kreps and Leaper 1976), and the pressures of role overload have not yet surfaced in visible and significant shifts in household behavior. The similarity in consumption behavior between households of employed wives and homemaker wives, despite the differences in occupational involvement of women, has been taken to imply lack of role overload (Reilly 1982). Various reasons have been advanced against role overload—including increased status and satisfaction from market work (Marks 1977). It is unlikely, however, that the "harried women" class can continue to survive without some fundamental changes in society. In order to outline the changes, it might be useful to examine the similarity of household consumption behavior by focusing on the meaning of and standard for the consumption experience.

The Consumption Experience

The consumption experience in the U.S. economy has been influenced by forces that created mass but individualized ownership of goods. The mass availability of goods reduced status differences among housewives and developed "an occupational culture of remarkable uniformity" (Margolis 1984, p. 134). It was the specialization of housework by women that facilitated the expansion of the consumption system. "Without the free services of the housewife the expansion of household consumption critical to the growth of the American economy in this century would have been severely curtailed" (Margolis, p. 132).

From a feminist point of view, the consumption experience has become a key issue because it is built on household activity done by women, because it disadvantages women, because it affects the social psychology of women, and because it leads to gender stratification (Ferree 1980). Although the production functions implied by the new home economics do not specify gender roles, it does take many things as given, such as current market wages that affect the cost and marginal productivity of male versus female labor (Berk 1985).

Ownership of Goods. One element of the consumption experience is the ownership of goods. In affluent western societies, ownership of specific material goods is a symbol of status and social success (Mason 1981; Belk 1982). For example, the symbolic significance of home ownership is very high in the United States (Mott 1978; Wilson 1980), particularly for the single-family, detached suburban home (Dillman, Tremblay, and Dillman 1979). However, home ownership necessitates possession of a whole array of "time-saving" durables such as washing machines and driers. The ownership of these durables is *nondiscretionary* (Dholakia, Dholakia, and Firat 1984). This suggests why research has failed to discover any relationship between occupational status of women and ownership of these durables (Reilly 1982; Strober and Weinberg 1980; Weinberg and Weiner 1983). While individual ownership of goods has created "an occupational culture of remarkable uniformity" (Margolis 1984), it has led to social isolation (Cowan 1983; Firat 1987). As Ferree (1980) comments: "The effect was to physically separate houseworkers in their individual homes and to tie them to their individually owned appliances" (p. 90), making housework isolated and culturally a marginal activity and less rewarding intrinsically.

Elaboration of Housework. The second element of the consumption experience is the "elaboration of housework" (Cowan 1983). This has affected the performance of household activities and the ownership of household aids. More and more goods—cooking ranges, vacuum cleaners, dishwashers—have become available as more and more work is performed at home to meet rising standards of performance (Margolis 1984). These standards of performance account for the relative stability over the past six or seven decades in time spent on housework despite modern technology (Berk 1985; Cowan 1983; Margolis) and the comparable number of hours spent on housework by full-time homemakers and employed wives.

Elaboration of housework had created a socially desirable role for women as managers of the consumption process. In the twentieth century, managing consumption has become a central feature of housework. Since consumption involves work, it takes time; the higher the standard of consumption, the more work and time it takes (Margolis 1984). So long as women stayed full-time homemakers, consumption management led to growth of the marketing sector, and an increasing array of goods were made available to facilitate the performance of housework. However, labor-saving devices still kept work at home and required a homemaker. For instance, in the first decade of the twentieth century, some 88 percent of middle-income families hired laundresses or sent some of their clothing and linen to commercial laundries; by 1930, only 15 percent of such families were sending their laundry out to commercial establishments (Margolis).

Gender Relations. As consumption management became time- and labor-intensive, it also became gender-stratified. The woman as purchasing agent made housework productive work; outside employment of women was seen as a threat to consumption management (Margolis 1984). In the process, however, consumption management became socially valuable but unpaid work.

The neoclassical explanation of specialization by women in household work because of lower market wages appears to be particularly weak. Available evidence indicates that even when market wages increase (for example, in dual-career professional families), household tasks do not shift significantly (Berk 1985). Actual disparities in husbands' and wives' participation in household work indicate normative constraints such as male and female stereotypes (Berk 1980). In fact, Berk (1985) goes on to argue that the household production function does not only combine market goods and time to produce commodities that provide utility, but it also produces gender relations. "The imperatives posed by the production of gender relations mean that the division of household labor not only is concerned with the rational sorting and optimal matching of tasks and time to household members but is also centered on the symbolic affirmation of the members or their 'alignment' with each other as husband and wife, man and woman, brother and sister" (p. 206).

The importance of the consumption experience has shaped public attitudes toward female participation in the labor force. First, the domestic sphere had become the domain of women, and home and employment were seen not only as separate but also as incompatible (Kreps and Leaper 1976; Margolis 1984). But as inflation and rising consumption expectations forced women to enter the labor market, the reality of women workers was rationalized by "economic need" and "consumption aspirations" consistent with the "helpmate" and "homemaker" roles (Chafe 1976). However, as women participate in the labor force for economic as well as personal needs and increase their commitment to outside employment, the threat to consumption management becomes an important societal concern.

The three elements of the consumption experience—individualized ownership of durables, elaboration of housework, and gender relations—have worked together to make consumption management a key feature of women's work in the twentieth century. However, with the increase in the ranks of women employed outside the house, these three elements of the consumption experience are under pressure. Because of strong social norms regarding individual ownership of goods and gender relations, it is likely that the elaboration of housework will yield to the pressures first. There is some evidence to suggest that in terms of discretionary behavior, employed wives are spending less time on housework, not performing some of the tasks (such as using coupons), and using more market goods and services (such as day care and restaurants) than full-time homemakers. The implications for managerial responses and the consumption process are examined below.

Marketing Responses and Their Implications

Marketing Responses

At the micromarketing level, emphasis on the household production function has emphasized the need for convenient, time-saving activities and products. As husbands and others participate in household activity, marketing questions are raised about their consumption behavior—do they buy/use products in ways similar/dissimilar to women and wives?

The changes in the household characteristics have led to responses by the marketing system as it adjusts its offering to meet the dynamic challenges. Some of these responses are described briefly below.

Product Responses. For both men and women, the pressures of managing a job and a career in single-headed or dual-career households have led to several changes in products and services offered to meet customer needs. They include day-care services for children (Lein 1979), care facilities for the aged (Edmondson 1986a), and cleaning services for households (Edmondson 1986b).

Upscale Emphasis. A large number of marketing responses appear to reflect the dual-income household and the aspirations for convenient, affluent lifestyles. The supermarkets that are doing well, for instance, are those with services such as gourmet goodies backed by in-store services (*Fortune* 1985b). Sales are growing quickly for goods with premium prices, such as expensive cars and fancy weddings (*Fortune* 1985a).

Greater Convenience. A characteristic of marketing's responses is the increased convenience in its offerings. Whether it be one-stop shopping, direct-response advertising, or computerized buying, the emphasis is to make products/services and the process of purchasing and using them more convenient (Baig 1986a; Bloom and Korenman 1986). Even big-ticket items are being marketed via direct-response advertising (Higgins 1986b; Baig 1986a), and predictions are being made for conveniences such as room service for house and apartment dwellers (Bloom and Korenman).

Price and Value. From designer clothes to garbage bags, there is increased emphasis on price and value. Various forms of sales promotions are growing faster than media advertising (Kessler 1986), leading to concerns about brand loyalty and customer franchise (Exter 1986). The emphasis on value accounts for marketing offers such as "imposter" perfumes (Higgins 1986a) and warehouse clubs (Saporito 1986).

The Target Consumer. The emphasis on the full-time homemaker is undergoing changes as marketers find more and varied members of the household participating in decision making, purchase, and use of products/services. The target consumer—the receiver of marketing messages and efforts—is being updated as marketers attempt to respond to the changing household characteristics.

The Impact on the Consumption Process

Marketers have looked at the changes in household characteristics and the role of women and responded to the opportunities for products and services such as day care, convenient hours and means for shopping, and restaurant facilities. At this level, marketing has attempted to remain adaptive and responsive to the changing socioeconomic scene. However, embedded in these responses are seeds of their own decline—particularly, in institutions and forms of marketing that have come to be associated with past developments. To put this in perspective, we have to examine the implications of the changing woman's role on the consumption process.

The Consumption Manager

In the postwar years, a consumer culture built on acquisition of goods was facilitated by the role of the woman as manager of the consumption process.

The working married woman was socially accepted so long as the second paycheck was used to bolster the standard of living (Margolis 1984). However, as more and more women work outside the home, combine a career with a family, and raise their children in settings other than the traditional home, their role as socializing agents for the consumption process is affected.

In various aspects of family behavior, including family planning and financial planning, the wife's education, occupation, and attitudes have proven to be more critical to the prediction of behavioral changes than any other household characteristic (Tauber and Sweet 1976; Schaninger, Buss, and Grover 1982). Consumer behavior has been equally influenced by changes in the role of women as socializing agents. Until recently, however, the traditional role of women as consumption managers has facilitated the growth of consumption. The new role of women in the labor force does not necessarily lead to similar developments.

Consumption Value

Changes in household formation and characteristics have many implications for consumption processes. For instance, decision making by nonmarried, cohabiting couples shows greater independence and self-centeredness (Murphy 1984). Similarly, two-income, dual-career, childless households indicate an orientation supporting a consumption-intensive life-style (Kinkead 1980). Households with women as head reveal income and time constraints that put severe pressure on consumption levels (Bane and Weiss 1980). Many marketing authors have examined these changes in the household and have recommended managerial changes in segmentation, promotion, and product strategies (Bartos 1979; Espenshade 1981; Scarpa 1982). Several of these are summarized by Murphy.

Two directly opposite kinds of consumption values may be emerging. One is upheld by the affluent, upwardly mobile consumers with visions of an expanding horizon. For them, more is likely to be better. However, the forces also appear to be putting downward pressures on consumption value. As women gain a sense of their own identity and self-worth, it is unlikely that they will depend on goods and tangible products to compensate for a lack of identity or to establish one. This may include lowering their aspiration level in a consumer sense in order to achieve a higher level in a worker sense. The creation of Superwoman's Anonymous (Edmondson, 1986c) to promote a life-style of "downward mobility" by reducing aspirations may be one expression of changing consumption values. More and more women appear to be questioning the "elaboration of housework" created in the past and its concomitant level of consumption.

In terms of more fundamental and macro-level marketing implications, the changes in household characteristics appear to be polarizing the consumption sphere, and the dynamics of these changes are still to be explored. On the one hand, we have households (single, married without children, etc.) with large discretionary income plus a hedonistic orientation with few constraints; they represent the "superclass" of consumers (Jones 1981). On the other hand, we have households—divorced women with children, older singles—with limited incomes and large unmet needs who are becoming the consuming underclass. Unlike the historical underclasses—such as minorities or citizens of Third World countries—many of these new underclass consumers in the affluent western world were in the middle-class consumers of yesterday. They were the foundation on which a mass marketing and mass consuming society was built. This new underclass of consumers has the aspirations and past experience of affluence but is saddled with a reality of diminishing means. In the past, aspirations always exceeded incomes but the current situation is unique because a large number of consumers are being forced to reduce their aspirations even though they had achieved a large part in the past.

We need to investigate the relationship between consumption behavior and consumption values. Kotler (1986), for example, has suggested that prosumers, a term coined by Toffler (1980), will produce their own goods and services—that is engage in "task elaboration." The concept of role overload makes this unlikely among employed women, particularly those committed to their careers. However, if women are blocked in their movement toward high-status and high-power jobs, then it is likely that conspicuous consumption will be used to compensate for "meaningless work" or slow advancement in jobs and real income (Belk 1986).

Consumption Volume

Based on changes in the woman's role in the household, a reduction in consumption volume may be predicted. This is likely to result from (1) the cumulative impact of cutbacks in mundane, daily activities and (2) the higher status of employed women. As women are forced to abandon "elaboration of housework" and its concomitant standard of performance, consumption volume per household is likely to decline. These cutbacks are occurring in tasks that are to some extent discretionary. For example, energy-conservation efforts have produced only small changes in behavior, such as reduced use of ovens and vacuum cleaners (Keck et al. 1974). Time pressures are likely to affect these daily activities too.

Ferber and Birnbaum (1980) have suggested fewer household goods and services to make management of the household tasks easier for working women. As a result, household appliances and household cleaning products may see a reduction in frequency of use and, therefore, a reduction in consumption volume. Several products and services have experienced a decline in consumption volume in recent years. Aside from health considerations, the per capita consumption of red meat has declined in the past ten years partly due to its time-consuming preparation (Baig 1985). Time pressures will continue to affect consumption in terms of what and how much of products/services are consumed. One effect will be a decline in consumption volume, particularly physical volume.

There appears to be some relationship between status of the employed wife and consumption volume. Higher-status employed women appear to own smaller cars, for instance (Schaninger and Allen 1981). Other forces are also likely to negatively affect consumption volume. For instance, surveys indicate that many household tasks required to maintain consumption levels are disliked by consumers, particularly by men, but by women also. It is likely that with time pressures and alternative sources of personal identity, these tasks will be minimized, which will have an impact on consumption volume (Hendrix and Qualls 1984).

We need to investigate the relationship between working women and usage, not ownership, of various goods and services and its implications for consumption volume. The consequences can be far-reaching if there is a significant shift in consumption behavior such as replacement of durable goods. Changes in industrial structure can result, having a wrenching effect on society. An analogy can be drawn from the automobile industry, where automobile usage and purchase declines resulting from the oil price shock affected the global industrial structure. While the emergence of women in the work force has not had as traumatic an impact yet, the indications are that dramatic shifts are likely due to changes in consumption volume.

One consequence will be in the growth of the service sector. Trends indicate that it is the service sector that is growing most rapidly (Hughes and Sternlieb 1986), that employs the most women, and that is leading to their "upskilling" (Kirkland 1985). Because of the growth of the service sector, there are concerns and debates over the "hollow" corporation (Jonas 1986), which will not manufacture any physical product. Even among analysts favorable to growth through services, there is concern about the difficulties of sustained growth. For instance, shopping center space per capita almost doubled between 1974 and 1984, but sales per square foot, after adjusting for inflation, declined over the same period (Mair 1985).

Consumer Socialization

The woman, as mother and primary nurturer, has also been the main transmitter of social values, including consumption values. With the mother away from home, other caregivers are fulfilling this role. Although data indicates that children (particularly preschoolers) are still being taken care of in home settings by relatives and other individuals (Luech, Orr, and O'Connell 1982), the issues of consumer socialization are likely to emerge.

Some evidence exists that there is an inverse relationship between quality of children and time invested in homemaking (Hunt and Kiker 1981). (Child quality has been measured by the parent's expectations of children completing college.) Research also indicates that employed women have different media habits and patterns (*Media Decisions* 1976; Schaninger and Allen 1981; Venkatesh 1980). Studies examining shopping behavior suggest that employed women are similar to men in terms of planning less, using information less, and spending more than nonworking women (Zeithaml 1985). Berry (1979) has suggested that the employed wife is a "time-buying" customer. Since imitation is the main form of consumer learning (Ward and Wackman 1973), it is likely that media and consumption behavior of the children of employed women are likely to be affected.

There is little or no research on the effect of working women on consumer socialization. There is some research to show that working mothers have more self-reliant and less anxious children who hold less stereotyped sex roles (Margolis 1984). Fundamental questions are raised regarding the production of gender relations. Gender ideals are at stake, and marketing as a visible social institution has to deal with problems of changing, maintaining, and reinforcing these relations. This needs further investigation.

Advertisements for products such as Enjoli perfume may attempt to emphasize the "superwoman" role, but it is likely to become increasingly difficult to effectively portray such role stereotypes. As in cigarette advertising, it is unlikely that marketing will precipitate a social trend instead of following it— women had started to smoke long before they were featured in cigarette advertisements. Similarly, women are likely to abandon the standards of housework portrayed in advertisements before advertisers change their portrayals. While the United States is still not seen as an egalitarian society in terms of sex-role stereotypes (Hyman 1972; Kandel and Lesser 1972), the consequences of more egalitarian roles are unknown, but role change has direct effect on the maintenance of gender relations.

Conclusion

So far, the role of women as consumption managers of the household sector has facilitated the growth of marketing. In the process, however, consumption management has become a full-time but unpaid occupation for women, tying homemakers to their individually owned appliances as they engage in the elaboration of housework.

The realities of life, however, no longer allow women to devote their full energies to the management of consumption. As a result, there are several threats to the consumer culture of the past. Due to pressure of role overload created by labor force participation and household work, the consumption experience based on individual ownership of goods, elaboration of housework, and gender relations is going to be transformed. It has been argued in this chapter that elaboration of housework will be the first to yield to the pressure since social norms favoring individual ownership and gender relations are so strong. However, the other elements of the consumption experience will not remain untouched. Individual ownership will come under fire as households increasingly substitute market-bought services for home-produced goods, and gender relations will be affected as alternative configurations of household members involve themselves in the performance of household tasks.

As a consequence, consumption values that facilitate ownership, consumption behavior that leads to high volumes of consumption, and consumer socialization processes that transmit these values and behavior will be under pressure. The challenge for marketing is to respond to these threats and pressures in a way that fosters a consumer culture without building on the gender inequalities of the past. It is a challenge that is unique in history.

References

Baig, E.C. (1985), "Trying to Make Beef Appetizing Again," *Fortune* (November 25): 64.

——— , (1986a), "Dial 800 for a PC," *Fortune* (February 17): 31.

——— , (1986b), "Consumers Back Off," *Fortune* (February 17): 31.

Bane, M.J., and R.S. Weiss (1980), "Alone Together," *American Demographics* 2 (May): 11–15.

Bartos, R. (1979), "Exploring Mysterious Markets," *American Demographics* 1 (March): 9–17.

Becker, G.S. (1976), "A Theory of the Allocation of Time," *The Economic Approach to Human Behavior*, G.S. Becker, ed. Chicago: University of Chicago Press.

Belk, R.W. (1982), "Acquiring, Possessing and Collecting: Fundamental Processes in Consumer Behavior," in *Marketing Theory: Philosophy of Science Perspectives*, R.F. Bush and S.D. Hunt, eds. Chicago: American Marketing Association.

——— , (1986), "Yuppies as Arbiters of the Emerging Consumption Style," in *Advances in Consumer Research*, Vol. 13, R.J. Lutz, ed. Provo, Utah: Association for Consumer Research, 514–19.

Berk, R.A. (1980), "The New Home Economics: An Agenda for Sociological Research," in *Women and Household Labor*, S.F. Berk, ed. Beverly Hills: Sage, 113–48.

Berk, R.A., and Berk, S.F. (1979), *Labor and Leisure at Home: Content and Organization of the Household Day*. Beverly Hills: Sage.

Berk, S.F. (1985), *The Gender Factory*. New York: Plenum.

Bernard, J. (1974), *The Future of Motherhood*. New York: Dial.

Berry, L.L. (1979), "The Time Buying Consumer," *Journal of Retailing* 55 (Winter): 58–59.

Bloom, D.E., and S.D. Korenman (1986), "The Spending Habits of American Consumers," *American Demographics* (March): 22ff.

Bose, C.E. (1985), *Jobs and Gender: A Study of Occupational Prestige*. New York: Praeger.

Bureau of Labor Statistics (1980), *Perspectives on Working Women: A Data Book*. Washington, D.C.: U.S. Dept. of Labor.

Chafe, W.H. (1976), "Looking Backward in Order to Look Forward: Women, Work, and Social Values in America," in *Women and the American Economy: A Look to the 1980s*, J.M. Kreps, ed. Englewood Cliffs, N.J.: Prentice-Hall, 6–30.

Cowan, Ruth S. (1983), *More Work for Mother: The Ironies of Household Technology from the Open Hearth to the Microwave*. New York: Basic Books.

Dholakia, R.R., N. Dholakia, and A. Fuat Fırat (1984), "From Social Psychology to Political Economy: A Model of Energy Use Behavior," in *Consumer Behavior and Energy Policy*, Peter Ester et al, eds. Amsterdam: North Holland, 43–60.

Dillman, D.A., K.R. Tremblay, and J.J. Dillman (1979), "Influence of Housing Norms and Personal Characteristics on Stated Housing Preferences," *Housing and Society* 6(1): 2–19.

Edmondson, B. (1986a), "The Demographics of Guilt," *American Demographics* (March): 32ff.

———, (1986b), "Merry Maids Clean Up," *American Demographics* (March): 20.

———, (1986c), "Business Reports: Superwomen Say Enough Is Enough," *American Demographics* (March): 18.

Espenshade, T.J. (1981), "Demographics of Decline," *American Demographics* 3 (February): 22–23.

Exter, T. (1986), "Looking for Brand Loyalty," *American Demographics* (April): 33ff.

Ferber, M.A. and B. Birnbaum (1980), "One Job or Two Jobs: The Implications for Young Wives," *Journal of Consumer Research* 7(3): 263–71.

Ferree, M.M. (1980), "Satisfaction with Housework: The Social Context," in *Women and Household Labor*, S.F. Berk, ed. Beverly Hills: Sage, 89–112.

Fırat, A.F. (1987), "Towards a Deeper Understanding of Consumption Experiences: The Underlying Dimensions," in *Advances in Consumer Research*, vol. 14, M. Wallendorf and P. Anderson, eds. Provo, Utah: Association for Consumer Research (forthcoming).

Fortune (1985a), "Marriage Megabucks" (June 22): 59–65.

Fortune (1985b), "The Giant of the Regional Food Chains" (November 25): 27ff.

Hendrix, P.E., and W.J. Qualls (1984), "Operationalizing Family Level Constructs: Problems and Prospects," in *Marketing to the Changing Household: Management and Research Perspectives*, M.L. Roberts and L.H. Wortzel, eds. Cambridge, Mass.: Ballinger, 25–40.

Higgins, K.T. (1986a), "Imposter Line from Parfums de Coeur Striving to Knock Off Designer Brands, Literally and Figuratively," *Marketing News* (January 17): 1, 12.

———, (1986b) "Big-Ticket Items Marketed via Direct Response TV," *Marketing News* (February 28): 25.

Hu, J. (1980), "Household Projections: An Alternative Approach," *American Demographics* 2 (October): 23–25.

Hughes, J.W., and G. Sternlieb (1986), "The Suburban Growth Corridor," *American Demographics* (April): 34–37.

Hunt, J.C., and B.F. Kiker (1981), "The Effect of Fertility on the Time Use of Working Wives," *Journal of Consumer Research* 7 (March): 380–87.

Hyman, R. (1972), "Marital Power and the Theory of Resources in Cross-Cultural Context," *Journal of Comparative Family Studies* 1: 50–67.

Joag, S., J.W. Gentry, and J.A. Hopper (1985), "Explaining Differences in Consumption by Working and Nonworking Wives," *Advances in Consumer Research*, vol. 12, E. Hirschman and M. Holbrook, eds. Provo, Utah: Association for Consumer Research, 582–85.

Jonas, N. (1986), "The Hollow Corporation," *Business Week* (March 3): 57–59.

Jones, L. (1981), "The Emerging Superclass," *American Demographics* 3 (March): 30–35.

Kandel, D., and G.S. Lesser (1972), "Marital Decision Making in American and Danish Urban Families: A Research Note," *Journal of Marriage and the Family* 34: 134–38.

Keck, C.A., N. Erlbaum, P.L. Milic, and M.F. Trentacosta (1974), "Changes in Individual Travel Behavior during the Energy Crisis 1973–74," Preliminary Research Report no. 67. Albany, N.Y.: Dept. of Transportation.

Kessler, F. (1986), "The Costly Coupon Craze," *Fortune* 101 (April 7): 74–84.

Kirkland, R.J., Jr. (1985), "Are Service Jobs Good Jobs?" *Fortune* (June 10): 38–43.

Kotler, P. (1986), "The Prosumer Movement: A New Challenge for Marketers," in *Advances in Consumer Research*, vol. 13, R.J. Lutz, ed. Provo, Utah: Association for Consumer Research, 510–13.

Kreps, J.M., and R.J. Leaper (1976), "Home Work, Market Work and the Allocation of Time," in *Women and the American Economy: A Look to the 1980s*, J.M. Kreps, ed. Englewood Cliffs, N.J.: Prentice-Hall, 61–81.

Lein, L. (1979), "Parental Evaluation of Childcare Alternatives," *The Urban and Social Change Review* 12: 11–16.

Linder, S.B. (1970), *The Harried Leisure Class*, New York: Columbia University Press.

Luech, M., A.C. Orr, and M. O'Connell (1982). *Trends in Child Care Arrangements of Working Mothers*, Current Population Reports, special studies no. 117. Washington, D.C.: U.S. Dept. of Commerce, 23.

Mair, J. (1985), "Merchants' Woe: Too Many Stores," *Fortune* (May 13): 62.

Margolis, Maxine L. (1984), *Mothers and Such: Views of American Women and Why They Changed*. Berkeley: University of California Press.

Marks, S.R. (1977), "Multiple Roles and Role Strain: Some Notes on Human Energy, Time and Commitment," *American Sociological Review* 42: 921–36.

Mason, R.S. (1981), *Conspicuous Consumption: A Study of Exceptional Behavior*. Hampshire, England: Gower.

Media Decisions, (1976), "The Working Woman" (February): 53–54.

Moore, T. (1986), "What's Taking the Punch out of Profits," *Fortune* (June 9): 114–20.

Mott, F.L. (1978), *Women, Work and Family: Dimensions of Change in American Society*. Lexington, Mass.: D.C. Heath.

Murphy, P.E. (1984), "Family and Household Changes: Developments and Implications," in *Marketing to the Changing Household*, M.L. Roberts and L.H. Wortzel, eds. Cambridge, Mass.: Ballinger, 3–24.

Nakamura, A., and M. Nakamura (1985), *The Second Paycheck: A Socioeconomic Analysis of Earnings*. Orlando, Fla.: Academic Press.

Nelson, L. (1980), "Household Time: A Cross-Cultural Example," in *Women and Household Labor*, S.F. Berk, ed. Beverly Hills: Sage, 169–90.

Pollak, R.A., and M.L. Wachter (1975), "The Relevance of the Household Production Function and Its Implications for the Allocation of Time," *Journal of Political Economy* 83: 255–77.

Reilly, M.D. (1982), "Working Wives and Convenience Consumption," *Journal of Consumer Research* 8 (March): 407–18.

Robinson, J.P. (1980), "Household Technology and Household Work," in *Women and Household Labor*, S.F. Berk, ed. Beverly Hills: Sage, 113–48.

Saporito, B. (1986), "The Mad Push to Join the Warehouse Club," *Fortune* (January 6): 59–60.

Scarpa, R.J. (1982), "Changing Demographics Bring Investment Opportunities," *American Demographics* 4 (January): 26–29.

Schaninger, C.M., and C.T. Allen (1981), "Wife's Occupational Status as a Consumer Behavior Construct," *Journal of Consumer Research* 8 (September): 189–96.

Schaninger, C.M., W.C. Buss, and R. Grover (1982), "The Effect of Sex Roles on Family Economic Handling and Decision Influence," in *An Assessment of Marketing Thought and Practice*, B.J. Walker, ed. Chicago, Ill.: American Marketing Association, 43–47.

Strasser, S. (1982), *Never Done: A History of American Housework*. New York: Pantheon.

Strober, M.H., and C.B. Weinberg (1977), "Working Wives and Major Family Expenditures," *Journal of Consumer Research* 4: 141–47.

Strober, M.H., and C.B. Weinberg (1980), "Strategies Used by Working and Nonworking Wives to Reduce Time Pressures," *Journal of Consumer Research* 6 (March): 338–48.

Tauber, K.E., and J.A. Sweet (1976), "Family and Work: The Social Life Cycle of Women," in *Women and the American Economy: A Look to the 1980s*, T.M. Kreps, ed. Englewood Cliffs, N.J.: Prentice-Hall, 31–60.

Toffler, A. (1980), *The Third Wave*. New York: Morrow.

Tracy, E.J. (1985), "The Gold in the Gray," *Fortune* (October 14): 137, 140.

Vanek, J. (1974), "Time Spent in Housework," *Scientific American* 231: 116–20.

———, (1980), "Household Work, Wage Work and Sexual Inequality," in *Women and Household Labor*, S.F. Berk, ed. Beverly Hills: Sage, 275–92.

Venkatesh, A. (1980), "Changing Roles of Women—A Lifestyle Analysis," *Journal of Consumer Research* 7 (September): 189–97.

Ward, S., and D.B. Wackman (1973), "Children's Information Processing of TV Advertising," in *New Models for Communications Research*, P. Clarke, ed. Beverly Hills: Sage, 119–46.

Weinberg, C.B., and R.S. Weiner (1983), "Working Wives and Major Family Expenditures: Replication and Extension," *Journal of Consumer Research* 10 (September): 259–63.

Wilson, J.O. (1980), *After Affluence: Economics to Meet Human Needs*. San Francisco: Harper & Row.

Zeithaml, V.A. (1985), "The New Demographics and Market Fragmentation," *Journal of Marketing* 49 (Summer): 64–75.

Part V
Toward a New Social Science
Discipline

20
A Modest Proposal for Creating Verisimilitude in Consumer-Information–Processing Models and Some Suggestions for Establishing a Discipline to Study Consumer Behavior

Russell W. Belk

A Modest Proposal

The first half of this chapter's title is borrowed from Jonathan Swift's (1729/1955) ingenuous solution to the Irish poor's burden of too many children during the great potato famine. After fattening the children for a year, sell them to the rich as sources of food and fine leather. This solves both the overpopulation and low standard of living problems characteristic of the poor while also adding some joy to the lives of the rich via new forms of haute cuisine and haute couture.

The problem to be addressed by the current modest proposal is itself more modest: The dominant paradigm in consumer behavior research—the view of consumers as information processors—is not an adequate representation of the way consumers behave. While this paradigm is an elegant synthesis of economics' rational man and cognitive psychology's metaphorical model of man as a computer, it just has not proven to be very useful in illuminating the rich mysteries of consumer behavior. The literature need not be reviewed here to convince the reader that consumers seek little or no information, ignore nearly

I thank Richard Semenik and Morris Holbrook for their helpful comments on an earlier draft of this chapter.

all information that they accidentally encounter, seldom if ever engage in problem-solving behavior, and, in general, process information far less well than the most modest grade school computer.[1]

The solution proposed for the inadequacies of the consumer-information–processing (CIP) model is as expedient as Swift's, even though it must take advantage of technological possibilities that could never have been envisioned in Swift's time. The technology derives partly from the same phenomenon that provides the metaphor for the consumer in the CIP view: the computer. Currently, this technology flourishes in the region of Northern California known as Silicon Valley. Here, the Apple, the Osborne, and a host of other computers and computer technologies have been born. The other part of the necessary technology currently flourishes in the region of Northern Utah known as Bionic Valley. Here, a blend of engineering and medicine has produced artificial hearts, kidneys, hands, arms, ears, and other parts of the human anatomy (*U.S. News and World Report* 1985).

From here, the solution to the problem of consumer-behavior departures from the CIP model should be obvious. If consumers are too naturally stupid to behave in the way the computer does, let us provide them with the artificial intelligence that will enable them to do so.[2] I am informed by scientists in both Silicon Valley and Bionic Valley that this is not only technologically possible, but long overdue.[3] With the surgical implantation of one small processor chip and another small coprocessor for added speed in numerical calculations, consumers should not only be able to live up to the models that have been developed to describe their behavior, but they should behave in a much more predictable, logical, and infallible fashion than is currently the case. No more self-indulgent splurges, overly generous gifts of love, nonnutritional eating, ignored advertising, or lamentable susceptibility to well-crafted personal sales appeals. These benefits are so self-evidently in the consumer's best interest that consumers will hardly need to be convinced to acquire the requisite package of artificial intelligence. The U.S. economy and society will also benefit from the perfect price competition and the elimination of wasteful emotional appeals that would result.

Given the savings that would accrue to consumers and society, it seems quite certain that medical insurance or perhaps even the federal government will cover all of the costs involved. Non-CIP behavior can, after all, be regarded as a form of mental illness. Furthermore, with the incorporation of a small portable transceiver during chip implantation, marketers should be able to continuously monitor the information consumers process and accurately anticipate their next purchases before they are made. (I am told that range will be greatly enhanced by a small six-inch antenna that could be installed at the top of the cranium and coupled with cellular mobile technology.) The evaluation of specific marketing programs will then become instantaneous and definitive.

This should allow both marketing and consumer research to come out of the dark ages of crafts practice and become true sciences at last.

But rather than stop with just monitoring consumers via this consumer–marketer link, it can also be used to transmit advertising directly to the consumer for processing without the necessity of wasting time with mass media to receive the information. The information can even be sent and processed as consumers sleep! The savings in advertising costs will benefit all of society, while consumers will be freed of endless hours of tedious and unproductive television viewing. The possibilities for test marketing are fully as enticing. Split-cable and UPC scanning systems will be quickly out-moded as consumer tests and marketing strategy duels are waged instantly and painlessly through the wonders of electronics. With dual implants, split-cable testing will be further antiquated by the possibilities of *split-brain testing.*

Having provided consumers with standardized processing units and assuring that all those in a designated target market will receive and process intended advertising data, one further step remains to optimize consumers' behavior. With the input of correct weights (values, importances, and evaluations) into consumers' multiattribute attitude models, consumers can all arrive at indisputable correct preferences. Of course, this means that we will all drive midsized brown sedans. But even if the lunatic fringe insists upon maintaining wasteful variety in consumer choices, we can always give some segments of people different objective function weights so that they will end up preferring, for example, green station wagons. Market shares will depend solely upon corporations' abilities to offer products that fit these objective functions. But since these function weights will be known to all, each marketer will have an exactly equal chance to serve a particular market segment.

On the consumer side, a direct consumer–marketer link will be similarly enticing. Interactive computer shopping? Outmoded! The consumer will need only to *think* that they would like a product and funds will be transferred as the product is being delivered. A hostile reaction to an ad? Think about it and the advertiser will be instantly apprised of your feelings. It will truly be as if everyone with sufficient purchasing credit were given the power to have all their wishes granted. Computerized consumers will then be their own fairy godmothers.

I cannot imagine that anyone could object to this proposal, for it is logical, economical, optimizing, and in tune with modern progress. Nevertheless, in order to be fair and to keep an open mind on the subject, the second half of this chapter explores the major alternative that I can imagine might be proposed: If consumers are not to be made to conform to our models, perhaps we could make our models conform to the nature of consumer behavior. I admit from the outset that this is a much more difficult course of action and one that offers none of the original proposal's advantages to consumers, society, and marketers, but, by examining it, I cannot be accused of failing to consider all alternatives.

Some Suggestions for Establishing a Discipline to Study Consumer Behavior

It seems to me that the obstacles to developing more adequate models of consumer behavior are largely the same as the obstacles that have prevented consumer behavior research from becoming a discipline. These obstacles will be considered one at a time along with suggestions for overcoming them.

Consumer behavior research has not studied consumer behavior.

As argued elsewhere (Belk 1984b), consuming (of both nondurables and durables) has been the subject of extremely little research. *Buying* and various preacquisition behaviors have been studied in some detail, but consuming and postacquisition behaviors have generally been ignored. This is much more than a matter of terminology, since consumer behavior is more fundamental to human behavior than is buyer behavior. Belk (1984b) discusses several important differences between these two types of phenomena:

1. Consumer behavior has always occurred and will always occur as a necessary part of human behavior; buyer behavior is a relatively recent phenomenon.
2. Buyer behavior is not a necessary antecedent to consumer behavior, although consumer behavior is a necessary consequence of buyer behavior.
3. We spend much more time engaging in consumer behavior than engaging in buyer behavior.
4. The objects of buyer behavior are largely interchangeable with similar appearing objects; this is seldom true for durable objects of consumer behavior.
5. Consumer behavior items acquire more symbolic meaning than buyer behavior items.

For instance, the symbolism noted in the final point has been considered for some time in *buyer* behavior when items are still relatively devoid of personal meaning (e.g., Levy 1959; Sirgy 1982), but has only recently begun to be investigated in postacquisition *consumer* behavior (e.g., Csikszentmihalyi and Rochberg-Halton 1981; Olson 1981, 1985; Wallendorf 1984). Nevertheless, postacquisition possessions play a significant part in our lives, symbolizing past experiences (Olsen 1981; Sherman and Newman 1977; Taylor 1981; Unruh 1983; Whetmore and Hibbard 1978), present status (Huber 1971; Mason 1981, 1984), future hopes (Hope 1980; Lewis 1969), love (Issacs 1935; Scammon, Shaw, and Bamossy 1982), friends (Caplow 1982, 1984; Levi-Strauss 1965), enemies (Clodd 1920), relatives (Volkan 1974), personal identity (Becker and Coniglio 1975; Churchill and Wertz 1985; Cunliffe 1976; Dixon and Street 1975; Harrington 1965; Kron 1983; Myers 1985; Prelinger 1959; Stein 1985), community (Greenbaum and Greenbaum 1981; Vinsel, Brown, Altman, and Foss 1980), and culture (Beaglehole 1932; McCracken 1985). All of these associations are rich in meaning, but they are relatively unexamined, especially within the domain that we now call consumer behavior. The obvious solution is to turn our attention from buyer behavior to consumer behavior.

Consumer behavior research has been seen as a subdiscipline of marketing.

This related problem has its historic origin in the fact that marketers were the first to aggressively study consumer behavior in a nonaggregate fashion. As Lutz (1985) noted in the call for papers for the 1985 conference of the Association for Consumer Research, nearly 80 percent of that association's members have titles nominally related to marketing. Even though not all of these members take the narrow marketing perspective on consumer behavior, it is that narrow perspective that makes this a problem. As Holbrook (1984) pointed out, it is as though consumer behavior were a football game that we sought to understand only by examining kickoffs (buying). We describe the game as kickoffs between which something of little interest happens which, with luck, leads to another kickoff. As argued above, the resulting focus on buying to the exclusion of consuming (or disposing) has caused us to neglect the most interesting and significant consumer behavior phenomena.

Fortunately, a growing number of scholars both within and outside of the Association for Consumer Research have begun to consider nonmarketing issues involving consumer behavior. They include historians Braudel (1967), Boorstin (1973), Williams (1981), McKendrick, Brewer, and Plumb (1982), and Fox and Lears (1983); sociologists Mukerji (1983), Rochberg-Halton (Csikszentmihalyi and Rochberg-Halton 1981), and Schudson (1984); anthropologists Douglas (Douglas and Isherwood 1979), McCracken (1985), Sahlins (1972), and Sherry (1983); literary critics Hyde (1983) and Shell (1982); psychologists Csikszentmihalyi (Csikszentmihalyi and Rochberg-Halton 1981) and Furby (1978); economists Easterlin (1980) and Hirschman (1977); communication theorists Leiss, Kline, and Jhally (1986); and geographer Tuan (1982). Unfortunately, most of those who identify themselves as consumer researchers have had little or no contact with any of these other scholars and their work is little known outside of their own disciplines.

What is needed in the long run is *not* a multidisciplinary approach to consumer behavior, but a *unidisciplinary* approach, with that one discipline being consumer behavior. However, for this to happen, a mass of consumer behavior theory and research first needs to be established. For this to occur, we must remove the marketing blinders from the majority of those working within the field. As argued elsewhere (Belk 1986), this means that consumer behavior should ultimately seek a status as an independent social science existing, in a university context, outside of the business school.

We have been micro, not macro.

It is symptomatic of the marketing approach followed by consumer researchers to date that the research agenda thus far given major attention has focused on a narrow set of micro issues such as:

1. How can we predict which brand a consumer will buy?
2. How can a product or service be designed that consumers are especially likely to buy?
3. How can we determine which market segments are most likely to buy a product or service?
4. How can we measure the effects of advertising on consumer brand attitudes?

These are clearly consumer behavior issues (or, more accurately, *buyer* behavior issues), but consider their relative importance compared to such macro consumer behavior issues as:

1. How do consumers make trade-offs between money, durables, and discretionary nondurables?
2. Does the acquisition and consumption of money, durables, and discretionary nondurables contribute positively, negatively, or not at all to happiness and feelings of well-being?
3. What roles do consumption objects play in interpersonal relations?
4. How does the consumption of products and experiences affect consumer sense of self?
5. Why and under what conditions do consumers share their goods, wealth, and services (and with whom)?
6. What will Chinese (PRC) consumers first want as income and discretion-

ary income increase? Will these consumers be better off for wanting and getting these things?

7. What is the consumer culture and when did it originate?

Somewhat more systematically, a very partial agenda of neglected but significant macro consumer behavior issues is outlined in table 20–1. In order for consumer behavior to move toward becoming a legitimate academic discipline, issues such as these must be addressed. This is not to say that micro consumer behavior issues are not also a legitimate part of the domain of consumer behavior, but it must be realized that the topic involves much more than micro issues. There have been other calls to examine macro issues in consumer behavior (e.g., Fırat and Dholakia 1982), but these have failed to escape the view that marketing (or, in this case, macromarketing) is a master discipline.

Yes, we have no theory.

In his 1984 presidential address to the Association for Consumer Research, Sheth (1985) characterized consumer behavior research as a field that had reached its maturity. Indeed, most consumer behavior texts and attempts at comprehensive models of consumer behavior also imply that the field has been pretty well explored and that the task is now one of synthesizing the vast knowledge that has been accumulated. However, I submit that the field is in its

Table 20–1
Suggestive Macro Consumer Behavior Issues

	Focus		
Process	*Personal*	*Interpersonal*	*Cultural/Cross-cultural*
Acquisition	Happiness/well-being Trade-offs Pathologies of acquisition	Gift Receipt People as Possessions Social exchange paradigm	Consumer culture Marketing effects on consumer values Political economies
Consumption and use	Tangibles versus intangibles Experiential consumption Symbolic consumption	Sharing Distributive justice Consumption rituals	Cultural artifacts Consumption institutions Media portrayals of consumption
Disposal and disuse	Conspicuous waste Moving and possessions Travel versus accumulation	Material rewards and punishments to children Wills and possessions Organ donation	Secondary marketing system "Kleenex culture" Fads and fashions affecting disuse

adolescence at best. (See Belk 1986.) We have bright prospects and abundant opportunities, but, as of yet, we know and have explored very little of the territory outlined above. And only by expanding our horizons to explore consumer rather than simply buyer behavior, nonmarketing rather than marketing perspectives, and macro rather than micro issues, are we likely to achieve our full potential. Only by striking out in substantially new directions from those explored during our adolescence are we likely to someday earn the status of being a mature discipline of consumer behavior.

This may necessitate new methods for conducting much of our research as well. Macro issues are not as susceptible to experimental research as are the micro issues that we have studied in the past. With such a perspective, the marketer joins the consumer as the subject. But marketer subjects are far less amenable to the administration of experimental conditions. In addition to quantitative survey research and content analyses, a shift to macro issues will necessitate post-logical-positivist techniques variously referred to as qualitative, hermeneutic, ethnographic, phenomenological, subjective, case study, and naturalistic (Lincoln and Guba 1985). A concurrent shift from deduction from borrowed theory to induction of original theory will also be needed.

Recognizing the enormous changes in our thinking and research that such recommendations entail brings me back to the issue addressed in the modest proposal beginning this chapter. Since it should be far easier and far more advantageous to all concerned to make consumer behavior conform to our models than to attempt to make our models conform to consumer behavior, why not take this easy way out? The computer is already an important part of the curriculum in courses in marketing and consumer behavior. It has become the dominant metaphor for consumer behavior with little difficulty or objection. Therefore, I humbly offer the modest proposal of computerizing consumers as an alternative to rethinking consumer behavior.

Notes

1. For reviews of these consumer frailties, see Belk (1984a), Firat (1985), Olshavsky and Granbois (1979), and Zajonc and Marcus (1982). Rather than ask "Why can't a woman be more like a man?" (Lowe and Lerner 1969), Henry Higgins should have more profoundly asked why can't a consumer be more like a computer? It may be true, as Turkal (1984) observes, that we are trying to become more computerlike as we compare ourselves to the computer, but it is evident we still fail miserably in the comparison. Thus, it was perhaps inevitable that Time magazine's 1982 man of the year was the computer (Friedrich 1983).

2. Attempting to produce artificial stupidity in the computer has apparently proved even more difficult than producing artificial intelligence. (See Ferris 1985 versus Dreyfus and Dreyfus 1986.) Thus the opposite solution of making computers more like consumers does not hold out much promise.

3. A number of authors (e.g., Cook 1981; Levin 1972) have envisioned android-like human computers before; Pohl (1983) has described the necessity for robot consumers. But to the best of my knowledge, I am the first to recognize the potential for computerizing consumers. However, lest this be construed as a self-interested recommendation, it can be verified that I have no direct or indirect financial interest in either silicon or bionic technology, nor do I stand to benefit in any way from the implementation of this proposal.

References

Beaglehole, Ernest (1932), *Property: A Study in Social Psychology.* New York: Macmillan.

Becker, Franklin D., and Cheryl Coniglio (1975), "Environmental Messages: Personalization and Territory," *Humanitas* 11 (February): 55–74.

Belk, Russell W. (1984a), "Against Thinking," in *1984 AMA Winter Educators' Conference: Scientific Method in Marketing,* Paul F. Anderson and Michael J. Ryan, eds. Chicago: American Marketing Association, 57–60.

——— ,(1984b), "Manifesto for a Consumer Behavior of Consumer Behavior," in *1984 AMA Winter Educators' Conference: Scientific Method in Marketing,* Paul F. Anderson and Michael J. Ryan, eds. Chicago: American Marketing Association, 163–67.

——— ,(1986), "What Should ACR Want to Be When It Grows Up?" in *Advances in Consumer Research,* vol. 13, Richard J. Lutz, ed. Provo, Utah: Association for Consumer Research, 423–24.

Boorstin, Daniel (1973), *The Americans: The Demoncratic Experience.* New York: Random House.

Braudel, Fernand (1967), *Capitalism and Material Life, 1400-1800* (Civilization Materielle et Capitalisme). New York: Harper & Row.

Caplow, Theodore (1982), "Christmas Gifts and Kin Networks," *American Sociological Review* 47(3): 383–92.

——— ,(1984), "Rule Enforcement without Visible Means: Christmas Gift Giving in Middletown," *American Journal of Sociology* 89 (May): 1306–23.

Churchill, Scott, and Frederick J. Wertz (1985), "An Introduction to Phenomenological Psychology for Consumer Research: Historical, Conceptual, and Methodological Foundations," in *Advances in Consumer Research,* vol. 12, Elizabeth C. Hirschman and Morris B. Holbrook, eds. Provo, Utah: Association for Consumer Research, 550–55.

Clodd, Edward (1920), *Magic in Names and Other Things.* London: Chapman and Hall.

Cook, Robin (1981), *Brain.* New York: G.P. Putman's Sons.

Csikszentmihalyi, Mihaly, and Eugene Rochberg-Halton (1981), *The Meaning of Things: Domestic Symbols and the Self.* Cambridge, England: Cambridge University Press.

Cunliffe, Marcus (1976), "Private Property: The American Way," *The Center Magazine* 9 (September-October): 16–21.

Dixon, S.C., and J.W. Street (1975), "The Distinction between Self and Not-Self in Children and Adolescents," *Journal of Genetic Psychology* 127: 157–62.

Douglas, Mary, and Baron Isherwood (1979), *The World of Goods: Towards an Anthropology of Consumption.* New York: Norton.

Dreyfus, Hubert, and Stuart Dreyfus (1986), "Why Computers May Never Think like People," *Technology Review* (January): 42-61.

Easterlin, Richard A. (1980), *Birth and Fortune: The Impact of Numbers on Personal Welfare.* New York: Basic Books.

Ferris, Michael (1985), "Last Word," *Omni* 7 (May): 118.

Fırat, A. Fuat (1985), "A Critique of the Orientations in Theory Development in Consumer Behavior: Suggestions for the Future," in *Advances in Consumer Research*, vol. 12, Elizabeth C. Hirschman and Morris B. Holbrook, eds. Provo, Utah: Association for Consumer Research, 3–6.

Fırat, A. Fuat, and Nikhilesh Dholakia (1982), "Consumption Choices at the Macro Level," *Journal of Macromarketing* 2 (Fall): 6–15.

Fox, Richard W., and T.J. Jackson Lears (1983), *The Culture of Consumption: Critical Essays in American History: 1880–1980.* New York: Pantheon.

Friedrich, Otto (1983), "Machine of the Year," *Time* (January 3): 12–24.

Furby, Lita (1978), "Possessions: Toward a Theory of Their Meaning and Function throughout the Life Cycle," in *Lifespan Development and Behavior*, Paul B. Baltes, ed. New York: Academic Press, 297–336.

Greenbaum, Paul E., and Susan D. Greenbaum (1981), "Territorial Personalization: Group Identity and Social Interaction in a Slavic American Neighborhood," *Environment and Behavior* 13 (September): 574–89.

Harrington, Molly (1965), "Resettlement and Self Image," *Human Relations* 18 (May): 115–37.

Hirschman, Albert O. (1977), *The Passions and the Interests: Political Arguments.* Princeton, N.J.: Princeton University Press.

Holbrook, Morris B. (1984), "Belk, Granzin, Bristor, and the Three Bears," in *1984 AMA Winter Educators' Conference: Scientific Method in Marketing*, Paul F. Anderson and Michael J. Ryan, eds. Chicago: American Marketing Associations, 177–78.

Hope, Christine A. (1980), "American Beauty Rituals," in *Rituals and Ceremonies in Popular Culture*, Ray B. Browne, ed. Bowling Green, Ohio: Bowling Green University Popular Press, 226–37.

Huber, Richard M. (1971), *The American Idea of Success.* New York: McGraw-Hill.

Hyde, Lewis (1983), *The Gift: Imagination and the Erotic Life of Property.* New York: Random House.

Issacs, Susan (1935), "Property and Possessiveness," *British Journal of Medical Psychology* 15: 69–78.

Kron, Joan (1983), *Home Psych: The Social Psychology of Home and Decoration.* New York: Clarkson N. Potter.

Leiss, William, Stephen Kline, and Sut Jhally (1986), *Social Communication in Advertising.* New York: Methuen.

Levi-Strauss, Claude (1965), "The Principle of Reciprocity," in *Sociological Theory*, L.A. Coser and Bernard Rosenberg, eds. New York: Macmillan.

Levin, Ira (1972), *The Stepford Wives: A Novel*. New York: Random House.

Levy, Sidney J. (1959), "Symbols for Sale," *Harvard Business Review* 37: 117–24.

Lewis, Oscar (1969), "The Possessions of the Poor," *Scientific American* 221: 114–24.

Lincoln, Yvonna S., and Egon G. Guba (1985), *Naturalistic Inquiry*. Beverly Hills: Sage.

Lowe, Frederick, and Alan J. Lerner (1969), *My Fair Lady*, rev. ed. New York: Chappel, 214–24.

Lutz, Richard J. (1985), "Call for Papers, 1985 ACR Conference," *Association for Consumer Research Newsletter* 15 (Winter): 5–7.

Mason, Roger S. (1981), *Conspicuous Consumption: A Study of Exceptional Consumer Behavior*. Westmead, England: Gower.

———— ,(1984), "Conspicuous Consumption: A Literature Review," *European Journal of Marketing* (183): 26–39.

McCracken, Grant W. (1985), "The Evocative Power of Things: Consumer Goods and the Recovery of Displaced Cultural Meaning," working paper 85–105. Guelph, Ontario: Dep. of Consumer Studies, University of Guelph.

McKendrick, Neil, John Brewer, and J.H. Plumb (1982), *The Birth of a Consumer Society: The Commercialization of Eighteenth Century England*. London: Europa.

Mukerji, Chandra (1983), *From Graven Images: Pattens of Modern Materialism*. New York: Columbia University Press.

Myers, Elizabeth (1985), "Phenomenological Analysis of the Importance of Special Possessions: An Exploratory Study," in *Advances in Consumer Research*, vol. 12, Elizabeth C. Hirschman and Morris B. Holbrook, eds. Provo, Utah: Association for Consumer Research, 560–65.

Olshavsky, Richard W., and Granbois, Donald H. (1979), "Consumer Decision Making—Fact or Fiction?" *Journal of Consumer Research* 6 (September): 93–100.

Olson, Clark D. (1981), "Artifacts in the Home and Relational Communication: A Preliminary Report," master's thesis. Salt Lake City: University of Utah.

———— ,(1985), "Materialism in the Home: The Impact of Artifacts on Dyadic Communications," in *Advances in Consumer Research*, vol. 12, Elizabeth C. Hirschman and Morris B. Holbrook, eds. Provo, Utah: Association for Consumer Research, 388–93.

Pohl, Frederick (1983), "The Midas Plague," in *Midas World*. New York: St. Martin's, 5–74.

Prelinger, Ernst (1959), "Extension and Structure of the Self," *Journal of Psychology* 47 (January): 13–23.

Sahlins, Marshall (1972), *Stone Age Economics*. Chicago: Aldine Atherton.

Scammon, Debra L., Roy T. Shaw, and Gary Bamossy (1982), "Is a Gift Always a Gift? An Investigation of Flower Purchasing Behavior across Situations," in *Advances in Consumer Research*, vol. 9, Andrew Mitchell, ed. Ann Arbor, Mich.: Association for Consumer Research, 531–36.

Schudson, Michael (1984), *Advertising: The Uneasy Persuasion*. New York: Basic Books.

Shell, Marc (1982), *Money, Language, and Thought*. Berkeley: University of California Press.

Sherman, Edmund, and Evelyn S. Newman (1977), "The Meaning of Cherished Personal Possessions for the Elderly," *International Journal of Aging and Human Development* 8 (2): 181–92.

Sherry, John F., Jr. (1983), "Gift Giving in Anthropological Perspective," *Journal of Consumer Research* 10 (September): 157–68.

Sheth, Jagdish N. (1985), "Presidential Address: Broadening the Horizons of ACR and Consumer Behavior," in *Advances in Consumer Research*, vol. 12, 1–2.

Sirgy, M. Joseph (1982), "Self-Concept in Consumer Behavior: A Critical Review," *Journal of Cosumer Research* 9 (December): 287–300.

Stein, Benjamin J. (1985), "The Machine Makes This Man," *Wall Street Journal* (June 13): 30.

Swift, Jonathan (1729/1955), "A Modest Proposal for Preventing the Children of Poor People in Ireland from Being a Burden to Their Parents or Country; and for Making Them Beneficial to the Public," *The Prose Works of Jonathan Swift*, vol. 12. Oxford, England: Basil Blackwell.

Taylor, Lisa (1981), "Collections of Memories," *Architectural Digest* 38 (April): 36ff.

Tuan, Yi-Fu (1982), *Segmented Worlds and Self: Group Life and Individual Consciousness*. Minneapolis: University of Minnesota Press.

Turkal, Sherry (1984), *The Second Self: Computers and the Human Spirit*. New York: Simon and Schuster.

Unruh, David R. (1983), "Death and Personal History: Strategies for Identity Preservation," *Social Problems* 30 (February): 340–51.

U.S. News and World Report (1985), "A Bionic Human Is No Longer a Pipe Dream," (March 4): 12.

Vinsel, Anne, Barbara B. Brown, Irwin Altman, and Paul Foss (1980), "Privacy Regulation, Territorial Displays, and Effectiveness," *Journal of Personality and Social Psychology* 34 (6): 1104–15.

Volkan, Vamik D. (1974), "The Linking Objects of Pathological Mourners," in *Normal and Pathological Responses to Bereavement*, John Ellard et al., eds. New York: MSS Information Corporation, 186–202.

Wallendorf, Melanie (1984), "Social Stratification, Object Attachment, and Consumer Life Pattern," paper presented at 1984 conference of the Association for Consumer Research, October 12, Washington, D.C..

Whetmore, Edward, and Don J. Hibbard (1978), "Paradox in Paradise: The Icons of Waikiki," in *Icons of America*, Ray B. Browne and Marshall Fishwick, eds. Bowling Green, Ohio: Bowling Green University Popular Press, 241–52.

Williams, Rosalind (1981), *Dream Worlds: Mass Consumption in Late Nineteenth Century France*. Berkeley: University of California Press.

Zajonc, Robert B., and Hazel Marcus (1982), "Affective and Cognitive Factors in Preferences," *Journal of Consumer Research* 9 (September): 123–310.

21
Rethinking Marketing

Nikhilesh Dholakia
A. Fuat Fırat
Richard P. Bagozzi

> Science attempts to study the unknown by pretending it is just like the known and then often forgets this was a pretense.
> —Richard Levins (1986)

> We simply no longer have any useful notions of how science works or what scientific progress is.
> —Thomas S. Kuhn (1986)

A message that reverberates through most chapters in this book is: Incremental change in marketing is not enough; radical restructuring is required. Collectively, the chapters are a clarion call for rethinking marketing.

But, to put it colloquially, here is the rub: It is easier to repudiate marketing than to rethink it. Vast numbers of powerful and not-so-powerful people have chosen to repudiate marketing—they do not like it; they will not have anything to do with it. Indeed, the rejection of marketing makes strange bedfellows. Josef Stalin and Milton Friedman, for example. The former would have liked to rid the world of this capitalist scourge. The latter abhors the imperfections, segmental monopolies, and barriers that constitute the very stuff of strategic marketing. Perfect communism or perfect markets would strangle marketing as we know it. Fortunately for the burgeoning number of M.B.A.s and their marketing mentors, we live in a lushly imperfect world which is growing more imperfect every day. Diagnosis and prognosis: Marketing will be growing, kicking, and spreading like a plague!

With the spread of marketing, the disillusionment with marketing is also spreading—a thin layer, like oil on water, but dangerous enough to choke off the oxygen from the vital organisms in the marketing ocean. The chapters here have clearly identified the sources of this disillusionment: naive empiricism, conceptual poverty, restrictive methodologies, excessive specialization, unidimensionality, opprobrious instrumentalism, and above all, a neglect of human interest. What, then, can be done?

We believe it is possible to rethink marketing—to reconceptualize it, to reoperationalize it, to redirect it. The very eclecticism of marketing, the eclecticism that gnaws at the self-confidence of struggling dissertation writers in marketing, also makes it possible to invent, import, and fuse new concepts. In the multidisciplinary pragmatism of marketing lie the seeds of its own renewal. Glimpses of such renewal occur in every chapter in this book. In this concluding chapter, we would like to pull together the many strands of renewal in marketing. We cannot and do not wish to offer a completely new and perfect vision of marketing. Such vision can only be achieved with efforts to seek it, with controversy, by generation of provocative ideas and perspectives during the process of changing and transforming marketing. Asking those who study marketing to wait until a perfect vision is achieved before launching a rethinking effort is a call for inaction, a call to continue the status quo, because a completely new and perfect vision can never be achieved standing still. At this juncture, we hope to suggest agendas for further work.

The Unfolding Paths

From the viewpoints expressed by the contributors to this book, many paths seem to unfold—new avenues along which knowledge and practice of marketing can be furthered. We discern fairly broad consensus concerning six ways of being radical in marketing:

1. Infusing humanistic values,
2. Fostering enlightened, responsible practice,
3. Adopting macrosystemic perspectives,
4. Using comprehensive causal models,
5. Developing holistic and integrative frameworks,
6. Deepening the historical basis of the discipline.

There are, of course, other ways of being radical—peering behind symbolisms (Levy 1981), analyzing the metaphors and the language of a field (Arndt 1985), questioning the metatheoretic structures (Zaltman, LeMasters, and Heffring 1982), exploring conflicts and antagonisms (Godelier 1972; Jay 1973), and adopting anarchic and unbounded perspectives (Bookchin 1971; Feyerabend

1975). We value all these perspectives and oppose the tendencies to convert any perspective—orthodox or radical—into a dogma. Let us examine briefly the six directions emanating from this book.

Humanist Values

A recurrent theme in this book has been to infuse humanist values in the knowledge enterprise of marketing. Belk, Benton, Holbrook, Karlinsky, Kilbourne, Mokwa, and Moorman explicitly or implicitly call their readers to adopt humanist perspectives when researching consumers and managers. Kotler even suggests that "humanism pays" and cites several examples of humanistic marketing in action.

We feel the injection of humanism in marketing is an uphill battle. This is because, even though humanism sometimes pays, foresaking humanism often pays more. A case in point is medicine, which started as a humanist discipline, but is being rapidly transformed into a business where human values are of secondary importance. This appears to be the way of capitalist (and perhaps even noncapitalist) development in the contemporary world—there is inexorable "marketization" of ever-widening spheres of life, as Grønhaug and Dholakia point out in their chapter.

There is a glimmer of hope in the growing discussion of humanist approaches in the academic forums of marketing and consumer behavior. (See Hirschman 1986.) Humanist approaches, however, can and are known to fall easily into the trap of utopian, idealist wishfulness. To keep, on the one hand, the vision and sensitivity of humanist values and, on the other hand, the realism required to achieve the purpose, a critical and radical understanding of the history as well as the present state of the human condition is an imperative. We hope that the chapters in this book will accelerate this trend.

Enlightened Practice

If marketing were practiced in a responsible, enlightened, and ethical way, many of the problems attributed to marketing would disappear. This is the position advocated by Fennell and Kotler in their chapters, and to some degree by Mokwa. We do not have a clear idea as to what the barriers to enlightened practice and thought are, though Fennell, Kotler, and, especially, Mokwa offer us many insights. The advocacy of enlightened practice has merit nonetheless. In applied fields such as marketing, practice often precedes theory. Unless enlightened practice can be fostered, radical marketing theories will remain merely critical and will not offer an agenda for change. Of course, the practice of *academic* marketing can become as hidebound as any other form of practice and needs to be redirected every so often, as Fennell insists. Let us hope there is a snowballing of enlightened marketing practice, not just in the corporate sector, but in the public and community sectors as well, so that we will have "people's marketing" much in the way people's science and grassroots medicine have taken hold in many countries (Beckwith 1986).

Important issues are raised by Fennell's practitioner's perspective and Kotler's humanist perspective when they are considered in conjunction, although these issues are not openly discussed in either chapter. While Fennell separates social advocacy from marketing, the demarcation point being the central approach—marketing as a *participant* in existing behaviors, social advocacy as a *change agent* of behaviors—Kotler's humanistic marketing sounds like Fennell's social advocacy. Humanistic marketing, according to Kotler, ought to advocate change if what is presently wanted by the consumers is to their long-term detriment. Marketing, in its humanistic phase, must take into consideration the long-term implications of present consumption as well as long-term benefits for consumers and society. Are the two approaches presented by Kotler and Fennell really that different? If not, what unites them? If yes, what differentiates them?

The two approaches may meet if one considers that long-term benefit could be a product that consumers demand. If so, according to Fennell, marketing ought to provide it. Consumers do not only demand immediate satisfaction of needs, but usually have a vision or purpose regarding their future lives. A consumer demand from the marketing system in society is that such a system should research, seek, and inform consumers on the possible alternative life forms and patterns for the future as well as on the ways of achieving these alternative lives. While this is a consumer need, marketing seems to fall short most in this responsibility.

A more complex issue is the identification of the beneficial ways. Who knows what is beneficial or beneficial according to whom? To know what is beneficial, one has to have information. Therefore, how and to whom information is disseminated in society become of prime interest. If everyone had access to total information about products as well as their direct and indirect effects, and each could equally participate in social choices, then again the Kotler and Fennell perspectives might meet.

When such information is available, however, will the necessity for persuasive communication in society disappear? In a way, Fennell asks for such disappearance when she argues for marketing as she defines it. The issue is, however, can anyone know what they want or need, can anyone articulate their demand *without social interaction* and, as a consequence, *without social influence*? If there is complete independence in demand, then pure marketing is fine. But if there is any interdependence, then persuasion through influence is a reality, and the problem is one of differential access to sources and means of persuasion. Those who have greater access will have greater persuasive powers.

In such a case, we need to study the causes of differential access to such sources and means.

Macrosystemic Perspectives

Marketers do not like to study themselves, we suspect for much the same reasons that executioners do not like to be psychoanalyzed. There seems to be an unwritten compact to avoid, as far as possible, reflexive, self-analytic, and systemic studies of marketing. At root perhaps is a fear of the Dr. Jekylls we may uncover. As a metascientific philosophy, positivism provides us with a handy excuse for this state of affairs. Positivism urges us to get on with the job, to banish doubts, to push ahead with our well-structured research programs (Blum 1974). In marketing, this generally implies forging ahead with research on microscopic consumer response to specific stimuli.

But chinks have begun appearing in the logical-empiricist armor. Several writers in this book have noted the lack of macro perspectives in marketing. (See, for example, Belk, Fırat, Hibshoosh and Nicosia, and Holbrook.) Several more have actually adopted macrosystemic perspectives in their chapters. (See, for instance, Ruby Dholakia, Fırat, Grønhaug and Dholakia, Pandya, Savitt, and Sherry.) Critically reflexive studies of marketing and consumption culture have started appearing in the mainstream journals of the field (Belk and Pollay 1985; Pollay 1986). We think that macrosystemic studies of marketing and consumption will prove to be a most fertile ground for restructuring marketing theory and practice. Methodological and measurement problems are a stumbling block in macrosystemic studies but not any more than in other new research endeavors (Venkatesh and Dholakia 1986).

Comprehensive Causal Models

The adoption of causal modeling techniques in marketing has opened the door for creating and testing much more complex and comprehensive theoretical structures than possible before, at least in the micromarketing arena. (See Bagozzi 1980; Bagozzi and Phillips 1982.) In their chapter for this book, Oliva and Reidenbach provide useful extensions of the causal modeling methods championed by Bagozzi. The chapter by Dant and Monroe, while not delving into methodological issues, illustrates the theoretical benefit of working with more comprehensive causal schema. Recognizing the complexity and dynamic nature of phenomena is a radical step, as Hibshoosh and Nicosia assert, because the more we abstract from reality, the more danger there is that simplified and ideologically "correct" relationships will supplant reality. Thus, the "perfect market" becomes not a convenient abstraction but an ideological prescription for the way the market system *should* work, and "consumer sovereignty" becomes not an abstract ideal but a widely endorsed view of how consumption choices *are* made.

We think that a great deal of work needs to be done in applying complex causal methods to macrosystemic marketing phenomena. Again, there are methodological and measurement constraints, but these can be overcome through determined research.

Holistic and Integrative Frameworks

The great chasm between the micro and macro aspects of marketing is only now receiving attention. The fracturing of knowledge systems across macro-micro dimensions, along ideological lines, and along disciplinary boundaries is a problem plaguing most social sciences. Dividing a discipline into narrow specializations has its benefits in terms of greater depth of research in each subarea. But the cult of specialization often becomes a tool for curbing critical inquiry—integrative perspectives are ridiculed, attempts to marry disparate perspectives are sabotaged on the grounds of theoretical or methodological inadequacy. We think the cult of specialization marks a fear of the whole—the whole may turn out not just greater but radically different than the sum of the parts. There is safety in the known terrain of specialization.

However, understanding, not safety, is the goal of enlightened research and a prerequisite for enlightened practice. Several authors in this book have argued for more integrative and holistic perspectives. Belk and Holbrook show what consumer behavior research would be like in a holistic frame. Hibshoosh and Nicosia sketch a model of consumer behavior where social and psychological perspectives are consciously integrated. Sherry adopts an integrative approach in exploring the link between global marketing and the emergence of a global consumption culture.

Holistic approaches are often woven together with tenuous links which are not firmly tested by extensive research. This is a risk worth taking, especially in marketing, where we seem to be losing the vision of the forest for the trees. Perhaps, sharp analytic inquiries will puncture holes in some of the integrated visions of marketing and consumer behavior. But without the visions, such penetrating inquiries would not even be attempted.

Learning from History

The idea of progress generally entails putting the past behind and engaging with the challenges of the future. In a pragmatic field such as marketing, this idea of progress gets easily corrupted into a *neglect* of history and the fostering of a mistaken notion that we can *escape* the past. We think that ahistoric pragmatism and historical determinism are equally sinister dogmas when it comes to the exploration of marketing phenomena. While people are products of their history, they also create history. In other words, while people cannot escape their historical roots, they can certainly transcend their past. In marketing, it is vital to keep our historical roots in focus and to learn from history even as we attempt to transcend the past and explore the future.

It is clear that the authors in this book do not fall into the trap of thoughtless ahistoricism. Kumcu argues that the use of historical methods will deepen our understanding of how marketing systems function. Fullerton makes a powerful case for including the historical method of research in the repertoire of tools and techniques used to study marketing and consumption phenomena. Savitt, who has previously advocated the use of historical methods in marketing, shows how the dynamics of marketing strategy can be better understood by situating the strategy in its institutional and historical contexts.

There is a gathering trend to learn from the history of marketing and we hope it will continue. There is a need to broaden the historical study of marketing on a global scale so that we may discern not just parallels across methods but also vital cross-cultural links that have helped transmit marketing ideas and institutions across space and time.

Altering Our Worldview

While the six directions outlined above will help explore marketing in new and radical ways, it must be recognized that being radical is ultimately not a matter of technique or style. Radical thought is a product of free, creative, and questioning minds. What we need most in marketing is a spirit of free inquiry which transgresses conventional boundaries, confronts established paradigms, and questions received wisdom. Why is such inquiry scarce in marketing? We think it is because of the illiberal worldviews engendered in the halls of academia and corporations alike.

The Barrier of Ideology

Ideology is a major barrier to the emergence of more critical and radical worldviews in marketing. The nature of ideology is such (it does not matter which ideology we pick) that it casts a veil of false consciousness over its adherents. By tinting our worldview, ideology renders it impossible to see the world in its true color—or even in a different color than the one in which we are encapsulated.

Our ideological moorings are being constantly reinforced by the culture and the media that surround us. We not only refrain from questioning motherhood and apple pie (or whatever is ideologically sacrosanct); we actually raise them to an unassailable pedestal.

Clearly, ideology serves the important function of maintaining social cohesion. But when ideology encloses a *knowledge system* in its iron grip, then critical and radical inquiry is stifled. In our view, the knowledge system of marketing has been stifled in this way because of the ideological worldviews of marketing scholars and practitioners.

The ideological bubble can be broken—the chapters in this book are a testimony to this. Escape from ideology is not difficult, but it is risky, especially for those with large vested interests in the present forms of marketing. We are encouraged that many well-known authors (in this book and elsewhere) are taking such risks. We hope this provides examples for those who have the best potential for radical inquiry: the young scholars and practitioners.

Going on a Creative Limb

As marketing becomes more "scientific," it becomes more difficult to take creative risks. The reason is the one-sided view of what is scientific. The logical-empiricist-positivist image of science which has permeated marketing (Hunt 1983) supports the context of justification, at least from a positivist stance, but subverts the context of discovery (Zaltman, LeMasters, and Heffring 1982). Marketing as art is often playful, irreverent, and creative. Marketing as science is usually serious, respectful, and bland.

Of course, we are not decrying the need for greater scientific work in marketing. We are saying, however, that the way science has been defined and understood by the marketing academia is one-sided; ignorant of the philosophy, history, and sociology of science discussions; and largely ideological. Equating science with a certain method of science, while refusing other philosophies and approaches to science is nothing but an effort by established "scientists" to ideologically control their fields and continue their set ways and paradigms.

Science, as defined by the establishment of scientists, has never been and is not now the only system of knowledge generation. If one sincerely believes that efforts at understanding the human condition in all its dimensions should flourish without rigid and ideological limitations, then views of science with which the art of discovery can coexist must be allowed. Also allowed must be the creative alternative approaches to the context of justification.

Renewal in a knowledge system occurs through creative thought, and our discipline cannot afford to close its creative channels, given the rapidly changing socioeconomic environment in which we operate. On the scale of critique and creativity, this book tilts heavily toward critique. We hope more creative aspects of marketing thought will be forthcoming in the future.

The Essence of Marketing

To illustrate how the altering of worldviews affects the structure of knowledge, we turn briefly to a question that has been central in marketing theory: What is the essence of marketing? The question of which phenomena are considered essential, central, and the defining phenomena of marketing (the worldview) has a profound effect on the thought, theory, research, and practices that ensue.

A Brief History

Whatever work has been done to study the currents of thought in marketing has principally been descriptive, primarily listing the dominating orientations in marketing thought through the history of the discipline (Bartels 1970, 1976). While descriptive work is useful in documenting facts, and, as such, is an integral part of scientific endeavor in any discipline, it falls short of providing insight into *why* and *how* the facts have come to be. That is, descriptive studies lack, on their own, analytical investigations required for explanation, which is the foundation of understanding.

The best known framework on the currents of marketing thought is the one introduced by Bartels. His scheme begins with the origins of the marketing discipline in economics. The interest in economics in the distribution of commodities from where they were produced to the markets where they were consumed is generally accepted as the beginnings of marketing as a discipline. This, of course, is a disciplinary perspective—one involved with the development of an interest area rather than with the development of the phenomena that eventually led to an interest and a discipline at the beginning of the twentieth century.

Broadening and Beyond

The more recent currents of thought, reflected initially in the art-versus-science debates and then in the "broadening" movement, consider that phenomena generic to marketing discipline or the essence of marketing process were always present in human history and practically in every human interaction. Two undercurrents are distinguishable in this general frame of thought which now dominates the academic marketing literature. One perceives marketing and its sister discipline, consumer behavior, to be pertinent only as far as some form of human interaction and, therefore (almost automatically, according to this undercurrent), exchange processes exist. The second undercurrent wrestles with this first one, in that it interprets the phenomena generic to marketing and consumer behavior as more integral to the human being, not necessitating interaction. Hence, the interest in consumption experiences. While for the first undercurrent, exchange is the generic concept of marketing, for the second undercurrent, the central phenomena are acquisition (not just purchase), consumption, and disposal of need-satisfying items through exchange or otherwise. Also, frustration due to nonsatisfaction, personal experience with consumption independent of acquisition, self-creation of items for need satisfaction, or even experiences of consumption without the specific purpose of need satisfaction (non-goal-oriented consumption activity) are all phenomena of interest. Since the most popular definitions of marketing proclaim the purpose of marketing activity to be satisfaction of human needs, the proponents of the second undercurrent tend to argue that limiting satisfaction of needs to *one* means, that of market transaction, is rather arbitrary.

A more radical current of marketing thought sees even the second undercurrent as a limited orientation. This is because, even in this second undercurrent, the satisfaction of needs or consumption experiences are studied with an emphasis on the present, not historically and not (yet) analytically. This radical current of marketing thought presses for an analytical understanding of this historic process which originates needs, transforms needs and consumption experiences, as well as transforms the means through which needs are satisfied or realized. This current of thought is critical in its orientation and always questions the universality of the present or even of the historic relationships upon which the present was founded.

The broadened, exchange-based concept of marketing is the reigning, widely accepted worldview in our discipline. The undercurrent focusing on consumption experiences as essential phenomena is gaining ground through increasing research and dissemination of results. This is beginning to provide an alternative worldview to understand marketing processes. The third, more radical worldview, in which historic formation and transformation of needs and need-satisfaction mechanisms are the focus, is as yet barely acknowledged in the knowledge system of marketing.

The point is that without acceptance or at least recognition of alternative worldviews, there is little possibility of alternative thought, let alone of sustained research and alternative practice. We hope this book opens the door a crack wider for alternative worldviews about marketing processes and phenomena.

Conclusion

Marketing is both an applied managerial technology and a social process (Fisk 1986; Sweeney 1972). While we comprehend this dual nature of marketing, our reward and value systems bias our knowledge endeavors in the applied direction. This applied bias is very understandable and even necessary for a field such as marketing, yet it is surprising how the social process aspects of marketing are largely neglected. The specialized work of marketing scholars and practitioners engenders a worldview in which the social constructs of marketing gradually fade away. When these social constructs are represented, as in the chapters in this book, most of us are shocked, confused, or incensed. It is easy to dismiss radical thought in marketing as soap-box muckraking and, having dismissed it, to get on with our specialized projects. We hope that the readers of this book choose the alternative route of critical inquiry and creative conceptualization. For without an alternative, even the freest-sounding concepts can become tyrannical.

References

Arndt, Johan (1985), "On Making Marketing Science More Scientific: Role of Orientations, Paradigms, Metaphors, and Puzzle Solving," *Journal of Marketing* 49 (Summer): 11–23.

Bagozzi, Richard P. (1980), *Causal Models in Marketing*. New York: Wiley.

Bagozzi, Richard P., and Lynn W. Phillips (1982), "Representing and Testing Organizational Theories: A Holistic Construal," *Administrative Science Quarterly* 27 (September): 459–89.

Bartels, Robert (1970), *Marketing Theory and Metatheory*. Homewood, Ill.: Richard D. Irwin.

——— , (1976), *The History of Marketing Thought*. Columbus, Ohio: Grid.

Beckwith, Jon (1986), "The Radical Science Movement in the United States," *Monthly Review* 38 (July-August): 118–28.

Belk, Russell W., and Richard W. Pollay (1985), "Images of Ourselves: The Good Life in Twentieth Century Advertising," *Journal of Consumer Research* 11 (March): 887–97.

Blum, Alan F. (1974), "Positive Thinking," *Theory and Society* 1 (Fall): 245–69.

Bookchin, Murray (1971), *Post-Scarcity Anarchism*. Berkeley, Calif.: Ramparts.

Feyerabend, Paul L. (1975), *Against Method: Outline of an Anarchistic Theory of Knowledge*. Atlantic Highlands, N.J.: Humanities Press.

Fisk, George, ed. (1986), *Marketing Management Technology as Social Process*. New York: Praeger.

Godelier, Maurice (1972), *Rationality and Irrationality in Economics*. New York: Monthly Review.

Hirschman, Elizabeth (1986), "Humanistic Inquiry in Marketing Research: Philosophy, Method and Criteria," *Journal of Marketing Research* 23 (August): 237–49.

Hunt, Shelby D. (1983), *Marketing Theory: The Philosophy of Marketing Science*. Homewood, Ill.: Richard D. Irwin.

Jay, Martin (1973), *The Dialectical Imagination*. Boston: Little, Brown.

Kuhn, Thomas S. (1986), "The Histories of Science: Diverse Worlds for Diverse Audiences," *Academe* 72 (July-August): 29–33.

Levins, Richard (1986), "A Science of Our Own: Marxism and Nature," *Monthly Review* 38 (July-August): 3–12.

Levy, Sidney J. (1981), "Interpreting Consumer Mythology: A Structural Approach to Consumer Behavior," *Journal of Marketing* 45 (Summer): 49–61.

Pollay, Richard W. (1986), "The Distorted Mirror: Reflections on the Unintended Consequences of Advertising," *Journal of Marketing* 50 (April): 18–36.

Sweeney, D.J. (1972), "Marketing: Management Technology or Social Process?" *Journal of Marketing* 36 (October): 3–10.

Venkatesh, Alladi, and Nikhilesh Dholakia (1986), "Methodological Issues in Macromarketing," *Journal of Macromarketing* 6 (Fall): 36–52.

Zaltman, Gerald, Karen LeMasters, and Michael Heffring (1982), *Theory Construction in Marketing: Some Thoughts on Thinking*, New York: Wiley.

About the Contributors

Russell W. Belk is N. Eldon Tanner professor of business administration at the University of Utah. His current research interests concern materialism and the relationships between people and possessions and between people as mediated by possessions. He is a frequent contributor to the *Journal of Consumer Research* and currently serves on the editorial boards of that journal and six others. He is a fellow in the American Psychological Association for consumer research this year. His Ph.D. is from the University of Minnesota.

Raymond Benton, Jr., is associate professor of marketing at Loyola University of Chicago. His primary interest is the study of economics and marketing as symbolic-conceptual worlds within which most Americans live and work and the differential impact each has on the social construction and interpretation of reality. He has published in the *Journal of Economic Issues, Journal of Macromarketing*, and *Review of Social Economy*. He has contributed to *Changing the Course of Marketing: Alternative Paradigms for Widening Marketing Theory*. He obtained his baccalaureate degree in marketing from the University of Arizona and holds an M.A. in anthropology and Ph.D. in economics from Colorado State University.

Rajiv P. Dant is assistant professor of marketing at the University of Mississippi. His recent research interests include behavioral issues in channels of distribution, quantitative integration of empirical research, and methodological issues related to data collection and data interpretation. He obtained his Ph.D. from Virginia Polytechnic Institute and State University and his M.B.A. from Bajaj Institute of Management in Bombay, India.

Ruby Roy Dholakia, professor of marketing at the University of Rhode Island, earned her B.S. and M.B.A. from the University of California at Berkeley in 1967, and 1969, respectively. She received her Ph.D. from Northwestern University in 1976. She joined the URI faculty in 1981, after two years at Kansas State University. Prior to 1979, Dr. Dholakia taught at the Indian Institutes of Management at Calcutta and Ahmedabad. Her research efforts in consumer behavior have been published in the *Journal of Consumer Research, Public Opinion Quarterly, Journal of Business Research*, and *European*

Journal of Marketing. Research dealing with macro and social marketing issues has been published in the *Journal of Macromarketing, Journal of Economic Psychology,* and *Decision.* Dr. Dholakia has presented her research findings on consumer behavior and social marketing of various professional meetings in the United States, Europe, and India. She has also served as a reviewer for professional conferences and the *Journal of Macromarketing.* Her research and teaching interests include marketing management of consumer and industrial goods, advertising and marketing communications, consumer behavior and consumer socialization, and macromarketing.

Geraldine Fennell is a consultant in marketing and consumer psychology. Previously, she worked in marketing management at J. Walter Thompson Company and Warner Lambert Company and as an economist at the Basel Center for Economic and Financial Research in Switzerland. Her papers reflecting research interests in a general model of action, the marketing concept, marketing ethics, and the academic-practitioner gap have appeared in *Advances in Nonprofit Marketing, Current Issues and Research in Advertising, Journal of Advertising Research, Journal of Marketing, Journal of Psychology, Motivation and Emotion,* and elsewhere. Her Ph.D. in experimental cognition is from the City University of New York. Her B.A. and M.A. degrees in economics are from the National University of Ireland in Dublin.

Ronald A. Fullerton is assistant professor of marketing at Southeastern Massachusetts University in North Dartmouth. He has training in both marketing and history. His current research interests include German marketing and social thought, marketing and development, marketing history, philosophies of knowledge, and trade policy. His work has appeared in the *International Journal of Advertising, Journal of Macromarketing,* and *Journal of Social History.* Professor Fullerton earned his B.A. from Rutgers, M.A. from Harvard, M.B.A. from Cornell, and Ph.D. from the University of Wisconsin.

Kjell Grønhaug is professor at the Norwegian School of Economics and Business Administration, and holds degrees in business administration, sociology, and marketing from the Norwegian School of Economics and the University of Bergen. He did his postgraduate work at the University of Washington, and has served as visiting professor at the University of Pittsburgh, the University of California, Irvine, and the University of Illinois at Urbana-Champaign. His publications include articles in leading European and American journals, contributions to several conference proceedings, and several books.

Aharon Hibshoosh began his undergraduate studies at the Hebrew University, where he studied with Louis Guttman and majored in mathematics, statistics, and social sciences. He received his Ph.D. from the Graduate School of Business Administration, University of California at Berkeley, in 1974, and is now associate professor in marketing and quantitative studies in the School of Business, San Jose State University. His research is on the interaction among marketing, statistics, and economics with specialization in building forecasting systems. Since the mid 1960s he has consulted as a statistician and marketing researcher for Kaiser Health Plan, AT&T, Longs Drugs, OLE's, F.T.I., the Pacific Stock Exchange, and other companies.

Morris B. Holbrook is professor of business at Columbia University in New York City. His research on marketing and consumer research has appeared in a number of journals. This work deals with a wide range of behavioral topics and spans a broad spectrum from quantitative to qualitative methods of inquiry.

Meir Karlinsky is assistant professor in the Graduate School of Industrial Administration at Carnegie-Mellon University in Pittsburgh. His research interests are development of marketing theory and research philosophy, development of consumer decision-aid systems utilizing home-computer technology, and the application of economics and psychology of decision-making models to marketing decisions. He holds a B.Sc. and an M.B.A. from Tel-Aviv University and an M.A. and Ph.D. from the University of California at Berkeley.

William Kilbourne is visiting associate professor of marketing at the University of Colorado at Denver. His previous research has appeared in scholarly journals such as *Journal of Marketing Research*, *Journal of Advertising*, and *Journal of the Academy of Marketing Science*. His current research interest is in the social impact of consumption in industrial societies. He holds an M.B.A. and Ph.D. from the University of Houston.

Philip Kotler is the Harold T. Martin professor of marketing at the J.L. Kellogg Graduate School of Management, Northwestern University, in Evanston, Ill. He is the author of the world's most widely used graduate textbook in marketing, *Marketing Management*, now in its fifth edition. He has also published twelve other books, including *Marketing for Non-profit Organizations* and *The New Competition*, as well as over eighty articles covering marketing strategy, marketing organization, marketing theory and models, and new products. Dr. Kotler has won several prizes for his original contributions to marketing, including the Leader in Marketing Thought Award (1975), Distinguished Marketing Educator Award (1985), and Award for Excellence inHealth Care Marketing (1985). He received his M.A. at the University of Chicago and his Ph.D. at MIT, both in economics.

Erdoğan Kumcu is on the faculty of the department of marketing at Ball State University in Muncie, Ind. His recent research interests have focused on bank marketing, marketing channels, and the role of marketing in development. He is the former editor of *Marketing Journal*, published by the University of Istanbul in Turkey. His works have appeared in numerous publications in North America and Europe. He has published a book on distribution channel behavior, and coedited several others including *The Role of Marketing in Development*, the proceedings of the International Conference on Marketing and Development. He holds a B.S. and Ph.D. in marketing from the University of Istanbul.

Michael P. Mokwa is associate professor of marketing and fellow of the Center for Ethics at the Arizona State University. He is the contributing editor to *Marketing the Arts*. His research has been published in the *Journal of Marketing*, *Journal of Business Strategy*, *Journal of Advertising*, and elsewhere. He earned his M.B.A. and Ph.D. at the University of Houston at University Park and formerly served on the faculty of the University of Wisconsin at Madison.

Kent B. Monroe is professor of marketing at Virginia Polytechnic Institute and State University. Known for his pioneering research on buyers' perceptions of prices, he has also contributed research on buyers' patronage behavior, marketing models, and research methodology. Currently he is chairman of the development of marketing thought task force of the American Marketing Association. He is the author of *Pricing: Making Profitable Decisions* and has contributed articles to the *Journal of Marketing Research*, *Journal of Marketing*, *Journal of Consumer Research*, and *Management Science*. He obtained a D.B.A. from the University of Illinois and an M.B.A. from Indiana University.

Christine Moorman is a doctoral candidate at the Graduate School of Business, University of Pittsburgh. Her interests include theory development and the philosophy of science, consumer information policy, planned social change, macroenvironmental concerns, and understanding the meaning of consumption activities. She has presented papers at the American Marketing Association and the Association for Consumer Research meetings and plans to pursue an academic career of teaching and research.

Franco M. Nicosia is professor at the University of California at Berkeley. He was director of the Consumer Research Program at the Survey Research Center, 1960–76. Academically, for more than two decades he has focused on consumer behavior and its applications to areas of marketing management and, later, to corporate management and public policy making. He was partner of Fredrickson-Nicosia, 1960–70, and has been a marketing associate at Teknekron since 1970. He was president of the San Francisco professional chapter of the American Marketing Association; a member of the executive council of the American Association of Public Opinion Research, 1973–75 and 1975–77; and president of the Pacific chapter of that association, 1986–87. In 1979, he was elected fellow of the American Psychological Association.

Terence A. Oliva, associate professor of marketing at the Graduate School of Management at Rutgers University, received his Ph.D. in operations management from the University of Alabama. He has eclectic research interests and has published in *Journal of Marketing Research, Journal of Marketing, Journal of Consumer Research, Journal of Macromarketing, Behavioral Economist, Journal of Collective Negotiation in the Public Sector,* and *Human Systems Management.*

Anil Pandya is assistant professor of marketing at Northeastern University in Boston. He has worked at Boston University and several leading corporations in India. His research on exchange in marketing has been published in *Research in Marketing.* His doctoral dissertation, *Technology Purchase in the Indian Public Sector,* is in the process of publication. He holds a B.S. in electrical engineering from the Birla Institute of Technology in Ranchi and a Ph.D. from the Indian Institute of Management in Ahmedabad.

Eric Reidenbach is director of the Bureau of Business Research at the University of Southern Mississippi. A graduate of Michigan State University, he has published in a number of business and marketing journals, including the *Journal of Marketing, Journal of Marketing Research,* and *Journal of Advertising.*

Ronald Savitt is the John L. Beckley professor of American business at the University of Vermont. In addition to his interest in marketing theory, he does research in marketing and economic development, marketing history, and retailing. Professor Savitt is the author, coauthor, or coeditor of eight books and numerous articles which have appeared in the *Antitrust Bulletin, California Management Review, European Journal of Marketing, Journal of Marketing,* and *Managerial and Decision Economics.* He holds an A.B. and M.B.A. from the University of California at Berkeley and a Ph.D. from the University of Pennsylvania.

John F. Sherry, Jr., is assistant professor of marketing at the J.L. Kellogg Graduate School of Management of Northwestern University in Evanston, Ill. His research interests include symbolic communication, hedonic and deviant consumption, secondary marketing systems, development, and ethnographic methods. His work has appeared in the *Journal of Consumer Research, Research in Marketing, Medical Anthropology Quarterly,* and *Florida Journal of Anthropology.* He obtained his Ph.D. in anthropology from the University of Illinois.

About the Editors

A. Fuat Fırat is associate professor of marketing in the Walker College of Business at Appalachian State University in Boone, N.C. He has taught previously at several universities including Istanbul, Texas at Dallas, Maryland, and McGill. His research on consumption patterns, distribution systems, and development policy has appeared in *Journal of Marketing*, *Journal of Macromarketing*, *European Journal of Marketing*, *Journal of Economic Psychology*, and elsewhere. He obtained his undergraduate degree in economics at Istanbul University and his Ph.D. in marketing at Northwestern University.

Nikhilesh Dholakia is professor of marketing at the University of Rhode Island, Kingston, R.I. He has also taught at the University of Illinois (Chicago), Indian Institutes of Management (Ahmedabad and Calcutta), Kansas State University, and Northwestern University. Among his many books is *Changing the Course of Marketing* (JAI Press, 1985) coedited with Johan Arndt. Nikhilesh Dholakia holds degrees in engineering and management from India, and a Ph.D. from Northwestern University.

Richard P. Bagozzi is the Dwight F. Benton professor of marketing and behavioral science in management at the School of Business Administration of the University of Michigan. Prior to this, he was on the faculties of the University of California at Berkeley, the Massachusetts Institute of Technology, and Stanford University. He holds undergraduate and advanced degrees in engineering and mathematics and an M.B.A. in general business. His Ph.D. is from Northwestern University, where he specialized in behavioral science and statistics in management. He has done extensive research in customer behavior, sales force behavior, marketing communication, and research methodology. He is the author of *Causal Models in Marketing* and *Principles of Marketing Management* and has authored or coauthored more than seventy-five articles in professional and scholarly journals. In 1982, an article he wrote for the May 1977 *Journal of Marketing Research* was given the O'Dell Award for the piece making the most lasting contribution in the five years after its publication. In 1985, an article he wrote earned the Maynard Award as the most significant contribution to marketing theory and thought in the 1984 volume of *Journal of Marketing*. Among other honors, Dr. Bagozzi has received the American Marketing Association's first-place award for his doctoral dissertation, a

Senior Fulbright Research Grant to do research in Europe, and, from University of California at Berkeley, the School of Business Administration Outstanding Teaching Prize and the campuswide Distinguished Teaching Award. Professor Bagozzi has served on the editorial boards of the *Journal of Marketing*, *Journal of Marketing Research*, *Marketing Science*, *Journal of Consumer Research*, *Journal of Macromarketing*, *Journal of Economic Psychology*, *Social Psychology Quarterly*, *Journal of Personality and Social Psychology*, and *Hong Kong Business Journal*.